BY MITCH ALBOM

LIVE ALBOM

Gone to the dogs

Credits

Editor: Tracee Hamilton

Associate editor: Gene Myers

Project co-ordinator: Dave Robinson

Copy editing: Bill Collison, Owen Davis, Steve Schrader and the Detroit Free Press sports copy desk.

Cover design: Keith Webb

Cover photograph: Andy Greenwell

Research: Chris Kucharski

Computer bailout: Ken Clover and Ann Mieczkowski

Special thanks to Kaila's Thundering Skye and his human, Larry Bliss.

Mitch's special thanks to Janine, Ken, Mike and Kerri. And, of course, Elvis.

© Detroit Free Press Inc., 1992
321 W. Lafayette
Detroit, Michigan 48226

To order additional copies of this book, or the original "Live Albom" or "Live Albom II," call 1-800-245-5082.

Once again, I would like to thank the editors and fellow writers at the Free Press sports department for putting up with my odd sense of deadlines and inch counts. Their patience with my work habits is remarkable. Special thanks to Tracee Hamilton, Gene Myers, Owen Davis, Keith Webb, and the boss, Dave Robinson, for their work on this project.

I would like to dedicate this book to my faraway sister, Cara, and my faraway brother, Peter. I wish they still slept down the hall.

Foreword

Joe Dumars says that Mitch Albom is the best writer he's ever met,
and while you might be tempted to dismiss Dumars' judgment —
after all, what other writers has he ever met, besides Joe Falls and
Charles Barkley? — you have to remember that Dumars comes from
Louisiana, which has nurtured such writers as Truman Capote and
Walker Percy and Tennessee Williams. I don't know whether Dumars
ever met any of them, but if he has, Mitch Albom is in very good
company, which he deserves to be.

Mitch Albom may not be the best writer I've ever met — I have met
Norman Mailer and Gunter Grass and John Fowles and Jimmy Breslin
and Tom Wolfe and Truman Capote and Tennessee Williams — but he
is at least a contender, certainly one of the very best among the people
who cover sports and athletes.

Mitch was a musician before he became a sports writer, and he
clearly understands the rhythm of a sentence, the rhythm of a phrase.
His words sound good, and they also make sense, a parlay that is not as
common a phenomenon as it should be. Albom makes me laugh and he
makes me think, another good parlay.

In his columns and on radio and television, Mitch applauds honest
effort and scorns hypocrisy. He is fortunate to be working in a field that
offers so much of both.

And Detroit is fortunate to have Mitch Albom and his talent. But it is
only fair. After all, Albom is from Pennsylvania, and since Detroit sent
Hank Greenberg to Pennsylvania in 1947, and sent Bobby Layne to
Pennsylvania in 1958, it is about time the city got equal value in return.

Mitch Albom, too, is a Hall of Famer.

It's a pleasure to introduce him, Sunday mornings on "The Sports
Reporters," and now, on these pages.

Dick Schaap
New York City
1992

Table of contents

1990

1991

1992

Etc.

(Columns from the Detroit Free Press Sunday Comment section)

1990

Take it from Jim Arnold:
Elvis lives, and loves football

August 17

I have good news for Elvis fans. He is not dead. Jim Arnold says so. Jim also says he and Elvis are good friends. They met at a doughnut shop. I am not making this up.

"It was a few years ago, at the Krispy Kreme in Memphis," recalls the Lions' punter. "I went in for some breakfast and there was Elvis, eating a jelly doughnut. I said, 'Hey, E.' He kinda looked up, then he looked away. He was wearing a hat and glasses, but I knew it was him. I got most of his movies. I said, 'Hey, E.' He said, 'Not here, man. Let's get outside.'

"So we went outside, and I said, 'E, don't worry, your secret is safe with me.' We started talking a little, you know, about football. Been friends ever since. He loves football."

"Really?" I say.

"Yep."

"You guys play together?"

"Sometimes. In the backyard. He can throw the ball pretty good, too. Maybe 40 yards. Not a real tight spiral or nothin' ..."

Now, it is not every NFL player who can tell you this story. But then, how many NFL players have a picture of Elvis taped inside their locker? Some have a poster. Some have Miss January. Arnold has the King, a color photo with the word "Remember" in pink letters, alongside a postcard from Graceland.

"Ever been there?" I ask. "Graceland?"

"Naw. Not yet."

"They have tours, you know."

Arnold snorts, then spits tobacco. "I won't take a tour. I'll wait until E wants to show me himself."

Of course. How stupid of me.

Now, you might have doubts about Arnold. But not me. I have learned to believe pretty much anything he tells me, ever since the time he sang "The Twelve Days of Christmas" in the voice of Pee-Wee Herman. Or maybe it was the time he did stand-up at the Comedy Castle. I once called his house when he was living with Eric Williams and Rusty Hilger, and his voice came over the answering machine sounding just like Robin Leach: "THREE ELIGIBLE BACHELORS LIVING IN A ROMANTIC PARADISE ..." Besides, the man might be the best punter in football. I figure if Elvis were alive, and he really did like football, he would want to hang out with the best, right?

"You never know with E, of course," Arnold says. "Sometimes he does the craziest things. He'll call up a fast-food place and order 147 cheeseburgers. And you got to help him eat 'em."

"Do you see him often?"

"Over the summer down in Tennessee. I been trying to get him up here for a game. But I can't just bring him in and say, 'Hey, guys, look who's here.' That's why he faked his death in the first place."

He sighs. "Barry Sanders wants to meet him."

"Barry's pretty big," I say.

"So's Elvis. I told him the other day, 'E, you're bigger than all cattle.' "

Did I mention how we got on this subject? Oh, Thursday was the 13th anniversary of Elvis Presley's death. Or supposed death. Arnold was clearly moved. This is a man who knows the entire sound track of "Blue Hawaii." In honor of the occasion, Arnold planned to wear black for tonight's exhibition against the Bills. Until Elvis called and said don't bother, seeing as he wasn't really dead and all.

"He told me, 'Jim, don't mourn for me, man,' " Arnold says. " 'I'm happy now. I got peace a' mind. Only thing I miss is puttin' on them sequins.' "

OK. I know what you're thinking. Arnold is crazy. Some of his teammates would agree with you. Then again, they all laughed at Jerry Glanville a few years ago when, as coach of the Houston Oilers, he left two tickets for Elvis at the Astrodome box office. Elvis never showed.

"Hmmph," Arnold sniffs. "Course not. He don't even like the Oilers. He's a Lions fan now."

"Will you leave him tickets?"

"I won't leave him nothin.' I'll give him the tickets myself. Just like he gave me this." Arnold fondles a gold necklace, with a charm in the shape of a lightning bolt, through the letters 'TCB.' I recognize this as an Elvis trademark. Taking Care of Business. He had one just like it. Hey. Wait a minu–

"The day E gave this to me, he said, 'Jim, I want you to have this. You been a friend, man.' "

He pauses. "I'll never forget that."

No. That would be hard to forget.

And so we wait. Arnold says Elvis has a standing offer to come to any Lions game, and if the crowd is big enough "so he can slip in unnoticed" he just might show. Stranger things have happened. Philadelphia's Tim Rossovich once ate live spiders before a game. Keith Jackson saw his pants catch on fire during a "Monday Night Football" telecast. Why not Elvis? I mean, I see people picking the Lions to win the NFC Central this year. When was the last time that happened?

"He won't be coming in a UFO, will he?" I ask.

"Come on," Arnold says. "I don't believe in that UFO stuff."

I didn't think so. ∎

Lions' No. 1 pick in 1950 demanded at least $8,500

August 24

Down in Houston, not far from where Andre Ware sits this morning — no doubt waiting for a phone call from his agent to find out if he has become a millionaire — there lives another Detroit first-round draft choice. He's a little older than Andre. OK, a lot older.

His name is Joe Watson. Forty years ago, he, too, was in Andre's position. With a few noticeable differences.

To begin with, the Lions never told him he was their No. 1 pick.

"Back then, there was no draft on TV or anything like that," recalls Watson, a retired oil company manager. "The day it happened, I was down at Rice, where I played college football. I think I was hanging around the football office. My coach told me I had a phone call. It was the Lions' coach, Bo McMillin.

"He told me Detroit had chosen me in the draft. That's all. Not No. 1. Nothing like that. Back then, you didn't even care what round you were taken. It didn't make much difference. Coach McMillin said he'd come down to Houston to talk to me. And a few months later, he did.

"I met him at the Shamrock Hotel. In his room. Just me and him. He said, 'Joe, we'll pay you $7,500 to play this year.' I said, 'Gee, I've got a good job with Gulf Oil. I don't want to play for less than $8,500.'

"He said, 'Joe, That's an awful lot of money.' I said, 'I understand. I'd rather not play then.'

"He said, 'Let me talk to my bosses and see what I can do.' "

Hmmm. You might have noticed the lack of agents in this story. That's because there were no agents back then. No agents. No press secretaries. No personal managers. No front-office bumbleheads.

Sounds like heaven, huh?

Which is not to say there weren't salary disputes. There are always salary disputes. I think salary disputes date back to the Egyptian pyramids, where one of the workers complained that a handful of water and some dusty bread was not enough for laboring all day in the hot sun. The taskmaster thought about this for a minute, then dropped a boulder on his head.

Today, things are more complicated.

Today, Andre Ware sits in Texas, demanding $1.5 million a year, even as the Lions play their next-to-last exhibition game without him. And today, quarterback Don Majkowski, with only one standout NFL season, sits at home demanding $2 million a year — even as his fellow Packers prepare for the season without him.

And back in 1950, coach Bo McMillin eventually called young Joe Watson on the phone and said, "OK, I talked to my bosses and I got you $8,500. Now get up here and start practicing." And Watson, an All-America center, came up the next day. And he started every game that season. He snapped the ball to the famous Bobby Layne. He blocked for the famous Leon Hart and Cloyce Box.

And when he wasn't playing center, Watson was out there on defense, playing linebacker. "There was never a game that I played less than 50 of the 60 minutes," he recalls. "You went both ways. That was just expected. They don't do that today."

Of course not. If they did that today, they would want twice the money.

I ask Watson whether there were any holdouts back then. He laughs and says, "Hold out for what?" I ask Watson whether anyone renegotiated in the middle of a contract. He laughs again. "Almost nobody had a contract for longer than a year to begin with."

I ask how he would have reacted had the Lions offered him a million a year, as they have offered Ware. "Well," he says, "I wouldn't let an agent stand in my way. I'd push the agent aside and say, 'Let me sign that contract. I'll deal with you later.' "

Things didn't quite work out that way for Joe Watson. After the 1950 season, the Lions changed coaches. Watson and the new coach, Buddy Parker, haggled over a $1,000 increase McMillin had promised. Parker said he would talk to his bosses.

"I told him fine," Watson recalls, "but I asked him to be sure to let me know at least two weeks before training camp, so I could square things away with Gulf Oil.

"Well, the day training camp opened, he called and said, 'I got you $9,500. Now come on up.' I told him, 'Sorry, Buddy. But I can't do that to my employers. I told them they'd get two weeks' notice and it wouldn't be responsible of me to leave now.' "

He stayed in Texas.

He kept his promise.

He never played football again.

You talk to guys like Joe Watson, a happy man with healthy knees who just turned 65, and you hear words such as "responsibility" and "maturity" and "who needed an agent?" And you start to realize a few things. Mostly, you realize sports were probably a lot more fun back in 1950.

"If you ever run in to Andre Ware, will you tell him your story?" I ask Watson before hanging up.

"Andre wouldn't believe me," he says, and he's probably right. ∎

Detroit's Big Four heroes share good time at a game

September 14

I t was two hours before the first pitch when Joe Dumars jumped in the car. He was late. He apologized. He stretched his long legs in the backseat and grinned like a kid.

"I hope Cecil hits one tonight," he said.

"Yeah," I said.

"And no singles or anything."

"Nuh-uh."

"I mean, it's like singles don't count with Cecil, you know?"

"Uh-huh."

"Got to be a home run."

"Yep."

A pause. "Preferably a long home run."

"A long home run," I repeated.

"Yeah," Joe said, leaning back.

We were going to a baseball game, Joe Dumars, Barry Sanders, Steve Yzerman and me. I had the tickets, which might be the only reason I got in the group. Then again, it's a pretty nice group. Considering these are the reigning superstars in basketball, football and hockey in this town, their egos are in nice perspective. You buy them a hot dog, they say, "Hey, thanks a lot." They meet Sparky Anderson, they act like impressed fans. A foul ball comes their way and they...

But I'm getting ahead of myself.

"What's Barry doing?" Joe asked as the car sped along Long Lake Road.

"He's got practice today," I said.

Dumars looked at the car clock. It read 5:30. "This long?" he said. I nodded.

"Man," he said, "football is really a job, isn't it?"

We pulled into the Silverdome parking lot. There was Barry Sanders, standing alone by his car. Hands in his pockets. Nobody around. This, remember, is probably the best running back in the NFL, the rookie who needed 10 yards in the final game to win the NFC rushing title last season, and told his coach, "Don't bother to put me back in. Let's just win and go home."

He shyly opened the door and slid inside, dressed in shorts and a pink T-shirt. "Hey, man," he said to Dumars. "Hey, man," he said to me.

"Thanks for coming," I said.

"No problem," he said.

"Should be fun," Joe said. "Cecil might hit one."

Barry smiled and nodded. The car pulled away. About 10 seconds later, Barry leaned in. He looked troubled.

"Um, to be honest," he said, "I don't really know who Cecil Fielder is."

One thing you will quickly learn about superstar athletes; they are not all alike. Take Dumars and Sanders, for example. Dumars can watch a baseball game on TV from beginning to end. He can watch volleyball. He can stare at ESPN while using the Stairmaster and absorb everything.

And then there is Sanders, who has never seen a Tigers game on TV. In fact, he has been to only one other baseball game in his life. "I don't have the time," he said, almost embarrassed. But then, out of the blue, he turned to Dumars and said, "I was a pretty good basketball player, though."

Dumars smiled. "You were?"

"I played three years varsity in high school."

"So you were better than me."

"Well … yeah, I guess I was."

And Dumars exploded in laughter. And so did Sanders. And from that point on, they were like pals. They chatted the whole ride down, about training, about mutual friends. At one point, Sanders gave Dumars his phone number and asked if maybe they could get together, hang around.

And here came the ballpark.

"We're meeting Yzerman here," I said. I looked at Barry. He had that same puzzled look.

"Steve Yzerman?" I said. "The Red Wings' captain?"

Well. Anyhow. There was Steve, right on time, and everyone shook hands, we all took the tickets and we walked toward the field. Tiger Stadium smelled of sausages and peanuts and greasepaint. "Nothing like a ballpark," Dumars said, sniffing. Yzerman waved at a fan. Sanders just looked around.

And then we were on the field. And there was Cecil Fielder, signing autographs. Sanders tugged on my sleeve. "That's him, right, No. 45?"

"Fielder," I said. "Leads the league in home runs."

Sanders nodded. "He's big."

Which is a compliment, I guess, coming from a football player.

Anyhow, I approached Cecil, mostly because these other guys were too shy to do it. And here was the moment I had waited for: Fielder. Sanders. Dumars. Yzerman. Talk about your basic elements. It was like hydrogen meeting oxygen.

"My MAN!" Fielder said, throwing an arm around Dumars. "Aw, man, this guy can hoop!"

"My MAN!" he continued, throwing an arm around Sanders. "Aw, man, this guy can scoot with the football.

"My MAN!" he continued, grabbing Yzerman's hand. "Uh, nice to meet you."

I don't think hockey is Cecil's big sport.

Anyhow, pretty soon it was like one big party. Cecil gave everyone a bat with his number on it. "Take some batting practice!" he insisted, pointing to the cage. They all just grinned and shuffled their feet.

"Football," Fielder said, turning to Sanders. "That's a sport!"

"You look like you could lay a few licks on somebody," Sanders said.

"Ha, man, I couldn't even catch you," Fielder said, laughing. He turned to Dumars. "And basketball! Now there's a sport."

"Nah," Dumars said, "baseball is a sport. I can't believe you guys stand in there with those balls coming in so fast. I'd be like, 'Whoa.'" He feigned a duck.

"Nah, man, basketball is exciting," Fielder said. "It moves, every night." He gazed out at the bleachers, mostly empty on this September evening. He swung at the air.

"Baseball is boring."

Did I mention Sparky Anderson? Oh, yeah. He snuck up and grabbed Dumars from behind and slapped his back. And he shook hands with Yzerman and Sanders. Barry had that awkward smile on his face again, so I slid up alongside him.

"Sparky Anderson," I whispered.

"Yeah," he mumbled, "I've seen him on the commercials. He's pretty famous, isn't he?"

And soon, we were heading for our seats. Barry. Steve. Joe. A couple of people oohed and aahed and a couple of kids wanted autographs, but mostly we were left alone and we stood for the national anthem. I asked Yzerman whether he had ever caught a foul ball at a baseball game.

"I never even came close," he said. "I sat on the third base side a whole game, and never even saw one."

Not long after that, the Yankees' batter fouled off a pitch and it lofted high in the air. For a moment, it was headed our way, but then it drifted toward the third base side, and a brown-haired young man caught it with his bare hands.

"Hey!" Yzerman yelled. "You know who caught that?"

"Who?" I asked.

"Tim Cheveldae."

I looked at the front row. Damn if he wasn't right.

Goalies get to catch everything.

Anyhow, the game went on and finally Cecil came to the plate. I would like to say he hit a home run in that first at-bat. He didn't. Actually, he struck out. But that didn't seem to dampen anyone's spirits. The Yankees' super rookie Kevin Maas hit a two-run blast into the rightfield seats. Next time he got up, Dumars leaned toward me.

"We got to pitch this guy tight and inside," he whispered. "Send him a message."

And Walt Terrell pitched him tight.

Dumars grinned. "Now we got to brush him back a little. Nothing too bad. Just a little."

And Terrell pitched him tight and Maas fouled it off his foot and hopped around the plate in obvious pain.

"Got 'im," said Dumars, crossing his arms.

Of course, it wouldn't be a game without hot dogs, and so I yelled for the vendor. "Four!" He passed them down, from Yzerman to Sanders to Dumars to me. And I passed him the money, me to Dumars to Sanders to Yzerman. And when Yzerman leaned over to hand me the change, he reached in front of Sanders. And he turned and said, "Excuse me."

And then Sanders reached around and said, "Thanks for the hot dog, man." I thought that was nice.

We had a few Cokes and we watched Terrell get out of a bases-loaded jam. The ice cream guy walked past and yelled "THREE-PEAT!" An older woman selling peanuts passed by and whispered "hi" to Dumars. Joe looked at Sanders, who was grinning.

"She likes you, man."

Everyone had to get home early, and pretty soon it was time to go. Steve said good-bye and drove himself back to Grosse Pointe, as unassuming as ever. And Sanders and Dumars could have gone home separately, but they talked it over and decided to go together. I walked them out, we shook hands. And they thanked me several times.

Earlier in the day, when the arrangements for this little idea were getting confused, my boss said, "God, why did we ever try this?" But you know what? It turned out OK. Barry. Steve. Joe. It wasn't three big egos trying to outdo one another. It wasn't three superstars who demanded luxury-box treatment.

It was basically three guys at the ballpark on a late summer night with a few hot dogs and a few Cokes and some unusual conversation. You couldn't do this in every city. Detroit is awfully lucky that the biggest guys in town are also the nicest and most unassuming.

I thought maybe that was the lesson of the evening. And just as I picked up the phone to send this story, in the bottom of the ninth, Cecil Fielder stepped to the plate and whacked a 2-1 fastball that hit the leftfield roof of Tiger Stadium. Home run No. 46.

You know what I figure? I figure it's a perfect ending. That's what I figure. ■

The Big Five-O, plus one!
Fielder caps a special season

October 4

NEW YORK — He swung the bat and he heard that smack! and the ball screamed into the dark blue sky, higher, higher, until it threatened to bring a few stars down with it. His teammates knew; they leapt off the bench. The fans knew; they roared like animals. And finally, the man who all season refused to watch his home runs, the man who said this 50 thing was "no big deal" — finally even he couldn't help himself. He stopped halfway to first base and watched the ball bang into the facing of the upper deck at Yankee Stadium, waking up the ghosts of Maris and Ruth and Gehrig.

And then, for the first time in this miraculous season, Cecil Fielder jumped. He jumped like a man sprung from prison, he jumped like a kid on the last day of school, he jumped, all 250 pounds of Detroit Bambino, his arms over his head, his huge smile a beacon of celebration and relief.

The Big Five-O.

"I'm so juiced now, I almost want to go out there and do it all again," said an exuberant Fielder, who became only the 11th player in history to hit 50 or more home runs in a season Wednesday night, and then put a cherry on top by cracking his 51st in his final at-bat. "I didn't mean to jump like that, but I couldn't help it, man! I couldn't help it! … Tony (Phillips) was running around the bases ahead of me, yelling, 'Daddy, you did it!' He calls me Daddy, you know."

Right. The rest of us just call him awesome. The 50th and the 51st? Five RBIs? Lord. Hollywood can't write scripts this good. Here, on the last night of the season — in the same stadium where, 29 years ago, also on the last day, Roger Maris belted his 61st to become the all-time home run king — Fielder did what everyone had been waiting for, but had pretty much given up on. Everyone except the man himself — and his family.

Last week, after he hit his 49th, Cecil's mother, Tina, flew to Detroit without telling her son. She had never seen him hit a major league home run in person. "I'm bad luck," she said. But like the rest of us, she wanted a peek. So she got a seat in the lower deck and hid behind a friend's hat whenever her son came to the plate. Didn't work. Still no home run. She went home. Cecil went to New York.

And Wednesday night, about 10 minutes after the big moment, I called the house in Rialto, Calif., where Tina and Kaory Fielder, Cecil's sister, had been watching ESPN, waiting for updates.

"I guess you heard," I said.

"Heard what?" Mrs. Fielder asked.

"Cecil hit his 50th."

"AHHHHHHHHH!"

"You're not lying, are you?" screamed his sister, who had picked up the other extension. "You wouldn't lie to my mother, would you?"

"I'm not lying."

"AHHHHHHH!"

"Say it again!" his sister said. "Say what you just said again!"

"OK. Cecil hit his 50th. Against the Yankees. Fourth inning. Leftfield seats. Two-and-one count. Wasn't even close …"

"Fourth inning, leftfield seats, two-and-one count …" Tina Fielder repeated, like a grandmother reciting the vital statistics of a newborn baby.

"AHHHHHHHH!"

The Big Five-O.

AAAAAAH! Isn't that the perfect response? The yelp of relief? The yelp of joy? Make no mistake. What Fielder did Wednesday night was perhaps more remarkable than all the things he had done up to then — come out of Japan, a heavyweight question mark, and hit 49 home runs in his first full-time gig in the majors.

By Wednesday night, however, like many heroes, Fielder, 27, had become a prisoner of his accomplishment. With each at-bat he could feel the eyes, the sighs, the moans, the groans, the enormous weight of all those expectations. When, Cecil? Now, Cecil? When, Cecil?

"After I hit the 49th, I started to get caught up in it all," he admitted after it was over. "It wasn't me up there anymore. I was trying to please everybody else. I was swinging for the fences."

Instead, he barely got the ball out of the infield. This last week was the most dismal: He swung wildly, his batting average drooped. He was fatigued. He had headaches. He shut himself off from reporters, but that only left him alone with the dragon. Every day was overkill. Every at-bat felt like life or death.

This is crazy, of course. America's fascination with numbers almost sank Fielder this season. Fifty isn't anything more than the number after 49; it just makes for a better headline. Fortunately, Fielder was smart enough to figure this out.

"Last night, my wife said to me, 'Hey, if you get it, you get it. If you don't, you had a great year.' That seemed to do something to me, the fact that my wife didn't care whether I hit it or not."

It did something all right.

It turned him loose.

The Big Five-O.

For those historians out there, here are the essentials: The pitch came off the Yankees' Steve Adkins, a 25-year-old lefty out of Chicago with a reputation for being wild. He had walked Fielder and retired him on a fly ball earlier. This time, he threw a 2-1 fastball and Fielder knocked it on a hooking arc into leftfield. The ball was retrieved by a blond-haired 21-year-old named Keith Harkness, from Connecticut, who saw it bounce down from the upper deck. He gave it back to Fielder in exchange for a bat.

"Pretty fair trade," the kid said, showing the proper baseball attitude.

The 51st? Oh, yes. Can't forget that one. Eighth inning, a 3-2 fastball by reliever Alan Mills that Fielder stroked over the leftfield wall so fast you barely saw it. That drove in three runs. The first homer drove in two. Nobody knows who retrieved the 51st ball, nobody really cares, which only shows you how misguided all this attention is.

But this doesn't diminish the accomplishment. Fielder wins the 1990 home run (51) and RBI titles (132), which means about one of every six Tigers runs this year came off a Fielder hit.

All this from a guy who played in Japan last year, a guy who left the Toronto Blue Jays in 1988 without a whimper from management. When he signed with the Tigers in January, Fielder had only one wish: "I didn't want them to think they'd made a mistake."

Mistake? He made the Tigers look brilliant, and their third-place season will always be framed by this picture: Fielder, that round, powerful body, leaping in joy along the first base line.

"It's your *fannnntasy!*" sang Lloyd Moseby to Fielder in the locker room afterward. Well. Yes and no. Cecil Fielder earned everything he got, he's a happy slugger this morning, he's world-famous. But most of all, best of all, he is still a man who has his priorities intact. When he walked into the interview room after the game Wednesday night, the first thing he did was find his wife, Stacey, and son, Prince. He kissed her. He hugged him.

"You're awesome," he whispered to his boy.

Right back at you, Daddy. The Big Five-O. Now that's the way you end a baseball season. ∎

Clemens, Cooney spoil finale by acting like overgrown kids

October 11

O AKLAND, Calif. — All Terry Cooney has to do is go out to the mound, lean into Roger Clemens' ear and whisper, "Young man, you say that one more time, and I'm throwing you out of the game."

He does that, he gets no arguments this morning. He does that, he looks smart and mature and patient, which is how umpires are supposed to look, right? As opposed to looking like a baby without his bottle.

Which, of course, is what happened. Cooney sank to Clemens' level, which means nursery school. And together, they dumped finger paint all over what had been a beautiful playoff clincher.

Here's Clemens, a guy who has become a real snot the last fewyears, shaking his head after walking Willie Randolph in the second inning of Game 4 of the American League playoffs. And here's plate umpire Cooney, an ex-Marine, and he sees Clemens shaking his head and decides he's going to show the boy who's boss.

So he yells, "I hope you're not shaking your head at me!" And Clemens says something. And Cooney says something back. Clemens says, "Take your bleeping mask off if you're gonna talk to me." Cooney says he won't. Clemens says something else. The whole thing is like Robert DeNiro in front of that mirror in "Taxi Driver." "Are you talking to me? ... Are you talking to me? ..."

I n the end, of course, Cooney pulls rank, he gives Clemens the thumb, you're outta here — in the second inning — even though Clemens is Boston's only prayer of avoiding complete humiliation by Oakland.

The Red Sox react by throwing a Gatorade bucket onto the field. Beautiful. This is what the baseball playoffs come to: a food fight.

I don't know who to give the bottle to first. Cooney says he threw Clemens out because "he said I was a gutless such and such. I had to eject him then, because everyone could hear it."

Yeah? So? What are they going to do, write it on the lunchroom wall? Remember, nobody at home or in the stands heard any of this exchange. It was just Cooney and Clemens and the players within earshot. Maybe Cooney should wonder if any of this would have happened had he not been playing DeNiro behind the plate. "I hope you're not shaking your head at me," he warns, like some schoolteacher wagging her finger. Unbelievable.

Not that it excuses Clemens, who never should have said what he did. But what do you expect? Clemens is basically a punk. If his head got any bigger, he would be the Great Pumpkin. He knows he's the only chance his team has to win a game off Oakland, and you don't risk that to knock an ice cream cone out of the umpire's hand. He does it anyhow.

According to Dave Stewart, one of the few baseball players I would trust, this is just part of what Clemens said to Cooney: "Put your - - - - - - - mask back on and get back behind the - - - - - - - plate."

Not once. Twice.

"He deserved to get tossed," Stewart said, with no apparent malice. "Those are the rules."

Clemens came into a postgame press conference and said, "I didn't curse at him. I just said, 'I'm not shaking my bleeping head at you.'"

As if bleeping means "gosh darn."

So you have your basic baseball crime and your basic baseball punishment. But what you don't have is some basic common sense. Common sense would have told Cooney to take the high road, ignore Clemens' mumblings, or at least give him a warning, since this was such a significant game and Boston's last chance at a dignified death.

And common sense would have told Clemens to keep his multimillion-dollar mouth shut. Not that he would listen. Clemens — who seems ready to become God in Boston — has developed a selective memory along with his sore shoulder. Someone asked about the umpire he shoved in the fracas after his ejection. He said, "I shoved an umpire?"

The shame of it is, this Clemens-Cooney mess obscures an otherwise magnificent performance by Stewart and the Athletics, who swept the Sox in four games without a single home run or triple and are now in the World Series for the third straight year. That's impressive. That's worth remembering. But Cooney and Clemens were willing to spit on this, and on the fans who bought tickets, and on the millions who skipped work to watch on TV, just so they could play "Liar, liar, pants on fire."

And instead of Stewart's MVP award, we'll remember another sad case of a ballplayer thinking he is bigger than the game and an umpire who has decided to tell us how important he is, as if we care. This has been happening more and more. In May, umpire Drew Coble ran to the Baltimore dugout to tell Frank Robinson to be quiet. Don Denkinger ejected Gary Sheffield for tossing his sunglasses. Dale Ford ejected Seattle manager Jim Lefebvre after Lefebvre reportedly said, "Bear down!"

Geez. Is this baseball or a nunnery?

"I didn't say anything," Clemens said.

"He said something," Cooney said. "By shaking his head, he told people, 'What an imbecile is back there behind the plate.'"

You know what? These two deserve each other. Let's give them a bunk bed, some cookies and milk, and lights out at 8. No watching the World Series.

After all, that's for grown-ups. ■

They played a World Series in Cincinnati without Rose

October 18

C INCINNATI — The Reds' locker room was stuffed with reporters, clamoring around any available ballplayer. Ron Oester sat by his locker, watching the fuss. He sipped a postgame beer. "This," he said, "is what it was like when Pete first got in trouble."

He took another sip and shook his head. "Pete should be here to see this."

A World Series is more than seven baseball games. It is a link to Octobers past, and the city it graces will usually spare no effort to trot out its baseball tradition. Were we in St. Louis this week, Stan Musial's statue would open the TV broadcasts. Were we in Detroit, Al Kaline might draw a bigger crowd than Moses. Yankee Stadium? The ghosts of Ruth and Gehrig would get no rest.

Pete Rose, on the other hand, is getting plenty of rest. And no attention. He is inside a prison in Marion, Ill., watching this World Series on a television set. Once he figured he would forever be synonymous with Cincinnati baseball. The idea of a Reds World Series without Rose, well, that made as much sense as a Disneyland without Mickey Mouse.

But it is happening now, this week. Rose is a non-entity, a taboo topic. There are no banners to him. No retired jerseys. No statues. And bigger than the prison sentence, bigger than the tax fraud, bigger than the gambling addiction that dragged him down by his fingernails, this might be Rose's worst nightmare: Baseball, Cincinnati baseball, has reached the end of the rainbow, the World Series. And you have to look hard to find anyone talking about old No. 14.

O ester is an exception. He wants Rose remembered. As a kid who grew up in this town, a kid who once had his favorite book, "The Pete Rose Story," signed by the man himself, a kid who played alongside Rose for six games in 1978 and who later played for him during Rose's managerial stint, Oester is not ashamed to invoke his name, as some others seem to be.

"Pete should be here throwing out the first ball or something," Oester said after Game 1, the first World Series in Cincinnati without Rose since 1961. "It doesn't seem right. You talk about Reds baseball and you can't not talk about Pete Rose. He's the greatest who ever played here. Hey, he made a mistake. Jesus. So what? If you looked into the closets of 99 percent of the guys in this room, you'd find something, I guarantee you.

"I know he's watching us in prison. I know it. I still can't get used to the idea."

He sighed and returned to his beer. When Rose was here, he and Oester would talk every day about the games they had seen on TV. Both had satellite dishes. Both would go home at night and stay up to 3 or 4 a.m., flicking the channels. "I'd see some great play and I'd say to myself, 'Pete is gonna ask me about that one tomorrow.' It was like studying for a test. And sure enough, he'd ask."

But just as they would always talk baseball, they would never talk about the problem. The gambling. Nobody wanted to bring it up. Not even Rose's friends, who suspected and often knew its extent.

Ray Knight, who played here for years, considers himself a friend. But he has not spoken with Rose. He has not contacted him during his troubles. "If you know Pete, you know how he wants to deal with this by himself. He doesn't want any outside advice.

"I was walking around Cincinnati today, going to the old places we used to go to, restaurants, stores, a golf course. And everyone asked me about Pete. A lot of them asked if I knew he was gambling. And I said absolutely. But we never talked about it. I can't explain. You just didn't do that with Pete."

Back in the '70s, Rose was all over the World Series. There is that picture of him sliding headfirst into third in 1975 against Boston. Back in 1972 — the first time the Reds met the A's — Cincinnati fell behind, three games to one. They had tickets to go home. Rose led off Game 5 with a homer. The Reds won that game and the next.

But that was then and this is now. The 1990 Reds bear the mark of Rose's image, but the fact is, with mostly the same talent, he could never muster them higher than second place. Rose was a pretty average manager, a guy who overworked his pitchers and wasn't much on discipline. He treated his players the way he probably wanted to be treated, which was to be left alone. He failed to realize that not everyone thinks like Pete Rose.

Perhaps, watching this Series on a prison TV set, he realizes it now. His old teammates are all over the place. Johnny Bench is here, and Tony Perez is here, and Ken Griffey is here, walking around, smiling. In fact, the Reds are wearing Griffey's No. 30 because he was part of this team when the season began. And, of course, there is no stigma in honoring Ken Griffey.

And Rose? There is only a street sign outside the stadium: "Pete Rose Way." Funny. It was the Pete Rose Way that got him where he is now.

Back in 1975, in Game 6 of the Series, one of the most dramatic ever played, Rose came to bat in extra innings with the crowd roaring. He grinned at Boston catcher Carlton Fisk. "This is a hell of a game, ain't it?"

Sure is. It has even, beyond his wildest imagination, managed to go on without him. ∎

World Series becomes circus for Reds, funeral for A's

October 20

OAKLAND, Calif. — First the circus, then the funeral. That's the way this World Series will be remembered, all those Cincinnati Reds circling the bases in the third inning Friday night like so many clowns on unicycles. One. Two. Three. Five. Seven. Seven runs? In one inning? Look, the shortstop got a triple. Look, the little second baseman got a single. Look, the funny-looking guy named Sabo with those Kareem Abdul-Jabbar glasses — he hit one out of the park, his second home run of the night.

First the circus, then the funeral. By the time the Reds were done with that inning — and done laughing — they were also done with this Series, they had buried the Athletics so deep, even Charlie Finley couldn't find them. "It was contagious," Eric Davis said of the hitting. "Like laughter."

Or a deadly virus. Oh, sure, there's Game 4 tonight in this Simply Red affair, and maybe Dave Stewart will make a last pitch for glory and push this Series one more night toward winter. But forget it. This one's over. It's Red October. Nobody has come back from a 3-0 deficit in a World Series, and we're going back to 1903 here.

The A's won't be the first. Heck, they're still trying to figure out 6:20 p.m. Friday, West Coast time, when the world as they knew it went flying over their heads.

How overwhelming was that one inning? You could wrap it up, put a bow around it and have a complete baseball set for Christmas. Singles. Double. Triple. Home run. Error. Stolen base. Wild pitch. Every Cincinnati hitter got a chance at the plate. Barry Larkin and Billy Hatcher got two. Only Hal Morris didn't reach base — and he knocked in a run.

Seven runs. Seven hits. One inning. Zero hope. Ray Knight, who four years ago was the most valuable player in the World Series, was sitting in the press box, keeping score on a large white scorecard. When the inning ended he stood up, turned around and this is what Ray Knight said: "Ahhhwoooooo! Ahhhwooooo!"

"What's that?" someone asked.

"It's the sound a dog makes when he just got his butt kicked."

Ahhhwooooo.

Ahhwooooo. That will teach us to make predictions. Nearly everyone had the A's not only winning this Series, but waltzing through it. Oakland was supposed to be unbeatable, stacked on every shelf. Some even used the dreaded word "dynasty" — because Oakland had swept last year's Series and at least shown up the year before. That makes a dynasty? Listen. Let's make a pact: From now on, "Dynasty" will refer only to a bad TV show with a lot of cleavage. You tag a baseball team with that word, it almost always gets embarrassed.

That is most likely how the A's feel this morning. Here was Rickey Henderson, running to the wall in that third inning, watching helplessly as Sabo's blast soared over his head. Here was Mike Gallego, diving to the basepath, a mouthful of dirt, as Mariano Duncan's hit went skipping past him into the outfield. Here was Mark McGwire, reaching for Paul O'Neill's shot down the first base line, and coming up with nothing but air as the ball ricocheted toward right.

The circus, the funeral. And, remember, the Reds — who have now scored 20 runs in three games — did Friday's damage on Oakland's home field, starting a pitcher, Tom Browning, who had about five minutes' sleep in the last two days after tending to his wife as she delivered their third child. "I was pretty hyped up," Browning said after the Reds' 8-3 blowout. "But once we got that lead …"

Say no more. Perhaps the most notable thing about that killer third inning is that it came after the A's scored two runs in the second to take the lead. The message was clear; it has been since Davis cracked a home run off Stewart when this World Series was still wet behind the ears. This is the message: We are not impressed.

N o. Instead, they are impressive. When the smoke clears, historians will have to race to the tote board and replace the names Canseco, McGwire, Henderson and Welch with Rijo, Hatcher, Sabo and Oliver. Who?

"I think the fact that we haven't been impressed with ourselves is what's enabled us to do what we've done," said first baseman Todd Benzinger. "We've done a good job where it counts — on the field."

And the A's? Bad job. First, Stewart gets racked in Game 1. Then Canseco plays pattycake with a fly ball, turning an out into a triple, and there goes Game 2. Then, Friday night, Mike Moore, who was supposed to be Mr. Big Game in the postseason, lasts only 60 pitches, most of them flying back past him and into the outfield. His exit after 2⅔ innings was the fastest of any Series pitcher since Dave Righetti got hammered by the Dodgers nine years ago.

What is it? Were the A's not as good as everyone thought? Not necessarily. They just ran into a Cincinnati steamroller. And their pitching went south when they needed it most. Then again, it's hard to stay sharp when all these Reds clowns are racing around your infield.

With the game just about over, Knight held up his scorecard, and he pointed to the third inning. It was full of black diamonds, indicating runs scored. "OK," he said, grinning, "who picked the Reds in four?"

Ahhhwoooo. ∎

Red Wings' Burr can't keep quiet, even when he's alone

November 1

"Holy Motormouth, Batman!"
— **Jimmy Carson, when asked to describe Shawn Burr**

He was 2 years old when he first heard the voices. They came from downstairs. Laughing. Talking. Beautiful noise. He had to find it. He pulled himself over his crib and wandered down the steps.

"Shawn, what are you doing down here?" his parents asked. They laughed and apologized to their guests. They carried the baby upstairs. Into the crib. Kiss goodnight.

Five minutes later, he was back.

"Shawn, what are you doing out again?"

Up the stairs. Into the crib.

Five minutes later, he was back.

This went on. And on. "I just wanted to be where all the action was," Shawn Burr recalls, laughing. "After a while, my folks put a lid on my crib. So I stayed put."

Today, there are still people who would like to put a lid on Shawn Burr. Maybe even a few of his teammates. But what do they know? To appreciate this suddenly excellent hockey player, you must not only appreciate his drive on the ice, his indefatigable spirit or the fact that he can lose 12 pounds in a single game, you must also appreciate his love of voices and the fine art of conversation, of which Burr, 24, is a master.

But then, he's had a lot of practice. From the crib to elementary school to junior hockey to the NHL, no one has ever had to say, "Hey, Shawn, what's on your mind?" You'll know what's on his mind. Believe me. If this guy were a radio station, he would be WBUR, 24-Hour Talk. Shawn knows a joke? The whole room knows the joke. Shawn has an imitation? The whole room hears the imitation. You think I'm exaggerating? Well. OK. Shawn doesn't really talk all the time. Only when he's awake.

"Yeah, I stayed up one night to see if I talked in my sleep, but I didn't." He laughs. Hyuk-hyuk-hyuk. Get it?

Oh. Yes. About that laugh. It's kind of like a hyena, all high-pitched and scratchy. But it's ... well ... the word I keep coming back to is charming. You hesitate to use that word with a hockey player — his teammates will tease him unmercifully — but, sorry, it's the best word I know for Shawn Burr. He really is charming.

He also has all his own teeth.

Shawn Burr on his athletic build: "I have the perfect body ... for a mailman."

On his female fans: "I usually attract the 15-year-olds who weigh 230 pounds. They come up wearing my sweater."

On his voice: "Sometimes I watch myself talking on TV, and I can't believe I sound like that. It's like one of the Muppets is behind me, lip-syncing."

Here, hockey fans, is a real rarity, the perfect blend of childhood innocence and NHL skill. It is true, for example, that Burr will watch cartoons on the road with his roommate, Sergei Fedorov. ("Sergei likes the Ninja Turtles. He doesn't understand the other shows.") It is true that Burr went to West Berlin and posed for a photo with a border guard — then stuck "the bunny ears fingers" behind his head.

It is also true that, as of Tuesday, Burr was second in the NHL in game-winning goals, had as many assists as Steve Yzerman and trailed only Yzerman in Red Wings total points. He is off to his best start ever and has become a force to be reckoned with on this Detroit team.

"Shawn is beyond a role player now," says his coach, Bryan Murray. "He has a chance to be a great NHL talent. He can be a 30-goal scorer. And he plays both ends real well. I can use him with a minute to go and us up by a goal, or with a minute to go and us down by a goal."

He can also use him with a minute to go and no commercials left. Give Shawn 60 seconds, he'll give you a nightclub act.

Example. Ask him about women reporters in the locker room. "I have a solution. We all take our clothes off."

Ask about injuries in the NHL. "It's rough. Unless the bone is sticking out from the skin, you better keep skating."

Now ask him about silence. Here's a subject that makes him uncomfortable. The child of a former Canadian football player, and the product of a loquacious family — for whom Christmas and Thanksgiving mean 10 relatives all talking at once — Burr is admittedly spooked in quiet rooms. He gets itchy. When he comes home to an empty house, he automatically flicks on the TV. Or talks to his dog. His dog?

"It's like fishing, right? I like to go fishing. But I don't like to go alone. It's too quiet. I start talking to the fish. I say, 'Come on. I know you're down there. Come on. Bite!' "

"Why do you like talking so much?" I ask.

He laughs. "I don't know, I feel like I usually have something to say."

You know what? He usually does. Although teammate Joe Kocur says, "Shawn talks enough for the both of us," Burr remains one of the most insightful guys on the Red Wings. He watches the news. He takes correspondence college classes. He has a refreshingly pure attitude, almost childish at times. Good is good. Bad is bad. People are pretty much OK, unless proven otherwise.

Not surprisingly, he adores kids — he plays with them, makes conversation, goes to their hockey games — and they gravitate toward him, perhaps because, with his blond crew cut and unwhiskered cheeks, he looks like a fourth-grader who just ran home from school. You half-expect him to burst in, yelling, "MA! GUESS WHAT I FOUND!"

A few years ago, Burr's teammates tried to get his attention on the bus. He deliberately ignored them because "I thought they were gonna throw a peanut at me." Finally, Adam Oates yelled, "Hey, SKIPPY!"

Burr turned, just for an instant. "I've been stuck with that nickname ever since," he moans.

Skippy?

Shawn Burr on alcohol: "I don't get hangovers, because I can't drink enough to get a hangover."

On what he would do if he weren't a hockey player: "Hmmm. Probably sit around and wish I was a hockey player."

On his Halloween plans: "My wife and I are going out, so I'll just leave a big bucket of chocolate bars on the porch and let the kids work on the honor system. I think it'll be OK. Unless some big fat kid comes along and eats them all."

Did you know this about Shawn Burr? He sometimes needs intravenous fluids after games. Goes to the hospital. Takes a needle. He has dehydration problems, and he plays so hard, he can drop pounds every period. His weight fluctuates from 185 to 200. Once, playing with the flu, he lost 12 pounds in a game. The sweat comes like rainwater.

So, sometimes, do the tears. I have seen Burr cry on several occasions, after tough losses. He is not ashamed of this. "He gives you everything emotionally," Murray says. "He is one guy who truly cares about the team first, himself second."

Lately, the team has been the greater beneficiary.

Which doesn't mean he's talking less. He still teases his teammates. And they still laugh and shake their heads. "Some of them think I say stupid things, but that's just me. I tried for a while to be quiet. I couldn't.

"It's like my body. Or my voice. I can't change it. But I wouldn't if I could. I believe you accept everybody for what they are.

"Besides, if everyone had a deep voice and a muscular build, the world would be pretty boring."

Holy Motormouth, Batman — he's a philosopher, too! Ah well. It's a perfect end to the story. In a lot of ways, Shawn Burr is still the same boy who crawled out of his crib 22 years ago, looking for the noise. Only now he makes it. You know what? I like the results. If talk-talk-talk be the price of success, well, pump up the volume. WBUR is on the air. Dogs and fish, are you listening? ∎

A handy guide to sports talk: Here's what they really mean

November 29

Well, personally, I want to say thanks to Zeke Mowatt. He did our business a real favor. After reportedly approaching a female reporter, sticking his naked body a few inches from her face and making several lewd remarks about what he thought she wanted — while some of his teammates egged him on — he then denied the whole thing. He made up a story. He told it to the NFL.

And after weeks of study, the NFL investigation came to the following conclusion: Mowatt's denial "is not credible."

Which basically means: Mowatt lied.

Now, some people are surprised at this. I don't know why. What did you expect, the truth? After all, most athletes are like politicians and actors; they figure the press is only there to make them look good.

As a result, most veteran sports writers have learned to distinguish what is said from what is meant. It's easy. You pretty much figure one has nothing to do with the other.

Of course, perfecting this can take years of hanging around steamy locker rooms. And who wants to ruin all those clothes? So as a public service to our readers, I am offering the following handy guide to the most common sports talk — from players, coaches, TV analysts — with the statement on top, and the translation on the bottom.

This way, next time you read something from Mowatt, you'll be able to laugh, like the rest of us.

Ready? Here we go …

"First of all, I want to give credit to the other team."
(WE KICKED THE HELL OUT OF THEM. HAHAHAHAHA!)

"Winning the MVP award is nice, but I'd rather we won the championship."
(I'm gonna hang this sucker right over my fireplace.)

"I'm Victor Kiam, and I liked the razor so much, I bought the company."
(I'm an idiot. Don't believe a word I say.)

"What quarterback controversy? If I don't play this weekend, then I'll root for whoever does."
(Yeah. I'll root for him to meet Lawrence Taylor, knee-high.)

"Gee, I'd like to stay with the team, but I have to think about my family."
(If I don't get $15 million for three years, I'm outta here.)

"I don't care what their record is, I guarantee they'll be fired up when they play us."

(That's all we need, to lose to these clowns.)
"That's the dumbest rumor I ever heard."
(I'm gonna kill the guy who leaked it.)
"He's a journeyman boxer with a solid reputation."
(He was the only guy available on half-hour's notice.)
"Gee, I don't know. You'd have to ask the coach about that."
(While you're at it, ask the fool when he's gonna retire.)
"We were extremely pleased with the production on our broadcast."
(PBS got higher ratings.)
"You know, Brent, some think he might be among the two or three most underrated players on his team."
(Quick, who is this guy?)
"Just because we're up, 3-0, in the series, we can't count those guys out yet."
(Boy, do they stink. What time's the parade?)
"THIS WILL BE THE GREATEST FIGHT OF ALL TIME!"
(It will cost $40, pay-per-view.)
"Son, I promise you'll be the starting fullback if you come to our university."
(And the other two kids I promised don't.)
"What I like about this kid, more than the way he plays, is that he's such a great person."
(He hasn't been arrested once this semester.)
"Sure, I'd be happy to sign your T-shirt."
(You bozo.)
"There's nothing wrong with the run 'n' shoot."
(That Jerry Rice couldn't fix.)
"I know my holdout might have hurt the team, but it really wasn't about money."
(It was about how much money.)
"He's a salt-of-the-earth guy."
(He can't read.)
"I didn't do nothin'."
(I did everything.)
"That's just something a reporter made up, trying to get a story."
(This excuse will work. It always does.)
"Statistics are meaningless."
(How many points did I have?)
"No comment."
(Drop dead.) ∎

Jacques Demers, radio man, returns to Joe Louis Arena

December 14

The bus pulled into the Joe Louis Arena parking lot, and the man in the blue suit peered out the window. He tugged on his canvas bag, which contained a pair of headphones and two media guides. Funny, he thought, have I ever used this entrance before? Last time he was here, and all the times before that, he had his own parking space, near the door. He would wave at the guard and drive right in, a VIP. Now he was riding the bus, with the visiting team. He did not even sit up front. That's where the head coach sits. Jacques Demers, radio man, sat a few rows behind.

Will they remember me?

The door opened. He stepped out. "Jacques! Jacques!" screamed a group of school kids, rushing at him like buffalo. "Jacques! Sign this, Jacques!"

They remembered him.

He smiled. He signed. He signed Red Wings banners and Red Wings caps. A man in a Red Wings sweater yelled, "Welcome back, Jacques!" and someone else, filming him with a video camera, yelled, "You're always at home here, Jacques."

"Good to see you again, Jacques!"

"Thank you."

"Hey, Jacques, you got a bum deal!"

"Thank you."

He had been unable to sleep all afternoon, missing his customary nap because, he said, "I was tossing and turning — like I was coaching the game or something." He was not coaching, of course, and that was the story. For four years Jacques Demers had been synonymous with Detroit hockey, he was the coach, the hero, the mustached Boy Scout who had found the team in the gutter and lifted it to its feet. He won a division title. Then he won another. He won coach of the year. But things soured. Players drifted from his grasp. Last season, the Wings missed the playoffs, and he was fired. This was his first trip back.

Jacques Demers, radio man.

"Hello, fellows," he said now, as the arena staff ushered him inside. "Hello. ... Hello, there. ... Nice to see you again. ..."

A small crowd floated around him. Cameras flashed. Reporters scribbled. A security guard stepped up and handed Demers a small blue credential, for visiting media.

"Sorry," the guard said, embarrassed, "you ... uh, have to wear one of these."

O nce, this building was the house of his dreams. "I thought I would live here forever," he said. But five months ago he got a phone call. Mike Ilitch, the Red Wings' owner, wanted to see him. Demers jumped in his Ford truck, thinking only good things. Maybe a promotion. Maybe the general manager's position. When Ilitch answered the door, Demers saw his face, and, as he says now, "I knew it wasn't a promotion."

He had been fired — for the first time in his life. On the way home, he pulled his truck off the road and his eyes began to water. This was always the Demers way. Heart. Emotion. It was his strength. Some say his weakness.

But that was then. This was now. He was Jacques Demers, radio man, and a local TV channel wanted an interview, and so he stepped into the empty arena and waddled a few steps onto the ice. Once, in 1987, he had done this same shuffle in front of a packed house, and the crowd roared with delight. His team, the laughingstock of the NHL, had come from impossible odds that night to beat the Toronto Maple Leafs in seven games and advance to within one round of the Stanley Cup finals. He shook his fists and threw a puck to his wife, Debbie.

Now, as he crossed the ice, he glanced up at the banner that commemorated that season, as if checking that it was still there.

"Are you going to go in the Wings' locker room?" he was asked.

"I'd love to see the players," he said, "but I don't feel right. Bryan Murray has a team to prepare for this game. I don't want to be a disturbance ..."

"Is it hard coming back?"

"It's difficult. Even now when I see that red sweater, I have special feelings ..."

"Do you miss coaching?"

"I miss it, but I enjoy what I'm doing now ... I ... "

He gazed across the ice. Without realizing it, he had stepped behind the Wings' bench, his old spot, the place he had sweated all those nights, and chomped on gum and thrown his glasses. Just for a moment, perhaps, some long lost feeling rose from those boards and pierced his flesh.

"I brought my heart here," he said, suddenly. "I brought my heart here. ..."

D own the hall, inside the Red Wings' locker room, Demers' former players dressed for the game. They had a new boss, a new attitude. Players don't get sentimental over coaches. It's not smart.

Still, each of them was shaped a bit by this man, as we are all shaped by the people we touch. Someone mentioned to Rick Zombo that Demers was out on the ice. Zombo smiled. He had been a marginal player when Demers arrived. He gave Zombo a chance — and the marginal player developed into a fine defenseman.

"I still remember the time Jacques and I flew to Toronto for a disciplinary hearing after I slashed a guy," Zombo said. "He was so nervous for me. He was popping peanuts in his mouth real fast, and chewing on ice.

"When we got before Brian O'Neill (NHL executive vice president), Jacques was so worked up, he was waving his fists and pleading with the guy. I knew we wouldn't get anywhere, but Jacques didn't give up. He just kept pleading for me, pleading, banging his fists. Afterward, when we got turned down, he felt really bad, he was all misty-eyed."

"He really went to bat for you, huh?" someone asked.

Zombo nodded. "Jacques went to bat for everybody."

The game drew closer. Demers did more interviews, more greetings, more interviews. Then, almost apologetically, he said, "Excuse me. I have to do my work."

He recorded a TV segment, in French. And a pregame radio show, in French. He wore the headphones and he spoke professionally about the Red Wings and their fine talent. Word is he's pretty good at this radio business. They love him in Quebec. The other night, after the Nordiques upset Vancouver in overtime, he sang, "Turn out the lights, the party's over. ..."

"He has a great future in broadcasting," said his partner, Alain Crete. "He is a natural on the radio."

Funny, isn't it? There was a time when you could not imagine this town without Demers, butchering the English language and pacing behind the hockey bench. Life goes on.

Still, every now and then what you give out comes back to you. So it was that during the final period Thursday, a fan bounced over to the radio booth and handed Jacques a construction paper sign that read, "We Love You. Thankx 2 U, Jacques." And when he turned the fan began to clap, and the row behind him began to clap, and the next row, then the whole section, and pretty soon, people were on their feet, facing the booth, cheering, one more time, for Jacques Demers. Radio man.

"I brought my heart here," he said later, wiping his eyes. Truth is, he left a piece of it here as well. ∎

A gentleman is wronged: Tigers dump Ernie Harwell

December 20

He entered the room with his heart already broken, yet he forced a smile; he greeted the reporters, told them thanks for coming. A gentleman does not forget his manners, no matter how much dirt is thrown at him. This has always been the quality that separates Ernie Harwell from the dim bulbs in baseball. And so he squeezed his lip when it began to quiver Wednesday morning, and he squinted into the lights of this, his first and only news conference in 72 years on this planet.

"I'm told it was a business decision," he said, when asked why the Detroit Tigers, had suddenly, after 31 years of the finest baseball broadcasting in America, told him he was out of a job after the 1991 season. "The Tigers said they wanted to go in a new direction. ... I would have liked to continue broadcasting, but ... this is what they decided. I have to accept that."

He refused to whine. He refused to grovel. Because he is a gentleman, he refused to slam his bosses for the lousy thing they had done.

Allow me.

Oh, you bet I'll slam them. And behind me is a line from here to Alpena waiting to do the same. What the Tigers did Wednesday was one of the most shameful acts I have ever witnessed from a sports franchise, and, considering the company, that's sinking pretty low. They took a man who is a national treasure and told him to start packing. They took a man who literally taught baseball to hundreds of thousands of fans, summer after summer, and they told him he's too old, his time is up. They fired Ernie Harwell? Is that allowed?

It is if you run the team and the radio station. So for this brilliant act of sports management, we can thank Bo Schembechler, the new Tigers president, and Jim Long, the WJR general manager, and Jeff Odenwald, the Tigers' new marketing man. (Everybody has a marketing man these days, right?) These three wise men, in a single 45-minute meeting a few months ago, made the biggest bonehead move of the decade. They killed the voice of baseball. They fired Ernie Harwell.

Oh, they prefer to call it "forced retirement," but that is a joke. Harwell, against his wishes, will be gone after next season — without a real pension, I might add, from the Tigers or WJR. Nice move, huh? Just in time for Christmas.

Hey, guys. Why not punch Santa in the face while you're at it?

Now, let's be clear on something. There is nothing wrong with Ernie

Harwell. No reason he should go, other than this "new direction" the Tigers keep spouting. Harwell looks good, sounds as wonderful as ever. "I feel better than I felt 20 years ago," he said Wednesday, looking quite fit in a blue sports jacket and red tie. "My blood pressure is 100 over 70, my cholesterol count is 179, the doctor said my eyesight is like a 35-year-old. …"

I heard this, and suddenly, something inside me began to twinge. Ernie Harwell, in this dimly lit room, defending his health — surely this ranks as one of the lowest sports moments in recent memory. His blood pressure? Good god. Why should Ernie Harwell have to give us his blood pressure? He has earned the right to stay in the booth until his teeth fall out.

Let me explain why this is: Here is a man who has been broadcasting sports since the end of World War II. A man who rode the trains with the old Brooklyn Dodgers, and who counted players such as Roy Campanella and Jackie Robinson among his friends. He goes back to the days of re-creations, which he did for the road games of the Atlanta Crackers of the Southern League. He would stand next to a ticker-tape machine and recite the play-by-play as it came across, while a sound man made the noise of bats and crowd cheers.

So Ernie Harwell is living history. And more than that. For the last three decades, he has awakened Michigan in baseball season with a favorite line from the Bible, "For lo, the winter is past, and the voice of the turtle is heard in our land." He has broadcast our World Series championships in 1968 and 1984. His phrases and soft Georgia accent were imitated by children who now have children of their own, doing the same imitations. "Here come the Tigahs." … "He stood there like a house by the side of the road." … "Thank-ya Mistah Carey."

There are countless reasons Harwell — and Paul Carey, his longtime partner, who announced that he also will leave after the 1991 season — must be considered the best in the business right now, not the least of which is the plaque in the baseball Hall of Fame that bears Harwell's name.

That alone is reason to keep him. But on top of all this, Ernie Harwell also has a characteristic beyond baseball, something that most of us lose with our childhood: He makes people nicer. I have seen the crudest of athletes turn into choir boys when Harwell walks past. "Hello, Mr. Harwell," they say. "How are you, Ernie?"

How does he do this? By being a good man, an honest man, a man who, as long as anyone can remember, has never stooped to insulting a fellow human being.

People like this, you don't fire. People like this, you pay off their doctors to keep them around.

So this move by the Tigers and WJR is so awful, so blatantly stupid, that I felt compelled to turn to Odenwald during Harwell's news conference and ask him why. I asked him five times. He never really answered me.

"We want to go in a new direction," he kept saying.

"Why?" I said again. "Is Ernie too old? Do you want to reach a younger audience? Are you unhappy with the way he broadcasts?"

"We just felt we wanted to go in a new direction."

Odenwald was stammering, looking for words. At that moment, he reminded me of some oil company executive, trying to sweep all his sins under the carpet of "it's not personal, it's just business."

But at least Odenwald showed up, which is more than can be said about Schembechler and Long. I think most readers know I have a lot of respect for Schembechler. But not on this. He gets one strike for the firing. He gets another if what Ernie says is true — and Bo says it isn't — that the Tigers and WJR suggested Harwell "announce his retirement" during the Tigers' press tour next spring, a cowardly thing to do.

Strike three comes with Bo's explanation when he finally surfaced Wednesday afternoon. "I don't want to get into all the factors," he said when asked for one good reason Harwell should no longer broadcast the games. "It's firm. It's not going to change no matter how much clamor is made over it."

Well, now. There's another bright statement from our baseball team. Who are they playing for — the fans, or themselves? Suppose the clamor turned to people refusing to buy tickets? Would they listen then?

L et me tell you something else about Ernie Harwell, something that makes this "new direction" even more despicable. For all these years, Harwell never used an agent to negotiate his contracts. Usually, he just walked into former Tigers president Jim Campbell's office, had a brief discussion and waited for the contract to arrive. The Tigers and WJR — both of whom have been known to be cheap — would sometimes not even give Harwell a raise between three- or five-year deals. WJR made him work without an engineer; he and Carey would have to lug their own equipment on road trips. I once asked Ernie if he would let me write this fact and he said, "No, I don't want to embarrass WJR like that."

And yet his station never hesitated to call on him to schmooze with potential clients. Ernie, go talk with this clothing store. Ernie, help us get this company to advertise. He never refused a request. What was he paid for this? Nothing. The truth is, while most people in Michigan saw Harwell as a treasure, WJR and the Tigers saw him merely as an employee. They squeezed him dry, like a dish rag. Now they want to toss him aside.

He never complained. He never demanded that money be put aside for his retirement. And now, because of this sudden dismissal, and because of the family he supports, he finds himself in a position where, most likely, he will have to work after his last Tigers season is over. Can you imagine? Ernie Harwell having to take a job with some other team, introducing himself to new players, maybe moving from his home? The Tigers offered him a limited role in 1992, maybe a pregame show. But as Harwell said, "A play-by-play man does play-by-play." Actually, if the Tigers had any class, they would take a million dollars they were going to give the next Willie Hernandez or Chris Brown and hand it over to Harwell, free and clear.

They won't, of course. This is your baseball team, Detroit, and your radio station, WJR, the "home of the Tigers." They want to go in a "new direction." They want to be the Pistons.

They can go anywhere they want. This will never change: This day, this sunny Wednesday in the middle of December, will forever be a black mark on the history of this franchise. Ernie Harwell, who gave and gave, deserved to pick his own exit, to take his bows when he thought he was finished. The Tigers and WJR have denied him this. They have killed the voice of baseball. Even worse, they have robbed a gentleman of his dignity. And in doing so, they have lost all of theirs.

Shame on them. ∎

Bowls by any other names don't smell as sweet as Rose

December 27

JACKSONVILLE, Fla. — If I had a dog — which I do, but I mean if I had a dog with me, right now, down here — I would say to him, "Toto, we're not in Kansas anymore." Or rather, "Toto, we're not at the Rose Bowl anymore." That's assuming his name was Toto, of course. And that he remembered the Rose Bowl. I remember the Rose Bowl. In fact, this morning I remember the Rose Bowl the way I remember my first girlfriend. I miss it desperately. I want it back in my arms. I spent the last three New Year's at that event, living in a hotel near the beach, where, each morning, they put a rose on your breakfast table.

They do that kind of thing in Southern California. Here in Jacksonville, things are a little different. Here, we are not far from Fat Boy's Real Pit Bar-B-Que, which is not far from Bubba's Bar-b-que, which is not far from Church's Bar-b-que which advertises, among other things, smoked goat. You just can't get that in Southern California. Also, there are no roses on the breakfast table here. There are grits.

None of this really matters — except maybe to the dog, who probably likes grits. What does matter — and the worst part of this No-Rose Bowl-for-Michigan-or-Michigan State Business — is this corporate thing. Allow me to demonstrate.

"Welcome to the Gator Bow–"

ZZZAPPP!

"Sorry. The Mazda Gator Bowl."

That's right. In case you were too busy decorating the Christmas tree with your official Kmart bulbs, and your official Pepperidge Farms Gingerbread Men, and your official Kraft candy canes, here is the news: College football has become one big corporate billboard.

"MAZDA GATOR BOWL!"

"SMOKED GOAT!"

Go blue.

Look around. It's everywhere. The Cotton Bowl is now the Mobil Cotton Bowl. The Fiesta Bowl is now the Sunkist Fiesta Bowl. The Holiday Bowl is now the Sea World Holiday Bowl. Companies have seized New Year's the way they seized every inch of a tennis player's body. Football, in their minds, is one big, blinking neon sign.

Now, I admit, I always thought it was kind of silly for mammoth defensive linemen to play in something called the Peach Bowl. Or the Raisin Bowl. But fruit — any kind of fruit — has to be better than this:

the Poulan/Weed Eater Independence Bowl. Weed Eater? Some team actually needs a winning season to get into the Weed Eater Bowl?

This stuff has to be a letdown for players. You can see them, years from now, with their grandchildren: "You know, Jimmy, when I was young I scored the winning touchdown in the Blockbuster Bowl."

"Wow, Grandpa! Did you get a free rental?"

What's next? I figure, with corporations footing the bills, it's just a matter of time before they tell the cheerleaders to mix in some product with the rah-rahs. Just imagine the cheers at this Mazda Gator Bowl:

Push 'em back,
Shove 'em back
Rooooootary engine!
Or the John Hancock Bowl:
Two, Four, Six, Eight
Assets will depreciate!
Or the Federal Express Orange Bowl:
Make 'em sweat, make 'em dirty
We deliver by ten-thirty!
Or the Domino's Pizza Copper Bowl:
Give 'em heck, give 'em hell. Our boss fired
Ernie Harwell!

Of course, it's not like college football didn't ask for this. Every November, greedy teams auction themselves as if part of a brothel. The final weeks of the season are repulsive, with little men in funny-colored jackets stuffing the press boxes, making deals, cursing when the team they thought they stole from old Billy Bob with Mobil turns out to be no better than the team Jimmy Joe suckered in with Blockbuster.

And you can bet, when you watch these bowl games on New Year's, you'll see logos, logos and more logos. The formula is sadly familiar: To advertise its product, the corporation wants the highest TV ratings. For that, it needs the best teams. For that, it spends a lot of money. And to justify the money, it needs to stick its name just about everywhere, including the lapel of your jacket. Yes. Most bowl games have pins they want you to wear on the lapel of your jacket. If the Mazda people throw in a car, I'll think about it.

Until then, I'll miss the Rose Bowl. Don't misunderstand. I'm happy for the Wolverines and Spartans players. They deserve a great bowl experience. But with all this commercialism, I can't help wishing one of them had made it to Pasadena, where tradition still rules: Big Ten champ vs. Pac-10 champ. No negotiating. No corporate name. Sure, some of the games have been as thrilling as two rhinos playing in the mud. So? You pick your poison.

I guess what I'm saying is this: In the end, I'd rather have a tiny rose on my lapel. It beats a tiny Weed Eater. ∎

Paralyzed, Ole Miss' Mullins has power to move people

December 31

JACKSONVILLE, Fla. — "It'll come back," he told himself, staring at the sky. "Just lie here. It'll come back." He could not feel his hands or feet. He could not feel his skin against the turf. Through his helmet he heard the dying roar of the crowd, which had suddenly realized the bad news: Chucky Mullins wasn't getting up. Try the fingers, he thought. Nothing. Try the toes. Nothing. Now the trainers were around him. They were screaming, calling for a stretcher. They pinched his arm. Nothing. "Everybody back!" someone yelled. "DON'T MOVE HIM!" … Chucky moaned. He blinked. He thought about the lick he had just laid on that Vanderbilt receiver. Man, it was a beauty, a real stick; no way he catches that ball. No touchdown for Vandy. Ha! But my toes, where are my toes? His body was limp; it slid where they pushed it. An airlift was called. The hospital was alerted. As they carted him off, tied to a wooden board atop a stretcher, Chucky Mullins was still waiting for his soul to return to his limbs. "Five minutes," he told himself, "it'll be back in five minutes. …"

This is the story of the last Mississippi player to arrive for the Gator Bowl. He came in a wheelchair Sunday. He rolled through the airport. He will make no tackles in Tuesday's game, but he will move people, more than any of his teammates will. That is the purpose for Chucky Mullins now, to move people. Back when he was a teenager, he used to throw his big body recklessly, wrestling with friends. One time this kid Tony came to the house, and Chucky greeted him with a bear hug, and the next thing you know they were rolling on the floor, and there's this big crash — BOOM! They broke the bed. They laughed. That was Chucky Mullins, smiling as he touched you. The crazy thing is, in a way, he's still doing it.

Fingers," says Carver Phillips. He takes Chucky's left hand and begins to move the digits, one at a time. Bend the pinky. Bend the pointer. Bend the thumb. Ten times. Now the wrist. Now the elbow. Bend, stretch, bend ...

This is daily life for Roy Lee (Chucky) Mullins, who was paralyzed from the neck down. He looks at his limbs, so soft now, so dead. Sometimes Carver, bending his knee, makes a joke: "Your leg is so loose, I might wrap it around your head." Chucky smiles. He keeps hoping for a tingle. An itch. Some feeling. He waits. He watches TV. He chews the food that Carver slides into his mouth. He talks into a special voice-activated computer — "Lights!" he barks, "Off!" — and the lights turn off. He sleeps.

He waits.

Carver Phillips waits, too. Here is the first person Chucky Mullins touched, long before the accident, before that football play in October 1989 that shattered four vertebrae and changed their lives forever. Back in the early '80s, Carver Phillips had been a young recreation worker with a wife and two children in Russellville, Ala., Chucky's hometown. One day he learned that Chucky's mom had died of pneumonia. He shook his head. He knew the Mullins kids from the rec center. He knew their father was out of the picture. "What will become of them?" he wondered.

He went to see Chucky, who was 12 and living with a nurse, an older woman. Carver took the boy to a few ballgames. They talked sports. One day, Carver's phone rang.

"Can I come live with you?" Chucky asked.

They have been together ever since.

Normally, Carver went to the Mississippi games to root for Chucky, who had grown into a 6-foot, 170-pound defensive back. But on the day of the accident, Carver's car broke down. When word came that Chucky was hurt he had to borrow a car to get to the hospital. On the radio, he heard about the play, how Chucky, a redshirt freshman, broke up a potential touchdown by slamming his helmet into the back of Vanderbilt's Brad Gaines — only his head was bent at a funny angle, and — crack! — he just dropped to the turf and didn't move. Medics later told Ole Miss football coach Billy Brewer that Chucky "should have been dead by the time he hit the ground. It was like taking a hand grenade and dropping it down his spine."

By the time Carver entered the hospital room, the doctors were cutting off Chucky's football pants. There were screws around Chucky's head, and weights and cords. His whole body was in traction. Carver saw that Chucky's eyes were open. He tried to smile.

"My football career is over," Chucky whispered.

Carver, his legal guardian, took a hotel room near the hospital. He stayed the next four months and never went home. Instead, he studied the doctors. He learned how to clean the tube in Chucky's throat, how to suction the saliva so Chucky could breathe, how to transfer Chucky's limp body from bed to wheelchair, how to work his toes and fingers and limbs. This wasn't his son. Did that matter? He had helped raise him. Fed him, clothed him. Two years earlier, Carver, who is only 35 himself, had contracted a lung disease. He could no longer work. He had trouble breathing. A religious man, he wondered what God was doing with him, banging him around this way.

"What is my purpose?" he remembers asking one night in prayer.

And now he had his answer.

Chucky.

C hris Mitchell was the second person to be touched. He and Chucky knew each other from high school, where both were star players. As freshmen at Mississippi, they grew close, they hung together in the dorms. Chris would come back from class sometimes and find Chucky and another friend, Tony Harris, wrestling on the floor.

"You guys are like a couple of kids," Chris would say.

"Aw, we just miss our girlfriends," Chucky would answer.

They built a friendship on fast food and football. And rides home to Alabama. One time the three of them were in the car with another friend. They drove over a hill — and froze. Coming up the hill were two 18-wheel trucks, side by side, trying to pass each other.

"TONY, PULL OVER! Chris screamed.

"OH, S---"

"LOOK OUT!"

They screeched off the road. The trucks passed. Chucky, who had been sitting in the front, had not said a word. Finally, he turned around.

"I wasn't scared a bit," he said.

The car exploded in laughter.

Chris Mitchell remembered that story the day they carried Chucky off the field. I wasn't scared a bit. He thought about it the first time he visited Chucky in the hospital. I wasn't scared a bit. What do you say to your buddy when you know he will never walk again? What can you say? You pretend you're not scared a bit and you go in. During one visit, the TV began to replay Chucky's final tackle. Chris froze. Should he shut it off? Ignore it?

Instead, the two friends watched it together, watched the bodies collide, the football pop away, and Chucky's hands suddenly drop as if his batteries had run out. When it was over, there was silence. Finally, Chucky took a breath. "It was a hell of a lick, wasn't it?"

"Yeah," said Chris, nodding, "you stuck him."

Mitchell sees Chucky all the time now. Last spring, Chris was chosen the best defensive back during football drills. Brewer, the Mississippi coach, came to him with an idea. Since they had played similar positions, would he wear Chucky's number this season?

"I got chills," Chris recalls. "Then I said yes,"

And so on Tuesday No. 38 in your program will be Chris Mitchell. And next year, the best defensive back will wear that jersey. And the best the year after that, and so on.

One life touches another and another.

Chucky.

H e still could not wiggle a finger. But the touching continued. The governor came to visit. President Bush. Janet Jackson.

And, most important, the embrace of his own backyard, the Mississippi campus, a place forever tainted by the bloody racism of the '60s. Attitudes change slowly here, and many think the school is still not far from the days when white men with rifles awaited James Meredith, the first black student. Only two years ago, a black fraternity house was burned to the ground. Last year, as a white fraternity prank, a pledge was stripped naked, painted with the words "nigger" and "KKK" and abandoned on an all-black campus.

But Chucky. Chucky seemed to cut through this color war. One week after his injury, students — including frat members — walked through the stands during the Rebels' game against LSU. They collected money. They were hoping to get $50,000. They got nearly $180,000. When Chucky was flown to the Liberty Bowl last year, white students called his name. Supporters waved banners. No one loses prejudice overnight. But the first step is to realize we all bleed the same.

"It was like Chucky had touched their conscience," Brewer says.

Or maybe become it. A university that once cried "NEVER, NO, NEVER!" to racial integration, has now built a black student a home near campus. Paid for the whole thing. Chucky lives there today. The touching continues.

And finally, to him, and here is perhaps the biggest surprise of all: Where you expect self-pity, there is none. Where you expect depression, there is laughter. He sits in the wheelchair, with the tube that helps him breathe still piercing his throat. When he wants to move, he taps his head against an electronic pad. The chair moves forward. Another tap. It stops. "One day," he says, "I'm gonna get out of this thing."

He laughs, but he is not joking. Chucky Mullins, his body frail now from atrophy, still watches his old films, still points himself out to visitors ("Look, that's me running there. ... Look, that's me making that tackle.") He is determined to move again — despite his doctors, despite the medical books. A few months back, his left arm began to twitch. He felt a flush of emotion. "Hey!" he told Carver.

"Do it again," Carver said.

He did it again. Today, he can lift the arm almost to his face. If they can rig a device for his still-limp hand, maybe one day he can feed himself.

"When this first happened, I kept thinking the feeling would come back. I thought that way for a couple weeks, even. Then eventually, I accepted it. But I never got depressed. I never felt sorry for myself. Why should I? I'm just another human being ...

"I'm not sorry I played football. I loved football. ... I would tell a young kid to play if he wanted. But I'd also tell him to never take one day for granted. That's what I'd tell him. Never take a single day for granted."

He will join his teammates today. And he will be there Tuesday when they play Michigan. Carver Phillips, who found his purpose, will be alongside him. And Chris Mitchell will be wearing his number. And the fans, white and black, will see him from the stands and maybe they will cheer.

You look at Chucky Mullins, who is 21 years old, and you ask, "Why him?" Isn't it enough to grow up poor? Isn't it enough to lose your mother and barely know your father? Isn't it enough to be a good kid through all this, a kid everybody loves? Isn't it enough? And the answer is, there is no answer. There is only this: Tuesday is New Year's Day, a traditional time to clean the slate, to plan our lives. And Chucky Mullins, who, incredibly, seems happier than most people, is here to remind us about priorities.

"What would you do," he is asked, "if your body finally came back to you, right now, this minute?"

"I would get up and run," he says. "And run and just keep running."

You see him smile. You want to cry. And your first New Year's resolution is this: Never forget his story. Never take a single day for granted. Run as far as you can, as fast as your feet will take you, because if Chucky could, he would.

Funny, no? Sometimes, the people who can no longer touch us are the ones who touch us the most. ∎

1991

Marcus Allen paints another silver and black Sunday

January 14

LOS ANGELES — The greatest myth about this football team, the Raiders, is that you only need a uniform to be a part of it. As if colors make the man. You slip on the silver and black and, suddenly, you're not just good, you're Raider-Good. You're tough. You're different. It is the reason that wherever you look, would-be heroes are wearing silver jackets and black hats. Look at me. I'm a Raider.

It doesn't work that way, of course. Marcus Allen, a real Raider, knows it. He has always known it. All during the stampede of TV cameras that plowed past his locker this season to get to Bo Jackson, he knew it. All during the clamor they made last year around new coach Art Shell — his former teammate — he knew it.

And now, at this moment, he knew it again. It was late Sunday afternoon at the Coliseum, like so many other late Sunday afternoons in his career, and Allen, now 30, gazed at the small crowd that was on its feet. The game was over. The freeways were thickening with traffic. But these fans stayed. They cheered. "MAR-CUS! MAR-CUS!"

He waved. He walked toward the tunnel. Security guards formed a human wall. Cheerleaders stood on their tiptoes to get a peek. O.J. Simpson, who, once upon a time, also made the No. 32 famous in this stadium, slipped into the circle and stuck a microphone in Allen's face.

Allen stopped. The cameras rolled.

"Great game, Marcus," said Simpson of the Raiders' 20-10 playoff victory over the Bengals. "Tell me, when Bo went out with the injury, did you feel you really had to pick it up?"

Allen grinned. He should have twirled the mike around O.J.'s neck.

Instead, this is what Marcus Allen said: "You know, I've been doing this a long time."

Spoken like a true Raider.

Hey, kids, all you non-shavers who think those silver helmets are just another marketing tool to make Bo Jackson famous. Listen up: Bo Jackson has yet to earn his Raiders uniform. He hasn't played a full season. He hasn't led the team in blood or courage. Most important, he has never been to the mountaintop. The motto of Al Davis' weird and crazy crew is not — despite what some think — "Bo Knows Football."

The motto is: "Just Win, Baby."

Marcus Allen knows how to win.

It was beautiful to watch him, cradling the football, busting into the open, gaining 140 yards, leaving Cincinnati defenders at his feet, the way he left the Washington Redskins that Sunday night in Tampa, Fla., seven years ago, when, with the world watching, he galloped for 191 yards and took home a Super Bowl MVP trophy.

That was back when Allen had the most famous feet in the Raiders' backfield, and some thought he was the best rusher in the game. That was a while ago. Things have changed. New faces. Losing seasons. Dwindling crowds. For a while, the Raiders seemed destined to go the way of Dillinger, Al Capone — legendary past, no present.

But now we see that for all those changes, Allen has not changed. At least not when it counts. Sunday was a big jump over the broom for this Raiders team, its first playoff game in five years. And once again, here was No. 32 leading the way.

He took a handoff in the first quarter and burst through an opening for 19 yards. A few minutes later, he ran off-tackle for 16 yards. It was this kind of day. Big holes. Big runs.

And then, in the fourth quarter, with Jackson on the bench with a hip injury and Cincinnati rising from the dead, threatening to steal this game, the Raiders gave the ball to Allen again and again. Do the old magic, Marcus. When he started running there was 5:41 left. When he finished, 19 seconds were left. He gained half a football field during that drive. He ate the clock. He sealed the win.

"I've been doing this a long time."

Allen entered the Coliseum tunnel, a place he has been going since his USC days. He showered. He took a pat on the back from Davis, like the old days. And then he came out to meet the press. A mob. The locker near his — No. 34, JACKSON — was empty and ignored.

"I was really pumped up for this game," Allen said. "I still know how to focus. I know what these (playoff) games are about. You get one chance. Sudden death. I was ready."

Old Raiders always are. Three times since 1977 they made the Super Bowl. Three times they won it.

So on Sunday, it was the old guys again. It was Allen rushing and Greg Townsend, the big defensive end, who slam-dunked Boomer Esiason just when Boomer was thinking about winning this game. And it was Shell, who was in his last year as a Raiders player when Allen joined the team. Shell guided the Raiders on Sunday the way John Madden once guided them. Have fun, but get it done.

Now someone asked Allen about the pressure.

"Pressure?" he said. "Pressure is what's going on in the Persian Gulf. This isn't pressure. We've been doing this a long time."

He got dressed. He went home. A long time. That's what the franchise is about. If the Raiders get back to the Super Bowl this year, don't be surprised if Allen — not Jackson — leads the way. Bo knows marketing. But Marcus knows how to make Sundays black and silver.

Go ask Al Davis which really matters. ∎

It was only a game, but oh, what a Super game it was

January 28

TAMPA, Fla. — All week long, they kept saying it's only a game, a war is going on, football, even a Super Bowl, can't mean much. It's only a game. Except that Sunday night, with eight seconds left and a group of New York Giants on their knees, praying on the sideline, and a nervous Buffalo kicker named Scott Norwood out on the field, lining up the ball, and every fan in the stadium on his feet and every fan in his living room on the edge of his seat, breathing hard — well, suddenly, it was more than a game; it may have been the best Super Bowl ever.

"The whole time I was saying, 'Miss it, please, miss it, please,' " Giants cornerback Everson Walls would say when this one was all over, when Norwood's kick went just wide, and the Bills sunk to their knees and those praying Giants sprung to their feet in another wild dance, the sudden winners of the championship of professional football, 20-19, the closest Super Bowl in history. "Please, please, please …"

Please. That was about the margin of victory, wasn't it? A please, a prayer, a whisper, an inch here or there. The best one ever? You might say that. Either team could have won. Either team would have deserved it. This was fine, mistake-free football with drama dripping from every corner. It was better than Baltimore-Dallas 20 years ago, the previous closest Super Bowl. It was better than San Francisco-Cincinnati a couple years ago and was probably even better than Pittsburgh-Dallas in the '70s, for that classic rivalry didn't come down to the final eight seconds, a team asking its kicker to do something he had never done before, make a field goal fly at least 47 yards through the uprights.

"Please, please, please …"

Wasn't this magnificent theatre? Jim Kelly, the Buffalo quarterback who'd waited his whole career for this chance, now pacing on the sideline like a caged cat, waiting for Norwood to seal his destiny. Kelly lumbered past defensive teammates Bruce Smith and Cornelius Bennett, exhausted, their chests heaving, they'd been on the field for what felt like a month. Now, they, too, could only watch.

And across the field, players such as Jeff Hostetler, Ottis Anderson, Dave Meggett and the rest of the low-profile Giants offense, these no-name guys who had kept the ball away from Buffalo for an incredible 40½ minutes — why? because that was the only way to win this game — but here, as they watched Norwood, they worried that maybe eight seconds too many had been left on the table.

"On my wrist I have written 'Just A Prayer,' " said linebacker Pepper

Johnson, one of the kneeling Giants Sunday night, "that's all we asked for, 'just a prayer.' And this time we were hoping Norwood would miss it. ..."

On their knees, heads down, the crowd roaring.

Only a game, right?

More than a game. Here was a clash of strategy, a battle of styles, a real showdown between flash and substance. It had terrific offense and crushing defense, it had running backs busting tackles and tight ends making big catches. It had a safety — a safety? — and a tipped pass that went for 61 yards. It had a starting quarterback, Hostetler, who, until last month, had been a career backup, and a defensive end who called himself "the best in the game."

And for all these ingredients, this Super Bowl was won with the simplest of philosophies: You can't be outscored if the other team doesn't have the ball.

So the Giants kept it. Like kids in a school yard. Our ball. Nyah, nyah. They moved slowly on offense, and I mean slowly, stringing together drives that seemed to stretch from one coast of Florida to another. "If our offense is doing its job," said Anderson, who would earn the MVP award for his 102 yards rushing, "then we're keeping the Buffalo offense off the field."

Indeed, for one incredible run — from late in the second quarter until late in the third quarter — New York kept Buffalo's offense virtually inactive; counting halftime it was nearly an hour. There were all these third downs the Giants kept converting that drove the Bills crazy. Mark Ingram taking a pass and twisting, spinning, juking and spinning again. The chains moved. Howard Cross, a tight end — Howard Cross? — finding a seam and sucking in a pass. The chains moved. More time. More time. The Giants' first drive in the third quarter took 9½ minutes. Their drive to start the fourth quarter took 7½ minutes. You could see Bills players such as Kelly and Thurman Thomas chomping at the bit, desperate to get back out there.

And yet, they showed great maturity. Remember that, unlike the Giants, the Bills have never been to a Super Bowl. You could expect jitters, mistakes, a collapse. Instead, when the Bills finally got the ball back with 2:16 left, trailing by one point with 90 yards to go for a touchdown, they simply shrugged and went to work.

They almost pulled it off.

"I just told my players we've gotta do it," Bills coach Marv Levy said. And here came Kelly, who loves this kind of thing, and he began with a scramble, then another scramble, and then came Thomas, bursting left for 22 yards and Thomas bursting right for 11 yards. Here, in the final seconds, was the situation the Bills were made for with that no-huddle offense. Panic? Nerve City? No problem.

Finally, with nine seconds to go Kelly took the snap and threw the ball to the ground. It was on the New York 29. It meant a 47-yard field goal try, longer than Norwood's personal best on grass. No time-outs left. Norwood trotted onto the field. On such decisions can a Super Bowl turn.

A moment here for Norwood. The problem with games that come down to the last play is that someone is destined to be the goat. Norwood's biggest concern, obviously, was that he had enough leg to make this kick. Turns out he got plenty of leg. But the ball never hooked. It went on a straight line just right of the goalpost, and as Giants cornerback Reyna Thompson, just a few feet from Norwood, began to leap up and down, Norwood began the longest walk of his life, back to the unhappy side of the field.

"I feel like I let a lot of people down," he said. "You only get one opportunity to do something like this. Maybe I tried too hard to get the foot into it. I don't know. I just feel like I let everyone down."

In truth, he didn't. Norwood's mistake wasn't the only one on the game. If anything lost this Super Bowl for the Bills, it was their inability to tackle on crucial plays. But then, there was also Hostetler's falling in the end zone, which led to a safety. And there were even a few bad decisions by Anderson, the MVP. So no one was perfect, no one expected them to be. Norwood's curse is simply this: He was the last guy on the stage.

But at that point, miss or make, it had been a terrific play, a Super Bowl in which, unlike previous blowouts, both teams felt the wrath of the other (listen, for all that New York dominance, Buffalo still racked up 371 yards, just short of New York's 386). In the end, as they say, it was a shame someone had to lose. But a disappointment? Not for the audience — particularly when the audience consisted of civilians in their living rooms and soldiers in a faraway desert.

Funny, isn't it? When you realize it's only a game, you realize how great a game it can be. ∎

Olympic experience just not complete without a mini-bar

February 17

N EWS ITEM — For the first time in history, NBA players will compete for the U.S. Olympic basketball team. This week, Sports Illustrated printed a "projected" Olympic starting five on its cover — Magic Johnson, Michael Jordan, Patrick Ewing, Charles Barkley and Karl Malone. While all of them are multi-millionaires, none will be paid for the Olympic experience. They say they can adjust ...

GUIDE: "*Buenos dias*, gentlemen, and welcome to the Olympic Village. I am Emilio, your guide. And these are your rooms."

EWING: "Whoa. You mean our closets."

GUIDE: "I beg your pardon?"

EWING: "These are the closets, right?"

GUIDE: "Uh ... no sir. These are the rooms. Each athlete gets the same accommodations. See the desk and the lamp and the two beds?"

MAGIC: "I only need one bed."

GUIDE: "Two athletes per room."

BARKLEY: "WHAT?"

JORDAN: "Relax, Charles. Look, man. We're tired from the trip, OK? We had to fly commercial. Let's just turn on ESPN and chill out."

MAGIC: "I wanna watch Sportscenter."

MALONE: "Hey, where's the TV?"

GUIDE: "No TV in village rooms, sir. But we have a splendid TV in the lounge at the end of the hall."

BARKLEY: "THE WHAT?"

JORDAN: "Relax, Charles. Look, we—"

THUMP! BRR-THUMP! CRASH!

MALONE: "What's that noise?"

GUIDE: "Those are your neighbors, the Yugoslavian wrestlers. I suppose they are — THUMP! — practicing."

EWING: "How am I gonna sleep with that?"

GUIDE: "Do not worry, sir, there—"

Bump-dump ... bump-dump-bump ...

MAGIC: "What's that?"

GUIDE: "Those are your other neighbors, the Romanian gymnasts. Tumblers, I think. Do not worry. They will stop by 10 p.m. That's when we have the silence curfew in the village."

BARKLEY: "THE WHAT?"

JORDAN: "Relax, Charles. Look, there's obviously been some mix-up. Let's call down to the front desk and get the rooms switched, OK?"

EWING: "Yeah, and then I'm calling my agent. No way this stuff is in my contract."

MALONE: "Mine, either."

MAGIC: "Let's send out for pizza."

JORDAN: "Emilio … where's the phone?"

GUIDE: "At the end of the hall, sir."

BARKLEY: "THE END OF THE WHAT?"

JORDAN: "Uh, listen, Emilio. I don't mean to be rude, but … I'll give you a dozen pairs of my shoes if you get us a nicer place, OK?"

MAGIC: "And front-row seats to the Janet Jackson concert I'm promoting."

EWING: "I'll give you a car! Two cars!"

MALONE: "My condo in Utah!"

GUIDE: "Please, sirs. I cannot accept anything. Like I said, all Olympians are treated equally, in the spirit of amateur competition. Why don't you relax, have some food?"

JORDAN: "OK. Where's the mini-bar?"

GUIDE: "I beg your pardon?"

MALONE: "No mini-bar?"

EWING: "How about the room-service menu?"

GUIDE: "All athletes eat in the cafeteria."

BARKLEY: "THE WHAT?"

MAGIC: "You mean like trays, and silverware, and big scoops of mashed potatoes?"

GUIDE: "Precisely."

EWING: "That's it. I quit. Where's Chuck Daly?"

MALONE: "He's downstairs, filming his TV show."

MAGIC: "But the Opening Ceremony is in three hours."

JORDAN: "Hey, how much appearance money do we get for that?"

GUIDE: "The Opening Ceremony? No money, sir. You march the around stadium with your flag."

MALONE: "You mean, like … for free?"

BARKLEY: "FOR WHAT?"

JORDAN: "And how do we get there?"

GUIDE: "By bus, with the other athletes."

MAGIC: "I think I got a hamstring pull."

EWING: "Bone spur in my foot."

MALONE: "Head cold."

JORDAN: "Look, Emilio. We got no TV, no phone, no room service, we gotta ride buses, march for free, hang out with people from Afghanistan, and Greece and Brazil. I mean, what do you call that?"

GUIDE: "The Olympic experience, sir."

BARKLEY: "WE CALL IT THE CBA!"

EWING: "How long till we go home?" ∎

Fame leaves Chris Webber precious little time to be kid

February 28

One coach, upon learning that Chris Webber goes to church every Sunday, dashed off a letter saying, he, too, was a regular churchgoer: "The other night we were singing a hymn, and I had the joy of Jesus in my soul — and then I started thinking about you, Chris, and how, if you played basketball for our school, it would bring joy to my soul, too."

Chris threw the letter away.

Another coach got wind that Chris was sensitive to family matters. So he called the teenager and began moaning about his divorce, how it was tearing him apart, affecting his work. "Chris," he said, nearly breaking into tears, "if you came to our school, it would make my life so much better ..."

Chris handed the phone to his father, who told the guy no thanks.

There was the coach from Southern Cal who wrote how he loved watching Chris play basketball, and how he had followed his career since junior high school — except that he spelled the name wrong, over and over, calling him "Weber" instead of Webber.

And then there was the coach from a college in Nebraska who called the house and couldn't get anything right.

"So, Chris, you guys play Class D ball, right?"

"No, Class B."

"Oh, right. So, how do you like living in Birmingham?"

"I live in Detroit."

"Oh, right. Say, uh, how's your Dad? I spoke with him just yesterday."

"My Dad's been out of town all week."

"Well, listen, we sure would like you to come to our school.... "

On it goes. Behind Chris Webber, in front of Chris Webber, above Chris Webber, below Chris Webber — this endless parade of college basketball characters. Coaches, recruiters, alumni, boosters, all tripping and stumbling and generally embarrassing themselves, chasing any lead, swallowing any tip — "Where will he go? Which way is he leaning?" — all because this tall, graceful, well-mannered son of an automotive worker can play basketball better than any other high schooler in the country.

He can swoop and dunk. He can pass like a point guard. His body, long and thick, can find the ball through any crowd of defenders, two, three, four, they can't stop him. One game, he scored 38 points and sat out the fourth quarter. Another, he had nine dunks by halftime. In a playoff game, an alley-oop pass went too high, over his head, but he just hung in the air until the ball ricocheted off the glass, then he grabbed it and stuffed it. Amazing. His coach at Birmingham Detroit Country Day, Kurt Keener, says Chris Webber plays the game "as if God built him to do it."

But God never had recruiting in mind. You thought you had a hard time getting through high school? Here is a teenager who has actually removed the phone from his bedroom because it never stops ringing. He has keys to four of his friends' houses — which he goes to even if they are not home — just to escape the madness. When he goes to school, people ask, "Which college have you picked?" and when he goes to the video arcade they ask, "Which college have you picked?" and when he stops at the supermarket they ask, "Which college have you picked?" — as if their lives will change with his decision.

Sometimes, he makes things up, just to throw them off. They swallow it anyhow. He could say he was going to Mars and recruiters would scurry to find what Mars was offering.

"It's embarrassing," Webber says. "All these grown-ups making this big fuss over me."

Embarrassing, yes. Also silly and sad. This is a story of the biggest prize in high school basketball, a 6-foot-9 specimen who can dunk, shoot, pass, rebound and hang in the air long enough to challenge a balloon.

But mostly this is a story of a kid who wants to be a kid. And can't seem to find the time.

A t first I loved all the attention, I admit that," Chris Webber says, "but now, I just wish it would stop." He is stretched across his bed at home in Detroit, a simple brick house on a street full of simple brick houses. Downstairs, the phone, as usual, is ringing. Chris ignores it. He looks around his small bedroom. On one wall is a huge poster of Charles Barkley. On the other, a picture of Big Daddy Kane, the rap artist. Near the bed is an open Bible and an old phonograph with a gospel record on it. Behind the bed is a plastic bag full of sneakers. And next to it, the huge box of recruiting letters from universities across the country.

Hundreds of envelopes. Name the school. It's in there. Unopened.

"I used to read every letter I got," he says. "Now I get maybe 50 a week, and I don't even look at them. They're so phony. I just give them to my younger brothers. I used to take every phone call myself, too. But now, my sister has a list of names of people I don't want to talk to, and she tells them I'm not home."

"When did the calls begin?" he is asked.

"Eighth grade."

It was that year that someone actually offered his father $20,000 to send Chris to a certain high school in Indiana. Ever since, Webber's life has only partly belonged to him. Basketball controls the rest, yanking him as if he were on a leash.

Although Webber desperately wanted to attend Southwestern High in Detroit, where many of his friends were going, his parents chose the prestigious Country Day School in Birmingham, a place that demands a coat and tie each day, has terrific sports teams and costs thousands of dollars a year in tuition — unless you get a scholarship, as Webber did. It was his parents' way of assuring that he got an education along with the athletics. But for the young Webber, it seemed like just another reminder that basketball made him different.

"When I first got to Country Day, it was really hard to adjust," he says. "It's pretty much a white, upper-middle-class school, and a lot of my classmates had these stereotypes about blacks from Detroit. They thought we all had big gold chains, that my mom worked in a Laundromat, that all my friends were thugs, that I wouldn't get good grades."

Eventually, Webber's personality — which, when he's relaxed, is friendly, funny and complimentary — won them over. But he never quite felt at home at Country Day. "I still don't," he says. He recently gave a talk to an assembly about racial prejudice, telling the story of how his great-grandfather was lynched by whites in Mississippi. It has become an important subject to him. Of all the kids in school, he remains closest to a small group of black teammates from his Detroit neighborhood.

"They're like me," he says. "Their parents made them go to Country Day."

But if Chris Webber feels funny, like a standout, let's be honest. He would stand out no matter what high school he attended. Basketball will do that — especially if you dominate the way Webber does. Watching him play, even against the better teams, is like watching a man among boys. He towers over most of the other players and is so superior in shooting and rebounding that he frequently gets bored and tries to make fancy passes or bring the ball up court just to stay interested.

Webber led Country Day to the Class C state championship two years ago and the Class B title last year. In his senior season, when Country Day again is ranked No. 1 in Class B, he is averaging 29 points, 15 rebounds and five blocked shots. More than that, he just looks like an NBA player-in-training. His sleek body moves, his strength, his shooting touch — even his trash-talking. For all his manners, Webber, on the court, is not to be taken lightly. He likes to dig at his opponents, mumbling, "Don't even think about coming in here. ... Don't even try to shoot that ball. ..."

Once, when a particular opponent got mouthy in return, Webber took a pass on the wing, drove straight at him, full speed, and nearly leaped over him en route to the basket, knocking him to the ground with his legs. "I thought the kid was dead," Keener said.

Talent. Size. Competitive fire. No wonder the recruiters drool. You can't get a college coach to compliment Webber on the record — that is forbidden by the NCAA until he signs — but off the record, they call him "a franchise ... he'll make your program ... the best in the country." Which is why, on any given day, at least several major college coaches will be in the Country Day gymnasium, leaning against a wall, watching Webber practice. They can't speak with him — more NCAA rules — but they come anyhow to make eye contact, to send a silent message: "We want you." For this, they fly in from all over the country. One remarkable afternoon, Lute Olson from Arizona, Mike Krzyzewski from Duke and Jud Heathcote from Michigan State were all in the gym to watch Webber play — in a pickup game.

It never stops. When Webber visits campuses, it's a red alert. He took a trip to Duke and was quickly roomed with Christian Laettner, the team's star player. When he recently attended a Spartans game at the Breslin Center, the student cheering section began to chant, "WEB-BER! WEB-BER! WEB-BER!" He was not impressed.

"It's so phony," he says, shaking his head and hooking his long arms across his chest. "I went there with Jalen Rose (another hot prospect, from Southwestern), and at one point, Jalen tapped me and said, 'Look at the bench.' There was this guy, maybe a student manager or something, and as soon as he saw us, he walked over and whispered something to another student, who goes over to the cheering section. And next thing you know, they're cheering, 'WEB-BER! WEB-BER!' I mean, the whole thing was set up. I saw it!" He shakes his head again. "So phony," he says. "I hate that."

N ow. Maybe you say it's a shame that a kid who will turn 18 on Friday has already become so cynical. But what did we expect? This is big-time high school basketball. Even Keener, Webber's coach, is not spared.

"I've already been on four or five radio talk shows from Kentucky," he says. "People call in and say, 'How y'all doing up there in Detroit? What's Chris thinking? How's he been playing? Does he want to come to school here?'"

Fortunately for Keener — and maybe everyone else — Kentucky has been eliminated from the picture. Webber has narrowed his choices to five schools — Michigan, Michigan State, Minnesota, Duke and Detroit Mercy. Which hasn't stopped the controversy. Just this week, the Detroit News reported that Webber had decided on Michigan. Webber flatly denied it in the Free Press the next day, saying the News' sources "might have been a 3-year-old, for all I know."

There have been nasty accusations flying across the battlefield, charges that one school is telling Webber that another school's coach is a racist, charges that Perry Watson, who coaches Southwestern, will become an assistant at Michigan and will bring Webber and Rose with him. It is crazy. Out of control. As Mayce Webber, Chris's father, says,

"This recruiting stuff, man, it's a dirty business."

And in the middle sits a thoughtful, smiling teenager who, were he not so tall and gifted, might be hanging around the mall with the other kids today. True, he might not have a future in pro sports that could bring him millions of dollars. But he wouldn't feel like a piece of meat, either.

"Sometimes I do feel like a prisoner of basketball," Webber admits. "I haven't gone on vacation during the school year in so long. A lot of my friends go to Florida and stuff. We always have to practice. In the summertime, I play in all these leagues, like 200 games a year. If I do go away, it's with a team to play basketball somewhere. It's not like normal kids."

Downstairs, the phone rings again. He ignores it.

"Do you think people would like you if you didn't play basketball?" he is asked.

"Well, I think they would like me, but it would take them a lot longer to get to know me. Right now, they like me without even knowing me."

"What if you couldn't play basketball?" comes the question.

"I think about that a lot. Did you ever see the movie 'Mo' Better Blues?' That trumpet player, what happened to him (his lip is busted in a street fight and he loses his ability to play), that was really scary to me. When he couldn't do what he wanted to do, he wanted to crawl up and die.

"I don't want to be like that. I want to have things balanced. In case one thing leaves me — like basketball — I don't want everything else to collapse."

Pretty smart, huh? For this perspective, he can thank his family: his father, who intercepts many of the recruiters; his mother, Doris, whom Webber says "couldn't care less about basketball, she just wants me to get a good education;" and his younger brothers and sister — Jeffrey, Jason, David and Rachel — who, when he plays a bad game, confront him as soon as he comes home. "Chris, you played lousy tonight."

"I like that," he says. "They're honest."

And every now and then, life provides its own lessons. Not long ago, Webber was at a camp with Pistons forward John Salley. "He was showing everybody this pivot move to the basket, and I was guarding him," Webber recalls. "I blocked his shot, kind of showing off. He did it again, and I blocked him again. He turned around and said, 'All right, rookie. I'm gonna teach you a lesson.' Then he turned to the crowd and said, 'I'm gonna go to my left and dunk on him with this hand.' He told me exactly what he would do and where he would go. I tried to stop him — and he dunked on me. Easy. He could have done it 15 more times if he wanted.

"I said to myself, 'No matter what everyone else keeps telling me, I got a long way to go.' "

And once again, it seems, the kid is smarter than many of the adults. Webber still gets the ridiculous phone calls, still gets the bundles of mail. "One coach called here to tell me he went to church, just like me. He said, 'Chris, the preacher gave this great sermon last night, from the book of Palms.' Can you believe it? He said the book of Palms. Not Psalms. Palms. I mean, I just had to laugh."

And maybe that is the best approach. Laugh it off. Still, teenagers shouldn't have to endure this kind of thing — driven from their houses, hounded by the mail and the phone, watched at every practice, every scrimmage, every game. After all, there is always another Chris Webber. There was Antoine Joubert before him and Earvin Johnson before Joubert. You would think these recruiters would have learned not to drool so much over any one kid. But perhaps they enjoy the chase as much as the capture.

Whatever. Webber will make his decision, and life will go on. Hopefully college will be more peaceful. But the normal high school life, the no-pressure, have fun, hang-out-and-be-kids years, they are gone forever for Chris Webber. And he barely knew them.

Back at the house, Webber lumbers through the living room toward the front door, where his father is returning from work. He goes outside to greet him. A photographer asks whether they would pose together.

"Yeah, Dad, let's take a picture," Webber says.

And they sit together on the porch, arms around each other, looking, for the moment, like a normal family. Inside, the phone begins to ring, but neither Chris nor his father makes any attempt to answer it. ∎

Why go to the dogs? Not one will whine about his contract

March 1

IDITAROD DIARY, CHAPTER 1: In which I travel to Alaska and learn that all dogs are not created equal, although most smell alike.

ANCHORAGE, Alaska — Mush!
Whoa!
Get off my leg!

All right. I admit it. Before arriving here for the Iditarod Sled Dog Race — or, as they call it in Alaska, the Last Great Race On Earth — my canine knowledge was somewhat limited. This, basically, is what I knew about dogs: If they urinate on your carpet, it's damn hard to get out.

And that isn't much help. Not in the Iditarod. When you ask a pack of huskies to pull your sled more than 1,000 miles through snow and ice and windstorms and frozen forests — well, let's just say you don't worry about the odor. You worry about other things.

Like moose.

Yes. A moose means trouble. It was a moose that killed two dogs and put Susan Butcher, the four-time champion, out of the Iditarod six years ago. It was a moose that attacked Rick Swenson's team and may have cost him the race last year. It was a moose that inspired the mushers to carry guns on their sleds. So I must be prepared. For a moose. And I am. Just let that big ugly creature make one move toward me — or my pilot — and he's asking for trouble. After all, I am from Detroit. We don't give moose the time of day. Although, I must confess, I've never actually seen a moose, besides Bullwinkle.

But I'm jumping the gun here. What am I doing in Alaska, you ask? Especially when the baseball teams are in spring training and the basketball teams are in midseason and the hockey teams are jockeying for playoff position? Alaska? Well. There are several reasons: 1) This is a sport, and I am a sports writer. 2) My boss wanted to get rid of me. 3) I love reindeer. 4) This is the only state in America that I have never visited. And now, having visited, I can safely say it is the only state in which I checked into my hotel and saw a polar bear in the lobby.

Also a mountain lion.

And on the way to my room, across from the ice machine, a musk ox.

They were stuffed. I think.

I didn't notice any moose.

But the real reason I am here is simple: If I write another story about baseball players' salaries, I am going to throw up.

I wanted to get away, to find a slice of the sports page unspoiled by owners, players and Dick Vitale. An adventure. Some history. The Iditarod — an endurance race from Anchorage to Nome in which the mushers often sleep on their sleds, fight blinding snowstorms and suffer hallucinations in the northern skies — is older than pro football. It dates to the early part of the century, the gold rush, when sled dogs were the only way to reach the treasure. In 1925, when an epidemic of diphtheria broke out in Nome, it was dogs on the Iditarod trail who delivered the serum to save the population.

You know what? Not one of those dogs demanded a three-year contract. So I like it already.

You've got danger out here. Collapsing ice. Wild animals. You've got natural obstacles. Mountains. Snowstorms. And then there are the characters who are nutty enough to do this, the mushers who have made the Iditarod part of their heartbeat. Like a woman I met Thursday morning, Beverly Masek, who grew up raising dogs in the small town of Anvik, Alaska. She met a guy, fell in love — he also was a sled dog racer — and they decided, what the heck, let's get married during the Iditarod. In the middle of the race! So in 1984, she flew into the fifth checkpoint on the course, Finger Lake, population 2 (that is not a typo, only two people live there), and she waited for her husband-to-be.

"He arrived in the late afternoon. He fed the dogs, made sure they were OK. And then we got married," she recalls. "We had one of the older racers do the ceremony, and several of the other mushers came and watched. It was beautiful, out in all that scenery. I had a bouquet made out of branches and flowers I collected in the woods. We said I do. And then, a few minutes later, he was back in the race."

Hmmm.

Beats the heck out of a Jose Canseco story, doesn't it?

By the way, you don't cover this race from a press box, either. You want to follow, you have to rent a plane. Fly from checkpoint to checkpoint. Sleep in a post office. Or on someone's floor. Or in a tent, in the snow. And the temperature can reach 40 below.

I'm not crazy about the tent part. But I do have a pilot, a trusty old sort named Jim Okonek. I will also have some company in the plane: two Japanese journalists. I don't think they speak English. They sent a representative to arrange their flights.

"How will I know you?" I asked when he called.

"I wear an eye patch," he said.

And he did. And he walked with a cane. And he spoke in a whisper. Before he left, I asked what happened to his eye and he said he fell on an icicle when he was a boy. Then he walked away.

The adventure begins.

I have gone to the dogs.

Now. Where's the damn moose? ■

Susan Butcher gets mushy about dogs, not people

March 2

IDITAROD DIARY, CHAPTER 2: In which we meet the champion, talk basketball, and learn that even mushers get jealous.

ANCHORAGE, Alaska — "Ha! You don't have enough fur." That's what one local told me as I sought to find the champion of the dogsled world. "Unless you got a cold nose and four paws," he said, sneering, "you ain't gonna get much from Susan Butcher. She don't much like people."

Butcher is Mush Master of the Universe right now, the reigning queen of the Iditarod, the 1,163-mile trans-Alaska dogsled race that begins today. Butcher has won it four of the last five years, lowering her time with each victory. She has more sponsors, more notoriety and more resources than most mushers. She is the inspiration for T-shirts here that read "ALASKA — WHERE MEN ARE MEN AND WOMEN WIN THE IDITAROD." But she hasn't exactly gone Hollywood. She still lives in a cabin way up north, in a town of 11 people, a place called Eureka. That's a gold miner's way of saying, "I found it! Gold!" In Butcher's case, the locals warn, it means "I found it! A place with no humans!"

But, what the heck? Sometimes, I'm not so crazy about people either. So as I park my car outside the veterinarian's office on a small, snowy, back road on the outskirts of Anchorage — someone tipped me that Butcher would be there — I do what any good reporter would do when hoping to interview a woman who lives with 150 dogs:

I practice barking.

To most Americans, Butcher, 36, is a parka-clad mystery, a hard-featured, no-makeup, rugged and weird adventurer. She's "the dog lady who wins that race every year," people say. They shrug. Any woman who takes a pack of canines, by herself, out in the frozen wilderness for 11 or 12 grueling, stormy days, and thinks this is fun — well, we are not dealing with Cher here. This is a woman who wants to be alone.

Surprisingly, I learn, her fellow mushers will gladly grant her wish. Not everyone is in love with Susan Butcher. Many of the male mushers, whom she has beaten over and over, quietly resent the attention she has gotten: the "Tonight Show" appearances, the articles in Sports Illustrated, those T-shirts. They mumble, "She just got lucky with some great dogs." Or, "It's the dogs who win the race, but in her case, because she's a woman, she gets all the credit." Butcher's closest rival, Rick Swenson, the only other musher to win the Iditarod four times, had a falling out with her a few years back, and now they're like Ali and Frazier. Swenson fiercely wants to beat her this year, and keep her from surpassing his victory total. Before Butcher defeated him for the first time, in 1986, Swenson reportedly boasted he "would walk from Nome to Anchorage if a woman ever beats me in this race." In which case he needs a whole lot of boots.

But Butcher doesn't seem to care. Or does she? She was not the first woman to win an Iditarod. In 1985, she was in the lead but had to drop out of the race after a moose attacked her dogs, killing two of them. First place was eventually captured by another woman, Libby Riddles, who received enormous attention for breaking the male barrier. Riddles, blonde and easy-going, became a mini-celebrity; she wrote a book; she picked up precious sponsors.

Butcher stopped talking to her.

"I don't think she ever forgave me for winning," Riddles told me the other night. "She's real competitive. Part of the reason people have a hard time with her is because she really does prefer dogs to people."

Great, I figure.

Where's my leash?

I enter the vet's office, prepared to be snarled at, and who should be sitting there but Butcher's husband, Dave Monson, a lawyer by training, a part-time dog musher, and now, pretty much, the man in charge of Butcher's small empire. Long-haired, bearded, smart and sarcastic, Monson met his wife in the early '80s, when he sold her some fish head scraps for dog food. (Hey, you do what you can to make money in Alaska.) Now he is reportedly the buffer between Butcher and the outside world.

So I tell him I'm from Detroit, and he says, "Detroit! All the way up here, huh?" And next thing I know, Susan Butcher comes pushing through the office door, wearing a T-shirt and blue sweat pants. She ignores me and approaches her husband.

"Hi, honey. Would you braid my hair?"

Now, this is not the opening I expected, given all the warnings. I sort of figured Butcher would say: "Grrrrrrrrrr, yip, yip, rrrrufff!" So, what the hell? I clear my throat and tell her, too, that I have come from Detroit.

And she looks at the floor and says: "Were you with Isiah?"

"Huh?"

Again, she looks away, batting her eyelashes in rapid-fire. "Were you with Isiah before coming here?"

Well, yeah, I answer. Actually, I saw Isiah at the Lakers game.

"He's my favorite. Isiah. We should name a dog after him, Dave."

"Yeah," says Dave. "Isiah and maybe Joe Dumars."

"Oh, yeah, I like Dumars, too."

"And who's that big mean white guy you got?"

"Bill Laimbeer?" I say.

"Yeah. We've got a few dogs like him. Don't we, Sue?"

"Oh, yeah," she says. "We've got a couple nasty ones."

"Uh, great," I say.

So right off the bat we learn several important lessons about Susan Butcher: 1) She is a basketball fan. 2) She needs help braiding her hair. 3) She names all her dogs. Personally. And we are talking hundreds here. She picks a theme for every litter — such as Russian novelists, Olympic athletes, names of rocks, even the stars of the "Tonight Show." (Yes, there is a Johnny Carson dog and a Doc Severinsen dog and even a Tommy Newsom dog.) And she remembers every one.

This she proves in the parking lot, when she introduces me to the 20 dogs she will run in this year's Iditarod. "Here's Sluggo," she says, still not looking at me, "and here's Hermit. And here's Stoney. But we call him Toooooooneeee! ... Hi boy, yeah, Toneee. ... "

Her voice is suddenly light and free and she pushes her face against the dog's muzzle, and he licks her all over.

And, I figure, what Libby Riddles said is just about right.

Dogs over people.

W hich is probably what makes Susan Butcher such a great musher. The art of sled-dog racing, more than anything else, is getting maximum performance from the animals. And Butcher's dogs — well-bred and extremely well-conditioned — are special. They seem willing to go though a frozen hell for her. Not only does she run with them through miles of long distance training; not only does she work them on ropes around a huge training wheel; not only does she feed them, massage their feet, and take them on solo treks to get a better feel for their personalities; but she supposedly talks to them like humans. And I don't doubt it. Butcher bonds with these dogs from the moment they are born. They drop from the womb and land in her hands. The trust begins.

It is what makes them trudge on through gulleys and mountains and 80 m.p.h. winds near the Bering Sea. Sometimes, this invisible connection they have with Butcher means the difference between life and death. Once, she was out on a long training run, and her lead dog kept disobeying, trying to leave the trail. Butcher, annoyed, nonetheless trusted the dog's instincts. Just as they pulled to the side, the trail collapsed into the river.

She missed death by two seconds.

"This is what I love to do," says Butcher, who, when she was 12 years old and living in Cambridge, Mass., wrote an essay for school titled "I Hate The City." "After this year's race, I want to get the phone out of Eureka. I want to get back to concentrating just on the dogs. There's been a lot of talk about my retiring, but that's not true. I just may not run the Iditarod again for a while. I want to have a child, and I won't race when I'm pregnant, obviously.

"There are some other races I want to try. Some other challenges. If I should win this Iditarod — and I will — I'll have five titles, and that may be enough for a while."

The part that catches my attention is the "and I will." She says it as if there is no doubt. I look at the dogs, as they parade in and are lifted to the vet's table. I see the way they look at her, ignoring other humans, just as she does for them.

And I figure I'd put my money on her to win, too, even if she doesn't want to look at me. I go to tell her, but she is back with the dogs and doesn't want to be disturbed. I leave without a good-bye, and without the chance to make a suggestion: When the Pistons litter arrives, name one of the dogs John Salley.

She'll never have to do an interview again. ∎

The real and the fake equal only at the starting line

March 3

IDITAROD DIARY, CHAPTER 3: In which The Last Great Race on Earth begins.

ANCHORAGE, Alaska — The streets were still dark when the horrible noise began, a yelping, screeching, howling sound that swelled to a frightening volume, until you wanted to cover your ears and run for shelter. It was the sound of dogs whose blood was boiling, the sound of dogs yanking on their chains, jumping over one another in anticipation. The sound of dogs, thousands of dogs, ready to run.

I walked these streets Saturday morning, between the hungry beasts, feeling the raw power that is Alaska on the morning of the first day of the Iditarod, the Last Great Race on Earth. I breathed in the cold air, the energy of the mushers, the naked power of these furry animals. I felt a kinship with my ancestors, a sense of history, a surge of passion.

Then I felt a squish beneath my feet.

So now I smell like a dog, too.

"You feel lucky?" I asked Joe Runyan, the 1989 winner, as he wolfed down an Egg McMuffin while the inspectors checked his dogs.

"I feel good," he said. "The dogs are ready."

"Last fast food for a while, huh?"

He grinned. "Yeah. Not many McDonald's on the Bering Sea."

All around were the trucks of his competitors, rolling kennels that house the dogs who will pull these mushers 1,163 miles the next two weeks, through mountains and rivers and forests. Seventy-five teams were in these Anchorage streets, some all business, others in it just for fun. Not far from Susan Butcher, the defending champion, was a businessman from North Carolina, in his first and probably only Iditarod attempt. Across from Rick Swenson, the only musher besides Butcher to win four Iditarods, was a lawyer who grew up in Michigan — in Farmington, for Pete's sake — a guy named Jim Cantor, who was wearing a gray suit over his long underwear, a costume he'll don for the first 20 miles.

"How did you get into this?" I asked. "Did you have mush dogs in Farmington?"

"Nah. I had a Labrador retriever."

There is a stockbroker in this year's Iditarod and there are mushers who spend all year with dogs, training hundreds of them in tiny villages in northern Alaska, just for this moment. The race will soon separate the real from the fake, but for now, the morning of the start, they are all together, the challengers, the hermits, the bearded, the demented. One guy actually has 10 poodles racing alongside his huskies.

"It's the Year of the Poodle," he told me.

I looked at his team.

Obviously it's the year of the puddle, too.

And suddenly, the announcer was calling and the teams were pushing through the packed snow on Fourth Street, in single file — "THREE ... TWO ... ONE ... GO!" — and the dogs, tethered together at the neck and body, sprang into action as if someone laced their water with amphetamines, galloping through the streets, the first steps on the odyssey toward Nome ...

W hat can happen out there, on the last frontier? Well, that is both the lure and the danger. You can, for example, fall though the ice on the Yukon River and be lost forever, frozen to death. A cheery thought. You can be thrown from your sled, crack your ribs, and only pray that someone finds you in the snow. You can lose track of the trail — maybe a snowstorm wipes it out, maybe you are so punchy from lack of sleep you simply make a wrong turn — and you are lost for days, your food runs out, your hungry dogs begin eating the leather that binds them together. This happened 15 years ago to Norman Vaughn, a well-known explorer who has been to the South Pole and back but nonetheless got lost during his rookie try at the Iditarod. He was saved, five days later, by snowmobilers who discovered his tracks.

This is the race that I will cover, by airplane, by foot, by curiosity mostly. And maybe stupidity. After all, why venture into the depths of the Alaskan wilderness, where the temperature can drop to 40 below, to observe an event in which even the best mushers can suffer frostbite, dizzy spells and hallucinations? They can be staring at 30 miles of wide-open, blinding white landscape and suddenly they imagine a tree, or a house, or the horizon turning into a stick trying to hit them in the face. "That happened to me several times," said DeeDee Jonrowe, a wavy-haired veteran Iditarod racer I met Thursday. "You start ducking and swiping at this stick, you keep thinking it's going to smack you, but it's just the horizon line, fooling you, playing tricks with your head."

Hmmm. Sounds like the '60s to me.

Of course, much of what you see out there is real and inspiring, like buffalo in a snow field, and much of it is natural and awesome, such as the Alaska mountain range, or the illumination of the Northern Lights, reflecting pink off the frozen earth. Then again, some things you don't want to see — like a charging moose, that big dumb animal who is a dog musher's biggest enemy. And mine, too. (Let's face it. I am hung up on this moose thing. And if one of them attacks me, I am not giving up my wallet.) Butcher, the master musher herself, had to drop out of the 1985 Iditarod — while she was leading — after being attacked by a pregnant moose. She held it off with a stick for half an hour until finally another musher came past with a gun and shot it dead. That filthy beast killed two of Butcher's dogs, trampled them to death. Most mushers carry guns now. I don't blame them.

It's you or the moose.

And then there are the mishaps with your own dogs. Some are tragic. Some are comic. Jonrowe — whom I really like, because she seems like the kind of woman who would laugh as her sled went off a cliff — tells the story of a recent race in which she was forced to stop her team when it went off course. On that day, she had 14 male dogs and two female dogs in her team.

The females were in heat.

"In the time it took to turn the sled around, Custard (a male) and Susitna (a female) couldn't resist each other, and they started to do what nature tells them to do. I kind of went 'Nooo! Custard!' But it was too late. And once they get started, naturally you can't separate them. I had to sit and let nature take its course. It took 25 minutes and cost me first place."

"What did you do?" I asked.

"What can you do?" she laughed. "I waited until they were finished, let them smoke a couple cigarettes, then we moved on."

"Weren't you angry?" I asked.

She smiled, as if explaining the Golden Rule to a child.

"It's the dogs who win the race," she said. "Above all, you have to respect them."

Back at the start the dogs were charging, leaping, howling as if someone were crushing them in a vise. So juiced are the animals at this point that the first 20 miles, mushers make them pull two people on two sleds. Just to tone down their adrenaline.

"What are you doing up there?" I yelled to Bill Peele, the 55-year-old North Carolina rookie musher who saved up three years of vacation time from his job to experience this race just once. He was standing on the roof of his truck, with a camera, as the early teams pulled out.

"I'm just trying to take this all in," he said.

"You nervous?" I asked.

"No. I just want to make it to Nome in one piece."

And that pretty much sums up my attitude. Because some strange things keep happening. Before sunrise, standing in the street, I once again encountered the mysterious, one-eyed man who is my liaison to the two Japanese journalists who will share my plane tomorrow. The man held a cigarette that glowed in the morning dark. He grinned.

"Are you ready?" he asked.

"Uh, yeah," I said.

"Be careful out there. It's tougher than it looks."

He tapped out his butt and limped away on his cane.

The dogs kept howling. I tried to ignore them. On Friday, I found a man who agreed to take me on a brief sled run, so I could better understand the power of these beasts. I hopped on, and the dogs looked back at me as if to say, "Great. Another tourist." And — ya! — they took off. And then they took a wrong turn and the musher yelled "whoa" and ran up and bit one of the dogs on the ear …

But that is a tale for the days to come, provided I can find a phone line out there between the snow drifts. For now, we buckle the hats and tug on the boot strings, we feel for that polypropylene underwear and, knowing it is there, get warm all over. We are following the call of the wild, the yipping and yelping that cuts through the darkness. The sound of the dogs, ready to go.

As soon as I change my shoes. ∎

Along frozen trail, simple pleasures simply aren't

March 4

IDITAROD DIARY, CHAPTER 4: In which we discover sleeping dogs, ice cooking, and witness a plane crash.

SKWENTNA, Alaska — As the wind curled over the frozen treetops, I glanced at my pilot, Old Jim, who used to fly burned bodies out of Vietnam — we'll get to that in a minute — and he pointed to a huge, frozen, snow-covered river in the distance. "Look there," he said.

On the surface, I spotted at least 20 rows of straw piles, each dotted with something black in the middle, and human figures bent over the snow. It looked like an outdoor hospital after a nuclear attack. We flew closer and I realized the black spots were dogs, hundreds of dogs, sleeping in straw beds. And the figures were mushers, cooking food. They have been out on the trail more than 24 hours and 150 miles, running through the sub-freezing night like silent messengers. Their faces, dog and human, were stuck with tiny icicles. They needed rest.

So this was, what, sort of a musher's Howard Johnson's? "It's a checkpoint," Jim said, "one of the more popular ones. There's a house, and the folks cook 'em food. They might even catch a little sleep."

He set the plane down on the ice, and we walked toward the husky dogs, sleeping in rows like kindergarten kids at nap time. I rubbed my back, which was sore from the mattress at the Latitude 62 Restaurant, Bar & Motel, the roadhouse where I had slept. No TV. No radio. No thermostat. But very low rates. Great place to take the kids. And leave them. But what do you expect? I have been here six days now, in the Lonely Country, and I have no one but myself to blame.

The mushers were toiling away on little fires. "Whatcha cooking?" I asked Kazoukojima, the only Japanese musher in this year's Iditarod. He stirred what seemed to be a plastic crockpot full of mush.

"For dogs," he said. "I make beef, honey, vitamins. They must eat."

"Yeah, but what will you eat?" He smiled and pulled out a plastic pouch and dumped it into a tin saucer. "Lasagna!" he declared. Then he yanked out a pair of chopsticks, tapped them together, and there, in the middle of this huge frozen river, with his dogs stretched out in front of him like furry soldiers, he dug in.

"Mmm," he said, the sauce dripping around his lips. "Is delicious."

The Last Great Race on Earth.

It takes 11 days, the Iditarod, if you're good. As much as four weeks if you're bad. And don't even think about trying it unless you know how to camp, fish, hunt and at least hold off a moose, if not shoot him dead. Above all, the Iditarod is about survival. One look around this Skwentna River, where mushers were hauling bags of food, starting fires, dipping into an ice hole for water, and sleeping inside their sleds — in 10 degree weather! — well, you know these folks passed the Boy Scout test.

Which is more than I can say. I used to think "roughing it" was a Motel 6.

I walked past Joe Runyan, who won this race two years ago. He said he was going into the cabin to try to sleep for an hour, alongside a dozen other mushers who were snoring away. Further down the ice was Susan Butcher, the defending champion, who, rumor has it, talks with her dogs like family. As I approached, she was moving them around on a tethered line, looking to get the strongest dog in front.

"Come on up here," she said.

Not to me. To a dog.

"What are you grumbling about?" she continued. "Oh, don't be that way. … And you, what's the matter? … I know, yeah, I know. …"

I figured it was best to leave Susan alone, seeing as I was not on a leash.

I should tell you about Old Jim, and the time he had to extinguish the burning body of a CIA agent and fly him back from Vietnam, and I should also tell you about my fellow passengers, two Japanese photographers, Sato and Suda, who work for a big newspaper in Tokyo. They don't speak much English. At one point in our flight, I turned around, real friendly-like, and said, "I am a newspaper columnist."

And they said, "You are communist?"

And I said, "Never mind."

But first, let me answer a few questions about the rigors of the Iditarod, seeing as you are probably reading this in front of a bowl of Cheerios.

1. How do the mushers carry all that dog food? It is flown, ahead of time, into designated checkpoints, thousands of pounds of beef, lamb, dried pellets, whatever. Each driver has his bags pre-marked, and only he can handle them, and only he can feed the dogs. Any help is breaking the rules.

2. What about sleep — can they sleep at the checkpoints? Well, some checkpoints are nothing more than a tent with a banner hung across two spruce trees. Not much sleeping there. Others are post offices, a community hall, a deserted cabin. You take your pick. Mushers sometimes sleep in their sleds, or in sleeping bags on the ice, to be close to the dogs so they won't run away.

3. Has that ever happened? Sure. One year, a team of dogs arrived in perfect stride at a checkpoint — without a musher. He had been plunked on the head by a low branch and had fallen out of the sled. The dogs, so excited to be running, never even stopped.

THE IDITAROD

4. If the checkpoints are so primitive, where do mushers, you know, relieve themselves? Anywhere they want.

5. The race is 1,163 long. How do mushers know where to go? The trail is marked. At least it's supposed to be marked. Sometimes a bad snowstorm will wipe out the trail, leaving mushers to figure it out themselves. It's not unusual for a team to wind up 50 miles off course. Still, that's better than what happened to a musher named Bert Bonhoff.

6. What happened to Bert Bonhoff? Six years ago, his team was behind the Iditarod race leader when the leader took a wrong turn, off the trail. Realizing his mistake, the leader turned his dogs around. But Bonhoff wasn't so quick. And the next thing he knew, his lead dogs disappeared — over a cliff. They were dangling helplessly 1,000 feet above a river, like something from an Indiana Jones movie. Bonhoff locked his sled in place, crawled to the edge, pulled on the ropes, and managed to save them from death.

A few more feet, and they would have been pulling him out of the water.

Which brings me back to Old Jim, the pilot who, as I said, used to do that sort of thing in Vietnam. Like a lot of people here in Alaska, he doesn't mind roughing it. He lived with his wife and two children in a remote house that had no electricity, no running water, and the way he tells it, no complaints. And I believe it. Old Jim is the rugged sort that survives here in the Lonely Country. And I trust him for two reasons:

1. He specialized in rescue operations — which is comforting, in case something happens between me and a moose.

2. He is prophetic. After we left Skwentna, we flew to the next checkpoint, an isolated, gorgeous spot called Finger Lake, nestled near the foot of the mountains. Jim landed the plane on a long, thin strip of packed snow. As I got out to walk toward the checkpoint — fwoooop! — I disappeared in a drift. Jim kind of laughed and I squirmed back to my feet. As I walked away, he said, "Hey, watch out for airplanes on this strip. They can sneak up on you."

I smirked. Very funny.

And 10 minutes later, I was sitting on a tree stump, interviewing Joe Garnie, the native Alaskan musher who is leading this race and who, by being the first to reach Skwentna, at 3 a.m., won himself a brand new Dodge truck. ("This is great," he said. "Now all I have to do is get a driver's license.") And suddenly I look up and a small blue plane is coming in for a landing. And it touches down and begins to wobble. Someone next to me mumbled, "Uh-oh." And the plane skids sharply to the left, toward four people who are standing there, and they run frantically — except one woman falls and the plane runs her over with its landing ski then crashes into two other planes parked nearby.

And the next thing, I am running, with the others, toward the ugly scene, and someone is yelling, "Medic! Get a medic! …" ∎

Mushers' misinformation is trash talk, Alaska-style

March 5

IDITAROD DIARY, CHAPTER 5: In which we make a rescue, cross the breathtaking mountains, and get nauseated.

RAINY PASS, Alaska — "Medic! Medic!"
Suddenly no one was thinking about the animals or the mushers or the thousand miles of frozen country still left in this trans-Alaska dogsled race. We were running down a narrow landing strip, toward a woman who was lying flat in the snow, her face contorted in pain. Just seconds earlier, a small plane had touched down, skidded off the icy runway, and veered toward four spectators. They scattered. Three men got away. The woman was not so lucky. She fell in the knee-deep snow and tried to cover up as the plane ran her over, its landing skis banging off her hip as it bumped past and went smack into two other parked planes, denting them badly. Now the woman was surrounded by a group of strangers, me included.

"Don't move her!" someone yelled.
"Are you all right?"
"CAN WE GET A STRETCHER?"
"We ain't got a stretcher out here."
"What happened?"
"DON'T MOVE HER!"
"Someone get that big piece of plywood by the tent. We'll make a stretcher."
"Who's got a plane that can get her to a hospital?"
"ARE YOU THE DOCTOR? WHERE'S THE DOCTOR?"
"What happened? What happened? … "

If anyone ever doubted the lonely dangers of the Iditarod, one need only have been on that frozen lake Sunday morning with no sled, no phone, no stretcher, no ambulance. We think of sporting events, we figure, hell, there's always somebody there, some trainer, some team doctor. In the Iditarod, the Last Great Race on Earth, there really can be nobody there. Night after night, for 1,163 miles, the dogs pull the sleds silently through the snowy landscape, through trees and over rivers and over mountains peppered with tall spruce, and only the headlights on the drivers' hats give any clue as to where they are. Accidents happen — they fall off the sled, they break an arm, a dog is injured and can't go on — and only the mushers' survival instincts will save them. It's the way of life in the Lonely Country; you fall in the woods, maybe nobody hears you.

So I suppose in a way that woman was damn lucky, even if she did get run over by an airplane. We lifted her onto the plywood stretcher, and loaded her into a small Cessna. She was conscious, weeping softy.

"The surprising thing," whispered Old Jim Okonek, my pilot, who has been in these Alaskan skies since the '60s, "is that the guy (landing that plane) is real experienced, one of the best."

We stood back as the Cessna rose into the white sky, heading for the hospital — even as another team of dogs trotted into the checkpoint with their tongues hanging out.

"Sometimes, out here," Jim said, shaking his head, "stuff just happens ..." Well, I could have told you that. I could have told you about the three mushers who already have dropped out. One neglected to put booties on his dogs' feet at the starting line in Anchorage, and by the time he reached the first checkpoint his team was staining the snow with bloody paw prints. I could have told you about trying to cover this race by airplane when your pilot likes to dip and drop and your stomach prefers to stay in one place. And maybe I will ...

But first, back to the race. On Monday morning, Day 3, we landed on a deserted patch of frozen valley known as Rohn Roadhouse, a place that in the 1800s served as shelter for dog teams delivering mail. Today, in the Iditarod, Rohn is special, like a medal on your chest. It means you've survived the perilous Alaska Mountain Range. It is there that a soul feels as alone as Adam, nothing to this Earth but God's massive granite mountains, covered in untouched snow. The race trail skirts ridges that drop sharp as cliffs and winds between the mountains in a narrow path that can disappear in a snowstorm and leave you stuck for hours, maybe days, praying for better weather.

You reach Rohn anywhere in the top 10 and you're in the big leagues in Iditarod. As they might say in Georgia, your dogs can bark.

Which explains my company there inside the one-room log cabin, where a cast-iron coffee pot sat on a coal stove, below shelves jammed with graham crackers, syrup and oatmeal; here, in one corner, taking a rest, was Susan Butcher, the four-time Iditarod winner and defending champion. Sitting a few feet away was Rick Swenson, a former champion and Butcher's rival, the guy who supposedly once said, "I'll walk home from Nome if a woman ever beats me in this race" — before Butcher did it four times. These two in one room could be dangerous.

Fortunately, a few other mushers were there, too — some taking their mandatory 24-hour stopover (each musher must make one during the race); some just grabbing a java after massaging their dogs to sleep.

"I am really sore," Butcher said, stretching inside her red snowsuit. "My arms are killing me. I think the handlebar on my sled is too high."

Swenson sipped his drink. He said nothing.

"Hey, Susan," said a smirking Terry Adkins, a retired Air Force officer. "If you're so tired, why don't you take a good long nap?"

They all laughed, but I wasn't fooled. I'd heard competitors' laughter before. It has a certain edge, like a steak knife. Don't let the word "mushers" fool you. These folks want to win so badly, they'd eat dog food. I think some of them do. Hey, would you want to spend 12 months in a kennel and have nothing to show for it?

So they play head games with each other. NBA players talk trash? Mushers give misinformation. It's not unusual for one of them to stop for a cup of coffee, give a yawn and say, "Well, I'm gonna sleep for a few hours and leave at 4 a.m." And another musher figures, great, he'll be smart, he'll only sleep until 3:30 a.m. and get a jump on the guy. And he gets up at 3:30 — only to learn that the first musher left two hours ago.

Head games. It's part of the way you win — along with nursing your dogs, picking the right weather patterns, bringing the right food, and, of course, if you have to — and never forget this — killing a moose. This is pretty much the Iditarod racer's philosophy: There's a lot of trail out there, and all that matters is who leads at the end, not along the way.

"Being ahead five minutes at this point," Butcher told me privately outside the cabin, "doesn't mean s - - - ."

W hich, now that she mentioned it, is how I felt a few hours later, as Old Jim Okonek — the white-haired pilot who once rescued the charred body of a CIA agent from a wreck in Vietnam — decided to show me some of the smaller points of interest, from inside the Piper Super Cub. We had ditched the two Japanese photographers, Sato and Suda, who, when I last saw them, were heading for a helicopter.

So it was Jim and me, in this tiny Piper, and he started dipping — and so did my insides.

"Look over the right wing," he said, "see the musher?"

"Uh, hang on," I said.

Another spin. "Whoa, look over there. There's another one."

"Jim, I …"

"Have you ever seen caribou? I think there's some over there. Let me drop down lower."

"Urrrpp."

"No, that wasn't caribou, sorry, just some brush. Hey, did you feel that wave of air come off that mountain?"

"Bleehhhhhrrrp."

Anyhow. You get the picture. I'd wait a few days before we take that Piper up again.

Jim was right about a couple things, however. He told me to duck when airplanes were coming in at Finger Lake. And then, on the airstrip in Rohn, he said, "Watch out for dog teams. They use the same area as the planes to come into the checkpoint."

And I thought to myself, "Yeah, right." And I turned around, and I was looking smack into the eyes of 17 panting dogs, running in perfect synch, heading straight at me … ∎

In the Last Great Race, right-of-way goes to the dogs

March 6

IDITAROD DIARY, CHAPTER 6: In which we come to an end.

ROHN ROADHOUSE, Alaska — I am shipping out. My orders came this morning. I have been called back from The Last Great Race on Earth, right in the middle, by my newspaper, which wants me to cover — if you can believe it — spring training in Florida. I hate to say it, sports fans, but, compared to the brave dogsled teams running through this frozen wilderness, baseball seems like a bunch of spoiled kids playing marbles. Monday, here in the Alaska Mountain Range, one musher's sled went over a cliff, and she crashed face-first into the snow. She got up. She pushed on. Another musher's line snapped and 17 of his 18 dogs sprinted off into the night. He was left with one dog and a heavy sled to drag through the darkness until he found his pack. He pushed on. That's the Iditarod. Rickey Henderson thinks he's underpaid? Let him try this sucker for a few hours.

Really. The thought of leaving these spectacular snow-capped mountains for the swamps of Florida baseball, it's enough to make me cry. But what can I do? The orders came from my boss. And I am but a mush dog on his leash.

A pity. For I was just getting used to that tingling sensation in my toes, and the wet spot under my nose. I was even catching on to the tricks of the trail — like staying off it. As you may recall when we left off in Tuesday's installment, I was walking along a snow-packed airstrip when I turned to discover a pack of galloping huskies right in front of me. And they were not slowing down.

"OUT OF THE WAY!" the musher yelled.

I dived into a snow bank. The dogs passed, panting. I think one of them laughed at me, but I'm not sure.

"You know," whispered Old Jim Okonek, my trusty pilot, as I got to my feet, "out here, the dogs have the right-of-way."

I know. I can tell by all the yellow snow.

But that is how it should be. These dogs were born to run. It's in their blood, it goes with the territory — and everything in this dangerous and wonderful 1,163-mile dogsled race is just about that: the territory. The rivers, the lakes, the mountains, the tall spruce trees that poke from the snow like giant needles. Beautiful? It's something beyond beautiful, something that wiggles in your stomach and makes you lose your breath when you look around. Alaska in winter: the Outback, the Great

Interior, the Bering Sea coast, the northern lights coloring the sky. I swear, it can bring you to your knees. Before this race began, I met a 40-year-old teacher named Urtha Lenharr who was entering Iditarod for the first time. He obviously had no chance to win. So I asked what he hoped to get out of it.

"The privilege of seeing this land," he said.

And I now know what he means. Just in time to ship out. Unfair? Yes. But maybe it is fitting. After all, many Iditarod mushers never get to Nome their first time out. They suffer exhaustion in the mountains, or they lose their dogs to bloody paws and sickness. Or maybe the animals just quit on them. It happens. It happened Monday — to Joe Carpenter. For nine hours he sat on the Yentna River with a team of dogs that refused to move. He fed them. He waited. He watered them. He waited. He went in front and tried dragging them. Nothing. "Something happened out there, I can't explain it," Carpenter would say.

In desperation, he took a tow from another musher, hoping that once his dogs started moving they'd get into it. But mushers are not allowed to accept a tow unless in dire emergency. Late Monday, the race jury disqualified Carpenter for breaking the rules.

A year of his life and $20,000 in dogs and equipment. Gone.

That's gotta hurt.

But this is no place for the squeamish, not in the wilderness, where at any moment you can come face to face with a moose. Which, fortunately, in my case never happened. Fortunate for the moose. Being from Detroit, I might have to show the beast how we do things downtown.

But no. The last action I saw came here, at Rohn Roadhouse, the lonesome checkpoint just over the mountains, 274 miles into the race. By the time I arrived, a half-dozen leading mushers were already there, hunkered down, grimy and tired. Here was DeeDee Jonrowe, nursing her huskies between the tall trees, rubbing ointment on their paws as they lay in beds of straw.

And a few trees away, Susan Butcher, everybody's favorite, cooking up chunks of beef, liver and fish to nourish her team back to speed. I want to say this about Butcher: I admire her determination, her total focus on the dogs and the environment. She probably wouldn't do real well at Spago, true, but when it comes to wilderness, the woman gets it done. I have no doubts she will win this race.

Also in the woods, in a sleeping bag: Joe Runyan, the 1989 Iditarod winner, a tall, lean man. Earlier, I had asked him about spending 11 lonely days with just a pack of dogs:

"That's one of the attractions," he answered. "You're so focused. You've got 11 days and nothing to think about but getting down that trail. For 11 days, you don't think about taking out the garbage, or taking care of the kids.

"It's kind of ironic, but for a lot of mushers, the Iditarod is just a super long vacation."

Without showers, of course.

Wait. Did I tell you about "talent night" at the Latitude 62 Motel, Restaurant & Bar in Talkeetna? The rooms are pretty basic — beds and window — but the people, like most people in Alaska, more than make up for it. This one night, I come back from the trail, and I'm at the bar, and the owner, a big, bearded fellow named Mac, starts telling me about the piano in the front — and next thing you know, I'm sitting there playing a few tunes for the guy. And he's dancing around like a big old polar bear.

"Whoooee!" he yelled. "If I played piano like that, I'd be a millionaire!"

And the piano was out of tune.

But this type of scene you get all over the Lonely Country, where the kindness of strangers makes you forget that it's cold enough outside to freeze a tank. I got such kindness at the Latitude 62, and I got it every day from Old Jim Okonek, my trusty pilot, a former Vietnam and Korean rescue operator who now runs K2 Aviation in Talkeetna. He greeted me each morning with newspaper clippings and a sack lunch his wife had made. When we flew, he would dip toward mountain or lake and tell me its name and what it was used for in the pioneer days. Here's a guy who's in the air more than the Goodyear Blimp, but now and then I'd catch him gazing at some mountain peak, and I'd hear him say, "God, it's beautiful out here, isn't it?"

If you had to be stuck somewhere for the rest of your life, you could do a lot worse than Alaska.

Back to the race. And who is going to win? All over the state, the media are betting on one guy or another to upset Butcher. Maybe it's male chauvinism. Maybe Alaskan men are just tired of women winning. After all, a female crossed the Iditarod finish line first five of the last six years.

But though Runyan is good, as is Lavon Barve, a balding 45-year-old musher, and Rick Swenson, the only driver besides Butcher to win the Iditarod four times, I still put my money on the defending champion. As the Pistons say, "You gotta know how to win when it counts." And Butcher is a fan of the Pistons.

But, hey, what do I know? Before coming up here, the only thing I'd seen a dog pull was my socks — from one room to another. I do know this: Whoever wins this year probably won't be a native Alaskan. And if the Iditarod has any dark side, that is it. Dog mushing wasn't invented in Indianapolis, you know. It is a proud tradition of the Alaskan Indians, the Eskimos, the people who settled this unforgiving land long before ABC Sports. Few of the 75 mushers entered this year have such roots. One who does is Tony (Wildman) Shoogukwruk. His nickname comes from his huge mop of hair and the unkempt black beard that frames his face.

"I've been trying to get into the Iditarod for years," he told me. "This is the first time I could raise enough money. The native businesses in Alaska, they talk a lot about helping our people, but they don't put their money where their mouth is. They would rather back a white person. They think the white man is a better musher."

He talked about his grandfather and great grandfather — hunters, trappers, men who used dogsleds for more practical purposes than racing. "The situation with our native people is very bad now," he said. "We feel cheated. Our children are confused. The elders in our towns, they like the old ways. The kids always feel like they're disappointing them. They become hopeless. They drink. Maybe they kill themselves.

"I want to race to show our kids that suicide is not the answer."

I looked at his team. It was scrawny compared to the rest and his equipment was used and shopworn. Some say this is the shame of the Iditarod. Others disagree. "I lived in the bush for a long time," said Libby Riddles, the 1985 winner. "A lot of the kids up there, they've been cleaning dogs and carrying their straw for years. They're sick of it. They don't want anything to do with dogs. There are plenty of opportunities for native mushers. But the kids in those villages would rather have snow machines and video games. It's sad, but it's true."

So even dogsled racing has its controversies. But they are small compared to the challenge. The Iditarod is not really about nationality, or even winning. It's about survival.

So as I head for the airport — and the sick, money-crazed world of baseball — I take these scenes from a week of Iditarod: I see the craziness of the start in downtown Anchorage, where serious racers mix with dreamers. I see all those dogs, hundreds of them, their snouts covered by icicles as they trudge on. I see mushers in the woods, cooking meat, dipping into an ice hole for water. I see Joe Garnie, the ebullient Alaskan who won a Dodge truck for being the first to reach a certain checkpoint, telling me, "This is great. Now I gotta get a driver's license." I see the solitary beauty of Finger Lake, the majesty of Rainy Pass. I see a line of dogs pulling a musher through white mountains as big as God's soldiers.

I see me cleaning off my boots, after stepping in a pile of you-know-what.

And I see the village of Skwentna, all 114 people, welcoming the mushers and their dogs with such enthusiasm. Everyone in this tiny town pitches in. Someone checks the racers, and someone operates the ham radio, and someone bakes a cake. A chubby kid was sitting on a snow machine with a sign that read: "TAXI RIDES, $1.00" So I hopped on, and he smiled, and he told me his name was Richard Price, he was 11 years old, and he went to school in Skwentna.

"How many kids in your class?" I asked.

"Just me," he said.

He was so unspoiled, this kid, so trusting and — I don't know — mature. There was no glint of Nintendo in his eyes. No talk of material things. When it came time to pay him, I pulled out a $20 and just handed it to him, and patted him on the head. And suddenly, he was hugging me like a brother.

It's hard not to be touched by the Iditarod.

"We used to have this guy in our village," Old Jim told me on our last morning, "and he was kind of a wimp. Even his name was wimpy — Carroll. And one day, he said he wanted to try the Iditarod. We all laughed, figuring, how's this guy gonna make it 1,100 miles, right?

"But Carroll rented a dog team, and he trained them, and then the race came. And darn if he didn't fall and break his arm in the first stretch. We figured, that's it. But you know what? They flew him to a hospital, he had the arm set and went back to the dogs. He finished the race, made it all the way to Nome. We couldn't believe it."

Jim shook his head. "It changed our opinion of him, that's for sure. And it changed him. He was different after that. That's the Iditarod, I guess. It changes people."

And maybe, I'm thinking, it changed me too. I know this: There's a golden retriever relaxing on my couch back in Michigan.

And when I get home, he's gonna start working a lot harder. ∎

When Free Press readers shout mush, we mush

March 8

I am about to tell you a remarkable story that not only restores my faith in newspapers, newspaper readers and humanity in general, but also makes my dog extremely happy.

Here I was in my house Thursday morning. I had just returned from the Iditarod Sled Dog Race in Alaska, a wonderful assignment that, unfortunately, was being cut short so I could get to Florida and write about — ahem — spring training baseball.

"Well, dog," I said to my golden retriever, as I unpacked the long underwear from my suitcase, "too bad I didn't get to see the end of that race."

"Mmmmph," the dog said.

"I mean, I know baseball is supposedly the national pastime, but all I see is a bunch of players complaining about their 'measly' $10-million contracts. Rickey Henderson? Barry Bonds? This is what we need to write about?"

"Mmmmph," the dog said.

"I don't want to complain," I said. "But between you and me? I'd rather be up north, witnessing the climax to the Last Great Race on Earth."

"Mmmmph."

(By the way, the reason the dog kept saying "mmmph" is that I have him tied to a sled, running up and down the stairs. After seeing those mush dogs in Alaska? He's not sleeping on the couch anymore. I can get a cat to do that.)

Back to the suitcase. I unpacked the sweaters and replaced them with T-shirts. I unpacked the Chapstick and replaced it with cocoa butter.

"North … to Alaska," I sang softly.

"Mmmmph," the dog said.

I looked at my watch. Just after 1 o'clock. I flipped on the radio in time to hear Ernie Harwell begin what, sadly, will be his last season broadcasting the Tigers. "Lo, the winter is past …"

Well. I had that to look forward to in Lakeland: I would get to see Ernie again.

"You know, dog," I said, packing my baseball cap, "I wouldn't mind spring training so much if only I had seen the Iditarod through to the end."

"Pffff … pffff …" the dog panted.

"I mean, you wouldn't leave the Indy 500 on the 100th lap, right? You wouldn't leave the Masters on Saturday afternoon."

"Pfffff ... puuh ... uhhhhhnnn—."

"You wouldn't leave the Olympics after the opening ceremony. Am I right? Am I right?"

Unfortunately, the dog had fainted.

I turned up the radio. I heard Harwell call a Dave Bergman sacrifice fly. I wondered who was winning in Alaska. I thought about those mushers, moving through the frozen night, dragging up mountains and gliding across frozen lakes.... .

"Stop it," I told myself. "It's over." I looked at my dog, who was flat on the carpet. "And you — get back to work!"

And then the phone rang. My boss.

"Go back," he said.

"Huh?"

"Go back. To Alaska. Find a plane. Find a horse. Get up there, before I throw you there myself."

"But Boss, I just got b—"

"I know that. The whole world knows it — after you wrote it in the newspaper. Do you realize we've had more than 300 angry phone calls? They say we're nuts for pulling you off Iditarod to go to Lakeland. They want to know what happens in Alaska. Some of them even called me a ... BOZO!"

"No! Not you, Boss."

"OH, YES, ME! Listen to this fax from a woman in Southfield: 'What is your sports editor thinking about? He sends Albom thousands of miles to Alaska ... and when the race reaches halfway, he pulls him out to cover Tiger camp? Who's crazy there? ... Has anyone thought that Albom would rather work for a paper where the sports editor is a little brighter?' "

"Well, Boss, now that she mentions it."

"GET ON THAT PLANE!"

A nd so, believe it or not, I am returning to The Great White North. "Hey, dog," I said. "I'm going back to Alaska."

His left ear lifted.

"By tomorrow, I'll be reunited with my trusty pilot, Old Jim Okonek, flying above the mountains."

His right ear lifted.

"And by Monday's newspaper, I'll be back on the trail, hunting down the weird and the wounded, the furry and the dirty, the mushers and the mushees."

His tail began to wag.

Who says you can't get things done by complaining? The readers have spoken. The readers have won. Actually, the readers have given my boss a massive headache. But it's a good headache. At least it'll seem good compared with the expense account I turn in from this sucker.

Alaska calls. I follow. The higher-ups at this newspaper have done a good thing. They have said, "We made a call; the customers didn't like it," and they have reversed their decision.

Now, if only the Tigers would apply the same logic to the Harwell situation.

But you can't have everything. For now, I thank you for your outrage — and your phone calls. It will enable the whole Iditarod story to be told. Also, my dog thanks you. As I left for the airport, I saw him through the window: on the couch, with a pizza.

So everybody's happy. ■

Fatigue and feuding set in after a week on the trail

March 11

IDITAROD DIARY, CHAPTER 7: In which we return to the land of ice and snow ...

KALTAG, Alaska — My trusty pilot, Old Jim Okonek, was waiting at the airport as I landed — again — in the Lonely Country. He tugged on his blue cap, his eyes dancing under his sunglasses.

"Nice to have you back," he said, grabbing a bag.

"Thanks."

"Might have been easier if you just stayed here, you know."

He smirked. OK. So I am the only journalist in history to leave the Iditarod on the fourth day, fly back to Michigan, then return to Alaska three days later. Hey. I needed to wash my clothes, OK? Besides, seeing what has happened in this gruesome race, I didn't miss anything except the chance to get my head taken off. Tempers have worn thin out on the frozen trail, and the lack of sleep, the long hours, the endless work — they're beginning to take their toll on the mushers. And the dogs. Apparently, one furry soldier decided he'd had enough of wearing a harness and clomping through snowbanks just to get a piece of lamb every few hours. His musher went to move him and — boom! He bolted. Took off into the wilderness, sprinting toward the black spruce at the base of the Alaska mountain range. A lost dog is disaster in the Iditarod, not just because anything can happen out in the abyss — mostly bad — but also because his team will be disqualified if he is not found.

"I let him go for a second and that was it, that was all it took," the musher, Bill Peele, told reporters after it happened. "Everything I worked for, for years, is shot unless I find him."

Peele tried calling the dog. Offering food. Hiding behind his sled. No go. Every time he tried to get close, the animal took off farther into the wilderness. Hours passed. It was a nightmare. The other dogs in his team were getting restless, and it was just Peele and that one damn dog and about a thousand miles of frozen wilderness in which to catch him.

My heart sank for the guy. I had gotten to know Peele before the race. He is one of those divided souls, a pharmaceuticals businessman from North Carolina who, deep down, has the heart of a wilderness pioneer. He has been coming to Alaska for years, climbing mountains, dreaming of the Iditarod — then going back to his 9-to-5 job in North Carolina. Finally, at age 55, he figured time was short, so he traded in three years' worth of vacation, borrowed $40,000 against his retirement and got into this year's race. His dream. His soul on fire.

And now a doggie had done him in. Bolted into the blue. At last look, Peele had dropped off his dogs at the Nikolai checkpoint and was headed back, alone, to try to find a single dog in a mountain range. "I gotta get that dog, no matter what it takes," Peele said. "Not for me. For the dog.

"All life is sacred to me. … All I thought about on the way to Nikolai was him out there freezing and starvin' to death, and dying …"

He had tears in his eyes.

The Last Great Race on Earth.

O f course, arguing with a dog beats arguing with humans, which is pretty much what's been going on near the front of the race. Since I've been gone, it seems, the Iditarod has become a machismo war, a boy-vs.-girl thing, kind of like those battles you used to have in grade school.

"He hit me!"

"She started it!"

It began with a 90-mile stretch of trail between tiny Ophir and Iditarod — two places never to be confused with Las Vegas and Reno — where a blizzard and high winds had obliterated most of the trail. Susan Butcher, the four-time champion, and DeeDee Jonrowe, maybe the world's second-best female sled driver, wound up breaking much of the trail for their mostly male competitors. They had to get off the sleds and hoof it in snowshoes. Their dogs, at times, were neck deep in drifts. Ugly stuff.

But when the other (male) mushers caught up, Butcher claimed, they didn't exactly volunteer to go ahead. Breaking trail is tough on the dogs, wears them out, and, apparently, the mushers behind Butcher — including her arch-rival Rick Swenson, the only other person to win this race four times — were just as happy to let her have the honors, thank you. "Hey," they seemed to say. "You're the champion. You go first."

Which began a mini-war of words in the press:

Butcher: "It's bad sportsmanship."

Swenson: "Hey, it's bad sportsmanship for her to bitch about it."

Butcher: "It's obnoxious of racers not to put in their turn leading."

Swenson: "I'm running my race on my schedule, and if that doesn't suit Susan, too bad."

Butcher: "Schedule is no excuse when the nose of his lead dog is near the tail of my sled."

Swenson: "What a bunch of crybabies."

At one point, reportedly, Butcher turned and called Swenson "a lazy son of a bitch." So I guess we have to keep these two away from any sharp kitchen utensils. Their little feud has caught the attention of the Alaskan public, and some actually find it amusing that out there, among the frozen rivers and bone-chilling winds, there is still room for a good, old-fashioned sports argument.

If you ask me, these mushers are acting perfectly normal for people who haven't showered in a week.

I myself have no such plans. I packed soap. Still, in the Lonely Country, you never know. Just before we took off in the small plane Sunday morning, Jim's wife, Julie, was stuffing food and flashlights and gas stoves — gas stoves? — into a duffel bag.

"You do have a lighter, don't you?" she said.

"A lighter? What do I need a —"

"And a sleeping bag?"

"A sleeping bag?"

But these were not my only surprises. Once we flew into the wilderness, it was clear that not only had the weather grown colder, but the Iditarod, now more than a week old, was no longer the happy hunting ground I had left behind. The checkpoint in McGrath, beyond the Alaska Mountain Range — where you land your plane on Main Street — was deserted, save for a few dozen dogs chained to a fence. These were the damned, the wounded, the animals the mushers had dumped along the trail, too sick or too injured to go on. They eventually would be shipped home. For now, they howled like prisoners in some medieval chamber. "Awwwooooooo! ... Awoooooo!"

Chilling. Then, in Shageluk, a lonely pit stop on the Innoko River, I encountered Jim Cantor, the Anchorage lawyer — and former Michigander — who raced the first few miles dressed in a three-piece suit, with a sign on his sled: "Send a lawyer to Nome."

Now he was curled up in the checkpoint cabin. His face was red, his eyes glazed. He looked like hell, like Charlie Sheen after the first battle in "Platoon."

"I've banged into everything I can bang into," he said. "I've had some rough going."

"You gonna make it?"

He looked at his feet. "I'm kinda groggy. I haven't had much sleep."

Chilling. Before the day would end, we would stick the plane in a snow drift, and everyone would have to get out and push. But that's a story for later. For now, as we lifted into the Alaskan skies, I pondered the dangers ahead and behind. I thought about the upcoming stretch along the Bering Sea, where the winds eat through your best winter clothes and burn you with cold. I pictured Cantor, back there, looking a hell of a lot worse than he ever does in court. And I saw Peele, the hard-luck North Carolina man who watched that dog take off with his dream.

Let's face it. This is not "Lassie," folks. This is the Iditarod, it's a damn long race and you never know how you'll spend it: arguing with a competitor, staring at your feet or squatting in the wilderness, looking for one stinking dog that doesn't want to come home.

And what did she mean, sleeping bag? ∎

Choices are sleeping bags or freezing to death? Bingo!

March 12

IDITAROD DIARY, CHAPTER 8: No rooms, no beds, no waiting.

KALTAG, Alaska — I'm going to be honest here: When it comes to sleeping, my first choice is rarely the floor. It is even more rarely the floor of an Alaskan bingo hall. And it is almost never the floor of an Alaskan bingo hall in the middle of a tiny village where the only heat comes from a huge metal drum converted into a stove, which needs new logs every few hours.

Unless the alternative is freezing to death.

Which it pretty much was.

And I have no one to blame but myself. After all, nobody made me come back here, to the frozen tundra, just to see which dogs were still chugging in the Last Great Race on Earth, the Iditarod. But here I was Sunday night, landing on a snow-packed airstrip in some dot on the map in the Alaskan bush. And I turn to Old Jim Okonek, my trusty pilot — who once flew Playboy photographers and their models onto Mt. McKinley for a spread called "The Women of Alaska," then managed to get his plane in the picture, which he figures is "pretty good publicity, huh?" — and I say to him, seeing as the sun is going down, "Hey, Jim, where do we sleep tonight?"

And he says, "Wherever we can."

And I remember the sleeping bags.

And I say, God help us, this guy's not joking.

Now, let me explain how you find a place to sleep in a village that just recently got running water: First you walk from the plane into town, which is about a half-mile of snow drifts. Then you come upon a dozen barking dogs, who look like they would chew you from your boots up. And then — hooray! — you see an Indian boy, and you smile and say, "Hello. Do you know where the Iditarod checkpoint is?"

And he runs away.

So we're making progress, huh?

And, eventually, you find the checkpoint, which is nothing more than a red house belonging to a local resident. And you go inside. And you see the other reporters, photographers and race officials who beat you to it and are already sacked out in the bedrooms. So you find the hostess, Violet, who is clutching a baby to her chest, and you say, "Pardon me, do you know any place we could sleep tonight?"

And she looks around her house, which is now a mess of bags, equipment, coffee cups, dirty dishes, wet towels and wet clothes, and she points to a space on the living room floor, near the baby's blanket, and she says, "You can sleep there, I guess."

And you say, "God bless you."

But wait. Someone has a better idea. The locals are playing bingo at the Community Hall, about 40 snow steps away. When they are done, you are told, you can sleep there; the building will already be warm.

"Great," Jim says.

"Great?" you say.

And then you sit around that living room, trading war stories for three hours, waiting for bingo to finish. (At one point, Susan Butcher's husband, David Monson, shows up, ahead of his wife, who is still out there in the frozen darkness, mushing for a fifth championship, and he sees you and asks that very important Iditarod question: "How are the Pistons doing?" But more on that later.)

And then, after what seems like only, oh, four days, it is 11:30. And you pick up your sleeping bags and walk out in the cold — and when I say cold, I don't mean someone-left-the-window-open cold, I mean, "Look, that guy just turned to ice" cold — and you crunch in snow until you reach the door.

And you chuckle and say, "This isn't really a bingo hall, right?"

And you hear a voice from inside. "G 47? ..."

Bingo.

I should mention here that Iditarod mushers don't get — or expect — better treatment. They, too, sleep on couches or floors or in empty school halls. Hell, some of them sleep in their sleds. For 11 days. But those people have an excuse. They're nuts.

Me? Well, as a sports writer, I have developed a ranking system of places to sleep on the road. In descending order: 1) Ritz-Carlton; 2) Marriott; 3) Days Inn; 4) my cousin's house; 5) the couch; 6) stay home.

And then — maybe — the floor of a bingo hall.

But in we go. The locals are packing up. They fold the chairs and tables. They unplug the machine with the little bingo balls. They point to the massive barrel-type stove and say, "Don't forget to keep throwing logs inside."

I walk up to the thing. It is warm, so warm. I hold my hands out, I wiggle my fingers. Warm, so warm. So I put my palms on its hot metal.

And I melt my gloves.

So now I have no gloves. I do have the sleeping bag. And some candy bars. And I guess, if I get restless, I can turn on the ball machine and play bingo.

I shut my eyes. Life on the road in the Iditarod. Somewhere in the darkness the dogs are sleeping on beds of straw and eating hot food.

"This is great, huh?" Jim says, as he pulls himself into his bag.

"Rrrrrufff!" I say. ∎

Weary, wary mushers know if they snooze, they lose

March 13

IDITAROD DIARY, CHAPTER 9: In which we encounter the sea, the sandman and the frozen soap.

U NALAKLEET, Alaska — Night has fallen. The cold winds howl. The villagers stand like statues atop giant snow drifts. In heavy coats and seal-skin hats, they gaze silently out toward the frozen water, like proud pioneers.

And I stand beside them, my knees shaking like Jell-O.

We are one big, happy family here at the End of the World, the Bering Sea, next stop Siberia. It is the last place anyone would come to visit. But tonight we look for a headlight in the wilderness. Tonight, someone is coming to visit. I hope. Or else I'm totally lost.

"There!" one of them yells, pointing into the darkness.

"Where?"

"Right there. See it?"

The villagers begin to buzz. The children squeal and slide down the snow drifts. Is that a headlight? Is that a dog team?

"Is it Susan?"

"It must be Susan."

"HERE SHE COMES!"

"Where?"

Church bells ring. Windows open. Mothers and children dart out of homes and converge on the narrow snow path, their feet sliding as they run. In a twisted way, it is like a scene from an MGM musical, this entire town, in the middle of nowhere, ready to burst into song.

It is the Night of the Dogs, the night the Iditarod drops in from the darkness. We are in the 10th day of the Last Great Race on Earth. The mushers are dizzy and exhausted — their dogs dropping, their sleds breaking — but they push on. And each evening, when they show up, some village like this comes to life, most of them places that won't have a night like this the rest of the year. Hunting villages, fishing villages. The frozen outposts of the Lonely Country.

"Hoooeee! I may stay open for hours!" howls Ray Caudill, cook at the Unalakleet Lodge, a coffee and sandwich place that doesn't see this much action in a month. He eyes the crowd — sponsors, journalists, townspeople — then dumps another basket of French fries into the grease. "Business keeps up like this, I may not close all night."

"What time do you normally close?" I ask.

"About 3 in the afternoon."

Gone to the Dogs

Suddenly, the first musher arrives from the darkness. It is Susan Butcher. (Of course it is Susan Butcher. She will win this race again, if you ask me, mostly because she owns it, which I'll soon explain.) As her dogs trot into town like Roman soldiers back from the wars, she is mobbed by the townspeople. They surround her. They want to touch her.

"IS THERE A CHECKER HERE?" she yells, like Mick Jagger yelling from inside his fan club. Someone rushes in with a clipboard. A little girl tries to tug Butcher's leg. An old man yells, "Give her room! Give her room!"

The winds are howling. The village has gone nuts. It is the Night of the Dogs, and more will be here soon.

Me, I'm just trying to find a shower. And I will do anything. I will beg. I will pay. I will sign on as sports columnist with the Unalakleet News — a lifetime contract — if only they provide some hot water. After three days of sleeping wherever there's an empty spot on the floor — and that includes a bingo hall one night and a school gymnasium the next — after three days of bumping along in sleds being dragged by snowmobile, three days of eating candy bars and Fig Newtons, three days of stepping — oops ... aww, damn it! — in doggie droppings, only to find at the end of the day that the only bathroom has but a sink and cold water, well, I don't normally resort to this, but I do find myself yelling: "Calgon, take me away!"

It doesn't work.

So I begin my own Iditarod: The quest for hot water. I crawl around the buildings; I sniff like a dog; I search for a trail, seeking markers such as "Men's Room." Finally, in the back of the town gymnasium, I discover ... a shower! OK, so it has no door. And no curtain. And the faucets are loose. And the floor tile is broken. And it smells funny, like raw eggs. So it's a shower Attila the Hun might look at and say, "Nah, I'll wait."

But I cannot wait because I smell like a raccoon. And so, while villagers clamor outside, I strip off my 43 layers of clothing and step gingerly under the water.

And I grab the shampoo.

And I squeeze.

And it is frozen solid.

In fact, everything is frozen solid: the shampoo, the conditioner, even the soap breaks apart in my hands. Also, I forgot, I did not pack a towel. So I basically let the water run for a few minutes, then step out, more wet than clean, and dry myself with a T-shirt.

And in bursts my trusty pilot, Old Jim Okonek, the combat veteran, and his eyes light up. "All right!" he says. "A shower, huh? This is first-class!"

I am beginning to wonder about him.

B ack to the race, which is a battle near the front: Butcher, followed by a half-dozen challengers, each hoping to destroy her dynasty. They will chase her the final 250 miles, down the homestretch, along the Bering Sea, through tiny Eskimo villages and miles of blinding white landscape. Their enemies, at this point, are not just Butcher's superdogs but their own desperate need for sleep.

Which, after waking up this morning between two snoring pilots, is something I can understand.

"I gotta find a place to lie down," says a bleary-eyed musher named Mike Madden, who was in 17th place when he stumbled into our little gym early Tuesday morning. If he was coming here to sleep he had to be desperate. "I've been out there all night, so tired that I tied myself to the sled then stuck my head between the handlebars. I did it so my headlamp would point forward and make the dogs think I was awake — and then I dozed off. I'm really beat."

He waddles toward a mattress and falls in.

They are all just as weary, these mushers. But the winners will not sleep, not more than an hour here and there. They will find a way to fight the drowsiness; they will stab it away like Zorro. Never mind that they have been pushing through the Alaskan landscape for a week and a half, through mountains and trees and the mighty Yukon River. Never mind that their bodies are exhausted, their minds dopey, their dogs panting and sore. Never mind that they soon will suffer hallucinations from lack of rest, mirages of buildings and sticks and monsters. Never mind. They are within 250 miles of Nome, the finish line.

You snooze, you lose.

B y morning the snow is blowing wild and furious, and the village has turned blizzard-white. "Too dangerous to fly," says Old Jim, shaking his head. A dozen mushers already have been here and gone. The village has settled back to its lonely routine. Tonight it will be some other town that lights up, ablaze with the annual Iditarod madness. And then the dogs will be off to the next stop, leaving a trail of memories — and plenty of yellow snow. Thanks for dropping by, fellas.

But let me tell you something that breaks this whole race apart. I am sitting in the bowels of the gym Monday, staring at my sleeping bag, dreaming of a Westin Hotel, king-size bed, and I notice a woman a few bunks over. She says hello. Her name is Donna King, wife of musher Jeff King, who led this race for a while. Donna has been here, sleeping on a mattress, for three days now, waiting for a glimpse of her husband. I ask whether she will get to spend any time with him when he stops.

"We're not allowed," she says. "Spouses are only supposed to say hello and good-bye, basically."

I laugh. "Nah, come on. I've seen Susan Butcher's husband hanging around her for hours."

Donna King rolls her eyes. "Things are a little different for Susan."

And after checking around, I find out she's wrong. Things are not a little different for Susan; they are a lot different. Major league different. All sorts of advantages, such as better accommodations, more sleds, her own airplanes circling overhead. Suddenly, as the mushers head down the homestretch of the Last Great Race on Earth, I begin to wonder whether this is even a fair fight.

So I set out in search of the race marshal. And I am walking in this blizzard — why? because I'm an idiot — and a snowmobile pulls up and the driver waves.

"Have you been on the trail yet?" he asks.

"The trail? Of course not. We can't fly."

He grins. "Do you want to ride with me out there? See what it's like first-hand?"

An intelligent man would laugh. An intelligent man would say, you don't take a snowmobile out on the frozen water. An intelligent man would say, "No, thank you, I prefer to live a healthy and productive life."

I of course say, "Sure. Why not?"

Because, as I said, I'm an idiot.

And off we go, into the storm … ■

It's dog eat dog out there as mushers hit homestretch

March 14

IDITAROD DIARY, CHAPTER 10: The homestretch, the lonely sea, and the rotten stench of money …

WHITE MOUNTAIN, Alaska — So there I was, speeding along the Iditarod trail, in the middle of a blinding windstorm, over the river and through the woods, where the real mushers mush and the real dogs dog — only I was on the back of a snowmobile. And we couldn't see a thing. And I yelled to the driver, who had a maniacal smile on his face, "HEY, MAYBE WE SHOULD SLOW D–"

And just at that moment, we hit a patch of frozen river and suddenly — WHOA-BUMP! — we were off the machine, spinning in the air …

But wait. Before I hit the ground in that tale — and before I tell you of the frantic homestretch in the Last Great Race on Earth, as the top mushers lope toward Nome, bleary-eyed, their sleds bumping along, their tired dogs panting — I want to say something about this event. Particularly its top attraction, Wonder Woman herself, Susan Butcher, whose team, at last look, was charging toward that $50,000 first prize like a pack of hungry greyhounds at a Florida dog track.

I like Susan, although she'd prefer that I had a tail and fur, and I like her husband, David Monson, even if he is a lawyer. But I must say — and I think, deep down, they know it — that Butcher, and a few other top mushers, have enormous advantages in this race.

Example: airplanes. Butcher and a few others hire planes to fly with them over the course. Ostensibly used to transport dogs and possessions, these planes also can relay valuable information, such as who's in what position, trail conditions, weather, etc. The information can be passed along as soon as Butcher pulls into a checkpoint. This is better than the way most poor mushers get news, which is to wake up in a sleeping bag on the floor of some old school house and mumble, "Who's winning? What's happening? Where am I? …"

Which leads to another inequity: accommodations. Butcher has a private home to stay in at almost every checkpoint, usually a warm place where, quite possibly, there is hot water waiting for her dogs, a comfortable bed and good food for her. Nothing illegal in this — nor is it illegal to use airplanes, if you can afford them — but the advantage in an 11- to 14-day race is enormous. The lesser-known mushers sleep where they can, heat their water over a fire, wolf down some fried food at the local cafe. How well can you mush when you're burping?

Another example: equipment. Butcher needn't worry should her sled get wrecked along the trail. She has a new one waiting at many checkpoints. While other mushers might spend precious time working on sled runners and patching dents, Butcher can unhook, rehook and be on her way. She also doesn't carry a cooker — an extra few pounds — because she has a new one available at most checkpoints, too.

Understand, none of this is against the rules — which is part of the problem — and several other top mushers, including front-runners Rick Swenson and Joe Runyan, also enjoy some of these advantages. But that doesn't make it right. If the Iditarod is supposed to be a pure and equal test against the elements, for all mushers, famous and not — well, let's just say money tips the balance.

You pick up 20 minutes a day; it's a four-hour cushion by the end.

"You're right, it's not fair," admitted Jim Kershner, the race marshal. "The top mushers like Susan have all this sponsorship money behind them, and so they have advantages. The other mushers can't possibly afford these things. I find it amazing that a musher can have an airplane overhead. Just amazing."

And this is the guy who enforces the rules.

Sixteen years ago, Kershner was a musher in the Iditarod. Those were the old days, before ABC and Sports Illustrated discovered it.

"Would you come back as marshal next year?" I asked him.

"Not unless we made some major changes in the rules," he said, sighing. "It's just not an equal race right now.. "

Of course, when I took all this to Monson, Butcher's husband — who travels the trail and confers with his wife, further angering other mushers — he said, "That's bull. That's jealousy. That's bull." And, yes, I'm sure there is plenty of jealousy toward Butcher because she is a four-time winner and a woman in what used to be a man's race.

But Monson is defensive, as if he knows his wife's success has turned into a year-round job, a big-money operation, that they planned this Iditarod as Gen. Norman Schwarzkopf planned the rescue of Kuwait.

"It's the winners versus the whiners," Monson sniffed. "People make charges against us because Susan wins. But there has always been griping in this sport, always.

"It's just the winners versus the whiners, that's all."

Which sounds a little whiny to me.

But it's not like Butcher isn't great with dogs. It's not like she couldn't survive in the wilderness without sponsorship. This stuff happens in every sport when the money comes in and the rules don't keep up. There is talk about changing those rules, making all mushers sleep in the same accommodations and park their dogs in the same open spots. Fine. Personally, I'd like to see all these big-money dogs trip over one another down the finish line, and have that 55-year-old rookie musher from North Carolina, who had to stop his team and chase a loose dog

around the mountains for a day, come trotting along and win the race.
But that's just me. And I can't even handle a snowmobile.

WHOMPF! I landed on the ice, on my head, then looked up to see my crazy driver brushing himself off as the snowmobile puttered down the river.

"I guess I shouldn't try to put my goggles on while driving, huh?"

I nodded. As my vision cleared, I saw a wooden stick with a red ribbon — a trail marker — and I realized, wow, this is what the mushers see, day after day, night after night. And what they see is this: nothing. Not a soul. Just white landscape, tall spruce trees, rivers so solid and snow-covered they look like ground — until you see a shiny, wet, green thing poking through the surface, ice that has popped from pressure, like a wrinkle in a carpet. The wind-chill is 30 below. The scene is eerie, like the Fortress of Solitude from those Superman movies.

I blew a mouthful of cold smoke. We were only 10 miles from the checkpoint, but the loneliness of it all was overwhelming. Here is quiet like you have never heard. Here, where the howling north wind blows snow horizontally across your face, the sun is but a blurry light in the white sky. What would possess a person to take a pack of dogs and run through this desolate landscape — or even further north, along the Bering Sea, or into the hills, through thickets and bushes and trees that, at night, hover like muggers to the sleepy dog-drivers? Are they crazy? Death-wishers? Or is the sheer beauty of it all, as Jack London put it, the call of the wild, what lures them?

It sure ain't the accommodations. Even as I nursed my bruises, miles ahead, between the villages of Shaktoolik and Koyuk, the leaders were huddled in a cabin in the wilderness: Butcher, arch-rival Rick Swenson, Martin Buser, Tim Osmar. Their dogs were resting while the snow blew up a white fog. They made small talk and watched each other like hawks, lest one sneak out and take off.

Suddenly, Joe Runyan — the tall, stoic one who says, "Only inexperienced drivers try to push things too early" — cruised past the cabin. And within minutes, the others were out on their sleds after him.

By the wee hours, they arrived at Koyuk, a village on the coast. And by sunrise, it was Butcher, again, in her familiar red snowsuit, out first onto the trail, followed closely by Swenson and Runyan. Out of Elim, a village on the sea where the winds are so cold they suck the breath from your chest, it was Butcher, Swenson, Runyan. Their dog teams were depleted now. Animals had been dropped along the way because of injury or sickness. But the ones that were left had their little booted paws moving in rhythm. And the mushers, droopy and fatigued from 11 brutal days in the Lonely Country, were nonetheless juiced on adrenaline. They could smell the end. It was time to run for the money.

It's a hell of a race.

And we could have a hell of a finish. ∎

Leaders approach Nome, but only rumors reach finish line

March 15

IDITAROD DIARY, CHAPTER 11: In which we learn absolutely nothing, except that someone might be dead out there.

N OME, Alaska — And the winner is … nobody?
"Have you heard anything?" someone asked in the confused headquarters on Front Street, where this grueling Iditarod dogsled race was supposed to have ended already — and I was now late for my plane back to planet Earth. "What's the latest? Have you heard?"

"I heard Susan turned around," someone answered. "She went back to White Mountain! And so did Martin Buser. They couldn't handle the storm. But Rick Swenson is still out there. He's gonna kill himself!"

"He's not gonna kill himself," interrupted someone else. "He's just lost. And so is Joe Runyan. But I heard Martin Buser is winning."

"Buser's not winning; he's going backward," someone else said quickly. "And Runyan turned around, too. But I heard Swenson has a secret cabin he's hiding in."

"A secret cabin? Really?"

Rumors flew. Rumors bounced. Where was everybody? Where was anybody? Suddenly, the Last Great Race on Earth was the Biggest Mystery in Alaska. Downtown Nome, normally a wild celebration at this point, was nearly empty, the finish banner hanging from two telephone poles, swaying in the wind. It seemed the entire population was inside the wood-paneled Convention Center, bumping into one another, trying to get some news. It looked like Republican headquarters on election night. "What's the latest? What's the latest? …"

Here was the latest: After 1,086 miles of unforgiving wilderness — frozen rivers, black trees and snowdrifts so high you could rent them for condos — after 11 days of weather shifts, snowstorms and raw ice that left the dogs' paws bleeding in the snow, after lead changes and strategy backfires and sleeping-bag nights on the icy frontier with only God as company — after all the Iditarod can be, suddenly the mushers were stuck. A ground blizzard had blown up during the final leg of the race, forcing Butcher, who had had a comfortable lead, to turn her dogs around after six terrible hours and seek shelter at the checkpoint, along with Runyan and Tim Osmar.

Swenson, however, her arch-rival — of whom one musher reportedly said, "He's gonna win this year or kill himself" — was more stubborn. He pushed on, into that blinding snow, hoping to find the trail, to find a miracle, to win this stinking race one more time.

No one had heard from him since.

"His dogs can handle this, he knows what he's doing," someone said.

"It's not safe, no one should be out there!" said someone else.

"It's his best chance!"

"Have you heard anything?"

I found the coffee pot and filled another styrofoam cup. So this is what it had come to after all those miles of Alaskan wilderness; sitting in a wood-paneled room, listening to radio reports. My trusty pilot, Jim Okonek took one look at the white skies this time and shook his head. "No way we can go in this," he said. And Jim used to fly through bullets.

No way to fly. But could they mush? And if so, who was winning? Did we have an upset here? The night before, we had been at the White Mountain Hunting and Fishing Lodge, just 77 miles from the finish line. There we ran into Charlie Butcher, Susan's father, who was smiling, in a jovial mood. And why not? His daughter, at that point, was about as sure a bet as Tyson vs. Douglas. Michael Douglas.

"Congratulations," Butcher said, hugging his son-in-law, David Monson, who had just come in from the trail.

"Well, we're not across the finish line yet," Monson said sheepishly.

You got that right, David. And in this race, if you're not across the finish, you're nowhere. In just one moonless night, Susan Butcher, the defending champ, had gone from hunted to hunter. She was behind. She could ... lose! After returning to White Mountain, she had smugly told reporters, "If Rick can make it through that weather, more power to him. But when I last saw him, he didn't have very high hopes." Maybe not. But unlike her, he was still out there, in all his macho swagger, battling that storm. And you can bet every leather jacket and tattooed arm in Alaska was pulling for him to get to that finish line and show the women of this state that the men weren't dead yet.

"They found him! He's moving!" someone said.

"He survived the storm. He's 40 miles away!"

"Nobody's confirmed that."

"What's happening?"

Hours passed. Night began to fall. I gulped another coffee and held a radio to my ear. What was the last sporting event I'd covered wherein I couldn't see the finish? There was the America's Cup final in Australia, but I missed that because I became nauseated on the boat. There was that NFL playoff game a few years ago, between Chicago and Philadelphia, where the fog got so thick you couldn't see the field. Yet even then, we figured the players were out there somewhere.

But this? Good Lord. Swenson could be on the trail, he could be in Siberia, he could be dead. Who knew? The planes couldn't fly, the snowmobiles couldn't run, and you can bet your butt nobody was walking out there. Not with 20-below temperatures, winds of 30 miles per hour, and the snow in such a maddening swirl that all you could see was white, white, white. Nuh-uh. For now, this was Swenson vs. the Wilderness, and they were playing on nature's home court. No tickets. No TV. Whatever happened down the stretch, we would not see it. We would only hear about it later.

Which, I figure, is just about the way Swenson would like it. Win the race, tell the story the rest of his life. Hot damn, the guy becomes a legend! Let's face it. Mr. Rick had played his hand here; he was going for the gusto. With weary dogs and a blizzard in his face, he either pushed on, found Nome — or he packed it in and kept right on driving back to Two Rivers. After all, he wasn't just trying to win this race. He was trying to beat Wonder Woman. His rivalry with Butcher is big stuff, the second most important thing you learn here in Alaska. (The first is to buy polypropylene underwear.) Rick was the king of the Iditarod — having won four — until Butcher came along. He has been winless ever since, while Susan has captured four crowns and more publicity then Rick ever dreamed of. The T-shirts tell the story: "ALASKA — WHERE MEN ARE MEN AND WOMEN WIN THE IDITAROD."

And the more he denied it, the more obvious it was that Butcher's success was driving Swenson batty. Once friends, they became bitter rivals. He moaned about her dogs. He said she "wasn't that great." He sniped at her. She sniped back. At one point during this race, Swenson told a reporter, "If she weren't a woman, I'd punch her lights out."

Now, in a way, he had the chance. Win this Iditarod — especially like this, with a good old-fashioned spit-in-the-face-of-death climax — and he'd be a hero in Alaska forever. The men in the bars would sing about him all winter, how he braved the wilderness while "the girl sat back in White Mountain." Hooh, boy, you can hear it already. Foolish, crude and sexist, of course. But then, we aren't exactly in San Francisco here.

"Someone saw him from a snowmobile!"

"He's 32 miles from Nome!"

"The weather's getting worse in White Mountain."

"No, it's getting better."

I turned off the radio. I went for the coffee pot. I thought of Butcher out there in White Mountain. Was she worried? Was she pressed against some window, cursing the skies? I thought of Runyan and Osmar. Were they second-guessing?

Finally, I thought of Swenson, the tough guy. Was he pushing his dogs too far now? Was this bravery or desperation? Maybe he was alone in that blizzard, with a radio plugged in his ear, enjoying all the fuss.

Then again, he could be in Siberia.

I filled another cup, found a seat and sighed. What the hell? A few more hours in the Lonely Country wouldn't kill anybody.

Would it? … ∎

Swenson's blind ambition stops women's streak

March 16

IDITAROD DIARY, CHAPTER 12: The Last Mile.

NOME, Alaska — Finally, from the darkness, came the dogs. They loped across the finish line, fell into the snow and wiped the ice from their eyes. The winning musher, his face barely visible inside a hood, trotted among them, patting their heads. Good dogs. Good job. From behind makeshift fences, shivering fans whooped and hollered, shattering the stillness of downtown Nome. It was 1:34 in the morning Friday. We had a winner.

"ALASKA!" someone yelled. "WHERE THE MEN WIN THE IDITAROD — AND THE WOMEN TURN BACK!"

"WHOOOOOOO!" the crowd answered.

And so it ends, between two telephone poles on Front Street, the Last Great Race on Earth — with drama and controversy, the way it should. The winner, the new king, is former champion Rick Swenson, a gruff, mustached, 40-year-old musher who was dumb enough to risk death, smart enough to avoid it, and fed up enough to walk through a blizzard and pull the dogs — that's how much he wanted this victory. And that's how much he wanted to beat Susan Butcher, his arch-rival, who was leading the race until 71 miles from the finish, before a storm forced her and other mushers to return to shelter — and gave Swenson his opening. For six years he had been hearing about women's victories in the Iditarod, and for much of that time he was made to feel guilty. "What's the deal, Rick?" the macho types would ask, gulping another beer. "You won this thing four times. How come these women keep beating you?"

Maybe a Wall Street exec would say, "Now, gentlemen, the women earn it the same as the men." And, of course, they do. But this is not Wall Street. Stockbrokers don't cook meat for their dogs, sleep outside in sled bags and snowshoe for miles in a blinding storm. Survival is the currency here in the Lonely Country. And Swenson was going to prove himself by surviving this race — and winning it. His chilling odyssey over the final 23 hours will go down in Alaskan folklore as truly remarkable. Which, around here, means all in a day's work.

"Weren't you scared?" someone asked Swenson in the bar of the Golden Nugget Motel, where he was already sipping a Jack Daniel's and Coke, less than an hour after he had won this trans-Alaska sled dog race in 12 days, 16 hours, 34 minutes and 39 seconds. "You went out in a blinding snowstorm when almost everyone else turned back. No one

Gone to the Dogs

could find you. You could have died!"

"Aw, hell, I wasn't gonna die," he snapped. "Not as long as I stayed on the trail. Besides, what's my life worth, anyway? If I had to go back and listen to 365 days of that crap — 'How come women keep beating you?' Blah, blah, blah — I'd just as soon be dead."

Like I said, this isn't Wall Street.

But it is the end. Which means a lot of things. Most of all, it means I can go back to sleeping in a bed. And eating something for dinner besides Hershey bars and coffee. It's a tough assignment, the Iditarod, pretty much back to basics. Or as Old Jim Okonek, my trusty pilot, might say: "Bathroom? Use a snow drift."

But, heck, my troubles were nothing compared with the homestretch of this race, out along the Bering Sea and deep in the treeless hills, where airplanes couldn't fly and snow machines had to turn back and nobody had a clue as to Swenson's whereabouts.

Butcher had encountered him not far out of the White Mountain checkpoint. His hands were freezing, his headlamp was broken. She tried to travel with him, arch-rivals thrown together by danger. But soon she lost him in the storm. Her dogs were tired. She had driven them hard in the first few days, trying not only for her fifth victory in six years but also to set a speed record. It cost her. Several windstorms had slowed her progress. And now, with another one burning her face, she made a fateful decision. "I can second-guess myself from now until I die," she later admitted, "but emotionally, at that point, my dogs could not endure another 55 miles in a storm."

She returned to White Mountain and prayed for a change in the weather. Because without it, she had just handed the race to Swenson. And she knew it.

Swenson didn't. He was still out there, poking around that blizzard like a blind man. Returning to White Mountain never occurred to him. What for? So he could lose the race, then listen to another year's worth of drunks asking why he couldn't beat the girls?

To hell with that.

He pushed on.

Understand what that means. It means walking in front of your dogs (the ones you have left) and pulling them along as you search for a stick with an orange ribbon on top — the only evidence that you are on the trail. Meanwhile, the whipping snow leaves you blind, and the wind — at a chill factor of 70 below zero — can rip the skin from your face. "I couldn't tell what was up, down, sideways," Swenson recalled.

But somehow, marker by marker, he made his way along the frozen flats and into Topkok Hill, pushing against the wind. He suffered frostbite. He was exhausted. Push on. Push on. After hours of this he came upon a shelter cabin on the far side of the hill. He poked the door open. And inside was a schoolteacher, sitting by a fire; his snowmobile had broken down.

"Wasn't he shocked to see you?" I asked.

"Nah," Swenson said. "He just nodded."

Alaska.

Which brings me to an important point. The Iditarod, I have learned, is not really about the $50,000 prize. And it's not really about the macho boasting that will soon begin, now that Butcher has been toppled. No. This race, first and foremost, is about Alaska.

How can I explain this state? It is an attitude, a frame of mind, the kind of thinking that makes men build cabins miles from nowhere, no water, no electricity, the kind of thinking that leads college graduates to abandon creature comforts and hunt for food, the kind of thinking that climbs mountains, hikes glaciers, welcomes strangers like family, teaches children to cherish nature, treats Eskimos and Indians and white men like brothers.

A quiet, simple, common sense. It's the kind of thinking that makes a lost schoolteacher in a snow-covered cabin look up from the fire and simply nod at a musher the whole state is looking for.

It's also the kind of thinking that uses snow drifts as bathrooms.

But it is magical. You can't deny that. Before this race started, I asked a rookie musher what he wanted from the Iditarod. He said, "The privilege of seeing this land." And you know what? He's right. It is a privilege.

If I learned anything from two weeks in this state, it's that America is lucky to call this place its own. You wander among these snow-covered mountains and frozen oceans and tall trees and rare animals and good, old-fashioned, terribly rare human kindness — and you keep asking yourself, "Does this really come with my passport?"

But enough mush. And back to the mushing. Hours after Swenson left that cabin, he was alone again, lost in the wind, when suddenly a snowmobile appeared, nearly running over his dogs.

"WHERE'S THE TRAIL?" Swenson yelled at the driver.

"YOU'RE ON IT!"

"WHAT HAPPENED TO THE OTHERS BEHIND ME?"

"THEY TURNED BACK."

They turned back? Swenson felt a rush. It was enough to get him over the hump and lead his team into Safety, the final checkpoint. There, it was confirmed: All the top mushers except Swiss-born Martin Buser were stuck at White Mountain, 55 miles behind.

And Buser was lost.

"What did you think then?" Swenson was asked.

"I thought I just won the Iditarod," he said.

And a few hours later, he had, the first five-time winner in Iditarod history. Weather made this the most dramatic finish in years. And weather surely cost Butcher her chance at a fifth championship. Despite an incredible team, she finished third (Buser came in a few hours ahead of her), and her reception, in the dark hours of the morning, was hardly a hero's welcome — maybe 50 people. A smattering of applause.

She held her head up.

"Turning back didn't lose me the race," she said. "I made the decision not to continue. …

"Could I have pushed my team more? Well, my whole strategy has always revolved around dog care; the better you take care of them, the better they perform. Maybe I could have popped a cork, got them to do it, but I didn't want to ruin their trust in the way I drive them."

"Are you upset at losing?" someone asked.

She wiped an icicle from her eyebrow. "I really wanted to win. It would have been a cute fairy tale. We (she and husband David Monson) could have hung up the harnesses and not raced Iditarod for a while. We want to start a family. And I think, even with this, we're going to do that."

She sniffed. Butcher takes a lot of heat for preferring dogs to people. But here, for once, at the finish of a life-draining race, she talked about children over dogs. Nice.

Meanwhile, back at the bar …

"How do you feel emotionally?" someone asked Swenson, who lives in Two Rivers, Alaska, as he nursed his drink. He grinned. His eyes rolled.

"I'm too brain dead to tell you."

Which about sums it up for me. I've learned many valuable lessons on this Iditarod trail: 1) Never sleep next to snoring pilots. 2) Avoid showers without doors. 3) Stay away from moose. (In Unalakleet, a tiny village, they had a dinner at the church: "Moose stew, all you can eat, five bucks." But I passed. One of them might be watching from the window.)

And 4) For those of you who, upon hearing of these brave dogs that run through ice and snow, now feel you must take your lazy pet and sign him up at Vic Tanny — well, let me say this. Before the race, I interviewed Joe Runyan, one of the best mushers in the business. He raises sled dogs at his kennel, dozens and dozens of top racing prospects.

"Let me ask you something," I said. "And answer me honestly."

"OK," he said.

"Can any of your dogs fetch a bone?"

"Uh, no," he said.

So there.

As for the race, well, let's remember that it's not over, that even as you read this, some of the 75 mushers who started this thing are still working their way across Alaska, from one little village to the next, with no hope of prize money, only the sense of accomplishment.

And that is enough. More than enough. They give an award to the last musher to arrive. It's called the Red Lantern. And right now, the leading candidate is none other than Bill Peele, the 55-year-old North Carolina businessman who traded money against his retirement to try this race just once before he died. He was almost disqualified after one of his dogs ran away in the Alaska Mountain Range. He had to tie up his team and go searching. Not finding that dog could have cost Peele a $30,000 investment and a year's worth of training. But as he set off that day, there were tears in his eyes — for the animal.

"If something should happen to him … " Peele said, breaking up. "I just gotta find that dog. …"

He did. He's still in the race. Back of the pack.

We'll leave the light on for ya, Bill.

Me? I leave Alaska with a certain sense of gain — and loss. Mostly, my butt is sore from sitting in Old Jim's plane for so long. All those stops. All those wonderful scenes. There's a song they wrote about this race, a playful little ditty that I heard a group of schoolchildren perform along the way:

"Oh, give me a team and a goodly dog
and a sled that's built so fine
and let me race those miles to Nome
One thousand forty-nine,
And when I get back to my home
Hey, I can tell my tale
I did, I did, I did the Iditarod trail."

And I did.
Now.
Where's the bed? ∎

Today's Casey at the Bat finds no joy in Mudville

April 7

Mudville 1991

The outlook wasn't brilliant
For the Mudville nine today,
The score stood 4-3 with just
One inning left to play.
The fans did groan when Jackson
Hit a dribbler to the mound,
Then Williams went down swinging
He barely got around.
But suddenly a hush did fall
The crowd began to shake …
Was that the Moody Casey
Walking toward the plate?
He flexed his arms and shook his chains
He checked his Rolex watch,
He spit, he chewed, he spit again
Then grabbed and scratched his crotch.
And when responding to the cheers,
He tipped his Nike hat
No stranger in the crowd could doubt
'Twas Casey at the bat.

"When did you sign?" the catcher asked
as Casey shook his girth.
"This morning," Casey answered
"Guess what my contract's worth?"
The catcher shrugged; he didn't know,
Our hero had to grin.
"Forty million for one year,
plus an island they threw in."
The catcher said, "Not bad"
as Casey stepped into the box,
"you hear about Tex Johnson,
who just signed with the Sox?"
"Tex Johnson?" Casey asked
as the pitch sailed toward his head.
"Fifty million," said the catcher,
"STRIKE ONE!" the umpire said.

Casey burped, then spit again
His cockiness did fade.
Just one pitch into the season
And he was underpaid.
"Tex Johnson ain't worth that much dough
You sure you got that right?"
The catcher nodded earnestly
And chuckled with delight.
The sneer was gone from Casey's lips,
His teeth were clenched in hate.
He pounded with cruel violence
His bat upon the plate.
He thought about Tex Johnson
As in the baseball sailed.
"Fifty million?" he repeated,
"STRIKE TWO!" the umpire wailed.

Now the fans began to stir
But Casey's eyes were slanted.
How dare his tightwad baseball team
start taking him for granted?
He sat down on home plate,
untied his Nike pumps,
"I want to renegotiate!"
He bellowed to the umps.
His manager came running out
And begged he'd reconsider.
His teammates said "Just swing the bat!"
lest they be late for dinner.
But with the count at 0-2
He sat there like a crate
And nighttime fell on Mudville
Moody Casey on the plate.

Soon a state of panic
Descended on the park.
How long would Casey sit there
Just sulking in the dark?
His agent flew from New York
His CPA came, too.
The owner of the team flew in
From a trek in Kathmandu.
The TV news reported live,
The headlines clearly stated:

"CASEY WON'T PLAY BASEBALL, SAYS HE'S NOT APPRECIATED."

Now all this time in Mudville
The scoreboard stayed the same.
The home team still trailed 4-3
Two strikes by Casey's name.
While on the field they argued
Over bonuses and cash,
As Casey sat there happily
and patted his moustache.
The fans began to boo and hiss
How long there must they linger?
Casey showed his deep concern
By giving them the finger.
"How can I survive," he asked
"On a measly 40 mill?"
If I don't get my way
I just may join the NFL."
Finally, the businessmen
who'd argued this till dawn
sighed that they were finished
"Play ball," the umpire yawned …

Now somewhere in this favored land
The sun is shining bright.
The band is playing somewhere
And somewhere hearts are light.
And somewhere men are laughing,
But here the money's saved
For justice has hit Mudville …
Moody Casey has been waived. ∎

In Amen Corner, even golf's Masters don't have a prayer

April 12

AUGUSTA, Ga. — Before I tell you, brothers and sisters, about the nastiest little golf hole ever put on God's good earth — "TELL US, BROTHER!" — before I tell you about the famous par-three that looks as temptin' as pumpkin pie on your grandma's windowsill, but will jump up and bite you faster than a caffeinated alligator — "LIKE AN ALLIGATOR, YES, TELL US!" — before I tell you about this evil hole, this wicked hole, this mean, hard, devastating, infuriating, head-knocking, teeth-gnashing sinner of a hole — "LORD, HAVE MERCY!" — before I tell you about the 12th hole at Augusta National ... can I get an amen?

"AMEN!"

Thank you.

We are, after all, in Amen Corner, the far end of the Masters course, Holes 11, 12 and 13, where supposedly, when golfers finish, they sigh "Amen." Thus, Amen Corner. Get it? And I am practicing my preaching. Because I cannot practice what I preach. Which, if I could golf, would be this: Get the hell out of here, fast. Before you embarrass yourself.

Especially on the 12th hole. You want no part of this. The 12th hole looks as if it belongs on a chip-and-putt course. But beware: It is Lizzie Borden dressed up as Liz Taylor; it will seduce you, then chop your head off. It is 155 manicured yards that plays like a construction site. A small green that you hit, and suddenly disappear from. Elements? Here's a quick story: A guy named Bob Rosburg once stepped to the 12th tee with a four-iron in his hand. Never known as a big hitter, he whacked the ball just as the wind died. It flew — and flew and flew, over the water, over the green, over the sand traps, over the fence. It landed on an adjacent golf course. Really. Embarrassed, he set up another tee shot — but kept the same club. This time, the wind picked up just as he swung. His ball landed 15 feet shy of the pin. Same hole. Same club. Same shot. That should give you an idea what a fickle little creature we are dealing with. What a nasty, fickle, evil little creature ...

Can I get an amen?

"AMEN!"

Thank you.

Let me tell you how I suddenly know so much about this hole. I have been sitting on a wooden platform overlooking it for five hours now. And everyone who comes by has a story. I have heard about the time Toney Penna hit the flagstick and still double-bogeyed. I have heard about Tom Weiskopf, who once hit the water five times before reaching the green, making a 13, a course record to this day.

I have heard about all the years the 12th has cost someone the green jacket. I have heard about 1934, the first Masters, when Ed Dudley bogeyed it four straight times and lost the tournament by three strokes. I have heard about 1959, when Arnold Palmer was leading on the last day, until he landed in the water, chipped over the green, took a six and finished third. I have heard about 1981, when Jack Nicklaus double-bogeyed it and lost the Masters by two strokes, and 1982, when Seve Ballesteros bogeyed it and lost by one.

"The hardest tournament hole in golf," Nicklaus has called it. You will get no argument from Ken Green. A colorful, outspoken golfer, Green was in the lead Thursday morning when he came to the 12th. He seemed confident. He swung. The wind blew.

Plop! In the water.

He took the penalty stroke, dropped the ball and chipped toward the green. Plop! In the sand trap. He blasted out, to the far end of the green, and needed two putts to sink it. A triple bogey. So much for the lead. Green could think of only one way to get even.

"I (snuck) into the woods," he said, "and ... uh, relieved myself."

Remind me to stay out of there.

B ut Green was not alone. Paul Azinger had a nice round going, until he hit the 12th. Plop! In the water. Give him a bogey. Nick Faldo, the two-time defending Masters champion, saw his tee shot bounce off the green and disappear down the backside. Another bogey. Same for Ray Floyd. And Sandy Lyle. And Arnold Palmer. And this was a nice day.

The crazy thing is, the 12th looks so genteel. It is a postcard: a short velvet fairway and a rippling creek, with a green surrounded by gorgeous pine trees, shrubs and honeysuckle. OK. So the green is about the size of your kitchen table. OK. So it slants to the water like an Olympic ski jump. OK. So there is one bunker smack in front and two bunkers right behind. OK. So the wind dances in the semicircle of trees, making it impossible to gauge.

Hey. This is the Masters. It's not supposed to be the American League East.

And in the end, the 12th always wins. So here I sit, watching it claim its victims. Having been here all day, in the warm Georgia sun, I find myself moved to compose a country song. I call it "12th Hole Love":

There's a bunker round your heart, and I fell in
will you hold me in your trap? there's no tellin'
I'm in 12th Hole Love,
Is that Ken Green I'm smellin'?
Can I get an Amen?
"AMEN!"
Thank you. ∎

Discrimination still is par for Masters' hallowed course

April 14

AUGUSTA, Ga. — "Sure, I'll talk to you," he says, sitting down on the porch. "Ain't got nothing else to do."

Leon McClatty tugs on his blue cap and smiles through crooked teeth. Once, he would have no time for interviews. Not during Masters week. He was a caddie at Augusta National, and there were bags to haul, golf clubs to polish. Mr. Nicklaus might be waiting. Or Mr. Watson. Or Mr. Moody. For nearly 30 years, Leon caddied for all three players, and many more, back when the rules required Masters golfers to employ a house caddie, all of whom were black. Leon — "That's all you gotta call me, just Leon" — was Watson's caddie for six years, including the two years he won here, 1977 and 1981. Leon carried his bag. Advised him on putts. Had this big feeling in his stomach when Watson slipped on the champion's green jacket. Leon calls it "My glory time."

Now there is no glory. Now no one is waiting. Augusta National changed the rules nine years ago: Golfers may bring their own caddies. Leon came out during Masters week the following April, looking for Watson, figuring to work together as they had done the last six years. "Then I saw he had this new guy with him. He didn't even tell me."

He looks off into the sky. "A man shouldn't do that to another man."

"Did you talk to him?" I ask.

"Naw. We ain't talked since."

He glances around the caddie barn. Big name golfers are coming and going, followed by their personal caddies, white men in crisp white uniforms. A few of the old black caddies wander aimlessly in street clothes, hoping someone shows up late or calls in sick.

There is a feeling in this magnificent golf course, a feeling beneath the dogwood tress and the magnolias and the velvet green fairways that stretch like endless pool tables. It is a feeling of discomfort. Of quiet bigotry. Never mind CBS and all those whispering announcers who would like to turn Augusta National into church at High Mass. This is a club for bigots, a place where there is one black member, added only because of outside pressure. Every other black man here seems to carry a tray or a broom.

"But we used to wait all year for the Masters," Leon recalls. "It was something, I tell you. Made you feel important. Walking up them fairways, all them people, all them TV cameras. And after the thing was over, we'd sit around and argue. We'd say, 'My guy woulda won if he'da listened to me.' "

When the rules changed, the luster disappeared from the caddie position; so did much of the money. Leon and his peers could make as much during Masters week — tips and percentage of winnings — as they made the rest of the season. Now they have only the $30 per bag they get from members and guests. And during the biggest week in Augusta, they sit around, doing nothing.

I ask about the one black member the club allowed in this year. Leon looks both ways, then lowers his voice. "They just did that to quiet everybody down."

I ask whether guys such as Nicklaus or Moody ever gave him anything to show their appreciation.

"Oh, yeah," Leon chuckles, "Mr. Moody did. He gave me a lot of dead presidents."

"Dead presidents?"

"You know, dead presidents on the dollar bills. Washington on the $1. Lincoln on the $5. Ben Franklin on the $100. Franklin wasn't no president, but he'll do."

L eon met a live president once. Back in the '50s, Dwight Eisenhower used to golf here. Leon, then a teenager, served as his caddie on several occasions. One time, Eisenhower, who wasn't much of a golfer, teed off into a water trap and went wading in after his ball. When Leon offered a club to help pull the President back up, Eisenhower, as a joke, yanked the club instead, pulling Leon into the water. The symbolism of that is too sad to address.

Leon McClatty has played Augusta National "more times than I got toes and fingers." He used to sneak on as a kid and play with one club — until they chased him out through the bushes. On Employees Day, he and the waiters played every hole over and over. "I love the game, see? You must play the game to be a good caddie."

He looks off, his eyes squinting. The sound of a golf cart rumbles, then disappears. "You can call me on the phone in the middle of the night, tell me what green you're on, and I'll tell you which way the ball's gonna break," he says. "I know this golf course."

And it doesn't seem to matter. Of all the famous players who once used the house caddies, a few still do. Leon and the others sit around, waiting. You'll hear a lot about the Masters today, its majesty, its tradition. And maybe, for some, that's true. But for others, Augusta National is just another southern place where it's no blessing to be a black man, and there's no work to be found this week. ∎

Root for George Foreman, and pass the cheesecake

April 19

ATLANTIC CITY, N.J. — You bet I'm rooting for George Foreman tonight. And so is every American male over 19 or 27 or 31 or whatever age your metabolism changes and suddenly, one morning, after eating the same healthy food you've eaten since you were a boy — namely, a bowl of Cap'n Crunch, a baloney sandwich, three Mallomars, two burgers and a half-liter of Coke — you wake up with Bill Murray's body. But not his sense of humor.

Which is the problem. If you have Murray's sense of humor, it might be a fair trade. You could tolerate all that sagging flesh because you could always say, "Did you see my last movie? It grossed $140 million. Pass the fries."

Alas, we cannot all be Bill Murray. But anyone can be George Foreman, with enough helpings at the buffet table. Big George, 42, is an inspiration to us all. Can you imagine if he wins tonight? Against young and svelte Evander Holyfield? All across America Saturday, men will be gulping pizza and milk shakes, and when their wives say, "What are you eating that garbage for?" they will reply: "Training for the heavyweight championship, honey. (Burp)."

This would be reason enough to root for Foreman. But there is more. The man is funny. I don't know when he became funny. I don't recall him being funny back in the old days, when he had hair. Maybe you get funnier when you're bald. (Don Rickles? Bob Newhart? That guy from "Night Court"?) Anyhow, I don't remember Foreman laughing much in the '70s, when he punched the lights out of, among others, Joe Frazier and Ken Norton. But these days, he has become, if you pardon the boxing pun, a stitch.

REPORTER: "You weighed in at 257 pounds."

FOREMAN: "I was hoping for 265. Shame on me. And I had dinner, too."

REPORTER: "The record for heaviest fighter ever is 270 pounds."

FOREMAN: "I'm on the verge of a record here? Somebody quick. Get me a ham sandwich!"

Of course there's a difference between being a stand-up comic and a contender for the heavyweight championship. At least I think there's a difference. And so people are wondering about this Foreman-Holyfield fight: Are we supposed to take it seriously? Is it sports or theater? After all, Foreman weighs as much as a small land cruiser. And his previous opponents are not exactly names you paste on your resume. Let's go through a few of them:

March 1987: Steve Zouski. Hmm. Never heard of him. Think I went to high school with his sister.

February 1988: Guido Trane. Not to be confused with cousins Soul and Midnight.

August 1988: Ladislas Mijangos. Don't know it. Can't spell it.

December 1988: Dave Jaco. Charles' brother?

February 1989: Manuel Clay De Almeida. Wait a minute, I ... hee-hee ... mmph ... I don't mean to laugh, it's just ... HAHAHAHA.

January 1990: Gerry Cooney.

Ah. Gerry Cooney. Now there's a name you can hang your hat on. In fact, given Cooney's shape, you can hang your coat, jacket, scarf and boots on him as well. Cooney is supposedly one of the "marquee" opponents Foreman has beaten to earn his $12.5 million tonight. Of course, that would be like telling my newspaper I scored a 98 on my third-grade spelling test, and Pete Iannuzzi, who sat behind me and always had his shirt untucked, scored only a 78 so therefore, I deserve a $500,000 raise. Wouldn't work. But then, my bosses are conservative.

The crazy thing is Don King isn't even involved with this fight. Not that it matters. Most boxing promoters are identical: They smell money, they dive in. And they aren't going to worry if the man they put in to fight for the heavyweight championship of the world is 10 years past his prime and has a training philosophy that can be summed up in one sentence: "Everything's better with Blue Bonnet on it."

Of course, some folks are concerned that Foreman's age, weight and track record will make this a slow fight:

ROUND 1: Foreman walks in circles, avoids heavy lifting.

ROUND 2: Foreman throws a punch, sighs, begins to salivate.

ROUND 3: Canceled for food break.

ROUND 4: Foreman walks in circles ...

But of course, by that point, it will be too late. You will have paid your $35 for pay-per-view. And boxing will have sucked another fortune from a public only slightly more hungry for entertainment than Foreman is for a roast beef on rye.

And so you ask, why am I here? And I am wondering the same thing. Curiosity? Boredom? Who knows?

What do we say to the people who moan that an event like this will ruin boxing? That Foreman's stepping into the ring is the biggest hoax since Milli Vanilli stepped to a microphone?

Relax. The whole sport is a joke. Has been for years. Might as well grab a laugh while you can.

Or as Foreman might say:

If you can't beat 'em, eat 'em. ∎

A sure thing about Laimbeer: You'll get stuck with check

May 9

BOSTON — The last time I had breakfast with Bill Laimbeer he stole my grapes. Just reached across the table and grabbed them. Didn't even say thanks — although he did close his mouth when he chewed. "These are good," he said, swallowing.

Then he stuck me for the check.

So it's risky business eating with Laimbeer. But I am doing it again, four years later. I am sitting here as he orders eggs Benedict, two bagels, cream cheese, large orange juice, coffee — and I am doing it because I want to know one thing: I want to know whether he is ready to quit.

Life without The Prince of Darkness? Well. There have been whispers that Laimbeer — who'll be 34 on May 19 — has considered retirement. Maybe next year. Maybe the year after. Some say he wanted to quit before this season, and was only talked into coming back by Isiah Thomas, who reminded him, among other things, that there is nowhere else on the planet where he can earn this kind of money. Bill admits the story is true. He also says,"Isiah was right — about the money." Call Laimbeer anything you want. Dumb, he isn't.

But he is not made of steel, and the years take their toll. Laimbeer, in his 11th season, could never run or jump worth a hoot, and now he says, "I notice I can't run and jump as well as I used to." So where does that leave him? If he got any slower, he'd be a mailbox. Any more earthbound, he'd be topsoil.

And yet, he can still change a game — sometimes more than any other player in a Pistons uniform. No wonder coach Chuck Daly has called him "the most important performer on our team." You want to win, you must rebound, you must box out, you must change shots and you must infuriate the other team. Laimbeer did all these things Tuesday in Game 1 of the Eastern Conference semifinals against the Celtics — especially the infuriation thing: In the first quarter, he took a charge from Kevin McHale and did a flop. The ref called McHale for the offensive foul. BOOOOOOO! Third quarter, Laimbeer pushed his way inside, grabbed an offensive rebound and tossed a quick shot as he fell to the floor. The ref called foul on the Celtics. BOOOOOOO! With less than five minutes left and the crowd on its feet, urging Boston to rally, Laimbeer took a pass and launched a 20-foot jumper. Swish! Silence.

Infuriation. He specializes in it. Maybe it's his sneer. Maybe it's the awkward way he carries his body. Maybe it's the faces he makes when he's called for a foul — as though a cop just gave him a speeding ticket and he wasn't even in the car. Whatever. He makes people crazy. Last week, in the Atlanta series, I was seated behind the Pistons' bench, and there was this fan, a fat guy with a baseball cap who never stopped yelling at Laimbeer. The entire game. "YOU'RE FILTHY, LAIMBEER!" he screamed. "YOU'RE FILLLLLLTHY!" Even when the game was no contest, even when Laimbeer wasn't playing, even when his voice got hoarse, this guy wouldn't stop. "YOU'RE FILTHY, LAIMBEER! YOU'RE FILLLLLLTHY!"

Infuriation.

So you might say, "Gee, why should anyone care if a guy like that said good-bye?" There might even be a party. Something small, like Mardi Gras.

And yet, I maintain that when Laimbeer goes — and he says unless he suffers a major injury it won't be this year — we will not see the likes of him again. A Bill Laimbeer comes along once a century. Which is good and bad. On the one hand, he is an inspiration, a guy who uses his brain and his nerve to became an NBA star. On the other hand, he wears a shirt to breakfast that reads: "Sometimes, I'm so bad, I don't even like myself."

"I think about quitting every day," he says, smearing the cream cheese on the bagel. "But it would be hard for me to leave right now because I'm still an integral part of an outstanding basketball team. I'd feel like I was quitting on my friends."

"What if they weren't such a good team?" I ask.

"Then it would be easier. I couldn't see staying around while we spent four years rebuilding."

"What if some of your teammates were traded?"

"That would make a difference. Guys like Isiah and Vinnie, we've been together a long time. If they were traded, I wouldn't feel the same things for the new guys."

"What about your family? What does your wife say?"

"Sometimes I complain about being tired, how I don't want to go through another season, stuff like that. She just says, 'You want to quit? Quit. Don't expect any sympathy from me.'"

He laughs. I should say that Laimbeer's wife, Chris, is a sweet, thoughtful, giving woman — and what she is doing with this lug I will never know. But that is part of the Laimbeer mystery. You want to know something? He infuriates me, too. He drives me crazy. Not like a Guillermo Hernandez or Roger Clemens. Those guys are just jerks. Bill Laimbeer gets to me because 90 percent of the time he behaves as if someone stole his cookies and milk: He is cranky, whiny, annoying, loud, rude, boorish and immature. But the other 10 percent he is one of the most astute, knowledgeable and thought-provoking personalities in the game.

Let me give you an example. After five minutes of complaining to me that all reporters "only want negative stories" and how he feels justified in "abusing young writers who ask stupid questions because they're stupid," after five minutes of that drivel, he suddenly switches gears. He wants to explain the life of a professional athlete. He is passionate. This is what he says: "We have this drill every training camp, the mile run? I hate it. I think it's stupid. So when we do it, I just look at my feet, putting one foot in front of the other. I never look up. I just watch my feet. One-two, one-two, one-two. I keep running and looking at my feet until someone tells me to stop.

"That's the way the NBA life is. That's how you survive, especially the regular season. You travel, you play, you eat, you fall into a routine. The way to get through it is to treat it like that mile run, looking at your feet: One-two, one-two, one-two. You don't look up until you get to the end and someone says you're finished."

And then he stops. He sighs.

Damn it. I hate when he gets smart like that.

Do you know what Bill Laimbeer wants to do when he retires? He wants to host an outdoors show. He is hoping to try it this summer. A sort of "American Sportsman" starring, of course, himself doing all those outdoorsy things he loves so much.

"I'd like to do a show where I take Vinnie Johnson salmon fishing," he says. "Or maybe a show where I take Dennis Rodman pheasant hunting. Stuff like that."

You can see this, right? Laimbeer goes onto the lake, looking for salmon, and when his line breaks he throws a fit, jumps up and down, splashes the water — and the fish are so scared they just jump into his boat. Here! Take us! Just don't hurt us!

"Of course what I really want to do is be a pro golfer," he says. (Laimbeer is already a one-handicapper.) "It probably won't happen, though. My age. And the travel.

"Of course, I could go into business with my father."

"Oh," I say. "What kind of business?"

"Corrugated boxes."

Corrugated boxes?

Hmmm. Somehow I don't see corrugated boxes. Not for Laimbeer. For one thing, nobody boos you in the corrugated box business. I mean, if they do, you must be really bad. And I think Laimbeer has gotten used to the boos. Maybe even come to like them. After all, he has been booed from Orlando to Los Angeles. It's not the best reputation, but it's his.

"It's funny," he says."I used to enjoy the booing a lot more two or three years ago. But now, when I'm introduced and they boo me, I really don't even notice. It's just noise. It's like the national anthem.

"Besides, people don't hate me the way they once did. I don't arrive in towns and read newspapers where they call me The Prince Of Darkness anymore. I think it's because we've won two world championships. They figure I must be doing something right.

"You know, I was reading a business magazine over the summer, and there was this item about conventional wisdom from the past versus the present. And they used the LA Raiders football team as an example. They said the old conventional wisdom was that the Raiders were only 'a team full of Bill Laimbeers.' The new conventional wisdom says 'maybe Bill Laimbeers are not so bad.'"

A whole team's worth?

Catch me before I pass out.

B̲ut all right. We are not talking about more Laimbeer, but less. So when will he retire? He says the only milestone he still covets is the 10,000-rebound mark — he needs 526 — to go with his 10,000 points. He says the money is not that big a factor, that he would leave even with years left on his contract. He says he will quit "when I wake up one morning and don't feel like going to work anymore."

(Under that principle, most of us would be unemployed by now.)

"The main thing is health. Right now I can still walk around a golf course. I don't have any permanent injuries. I don't want to push my luck. Every summer, it gets harder and harder to come back. I think about training camp and I say, 'God, I don't want to do it anymore.'

"People don't realize how hard this is mentally. I don't mean playing basketball. I mean trying to win a championship. It's excruciating, mental torture. You can't do it forever."

So when will he leave us? This year? "Probably not." Next year? "Maybe." The following year? "I don't know."

He chomps the last of the bagel and washes it down with coffee. In the book, "The Natural," Roy Hobbs tells his sweetheart that one day he wants people to point at him and say, "There goes Roy Hobbs, the greatest to ever play the game." I ask Laimbeer how he would want people to finish the sentence "There goes Bill Laimbeer ..."

"World champion," he says.

"That's it?"

"That's it."

"But they can say that already."

He grins. "I know."

I bet I get stuck for the check again, too. ∎

Hardscrabble Chicago home is where Aguirre's heart lies

May 23

C HICAGO — Pressure is a funny word. There is the pressure a sports team feels when it needs to win a playoff game, like the pressure the Pistons are feeling, celebrated, famous pressure that inspires big stories on the 11 o'clock news.

And then there is another kind of pressure. More subtle. More powerful. It affects athletes every day, but it never makes the news, never makes headlines. You might not know about it at all unless you go to see it, unless you drive down the streets where Mark Aguirre is driving now, past the boarded-up houses and the old churches and the weeds that poke up wild amid the asphalt.

Home.

"Right there is the first place I became aware of Isiah as a basketball player," Aguirre says, pointing out the car window at a cream-colored recreation building. "We played in the 'Bitty' league together. We were maybe 9 years old. You see that brown door right there? That's where we would sneak out to get away from the gangs. They wanted our money. They knew we had to have 25 cents for the bus, so they came after us."

"Did you get away?" he is asked.

"Sometimes."

"And when they caught you?"

"We gave them the money."

"Then what did you do?"

He laughs softly.

"Then, you walked home."

He turns the car and continues on. Past corner groceries where the windows are taped shut. Past row houses with seven or eight children sitting on each stoop. Past deserted playgrounds where the fences are torn and the basketball rims are bent and the nets are not even a memory.

"See that playground there?" Aguirre says, pointing to a small area behind a building. "That's where I learned to play. Bryant Park. Me and my cousin got this spotlight — actually, he stole it from the back of a store — and we rigged it with wire on the side of that building. We pointed it up so it would shine on the court. We played all night, man. That spotlight was great. We'd unhook it when we went home, then hook it up when we wanted to play."

He nods silently, as if seeing himself there now, shooting baskets on a hot summer night. He steps on the accelerator. He drives on.

"Yeah, that spotlight was fun," he sighs, "but we should have taken it down when we were finished."

"Why?"

"One night, someone stole it back."

Home.

M ost fans don't really know Aguirre, the Pistons' forward. But then, most fans don't really know any pro athlete. They see the gravy — the money, the fame, the endorsement contracts, the pretty women. They don't see what each man had to rise above to reach all that.

Here, on the West Side of Chicago — or in 1,000 places just like it across the country, places where poverty is a blanket, where liquor is medicine, where jobs come and jobs go and fathers and mothers interchange with aunts, uncles, grandmothers, friends, so you may have three different homes and you may sleep four or five to a room, you may have gangs chasing you for a quarter and friends who are alive one day and dead the next. In places like this, there is a pressure that has nothing to do with NBA trophies and playoff victories, a pressure that comes before all that. This is the pressure: to hold on tight to a basketball, tight enough to pull you high above your life, high enough to escape.

Many try. Few succeed.

Home.

"This," Aguirre says, pointing to the streets, "is who I am. This is where I come from. I've seen everything here. A friend of mine was shot point-blank in the face. Another friend was pushed from a third-story window. I had an uncle who was stabbed 27 times.

"But in a way, I'm glad I had this. You can survive this, you can survive anything. Sometimes I think about where I am now … like, we're staying downtown at the Ritz Carlton Hotel, right? When I was a kid, I never saw that part of town. I didn't know what a Ritz Carlton was!"

He laughs, and waves his hands for emphasis. "Ritz? Shoot, I thought Ritz was a cracker!"

Aguirre, 31, comes back to the West Side each spring during the Pistons' seemingly inevitable playoff series against the Bulls. He rents a car after practice and drives out to visit the people who raised him. Aunts. Uncles. Neighbors.

Even teachers. As he turns past Westinghouse Area Vocational High School, his alma mater, he notices hundreds of students lounging on the sidewalks and the front grass.

"What the hell is going on here?" Aguirre says.

He spins the car around and pulls up near the front door. A group of teachers, wearing security identification badges, peers inside the vehicle, shielding their eyes from the sun. When they make out the driver, their faces go from annoyance to delight.

"Mark!"

"What are you doing in that car? Come on out here, man!"

"Look who's back!"

"It's Mark Aguirre!"

He steps outside slowly, and he is all smiles. He remembers every name. Mrs. Nelson. Mr. Lamont. The shop teacher. The history teacher. The English teacher. They hug him. They slap him. They tease him about the playoff series.

"Why is everybody outside?" Aguirre asks.

"Fire drill."

"Oh."

"Hey, Mark, we saw you and Michael Jordan doing some talking. You two gonna fight or what?"

"Nah, we were having a little conversation."

"Don't hurt Jordan, Mark. He wants a ring."

"He can have a ring. Not this one, though."

"Oh, Mark. Listen to you, man!"

"Yeah, listen to you, man!"

A warm breeze blows. A small crowd begins to gather. Above the entrance to Westinghouse hangs a fading sign that reads: "Our Children, Our Future."

Listen to him.

He is home.

M ark Aguirre was nearly born on a train. His mother, Mary, was only 16 years old, living in Arkansas, when she became pregnant. In her ninth month, she rode north to Chicago, where some of her family lived, thinking perhaps she would give this baby to her sister, Daisy, who wanted a child and was better prepared to raise it. By the time Mary arrived in Chicago, however, she was in labor. Her family rushed her from the train station to the hospital. A few hours later, Mark was born.

"It's too bad," his Uncle Frank, a middle-aged man in a bright-colored sweat suit, is saying now. "If you'da been born on that train, you'da been able to ride free for the rest of your life. You know that, Mark? You could take a train ride from Chicago to Los Angeles right now if you wanted! Free of charge. Yes, sir. They do that for babies born on trains, you know."

Aguirre laughs. He is slumped in the sofa in the front room of his Aunt Daisy's home, a row house on a street full of row houses, where the door is open and children race in and out, squealing and chasing each other, crawling into Aguirre's lap and wrapping themselves in his long arms. The room is warm; there is no air-conditioning. The pale walls are dotted with photos of the family. There is a picture of Mark and his wife, Angela, on one. In the corner, above the TV set, is a certificate. "The James Naismith Trophy ... Mark Aguirre, DePaul University ... as the most outstanding college basketball player in the U.S."

Aguirre was raised, at least a little bit, by everyone in the room and on the picture walls. His grandmother, who died in the 1970s, took care of him for years. He also shuffled between aunts' houses and his mother's place. His father figures were his uncles and his cousins. "The first time I met my real father was when I was 6 years old," he says. "I don't even remember where it was. It was like, 'I know who you are, and I know you are not living with my mother.' After that, I didn't see him for a while."

Mark Aguirre has taken a lot of criticism over the years. In Dallas, for whatever reasons, the press hated him so much, that when he was traded to Detroit, one Dallas columnist declared it "the greatest day in Mavericks history." Aguirre was seen as moody, rude, aloof and lazy — although he has not taken those traits to Detroit. Still, if you are being fair, you must wonder about the people criticizing; you wonder whether those people had one mother and one father and one nice roof over their heads when they grew up. It is a difference. It is a problem in sports. It is the gap that separates the American Season-Ticket Holders from so many of their American Sports Heroes. They come together as adults, but they were so different as children, so different in the part of life that forms all the things we are to be.

Home.

R ight there," says Aguirre, slowing the car and pointing to a wood-faced building called the Pleasant Green Trinity Church. "See that? The preacher there had a daughter that I was so in love with. Oh, man! I was 11 years old and I'm telling you, this girl was on my mind from the minute I got up in the morning. Her name was Yolanda, and I used to pick dandelions and give them to her. I mean, I was crazy about that girl.

"And then one day, she died. She got sick and died. I snuck down to the funeral, and I went in the church. And I saw her inside the coffin, they had it open, and it just really messed me up. I realized that she was never coming back. That was it. She was gone forever. With all the stuff that happened in my neighborhood, I never really understood about death until then. It screwed me up for a long time."

It would not be Aguirre's only loss. His grandmother, whom he adored, would die a few years later. His mother, Mary, would die of cancer in the mid-'80s. "They taught me so much," he says now. "My mom really tried to keep me straight. And my grandmother used to tell me, 'Don't run to trouble. Run away from trouble.'"

He stops at a corner grocery on Karlov Street in K-Town, another part of the West Side. The windows are old and the merchandise behind the counter, candy and chips and cold cuts, is protected by glass. This is another place where Aguirre grew up, in the house behind the small grocery, and another group of family is waiting here for him: his Aunt Tiny — "She raised me, too" — his sister Angela, more uncles, more cousins, more nieces and nephews. Some kids passing by stare at the tall man in the fancy car who is hugging and kissing all these neighbors.

"Hey, Mark Aguirre!" one yells.

Aguirre looks up and smiles.

"Y'all gonna lose to the Bulls!"

Ah, yes. The Bulls. Basketball. The pressure to win Game 3. It is all fans will talk about between now and Saturday, and many will marvel at where the Pistons get their resilience, their will, how they can keep coming back against the odds.

You drive out to an athlete's roots one day, and you may find an easy answer. You could find it on the streets in Brooklyn, where John Salley and Vinnie Johnson grew up, or in the dusty heat of Natchitoches, La., where Joe Dumars grew up, or here in Chicago, the West Side, where Aguirre and Isiah Thomas used to sneak into Chicago Stadium with the concessions workers to watch the Bulls, the same team — and the same building — they must now defeat to reach their dream of a third NBA title.

"Memories are really important," Aguirre says, holding two nephews and a niece on his lap. "No one who watches me play will ever know about this. You can take pictures. You can tell stories. But you'll never know what it was like to grow up here unless you did it. Never."

He shrugs and we leave him, in the midst of family, all of whom are still here, basking in the glow of their "famous" relative and dreaming of a way out for themselves. Aguirre is right. You never know unless you live it. But you think about growing up and you think about survival and you realize maybe winning a basketball game isn't really such pressure after all. ∎

Reigned out: Pistons shed the dream, not the tears

May 28

O ne by one, they walked off the court, surrendering the title like old sheriffs turning in their badges. Joe Dumars dropped on a table and tossed his head back. Isiah Thomas hugged Bill Laimbeer. Dennis Rodman, who looked stunned enough to cry, found Vinnie Johnson and slapped his hands. Then, with a few seconds left on the clock, they exited the Palace floor together, the deposed kings, heading down the tunnel where their wives stood clapping in the echoing silence.

Say good-bye to glory.

No tears.

Not here. No way. Never mind that this championship reign ended like a car crash, a four-game sweep by the arch-rival Chicago Bulls. Never mind that the whole series seemed as if the aging Pistons were playing in quicksand, two steps slow, two steps behind, rebounds going over their heads, Bulls racing past them at warp speed. Never mind. That was just the final chapter, not the whole book. This was a hell of a run — this team, this town, this Detroit turn atop the NBA pile.They played, they won titles and we had a ball. We laughed, we sang, we wore Pistons caps and Pistons T-shirts the way rebels wear their colors. Three NBA Finals? Two straight championships?

No tears.

"When will it hit you?" someone asked an exhausted Dumars, after the Bulls crushed the Pistons in Game 4, 115-94, to capture the Eastern Conference final and end the Detroit dream of three straight titles. "When will you realize it's over?"

"I realize it right now," he said. "I realize that someone else will be having that parade, and someone else will say, 'I'm going to Disneyland,' and someone else will lower that championship banner next year."

He smiled. "And you know what? If it doesn't rain tomorrow, the sun will still be up in the sky."

No tears.

So many times these Pistons went to the well and found an extra bucket of power, of confidence. So many times they were down, seemingly out of it, only to come back, win and laugh at the doubters. Isn't that why, until 5:45 Monday afternoon, some of us still believed a miracle would occur? Didn't you keep waiting for the happy ending?

It never came. Finally, this time, they lowered the bucket and the well was dry. "No TV, no refs, don't blame anything else," Thomas said. "They beat us because they were the better basketball team ... and they caught us at the exact right time."

Looking back, that was apparent from Game 1 of this series. And maybe it should have been apparent even earlier. Don't forget, the Bulls had the second-best record in the NBA this season — the Pistons had the ninth. The Bulls raced gleefully into this Eastern Conference final, leaving New York and Philadelphia in the dust. The Pistons, meanwhile, went the five-game limit against Atlanta, and needed six to get past Boston. Thomas was injured. Dumars was injured. James Edwards, Bill Laimbeer and Mark Aguirre were injured. Fatigue? Mental pressure? Only their reputation made the Pistons scary in this series; the truth was they were exhausted before it even began.

So we should not be surprised that it ended, ironically, on Memorial Day, when you honor fallen heroes, and we should not be surprised that it ended this way: with the Pistons sagging like an aged heavyweight on a humid night; with Chicago's Scottie Pippen, last year's head case, now dunking, rebounding, having a blast; with Michael Jordan slamming on a fast break, and Horace Grant slamming on a fast break, and Scott Williams — who? — slamming on a fast break, while the Pistons could only scream and moan about the fouls, drawing technicals like raw meat draws flies.

"Before today, I thought it took an awful lot to win a championship, I thought it was the hardest thing I'd ever done," Aguirre said, shaking his head in the post-game locker room. "But now I realize that it takes more to admit defeat. That's harder."

And what made it even worse?

The Pistons created the Bulls.

That's right. The team that now goes to the NBA Finals owes its rise to Detroit as sure as the monster owed its life to Dr. Frankenstein. All those years Chicago took a beating from Detroit, losing in the playoffs the way the Pistons used to lose to the Celtics? All those years, Chicago was learning. Studying. Imitating. Until this season, finally, Chicago was better at being Detroit than Detroit was. Think about it. The Bulls won the East with defense, rebounding, a strong bench, a superstar guard and an indomitable spirit.

Sound familiar?

"They definitely paid attention over the years," John Salley said. "They told themselves, 'We're not gonna do the old stuff anymore. We're not gonna make the same mistakes.'"

They didn't. In 1988, the Pistons beat the Bulls, 4-1. The next year, it was 4-2. Last year, it was 4-3. And this year? Whoa. This year, Chicago refused to bleed. It was like Arnold Schwarzenegger in "The Terminator." It did not even blink.

When Jordan was covered, he dished to John Paxson or Bill Cartwright. Score! When Grant missed, Pippen came flying overhead to slam down the rebound. Score! When the starters went out, guys you never heard of — I still can't get used to Cliff Levingston making a pressure shot — came in to carry the load. The Bulls won because they had two men, it seemed, on every Detroit player. Because they had two men going for every rebound. And because they knocked down their shots. Make no mistake. That is the biggest difference. No matter what the pressure, what the defense, what the score, what the arena, these new Bulls did not flinch, they hit their baskets, something the old Bulls did not always do.

"We knew we could beat the Pistons," Jordan said after winning his first Eastern Conference title, "but with the sweep, we even surprised ourselves."

A word here about Jordan. A brilliant player, yes, but he has a few things to learn about dignity and championships. His comments over the weekend were enough to make you ill: "The people I know are going to be happy (the Pistons) aren't the reigning champions any more. We'll get back to the image of a clean game. ... When Boston was champion they played true basketball. Detroit won ... but it wasn't the kind of basketball you want to endorse."

Well, as Mr. Endorsement, Michael ought to know. But before he reduces the world to good guys and bad guys — the good, of course, being players like himself who will talk trash non-stop, while getting fouls called whenever another player breathes on him — he should understand that there are many ways to reach the playoffs but only one way to win a championship: You must be the best. The Pistons were. For two years. They didn't win because they were dirty. They won because they were unselfish, because they played great defense, because they never gave up hope, and because they didn't put one player on a pedestal above the others. You may notice, Michael, that your team didn't get past the Eastern Conference until it did exactly those same things.

"If Jordan thinks we're so bad for basketball, let him buy the league and replace us," Rodman sniffed afterward. "He's got all the money, anyhow."

"Bad for basketball?" Dumars said, when informed of the comments. "Hey, if us winning two championships was bad for basketball, it was damn sure good for me. I got two rings in my closet."

No tears.

A nd that's the spirit we ought to wake up with this morning. In the days to come, there will be talk about changes — trades, free agents — there is always such talk after a crown is lost. But for today, as the final embers of this championship era die, better to remember the Pistons for what they were.

Can you ever forget their dance off the Silverdome floor the night the Celtics were finally vanquished? Or their champagne shower in the visitors' locker room of the Forum, after sweeping the Lakers and claiming the crown? Or the stunned silence of the Portland Memorial Coliseum after the Pistons went there and did the impossible, three straight road victories to win Title No. 2?

Can you ever forget the slogans? "Bad Boys"? "U Can't Touch This"? "Three The Hard Way"? Or the music that played when they took the floor, the trumpets of that "Final Countdown" song that sent shivers down your spine? Can you forget the sight of Chuck Daly, Mr. Dapper, croaking out instructions, waving his arms like a mad scientist? And the players. Most of all, can you ever forget the players? Thomas, hitting those magic shots against Boston in overtime, or Dumars, coming back from his father's death last year to lead the title charge, or Laimbeer, defying the boos in every arena, or Rodman, waving that fist after his 16th or 17th rebound, or Edwards, turning and sinking yet another fallaway jumper, or Aguirre, lighting up the nets from long distance, or Vinnie, who goes all the way back to the embarrassing years with this franchise, hitting that jumper last spring in Portland that now and forever will be known as :00.7?

"How do you think history will remember this team?" came the question.

Salley: "As the blue-collar guys that beat the glamour boys in LA."

Aguirre: "As a team that defied the odds and kept coming back to win."

Thomas: "As one of the greatest that ever played."

In the final seconds Monday, the scoreboard flashed the image of two fans, holding up signs that read "THANK YOU FOR 2" and "YOU'LL ALWAYS BE CHAMPIONS IN OUR HEARTS." A nice way to say good-bye. Hell of a run, guys. Hell of a team. No tears. Just a handshake and a nod of thanks.

Now.

How are those Tigers doing? ∎

'People without butlers' bring new life to Wimbledon

July 1

WIMBLEDON, England — Well, I finally arrived at the world's greatest tennis tournament and just in time, it seems. Things have gotten pretty weird around the old green yard. And I'm not even talking about Andre Agassi taking his clothes off. I'm not even talking about the British tabloid reporter who disguised himself as a bum — I swear this is true — and went knocking on the doors of the top tennis players' houses.

REPORTER: Spare some change, sir?

IVAN LENDL: Get lost.

REPORTER: Can I quote you on that?

Now. This is not normal behavior, even for a Brit. But wait. It's small potatoes compared with the really weird stuff that happened Sunday:

1) For the first time in history — due to countless rain delays — Wimbledon was forced to play matches on what always has been an off day.

2) They actually allowed REGULAR PEOPLE inside the stadium. You know, like, PEOPLE WITHOUT BUTLERS.

3) They did the wave at Centre Court.

Hard to believe. But it all happened. It began Saturday night with thousands of regular people sleeping in the streets just to get the first-come, first-serve tickets made available for this special Sunday session. General admission? At Wimbledon? Whoa. Next thing you know, they'll be serving hot pretzels.

"How long have you been waiting here?" I asked a pimple-faced teenager near the front of the line, which, at 10 a.m., stretched for more than a mile.

"Well, I got 'ere 11 hours ago," he said. "Me and my mates came down from Basildon. Slept in the street. Not bad at all. We ate some sandwiches. Sang some songs. Then, a few hours later, it started raining."

"Ooh, tough break."

"Not really. I needed a shower."

This, as you might figure, was not your typical Wimbledon crowd. No stiff jaws. No ascots under their collars. These people wore sweatshirts, carried sleeping bags, chewed gum. I personally saw three guys in Oakland A's jackets, at least a dozen in tie-dyed T-shirts, and one long-haired fellow in a leather coat that read: "CROAK LIKE A MOTHER."

You wonder what the queen would make of that one.

Of course, the queen wasn't there Sunday. Neither were any other regulars of the Royal Box. No dukes. No earls. No Duke of Earls. Heaven forbid they hould break with tradition. Show up on the middle Sunday? Mix with common people? They were probably afraid of catching a disease.

Wait. Did I mention the wave? Yes. Once they burst through the gates, made a dash for Centre Court and filled up that venerable stadium with backpacks and Sony Walkmen, these rookie fans actually did the wave. Up, down, up, down. "YAAHHHH!" The tennis players loved it. Before Sunday, the only wave at Wimbledon was when the Duchess of Kent swatted a fly.

The whole day was unique that way. Normally Wimbledon applause is polite and brief. On Sunday, it was loud. It was irreverent. "Like a football game," John McEnroe said. Yeah. With the same respect for authority. Upon entering the front gate, the guards give you a sticker to wear on your shirt. I saw several fans slap them on their foreheads. SMACK! Hey, Ma, look at me.

When Gabriela Sabatini took the court, these fans whistled like construction workers. When Jimmy Connors came out, they roared as if Paul McCartney had taken the stage. Sure, it broke with tradition a little bit ...

Typical Day at Wimbledon:
FAN 1: Smashing good shot!
FAN 2: Indeed.
FAN 1: Shall we dine?
Sunday at Wimbledon:
FAN 1: WOOF!
FAN 2: WOOF!
FAN 1: WOOF! WOOF!

You know what? It was terrific. Like letting a pack of Cub Scouts loose inside the White House. When they weren't playing around, they were snapping pictures. When they weren't snapping pictures, they were chomping on homemade sandwiches. And when they weren't eating, they were screaming their heads off, as if at a rock concert. When the games ended, I half-expected them to light matches.

"What did you think of the crowd?" came the question, over and over, as the players finished Sunday afternoon.

"It should be like that every year," Sabatini said. "I thought it was great."

"They were true tennis fans," gushed Martina Navratilova. "They didn't sit on their hands, they actually used them."

"My kind of crowd," Connors said. "Not the traditionalists who give you the old 'jolly good.' These fans were unbelievable! Where were they the last 20 years?"

Shut out, Jimmy. Stuck at home, watching on TV. Each year, nearly half of Wimbledon's tickets go to club members, sponsors and royalty. The other half are distributed through a lottery system, with the prices fairly expensive, about 25 British pounds per day, which, of course, in American money, given today's economic conditions, is about $3,428,377.68.

Ha! Just kidding. But I'm not kidding about this: I have been coming here for nearly a decade, and I never knew there were tennis fans like this in England. And if the folks running Wimbledon don't figure a way to get more of them inside these green walls, they're nuts.

Then again, this is a country where the next bum who rings your bell could be a reporter for the Daily Mirror.

I wouldn't hold my breath. ∎

Jennifer Capriati: She lost the match, saved her youth

July 5

W IMBLEDON, England — I don't want to sound cold here, but losing Thursday was the best thing that could have happened to Jennifer Capriati. She needed to win Wimbledon like she needed a bleeding ulcer.

Better to exit in the semifinals, still smiling, still saying things like "I had a great time," packing the suitcase with nice memories and one huge moment: the straight-set destruction of Martina Navratilova, the defending champion. Capriati took her out Wednesday, in the quarterfinals, the first time in a decade someone had beaten Martina here before the finals. That was like blasting a trumpet into the tennis world's ear.

And that's plenty. Go home, kid, soak it in, listen to a few M.C. Hammer albums. Let people buzz about the things you will achieve in this game. But win it all now? At age 15? Become the youngest Wimbledon champion in history?

Why not walk down to London Bridge, tie weights to your ankles, and jump off?

I f the overglitzed, overhyped and overpaid world of tennis has shown us anything in the last 20 years, it's that the top is no place for teenage girls. Not unless they want to spend the rest of their lives on a psychiatrist's couch. Take a quick look at a list of victims: Tracy Austin, who played her best tennis when she wore braces, now a dizzy 28-year-old woman still hounded by her unachieved potential; Andrea Jaeger, who before Capriati was the youngest player ever seeded at Wimbledon, a star at 15, a has-been at 20, out of tennis now, her career one big explosion and a lot of dust.

Monica Seles, the No. 1 woman in the world today; she had an ulcer by the time she was 12, and has been the subject of more "reported nervous breakdowns" than a soap opera star. Last month, at age 17, she disappears, skips Wimbledon and is spotted at Donald Trump's mansion in Florida, with half the world reporting she's pregnant and the other half passing judgment on her frenetic career. You need that when you're 17? People passing judgment? Come on. When you're 17, the only things you should worry about passing are 1) notes; 2) your driver's test; 3) that cute kid's locker.

Tennis stardom chokes all that. Steals the youth from thousands of girls who never reach a major tournament. Even those who survive are scarred; Steffi Graf's reputation went from invincible to unstable in about two years. (I have personally watched her smile disappear in press conferences, replaced by a permanent scowl.) Gabriela Sabatini, the Argentine star who beat Capriati on Thursday, endured bouts of homesickness and depression coming up.

And none of these women did what Capriati was threatening to do this week: win Wimbledon before her 16th birthday. Can you imagine? You'd have to throw her a life preserver. Newspapers. TV shows. Endorsement deals. Tournament directors. She'd be smothered. Every match she'd play would carry the introduction, "Ladies and gentlemen, the youngest Wimbledon champion in history ..."

Try living up to that the rest of your life.

No, Capriati deserves better. We have something special in this long-legged American teenager who seems to know instinctively that, at 15, the most important things in life are to be cool and laugh a lot. She still attends high school (albeit a rich, private academy). Her speech is peppered with "you know, like, you know, like ..." She sits down for press conferences as if flopping on her bed, elbows out, palms on her ears. All that's missing are the gum and the phone.

Good. That's how it should be. Bad enough she already has an agent, millions of dollars and Texaco and Oil of Olay patches on her tennis outfit. Bad enough that her father, who says "she's only doing it because she loves to" — all the tennis fathers say that — still pushes her too far, demanding workouts when she wants to be with friends.

The best we can hope for is that success comes slowly for Capriati, the way it did years ago for Chris Evert. Evert didn't turn pro until she was 16, didn't play in Europe until she was 17, made her first Grand Slam final at 18 and won her first one at 19.

She also lasted nearly 20 years.

Sadly, Capriati may be too talented for that pace. A pro at 14, she already has the big serve, hits like a rocket and fires passing shots better than Kevin Costner fired arrows in "Robin Hood." Guts? She made Navratilova, who could intimidate stone, look positively useless Wednesday. Even in losing to Sabatini, who has matured tremendously as a player, Capriati held off match point four times, whipping the ball out of reach, Sabatini flailing, looking bad, asking herself, "Hey, who's winning this, she or I?"

In the end, it was Sabatini, which, trust me, is the best news for Capriati. A semifinalist? In her second visit? That's enough. More than enough. Take it home, Jennifer. Put it in your scrapbook. Call your friends and say, "How cool."

"Memories?" she said, when asked. "I'll have great memories. I'll leave knowing I beat a great champion and that I got to the semifinals."

And, smiling broadly, she left the room, in that clumpy way teenagers have of leaving rooms, playing with her ponytail and never knowing how lucky a loser she really was. ∎

Even in his worst moment, Scott Hastings gets a laugh

August 25

I never got to say good-bye to Scott Hastings. Neither did anyone else around here. He was traded a few weeks ago, to Denver of all places. Jack McCloskey, who moves the pieces on the Pistons' board, made the deal, then called Hastings in Atlanta, where he lives in the off-season. "Hello, Scott?" Jack said, and Hastings acted surprised, like he was hearing from an old college buddy. "Hey! Jack! What's up?" And Jack chuckled and said, "Come on. You know what's up."

So even in the worst moment, Hastings got a laugh. And that seems fitting. In his two years with the Pistons, Hastings, 31, laughed just about everywhere he went, on the court, on the bench, at the airport, in a Boston bar at 1 a.m. I ran into him there, during the playoffs. Hastings was all sweaty. He was not drunk. He was leading a karaoke singing contest.

"Hey!" he croaked when he saw me, running over with a microphone in his hand, "you gotta come up here! We just did Elvis' 'Heartbreak Hotel.' Awesome!"

That was Hastings. If there was a weird place, or a strange crowd, he found it. He had fun. He laughed. He never seemed to mind that he was last on the totem pole, the 12th man on a 12-man basketball team. "My job," he would say, deadpan, "is basically to get stiff for two hours. And I understand that."

And no one ever got stiff like Scott Hastings. Instead of whining about playing time or demanding a trade, he invented games to make the idle time pass. He would trick fans into buying him popcorn during the game, then hide it under the bench. He and David Greenwood wore rubber bands on their wrists, so that, during slow moments, they could snap each other's elastic and yell "WAKE UP!" During 20-second time-outs, Hastings and Greenwood would quickly circle their teammates, tap each of them on the butt, then return to their seats and grin.

It was a race.

I remember the night Hastings spoke at a charity roast of his coach, Chuck Daly. He began by saying there was someone in the room he'd always wanted to meet, and, if the crowd didn't mind, it would only take second. Then he turned to Daly, held out his hand and said, "Chuck? My name's Scott Hastings. Damn glad to meet you."

He joked so much about his playing time — or lack thereof — that it became a citywide chuckle. Fans would roar when he pulled off his sweats. The rare times he actually got in a game, his benchmates would yell, "Get the ball to Scottie!" then urge him to shoot before the buzzer. Of course, this was usually when the Pistons were ahead by 30 points.

It was funny. It was cute. But no one ever thought about how hard it was for Hastings. Remember, for every 12th man in the NBA, there is a 13th and 14th and 15th man who didn't make the cut. And hundreds beyond them, and thousands beyond them. The fact is, every fellow like Hastings who sits on an NBA bench is still an amazing player, certainly the biggest star in his high school, and most likely in his college. Can you imagine reaching the top of your profession — the top one percent of your field — and being seen, mostly, as a joke?

"I guess I'm the player the average fan can relate to," Hastings said when I called him this week. "They'll put that on my tombstone: 'Scott Hastings. We Could Relate To Him.' "

I asked whether people appreciated the difficulty of being the last guy on the bench.

"Well," he said, "people do forget only a select few ever make the NBA, let alone play for years. In that respect I guess I've done something OK.

"Personally, I feel there's some value to being a 12th man. I mean, a 12th man can destroy the chemistry of a team as easily as a star. If I'm the general manager I want to be sure my 12th man doesn't have a bad attitude.

"I always felt if I was taking a paycheck, then I owed the team something. Work hard in practice. Cheerlead for the starters. I never rooted for the starters to foul out, because my biggest fear was that they'd put Vinnie Johnson in at power forward before me."

Hastings said he had a good time here, and now, hopefully, he will have a good time in Denver. This will be his fifth team in nine years, but he looked at the trade this way: It wasn't that the Pistons didn't want him, but that some other team did.

I asked whether he had any regrets.

"Regrets?" he said, and then he began to sing, "I've had a few, but then again, too few to mention … "

As a sports writer, you're not supposed to like the athletes. Keep a distance. Stay professional. Sometimes, that just doesn't work. I thought about the popcorn, the rubber bands, that night in Boston, Hastings running over with the microphone, and I listened to him sing now on the phone. I told him I would miss him, and for once, he didn't laugh. I thought that was nice. ∎

Still elusive, less reclusive, Barry is now one of the guys

August 29

B arry Sanders has something on his mind. He walks over to Jim Arnold, the punter, and sits on a stool nearby. Arnold is talking to a reporter, but his words grow jumpy as he glances at Sanders just sitting there — What does he want? Why doesn't he interrupt? — and finally, Arnold stops talking to the reporter altogether. It is damn near impossible to ignore Barry Sanders, even if he is sitting still.

"What's up?" Arnold asks.

"I need a favor from you, man," Sanders says.

"Name it."

Sanders grins, sort of embarrassed. "Nah, really, man," he says.

"Really," Arnold says.

"OK. Yo, um …"

Sanders rubs his face. His eyes dance back and forth. Arnold leans in. What is this favor, for god's sake? Lend him money? Kill somebody? What?

"Lemme have one of your cookies, man," Sanders says.

Cookies?

Arnold grins and drops his head. He reaches into the back of his locker, finds a small box and pulls out a fat, round, chocolate chip cookie. He hands it over.

"Thanks, man," Sanders says, lifting it to his mouth. "I just had to have one of these."

He takes a bite and grins like a kid riding his first bicycle.

"You're OK, man," Sanders says as he walks away. "You and me are gonna be all right."

Arnold beams.

Barry Sanders is coming out of his shell, and not only when his sweet tooth acts up. He no longer sits with his back turned. He actually initiates conversation. True, you still won't find him at nightclubs, and he is hardly a ladies man, and he dresses, well, "casually" is a nice word, and last year, when the police stopped him for speeding, and the officer looked at his license and said, "Are you *the* Barry Sanders?" he would only say, "Um, my name is Barry Sanders." The officer shrugged and wrote out the ticket.

"You big dummy!" safety William White, who was in the car, said afterward. "All you had to do is tell him who you were and you would have gotten off!"

"Nah, I can't do that," Sanders said. He paid the ticket.

And that's not even the best story.

"The best story," says White, who has grown close to Sanders recently, one of several signs that the recalcitrant superstar is finally reaching out, "the most unbelievable story, is when this Jeep dealership called Barry up and was gonna give him a free Jeep — brand new! — just for signing autographs at their place for an hour and a half. That morning he asks me if I could drive him over there. But that afternoon, he said, 'I don't think I'm gonna do it.'

"And he didn't. Passed it up. I guess he didn't feel comfortable or something. I couldn't believe it! A free Jeep? That had to be worth close to $30,000! For signing autographs? I said to him, 'Man, if you don't want the Jeep that badly, you could have given it to me!' "

White laughs and shakes his head. "But that's the man. B. Sanders. Yes, sir, he is unique."

W ell. No argument there. It's not everyone who wins the NFL rushing title in his second season, after missing it by only 10 yards as a rookie. It's not everyone who stands 5-feet-7 (don't believe the publicity reports), weighs 203 pounds and has barely an ounce of fat. It's not everyone who can accelerate from the backfield, leave one defender groping, another defender reeling, another defender falling — and none of them touches him.

Still, there are changes in Sanders. They show that, in addition to being perhaps the best at his position, he can be one of the guys. Sanders is loosening up. Lightening up. Growing up, too. "I'm the big two-three now," he reminds us, referring to his age, 23, and if that seems a funny statement, remember that when the Lions drafted him, he was only 20. How mature were you at 20?

"What I've learned since then, man, it's so much, it's unbelievable," he says. In his rookie season, Sanders was an emotional hurricane in a solid steel case. He had a million thoughts — on religion, football, fame, money — but he never felt right talking about them, or talking about much of anything, for that matter. Quiet. Quiet was better. For years he had watched his mother, with 11 sons and daughters, take on life with a shield of quiet, while his father screamed and tried to beat the crap out of it. Barry preferred his mother's way.

So when he left college early, and the critics said, "Mistake" — he kept quiet. And when he held out that first year, wanted more money, and people called his house and said, "Shame on you" — he kept quiet. And when he finally joined the Lions, and he took his first handoff and scampered 18 yards against the Phoenix Cardinals, he returned to the huddle, breathing hard — and kept quiet. "Even now, I never say anything in the huddle," he admits.

But the huddle is not real life. Real life calls for interaction. And in his third year of professional sports, Barry Sanders is lowering the gloves. He is letting people inside. But here's the surprise: What's behind the facade is often the same as the facade.

"People think Barry is putting on an act with that humble stuff," says White, grinning. "But I'm telling you, he really is that humble. He's too humble, probably. Like my wife sometimes will tell him, 'Barry, that was a great run you made against Washington, you ran for a touchdown!' And Barry will say, 'Is that right?'"

White cracks up. "'Is that right?'" he mocks. "'Is that right?' That's like Barry's favorite thing to say."

Is that right?

H ere are pieces of conversation from an hour with Barry Sanders: "Most people don't know this, but as a kid, I used to get whuppings every day of my life. I was always doing something wrong. I was loudmouthed. Fighting. Discipline problem. Got suspended from school. I remember this one time, in junior high, I called my gym teacher a punk. He didn't pick me for the ninth-grade basketball team and I was upset, so in class, in front of everybody, I called him a punk. I can't believe I did that. …

"When I run with the football, it's this feeling, man, I can't really describe it. It's like being a kid and playing tag, and that fear you have. I'm just trying to avoid the guy out there tagging me, that's all.

"If I could change anything in football, it would be how people worship the athletes. That's wrong. I go to Winans concerts, and I like them a lot, but I don't worship them. I know they're no different than the desolate man in the street.

"When people ask me for an autograph I say to them, 'Why is this piece of paper any more valuable if I write my name on it than if you do?' And most of the time they can't answer. That's amazing to me, man. …"

Between these sentences, Sanders looks at his feet, bites his lip, nods with a faraway look, as if listening to a running voice inside his head. This is Barry Sanders, too. More than just "Is that right?" Fact is, he can talk philosophy longer than the average athlete. And when it comes to religion, he can talk you under the table. He wonders about the fate of man, he wonders how we can adore the beautiful and ignore the ugly. He says things like "when you are treated special like athletes are, you don't have to develop any character." Maybe part of the reason he likes to be alone so much — and you wouldn't say this about every athlete — is that he likes to think.

Then again, given his refrigerator, he's not exactly expecting company.

"You go over to Barry's house, all he has in there is apple juice, water and banana pudding," says White, laughing. "And maybe some four-month-old milk."

W hich brings us to the money thing. Certainly, Sanders can afford to stock the fridge with Dom Perignon (if he drank it, which he doesn't) and caviar (if he ate it, which he doesn't). He earns, on average, more than $2 million a season. But it did not come easily. For the second time in three years, Sanders held out of training camp because of his contract. Teammates were supportive. Fans were divided. One disgruntled person drove past Sanders' house and yelled out the window, "There ought to be a salary cap for you guys!"

Sanders shrugs. He says this renegotiation was planned all along. He says the contract he took as a rookie (five years, $5.9 million) was less than what he thought he deserved, given his college statistics at Oklahoma State, where he won the Heisman Trophy. But he figured, fine, he'll play two years, prove himself, and then, like the Terminator, he'd be back. Make no mistake: Barry might be shy, but he will go to management when things get serious. He did it when he thought he wasn't getting the ball enough. And he did it this summer, after gaining 1,304 yards and the rushing title last season.

"I wasn't breaking a contract," Sanders says. "The Lions agreed to renegotiate. They felt something should be done, too. The only difference was how much. People forget that. This was a mutual thing."

The funny part is, you wonder where the money goes. Not for groceries, obviously. And not for clothes. "I went clothes-shopping with Barry not too long ago," White says, "a really nice store in Birmingham. Great stuff. And he picks out the ugliest sports jacket in there; this thing looked like some old English professor would wear it. Tweed job, had patches on the sleeves. I said, 'No. NO! You are not buying that! Put it back.'

"He ended up getting a nice blazer and a couple of slacks. He was gonna buy two suits, but then he said it was cheaper to get one jacket and two pants. It's funny. Everything he looked at, he still checked the inside sleeve for the price. I think it goes back to when he didn't have any money, his mom and dad and all."

Those were the Kansas days, the cement of Sanders' life, the days when he and his brothers would follow their father to a roofing job, working with the shingles in the hot sun, hours at a time. Barry never got an allowance — "Your allowance is that I pay the damn bills around here," his father would say — and never spent a penny foolishly, not without repercussions. To this day, Sanders admits, "I basically live on about $30,000 a year. That's all I need. The rest is put away or shared with others." He still gives 10 percent of everything he makes to his church. He owns no fancy cars. Even with his new contract, Sanders still drives an Acura, eschewing Mercedes, Porsche, BMW, Jeep.

"Hey, if they still made the Pinto?" says safety Bennie Blades. "Barry would be driving a Pinto, guaranteed."

So he'll never be John Salley. So he'll never grab the microphone and tell the city how wonderful it is. Big deal. What you get with Sanders is real. And as time passes, we are getting more.

"I think deep down he always wanted to be one of the guys," says

Lomas Brown, the offensive tackle. "It just took him awhile to get comfortable."

"He's looser now," White says. "He feels more relaxed around us. The dude has a sense of humor, too, and he doesn't even know it."

The man with the normal car and the apple juice in the fridge only shakes his head and laughs at himself. "I guess I am getting more comfortable being with people. I guess ... um ... before I almost preferred to be alone, but that's not the case now. It's different."

He sighs. He smiles. "It's good," he says finally, and it is. Fall is coming. Football is here. And the biggest player in the room is getting comfy with his life, one cookie at a time. ∎

For once in your life, Jimbo, act your age!

September 3

NEW YORK — Near the back of the men's locker room, on a wooden bench, Aaron Krickstein sat by himself, counting down the minutes. Soon he would become the loneliest man in the city, the man who would try to beat Jimmy Connors, a former tennis bad boy who just turned 39, and suddenly everyone wants to take him home and hug him.

"When was the last time you played a 39-year-old?" someone asked Krickstein.

"My coach," he said, smiling.

This would not be his coach. This would not be his peer. This would be unlike any tennis match he had played before, like playing Castro in Havana, like playing Superman at Krypton Stadium. Jimmy Connors now owns the U.S. Open, I guess because he is brash and crude and would kick your mother in the crotch to win a fight and therefore New Yorkers figure, hey, he must be OK. Go, Jimbo! Connors, a five-time Open champion, has become The Hot Story in The Big Apple this week, and what's hot in New York gets hot across the country, it grows real fast, until now meeting Connors at Flushing Meadow is like meeting the Libyan army at Tripoli.

"How many seats here, 20,000?" Krickstein asked. "I figure 19,800 will be rooting for him, and 200 for me. I think I gave out that many tickets. I just hope they make some noise."

Well. If they did, they were drowned out. Krickstein and Connors pounded each other for four hours and 41 minutes Monday. Five sets. It was the longest and best match of this U.S. Open so far.

It was also the most unfair.

YOU SON OF A B - - - - ! GET YOUR A - - OUT OF THAT CHAIR!" This was Connors to the umpire at the end of the second set, on a ball that was pretty clearly out. He didn't like it, so the fans didn't like it. They hooted at the ump, as Connors jerked his thumb repeatedly in the "you're outta here" fashion.

"KISS ME WHEN YOU DO THAT NEXT TIME! I LIKE TO BE KISSED WHEN SOMEONE DOES THAT TO ME!" This was Connors in the fourth set, same umpire, after another disputed call. The fans cheered Jimmy. They clapped on Krickstein's mistakes.

"YOU'RE AN ABORTION! AN ABSOLUTE ABORTION, YOU KNOW THAT?" This was Connors in the fifth set, same umpire, another disputed call.

"I'M TOO F - - - - - - GOOD! TOO F - - - - - - GOOD!" This was Connors yelling to fans after he tied the match at 5-5 in the final set. They roared like teenagers. This was tennis? A major tournament? Did Krickstein count at all?

Apparently not. For all this abuse — and there was plenty more that I left out — there were no penalties from the umpires. No fines. Not even a warning. Connors steered this match brilliantly and diabolically, intimidating the officials and playing the crowd like a piano. I point this out only to remind you that while Connors is a great story, a brilliant competitor, he is still, quite often, a jerk.

Which is why I question all the hype he is getting this week. Sure, what he is doing at the Open, at his age, is terrific — two five-set victories in his first four rounds — but the light that is shining on his courage and guts, which he has always had, seems also to be casting him as some sort of good guy. And you shouldn't buy that. This clever marketing campaign (the PaineWebber commercials) and the way Connors works the TV cameras — now that he has become a network analyst, the kind of job he once spat at — has not fooled me. This is the same temperamental guy who would bite your nose off, tell your kids to get lost, give fans the finger. What you saw in the second set Monday, and in the fourth, and in the fifth — the crude abuse, the me-first, me-only attitude — that's Connors. Always has been.

Having said that, you must give him his due. He came back from a set down, and from three games behind in the fifth. At 29 that's impressive. At 39 it's incredible. Time after time, Connors would charge to the net like a wild beast, slapping away returns. He played through injury, fatigue, his chest heaving, his hair dripping sweat. He seemed destined to win, convinced it was just a matter of time.

And maybe that is the difference between Connors and Krickstein, who has always been a little too nice for his own success. In six tries, Krickstein, 24, has never beaten Connors. Mentally, perhaps, he doesn't believe it can be done. "I should have been more aggressive," Krickstein admitted after blowing a 5-2 lead in the fifth.

Then again, he was taking on the entire stadium.

And things will not change for the next opponent. Connors is New York City this week, they are all behind him. And that's fine, I guess — as long as Connors isn't allowed to chew the rules and spit them out.

Personally, this whole Let's-Celebrate-Jimmy bandwagon seems a little too orchestrated for me. He's 39? Great. So's my barber. I pay more attention to little things, like behavior, like history. Like after the match, when someone asked Connors if he felt compassion for Krickstein. This is what he said:

"Hey, nobody ever had compassion for me."

A New York hero, if there ever was one. ∎

Giggles and shrieks are OK, but let's skip the tennis talk

September 4

N EW YORK — That does it. I am drafting a petition to the Women's Tennis Association: No more press conferences for girls under 18. Let them play. Let them shower. Let them go home to their Sting records.

But keep them away from the microphone. Really. It's for the best. And I have been thinking about this for a while, ever since Steffi Graf mumbled through her first few years, and then Gabriela Sabatini mumbled through her first few years, and then Jennifer Capriati laid about 400,000 "you knows" in a single sentence.

But what really pushed me over the edge was Tuesday, when Monica Seles, 17, came into the interview room after destroying Gigi Fernandez in about the time it takes to make an omelet.

Seles, as you know, has been quite a little pistol in her young career. The first thing anyone remembers her saying is "UNNNNYYEEEEE," which she shrieked whenever she hit a ball. Opponents were so distracted, they wanted to put a sock in her mouth.

The next thing we remember is her giggling during interviews, which made her sound — use your imagination here — like Woody Woodpecker on helium. "Well, I ... hehehehe ... think I ... " Reporters wanted to put a sock in her mouth.

This summer was Seles' silent period, when, ranked No. 1 in the world, she mysteriously disappeared and pulled out of Wimbledon. The official explanation was an injury. Others blamed: 1) fatigue; 2) pregnancy; 3) a love affair with Donald Trump; 4) publicity stunt. When Seles finally emerged, weeks later at a press conference, reporters watched her breeze in like a movie star, holding a little dog that was yapping like something out of a Zsa Zsa Gabor kennel.

They wanted to put a sock in the dog's mouth.

N ow comes the U.S. Open, where young Seles already has reached the semifinals. She could win the whole thing. But there's one problem.

This year, the Open, in an effort to increase accuracy, has hired a court reporter to type everything players say during press conferences. It's a good idea. The guy taps on a stenographer machine, like something out of "The Verdict."

And then along comes Seles. And the stenographer panics.

I don't want to say Seles talks fast. I will say that, after her, the guy from the Federal Express commercial makes perfect sense. The big problem — besides her favorite subjects being clothes, Madonna and Alec Baldwin — is that Seles, like most teens, forgets to come up for air between sentences.

Example: Someone asked her about equal prize money for women and men. She said: "I think a lot of times when you watch men's tennis and they go into five sets and you are up to here with them, 6-1, 6-1, you are sitting there and just waiting and the point, there are no points, I mean, he serves an ace and that is it, he serves, this is it, while in women's tennis not everybody is going to finish him with a big serve."

How about when they asked Seles whether other players said anything about her Wimbledon controversy?

"To me personally, nobody, really even from the top players and from the lower-ranked players, you know we don't talk, just say hi, I just walked by her and she walks by me."

I am not making this up. The stenographer, Peter Paul Balestrieri, was having a whale of a time with a question about Steffi Graf:

Seles: "Me and Steffi don't sit down much, we just say hi, how are you, and I ask her — I say congratulations for Wimbledon, she says congratulations for the French, and afterwards, you know, but, you know, the thing that — it's not that — we don't hate each other, I mean, we have respect but we are not — I am not going to ask her about her personal life, and she's not going to ask about mine."

Of course not. She'd be gone for days.

After Seles finished her press conference, I approached Mr. Balestrieri, who was shaking his hands out, trying to get the blood back to his fingers.

"Is she the fastest talker on the tour?" I asked.

"Oh, easily," he said, sounding fatigued.

"Do you know how fast she talks?"

"Over 300 words a minute."

"You're kidding."

"No. I won the New York State court reporters competition by typing 280 words a minute. And she's much faster than that. She's unbelievable. She's the fastest person I've ever listened to. She's ..."

I wanted to talk more, but he passed out.

All of which leads me to my point: Do we really need to hear 300 words a minute from Monica Seles? The girl just got her driver's license, for Pete's sake. How much wisdom can she impart?

Come on. Let her be a kid. Let her have fun. Let her play tennis, win tons of money, then go home and buy her own high school, if she wants. But enough with the microphones. To paraphrase a teenager: It's, you know, like, ˜mbarrassing.

At least wait until she's 18. Then, having reached voting age, she can tell us about her newest outfit, and how much she adores Madonna. And we can tell her what hospital the stenographer was sent to. ∎

Micro-waived: It's business, but hearts are still broken

September 5

He answered the door with a dazed look, like a man who had just been slapped in the face. "I don't know why they did it," he said, letting his guest inside and digging his hands into his pockets. "Maybe it was my birthday. I just turned 35. Maybe that's it."

He looked around his house, a new place, on a lake. He bought it a few months ago. They say never buy a house if you're a professional athlete; it's the kiss of death. "We were supposed to start some construction on Monday." He forced a laugh. "Better hold off on that, huh? Aw, maaan."

Aw, maaan, indeed. The Microwave has been unplugged. Cut. Cut? Can they do that? Can they really cut the man who has played more games, taken more lumps as a Piston than anyone else in history? Can they cut the man who, just last summer, on a raucous night in Portland, threw in that final jump shot with :00.7 on the clock, the shot no one else wanted to take, the shot that won the Pistons their second consecutive NBA championship? The Microwave? VJ? Cut? Can they do that?

They just did. Johnson is gone because he is aging and because he costs too much and because general manager Jack McCloskey — who just a few months ago, after the brutal playoff elimination by the Chicago Bulls, insisted there was "no reason to shake up this team" — now seems intent on doing just that. Johnson is tossed off the roster in hopes that another team will take him and his salary so the Pistons can make more moves, as if the five guys they've dumped isn't enough.

"I don't know about all that," Johnson said. "None of my business now, anyhow."

He gazed out the window at his patio furniture and the lakefront. It was a beautiful summer afternoon, cool breeze, warm sun. Far too nice a day to die. "If this was illegal," Johnson sighed, "I could call the police. I could say I was robbed.

"But it's not illegal. It's business."

It's business. It's business. Why is it every time someone says, "It's business," someone else's heart is broken? Vinnie Johnson was the historical cornerstone of this team, the brick laid during the hungry years, when the Pistons were names like Paul Mokeski and Larry Drew and they couldn't sell out if they gave away dinner. Johnson arrived one November day in a trade for Greg Kelser, a local hero. Fans said, "Bad move! Kelser is better!" Today, Kelser announces the games. Vinnie still plays them.

Or he did until Wednesday. Oh, another team will almost surely pick him up. But what does he do with all those Detroit memories? Vinnie Johnson can remember nights at Joe Louis Arena, nights at the Silverdome, nights at the Palace. He remembers when Atlanta was the hated rival, then Boston, then Los Angeles, then Chicago. He remembers conking heads with Adrian Dantley in that horrific seventh game at the Garden. And he remembers running off the court in LA, diving into a pile of champagne-soaked teammates, screaming, "WE DID IT, BABY! WE DID IT! BAAAD BOYS! BAAAD BOYS!"

He remembers all of it, good and bad. And yet the legend of Vinnie Johnson is not what he remembers, but what all those other teams will never forget. Folks in Boston still wince when you speak his name. New Yorkers just blow cheekfuls of air and shake their heads. Portland fans? They still haven't forgiven him. All those blind turnaround jumpers, the spinning, twisting, no-way-he-makes-that-shot baskets? Raised on the playgrounds of Brooklyn, Johnson was that rare player who actually felt the basket; seeing it was unimportant. In a game in which defense wins and quickness decides, scoring is still what makes your heart race.

And Vinnie Johnson could score like God.

H e leaned now against the clean white counter of his new kitchen. Friends sat around, saying nothing, everyone sort of stunned. From the other room you could hear the TV playing softly.

"I don't want to say anything bad," Johnson said. "It's been 10 great years here. I don't want to be remembered for a controversy. I want to be remembered as making that last shot in Portland. As a champion.

"When I came here, this team was 21-61. It worked out. So maybe things happen for the best."

He said it, but he didn't mean it. The Pistons had just told him, in essence, that they would rather pay him not to play here than pay him to stay. How would you feel? A guy like William Bedford stays on the roster, at nearly $1 million a year, and Vinnie goes? Where's the justice in that? There is talk that Detroit is dropping Johnson to make room for Washington's Darrell Walker. There is talk of an even bigger trade about to come. There is always talk. It doesn't change this: Once again, a player who gives his best years for a team is, in the end, tossed aside like smelly sneakers.

"Hey, if you're writing a story, tell all those realtors out there not to call me," Johnson said. "I ain't moving. This is my home. No matter what happens. I've been here too long to change that."

He walked the guest toward the door, passing a portrait of himself in mid-jump shot, the wrist about to flick another low-flying missile at the basket. "It's business," they say, but that doesn't take the sting out of it. The face has been slapped. The Microwave has been unplugged. And things just got a little colder around the Palace. ■

Lions' goal-line heroics cap a weekend of wonder

September 16

I can retire now. I've seen it all.

In one weekend, I watched Michigan finally beat Notre Dame, on a fourth-down bomb that surely would have made Bo Schembechler quit the game and go into baseball, if he hadn't done that already. Then I watched the Chippewas from Central Michigan, who were supposed to be happy with the invitation to play Michigan State, stuff their RSVP down the Spartans' throats and beat them, 20-3. Thanks for having us, George. We had a great time.

And now, the *piece de resistance*. On Sunday, in a sweltering Silverdome — and wouldn't it be nice if they saved these indoor games until the weather got cold? — I watched the Lions, our Lions, you know, Detroit, actually beat the mighty Miami Dolphins — Dan Marino, Don Shula, the whole cast — by stopping them not once, not twice, not thrice (thrice?) but four straight times within the shadow of the Lions' end zone.

Defense? The Lions won with defense? Somebody get me a Maalox.

"What do you think now, huh? Still pick us to lose?" Chris Spielman gloated when he saw me in the locker room, after the Lions' biggest victory in a long time, 17-13 over the Dolphins. To his credit — and my luck — he was laughing. Still, I was hardly alone in predicting Miami to beat the Lions on Sunday, based on past experience. And with five minutes left in the game, when Rodney Peete threw a desperation pass smack into the palm of a blitzing Vestee Jackson, and the ball bounced high into the air, and it came down in the hands of a big Miami lineman named Shawn Lee, who lumbered to the Lions' 3 — well, I would say the doubters looked pretty prophetic, no?

But wait.

There comes a point when you get sick of the big kids stealing your milk money. One day they rough you up, and, for the first time, you swing back. So here was the Lions' defense, the butt of more jokes than Dan Quayle, trotting out to do the impossible, keep Marino, football's answer to the Veg-O-Matic, out of the end zone when he could almost walk in. If there were five people in the Silverdome who thought they could do it, it was a lot.

First down, Marino drops back to pass, the coverage is tight, he throws it into the turf. "THAT'S ONE!" yelled the Lions in the huddle. "THREE MORE TIMES, BABY!"

Second down, a handoff to Tony Paige, a former Lion. Detroit has taken a lot of abuse for letting this guy go. Wouldn't it be typical if he beat Detroit with a touchdown? "GET HIM!" the fans yelled — and Spielman got him, leveled him after a one-yard gain. "THAT'S TWO!" Spielman hollered.

Third down. Another handoff, this time to Mark Higgs and — whoa! Dan Owens, the second-year lineman, bolts into the backfield and makes the tackle. A three-yard loss. "THREE! THAT'S THREE!"

Now the final test. Fourth down. Less than four minutes left in the game. Against another team, trailing 17-13, the Dolphins might have chosen a field goal. Figured a touchdown was too tough, they'll take three and hope for another chance. Instead, Marino and company stayed out there, banking on a touchdown, the big kids saying, "Give us your milk money." The Lions dug in.

"Did it surprise me they went for it?" Bennie Blades would say. "Not at all. Nobody respects our defense. But this was now or never for us. We had to do it or live with ourselves the rest of the season."

Ball is snapped. Marino looks right. Throws to Tony Martin in the end zone — and Detroit's Ray Crockett dives and bats the ball down. No flags. Fifty-six thousand fans suddenly realize what they've witnessed — the growing up of a football team.

They explode in noise.

I am looking for that Maalox.

This is the first time since I've been here that everybody did what they had to do to win," Spielman gushed in the locker room afterward. "Maybe, finally, we have learned how to win."

"A game like this two years ago, after that interception?" Lomas Brown added. "Maybe one or two guys would say, 'Let's go!' and the rest would have their heads down. But this time, everybody was on the sideline screaming, 'We can do it!' "

They did it, they actually have a winning record after three games, and they got it by beating a marquee team, not Green Bay, not Tampa Bay, but a team that goes to the playoffs and even wins sometimes. And it was not only that fourth down. The Lions actually outperformed Miami in — sit down, this could make you dizzy — rushing yards (Barry Sanders, a brilliant 143), net yards passing, third-down efficiency, sack yardage and time of possession. They also won the Punt, Run and Hide Competition when Jim Arnold, realizing he was about to get blocked, tucked the ball under his arm in the second quarter and raced 21 yards for a first down. OK. Maybe "raced" is too nice a word.

"That's the farthest I ever ran with a football," Arnold panted afterward. "But I would like to announce that, based on today, I will be entering the 1992 Olympics, in the 100 meters, thank you."

After everything I've seen this weekend — the end of the Irish, the rise of the Chippewas, and the sudden maturity of the (gulp) Lions' defense — it wouldn't surprise me a bit. ∎

For U-M's Greg Skrepenak, it's tough to be a gentle giant

September 27

I t was the great philosopher Kermit the Frog who said, "It's not easy being green." He should try being big. He should try being 6-feet tall in grade school. Or 300 pounds in high school. He should try sitting in a kitchen chair, only to have the chair snap in two.

He should try getting weighed on an industrial shipping scale. Or going to the all-you-can-eat places and seeing the owners gulp. He should try shopping for 17EEE shoes, or walking through life as "Ohmigod, did you see that?"

He should try being Greg Skrepenak, 6-feet-8 and — after a severe diet — a svelte 320 pounds. Yo, Kermit. Being green is a breeze.

"All my life people have thought I'm not normal," says Skrepenak, a major part of Michigan's celebrated offensive line that faces No. 1 Florida State on Saturday. "They think my size makes me different. But I'm not. I'm no different than an average person. I think. I bleed. I have emotions. I cry."

Ladies and gentlemen, meet the Gentle Giant.

W hat did you expect? For Skrepenak, football is less a passion than a given. When you tower over the kids in your class, when you accidentally push one and see him fly across the lawn, when every adult who crosses your path seems to say, "Hmm, I bet you're gonna play football," well, sooner or later, it sinks in. In a town like Wilkes-Barre, the same rugged Pennsylvania soil that gave us Andre Reed and Rocket Ismail and, farther west, Joe Namath and Dan Marino and Joe Montana, well, not to play football — at Skrepenak's size — would almost be sacrilegious. So it was that young Greg, 9 years old, signed up for his first league and arrived with his helmet, all excited, ready to find his destiny. And the opposing coach took one look at him and said, "He can't play with these kids. He'll kill them."

Skrepenak was barred from his very first game.

"I cried my eyes out," he says.

In the years that followed, his mother would carry his birth certificate in her purse, just to prove to people that her son really was as young as the others. Didn't matter. He soon towered over his teachers. As a teenager, he shopped at Big & Tall stores. When it came to sports, he was constantly plucked from his peers and dropped in with older kids. By junior high he was practicing with the varsity, and upon making the varsity he was the biggest guy on the team. His jolting growth left him awkward for a while, bumping into things, tripping, dropping, as if the boy inside didn't know what to do with all this muscle — or this strength.

"One time we were playing, and I drove up into this other lineman and he just went flying backwards and landed flat," Skrepenak says. "He wasn't moving. He just kind of moaned. I thought I killed him."

He shudders. "I couldn't have lived with myself. I mean, God, if I had really hurt him. ..."

Y ou talk to Skrepenak, it is hard to imagine he would hurt anyone; the deep but innocent voice, the quick smile. He looks like Gerry Cooney. He walks like Frank Bruno. Everything about him seems to suggest a large fellow who stoops over to talk to a child and immediately the child thinks "friend."

Of course, things change when you put on a helmet. Take the first play of the Michigan-Notre Dame game two weeks ago, when Skrepenak basically drove his man into the grass and mowed him. "That one play set the tone for all of us," says teammate Dave Diebolt, the tight end, who also shares a house with the big guy. "It was like, man, Skrep's really serious."

"I was so tired of Notre Dame," Skrepenak says. "I just wanted to win that game so bad. I felt mean."

And that has been a problem in the past. Like many a big man before him, Skrepenak found that outsiders expected his meanness to match his weight. Coaches especially. They kept yelling, "More aggressive! More aggressive!" — that is, when they weren't yelling, "Less pizza! Less pizza!" Skrepenak's weight, like his aggressiveness, has been an issue for years. He once ballooned as high as 370 pounds, mostly on late-night Italian food and boxes of cookies. During the Bo Schembechler era, Skrepenak was taken to a shipping company and weighed on an industrial scale. Some feel that this was done to embarrass the weight off. "He never said anything to the coaches, but, deep down, I think Skrep was really bothered by that," Diebolt says. "It was like, why are you taking me out in front of all these people and doing this to me? What did I do wrong?"

The answer is, nothing. He was playing well. He has played well for years. He has started 38 straight games for Michigan. How bad could he be? "That's my point," he says, waving those huge hands. "If I'm doing the job OK, leave me alone about my weight."

A h, but when you have all that flesh, people can't help trying to mold it. They have always been reshaping Greg Skrepenak, the coaches trying to make him meaner, the trainers trying to make him lighter, the other students trying to make him fit their stereotype.

And outwardly, the Gentle Giant with the legs like tree trunks goes along with just about anything. When a TV reporter asked to be held upside down while he did his report, Skrepenak shrugged and held the guy upside down. When another TV station wanted him to growl like a madman, Skrepenak shrugged and growled like a madman. When people ask to see his hands, he holds them up like souvenirs. When people ask, "Can you fit in my car?" he smiles and says, "Sure. I've fit in smaller ones than that."

Of course, now and then, off the field, he likes to throw his weight around — but only against inanimate objects. "I've broken beds, chairs, you name it," he says, sighing. "My girlfriend has a hair salon, and I sat down in one of her chairs. Now it's a recliner.

"It's gotten so that if the chair isn't a La-Z-Boy, or at least real sturdy, I'd just as soon stand up. It's embarrassing when you break a chair. Not only that, you can really kill yourself."

And then there was The Night of the Cube. This, he admits, is a little weird. Skrepenak and a few friends were coming home. They walked past the Cube, the giant steel sculpture that sits near the student union, a modern art black box nearly 20 feet tall and wide enough to dwarf even Skrepenak. "I don't know what got into him," Diebolt recalls, "but he decided he was going to block the Cube. He said, 'I'm gonna try and knock it over.' He set himself and rammed up into it. It didn't move. The next day, though, he had a big scar on his shoulder. It was kind of nuts, if you ask me."

Skrepenak laughs at the memory. "It was kind of nuts. But I just felt like trying."

Which is more than he can say about his coach's less nutty request: lose the fat. "I want you down to 320," Gary Moeller told Skrepenak last season. "No ifs, ands or buts." The big guy shrugged — OK, maybe it was more than a shrug — but he did it. He cut out the pizzas before bedtime. He concentrated on (ugh) vegetables and fruits. He got down to 320.

"I know it wasn't easy for Greg and he didn't exactly love doing it," Moeller says now, "but the important thing is, he did it. He's lighter, he's faster, and I haven't noticed any drop-off in his strength."

B ut whatever they do to Skrepenak's exterior, beneath all the flesh beats the heart of a kid, and that heart, somehow, remains impervious to cynicism or anger or revenge. Example: Skrepenak and Rocket Ismail come from the same hometown, and the year Ismail beat Michigan almost single-handedly — and went on to become the most over-hyped name in college football — it would have been easy for Skrepenak to turn jealous. After all, this kid is even stealing the glory in his hometown — and he's so small, and sleek and fast.

Instead, this is what Skrepenak says: "If someone had to beat Michigan, I'm glad it was a guy from Wilkes-Barre."

The Gentle Giant.

"A lot of people have said bad things about me," he explains, "called me fatso, or an overrated fat guy or whatever. But I don't want to sink to their level. I'm a religious person and I figure they'll get theirs in the end. ...

"Are there times when I wish I was just Joe Average, maybe 6-foot tall, 180 pounds? Yeah, sure there are. Even if it meant giving up football, I think sometimes I would do it. Football is just a game. It's not my life. It's not who I am. I think I'm smart enough to get by in life if football ended tomorrow. And the people who love me are gonna love me even if I don't play the game."

But football will not end tomorrow. Tomorrow Skrepenak will slam himself into a Florida State lineman and open holes and pancake opponents. And next April he will no doubt be a high draft choice in the NFL and make a nice load of money, and finally be rewarded for all those years of being too big. Before all that happens, however, a message from the man himself to all those people who whisper behind his back:

"Us big people are just like you. We have emotions. We feel things. So don't talk behind our backs; come up and talk to us like regular people. We're not going to kill you or anything."

It's not easy being big. The Gentle Giant has spoken.

Now. Let's hear from those frogs ... ∎

Ernie's long gone, and the good-byes aren't easy

October 1

On the morning of the last day of the best days of his life, Ernie Harwell got up and put a cassette into the small recorder he had plugged in under the sink. "This is Sammy Fain singing," he said. The recorder spit out scratchy sounds of an old man and a piano, a ballad, a pretty melody.

> *We came together young and strong*
> *The summer smiled and touched us with a song*
> *for that one summer*
> *that one sweet summer*

It was a song Harwell had written, years ago, in happier times, when there was no end to his rainbow, and no one was telling him Monday would be his last day broadcasting from Tiger Stadium, whether he liked it or not. Harwell has always been a songwriter, back to the time when he was calling home runs for Jackie Robinson's Brooklyn Dodgers, and in the later years he kept his tapes and sheet music in the booth, just in case. "One time, these two fellows, Homer and Jethro, they were a singing act, they came in before a game, and I played them a song and they said, 'Hey, we like it. We'll use it on our next album.' And they did. That's how I got my first song recorded."

He smiled at that memory and walked stiffly to his guest, holding his back, a reminder of all those years in the booth, the hard chair with no cushion. Carpenters get wobbly knees. Coal miners get dust in the lung. Guys in the booth get bad backs. Price you pay.

Ernie Harwell would have paid it longer, if they let him. Instead, he sat in the small living room in the house on Witherspoon Street, a house that still has no answering machines and no stereo system, just transistor radios, everywhere you look, on the couch, on the kitchen counter, on the hall table, transistor radios and Bibles, a book of Psalms, a book of hymns. Here, between the word of God and the sound of the radio, Ernie Harwell awaited the good-bye hour. His last game at Tiger Stadium. Outside the weather was autumn, and through the white curtains he could see his wife, Lulu, picking flowers from the garden.

"I've prepared something to say tonight," Harwell said, holding up a piece of Detroit Tigers stationery. "I wrote it out a few days ago. I figured since the stadium has been such a part of my life, maybe I should say something."

He handed over the paper, creased in half. The typing was like that of a college student. A few misspellings. Some ink notes on the side. It was probably the millionth note he had written himself to say on the air — hello to a fan in Alpena, a reminder that Picture Day was coming up, good seats still available, the batting average of some broad-shouldered rookie who just got off the bus and was now at home plate.

"Good-byes are never easy ..." the paper began.

G ood-byes are never easy. Especially when they aren't necessary. Ernie Harwell needs to leave Detroit the way we need a tax on breathing. But leave he will. After 32 seasons on the job — and nearly 50 in the business — the club and the radio station no longer want him. This was a bombshell last December. Now it is something worse; a dull pain too draining to fight. The protests have been ignored. The club is auditioning new announcers. And the voice of baseball packs his bag. You say to yourself, if they can make Ernie Harwell leave, they can do anything to anybody.

"Here we go," he said now, getting into the car for that last ride to the stadium, wearing a blue overcoat and his trademark beret, which always made him look more like a French professor than a booth man. Thirty-one years ago, on a warm day much like this one, he left the lobby of the Book Cadillac hotel in downtown Detroit and walked to Tiger Stadium, his first home game as the new announcer. He made his way down Michigan Avenue, past a place called The Crow Bar and past the down-and-out people who would ask him for a dime. He got behind the microphone and began to immortalize names such as Cash and Colavito and Kaline. In the years to come, there would be Lolich, McLain, Fidrych, Gibson, Trammell, Whitaker, Fielder.

Now he drives to work, staring at the landscape that has collapsed during his time. The Crow Bar is gone and the Book Cadillac hotel is gone. The down-and-out people are still there. They ask for a dollar now.

"What will you remember most about the booth at Tiger Stadium?" Harwell was asked.

"Well," he said in that rich baritone, "the booth we're in now is not the one we started in. The one we started in was on the first-base side, and you had to climb down into it, like a submarine. It even had a hatch on top, and you would climb down the ladder to get in.

"One time, the mayor of Pinconning stopped by to see us and he brought a present, a big round of cheese, Pinconning cheese, oh, it was so big, maybe 50 pounds. But the problem was, the mayor was a little, shall we say, inebriated. And when he lowered himself down the hatch, he lost his grip on the cheese and it rolled down this slanted roof and over the edge and landed in the seats."

He chuckled. "That booth wasn't for everybody."

No. Only for those who wanted to rub elbows with baseball history. Milton Berle once came to that booth, and Bob Hope came, too, sliding down the hatch to talk with Ernie Harwell. Jerry Vale. The Peach Queen of Romeo. Every senator and congressman you can think of.

"Each game, around the third inning, someone would come by with a bag of cold hot dogs and warm Coke, and they would lower it down the hatch," Harwell recalled. "That was our dinner. Back then, the Tigers didn't even allow the announcers to eat with them in the food room."

So you can see where the tradition began.

Now Harwell was walking up the steps in the empty stadium, a walk he has taken every game day for the last 32 seasons. "It's easier if you just use one foot per step," he said over his shoulder, like a kid explaining hopscotch. "You're less tired when you reach the top."

At 73 years old, he reached the top with barely an extra breath. He turned and headed for the booth, walking along the blue girders and grimy cement passageways that make up this marvelously decaying ballpark. Two teenagers are waiting for him already, holding baseballs.

"Mr. Harwell, will you sign this?"

"Why, sure."

"Can you put 'Ernie Harwell, Final Broadcast, 9/30/91?' "

"All right."

When he handed over the balls, the kids thanked him, then ran away, waving their fists in a collective "ALL RIGHT!" Maybe to someone reading this from afar, the fuss seems strange. All this for an announcer?

To understand, you must first understand a summer night on Lake Charlevoix, or a traffic jam on the Lodge Freeway, or a clock radio in your bedroom when you're too sick to go to school but there's a day game on and you turn the knob and there it is, that voice, genteel and comforting, a trace of Georgia accent. "The Tigahs," it says. "IT'S LONNNG GONE!" it says. "Strike three … he stood there like a house by the side of the road."

Call it age. Call it nostalgia. But fathers here remember that voice in 1968, the afternoon McLain won his 30th — "HERE COMES McLAIN RUNNING OUT OF THE DUGOUT" — and sons remember that voice in 1984, the night Kirk Gibson turned October into here madness — "IT'S GOING, IT'S LONG GONE, A HOME RUN!"

Fathers. Sons. Mothers. Grandmothers. Can't everyone here remember something or someplace where that voice was in the background? In this part of the country, Ernie Harwell is the growth chart on the kitchen wall. You stand up against him and chart your life.

It was 7 p.m. now and photographers were crammed inside the booth. A local TV anchor requested a few minutes. Out on the field, a guy named Bob Taylor, who has sung the national anthem here for years, was about to dedicate this last one to Ernie and Paul Carey.

Harwell had his jacket off and his tie loose, hot from all the visitors. Many of them looked around, this being their first time inside the booth. So this is where he does his stuff, huh? It hardly seemed worthy. A cramped metal room with a dropped ceiling, bare walls, a beige Formica table top that holds two microphones: Ernie Harwell, Paul Carey. There is a naked light bulb taped to the table with black electrical tape. It tells them when they are on the air.

"Has it been tough for you, Ernie?" the anchor asked.

"A little bit tough. But the affection of these fans has made it much easier to bear."

"Will you savor this final game or survive it?"

A laugh. "I think I'll survive it."

To the end, he refused to badmouth anyone. Not the radio station that turned its back on him. Not the front office that begrudgingly gave him a day in his honor, then sent nobody important from its staff. "The only regret I have," Harwell said, "is that we're not ending with friendly feelings. I'm not comfortable with people being upset or unfriendly." Now the booth began to clear and he took his seat again, next to Carey, who also is leaving after this season. When the little lightbulb flickered on, they began.

"This is kind of a special night for both of us," Carey said, "because it's our last broadcast at Tiger Stadium. …"

"Thank you, Paul," Harwell said, "and it's great to be with you for all these years and great to be in this old ballpark. …"

The place was nearly empty. A breeze blew through the seats. In the seventh inning, the small crowd would rise, turn to the booth, and begin to clap. There should have been a sellout, of course. There should have been 50,000 people inside, and 50,000 more outside, on their feet, in a salute. But the club didn't care and it was Monday night and the Tigers were out of it, and, hey, life goes on.

But it doesn't go on, not the same way, not this morning. You can go to work, you can eat in the restaurant, you can check your bank account and see that everything is still there. But if you live around here and you love baseball, a piece of you was just waved out of town, and come next March, when the first game from spring training is called, you'll feel it.

I will feel it sooner. I was the one in the living room Monday morning. As I write this, I can hear old Sammy Fain, playing the piano and crooning, from that little tape recorder, the words Ernie Harwell wrote in a happier time:

Let autumn come on distant wind
I'll treasure still
the time you called me friend
for that one summer
that one sweet summer

The man in the booth is gone.
Tiger Stadium just lost the best friend it ever had. ∎

Amazing! Lions score 21 in final seven minutes

October 7

The fans were screaming and the players were hugging and the scoreboard lights were changing for the third time in seven minutes, touchdown, Detroit, touchdown, Detroit, touchdown, Detroit, and, good Lord, this was unbelievable. Big Jerry Ball did a forward flip, all 320 pounds of him. Rodney Peete tried to slap every hand in the Silverdome. Barry Sanders, who had just squirted past one of the best defenders in football for that final score, was a grinning birthday cake now; all his teammates wanted a piece. Horns blared. The building shook with noise. If they never do another thing this year, the Lions will have this moment.

You know what?

It might be enough.

"I have seen a lot of football in my life," gushed coach Wayne Fontes, after the best finish around here since, man, who knows when? — a thrilling 24-20 comeback victory to claim sole possession of first place in the NFC Central, "but I'll tell you, I have never been associated with anything like that fourth quarter. When they ask me one day what do you remember about football, I'll remember this."

He'd have a hard time forgetting. Here was the moment when the Lions officially crawled out of the lime pit that had nearly fossilized them as losers, and became — not just in their minds but all those jaded minds in this weary city — winners. Trailing 20-3. Seven minutes left. Fans heading for the exits. Maybe San Francisco wins games like this. Maybe the Giants. The Lions?

They do now. It was as if a little voice had crawled inside their ears and said, "Do you really want to lose again? Do you really want to go back to being what you've been all these years?" They were 4-1 coming into this game, but few people believed they had turned the corner. "Easy opponents," the critics said. "They'll blow it against the Vikings, just watch."

Now, down by 17 points, with three quarters behind them as flat as last week's soda, Detroit was on the verge of proving the critics right.

And then, something happened …

What's that kissing game you play as a teenager? Seven minutes in heaven? Here, at the Silverdome, was the Detroit rendition. The first kiss was a stunner, Peete found Robert Clark running a straight post route after the Vikings somehow went for a fake, a terrible play on their part. Clark sucked in the pass and dashed 68 yards untouched for the score. Vikings 20, Lions 10. Out in the parking lot, several departing fans mumbled, "What was that?"

"We're going for the win!" Fontes yelled at his staff as the Lions prepared to kick. "Squib it!"

Squib it? This was the second kiss. The Vikings trotted out expecting a deep boot, and were stunned when the Lions ran to one side. Too late to change, Minnesota's big blockers tried to handle the bouncing ball. Oops. Derek Tennell, the Detroit tight end who has caught only two passes all year, saw the pigskin free on the turf. "I fell on it and I said, 'It's mine, you can't take it, I don't care how many of you jump on me!' " he laughed afterward.

Peete was watching when Tennell came up waving that ball on the Lions' 43, the crowd going nuts. Suddenly, the quarterback felt a shiver, something he hadn't felt since college, when he was leading Southern Cal to the Rose Bowl, call it Popeye's spinach, or Zorro's sword. "It's a feeling like you can't do anything wrong," Peete said, "like you're supposed to win."

Down the sideline, Sanders felt it, too. The two men trotted onto the field, and from that moment on, they were unstoppable, accounting for most of the magic in the last two kisses. The first was Peete's beautiful 16-yard touchdown pass to the outstretched arms of Willie Green, which pulled the Lions within three points. And then — after an inspiring series by the defense, which stuffed the Vikings like a boneless chicken breast — the *coup de grace*, the end of the rainbow, Sanders' brilliant run to win the game.

Goodness. Has there ever been a guy like this, who goes through defenses like a school kid racing through the forest, his shirttail flying, his legs churning, skirting tacklers as if they were heavy trees rooted to the earth? Sanders beat all five Vikings trying to stop him on that last draw play, going 15 yards of highlight film and ducking under the intimidating Joey Browner to cross the stripe and hang six on the scoreboard. All told, he collected 70 rushing yards in those final seven minutes, 15 more on receptions, six first downs and a score. Hey. That's a day's work for most backs. Everyone knew Sanders was a gleaming talent. They now learn something more important: He is a winner, too.

"Were you excited?" someone asked the normally unexpressive Sanders.

"Oh, yeah, I was very excited," he said. "I, uh, may not have shown it like everyone else, but I was."

"He was excited," Peete confirmed. "I actually saw him smile in the huddle."

S mile? How could you help it? This was the day the Lions truly grew up, shed their old skin. On the NBC broadcast later in the day, Bill Parcells, who coached last year's Super Bowl champion Giants, said a victory like this "is good for five or six weeks, because the Lions will never believe they can lose a game now, after what they did."

Exactly. The way the overtime loss to Washington torpedoed last season, so could Sunday's victory galvanize this one. The Lions think like winners now. And if that isn't the biggest difference in this franchise, then this newspaper is printed on goat skin. "It's never ever been like this before," said offensive tackle Lomas Brown, who has endured plenty of dismal years. "In the past, losing in the fourth quarter, we would have folded — heck, we would have folded in the third quarter! This is the best moment I've ever had in pro football, better than the Pro Bowl, better than anything!"

Someone asked Ball: "Is this your best moment in the pros, too?"

"The pros? S - - -," he snapped. "This is the best in the pros, college, high school, all 20 years I been playing football."

That feeling coursed through the locker room like blood through a vein. Lost in the euphoria was the fact that Detroit has won five games in a row — only Buffalo and Washington can make that claim — and is solo atop the NFC Central, a game ahead of the Bears, three games up on the Vikings, four up on Green Bay and Tampa Bay. Then again, maybe it's not lost. Maybe it's put in perspective. You crawl before you walk. You walk before you run. Streaks are nice, and winning the division would be gravy, but the meat of this season was — and is — to wash off the old dirt, lose that losing image.

Consider it done.

Seven minutes in heaven.

"You know," said Peete, sitting alone by his locker after most of the room had cleared out, "this was one of those games that you think about when you're driving at night, by yourself. You imagine your team is down by three touchdowns late in the fourth quarter, and they rally and come back to win. It's a dream. The kind of game you always look forward to."

"And now?" he was asked.

"And now," he said, grinning, "I'll be able to look back instead of forward."

Hang onto your hats, folks.

We just got ourselves a football team. ■

On the field and off, Howard is a cut above

October 17

F irst of all, about the haircut. Hair on top. None on the sides. Then sideburns. He cuts it himself. Before each game. Calls it the "high inside fade." When he explains this, he rubs the naked skin above his ear and smiles, a huge smile, a smile that will make him famous one day.

"The sideburns," he proudly notes, "are my personal thing."

Next, the earring. Little gold thing. Goes with the sideburns, I guess. He wears it only off the field, away from the football team. Coaches just don't understand. You know how it is.

And then there are his quirky habits, such as meditating, or picking up the phone and saying, "Magic."

"Oh, I've been doing that since the eighth grade!" he says, bursting into laughter. "Hey! You got to be a little different!"

What are you saying, Desmond? Catching all those touchdowns isn't enough? Diving into the air and sucking that ball in with your fingertips, that's chopped liver? Anyone can do it? The miracle catch that beat Notre Dame? The four touchdowns against Boston College? The Heisman Trophy talk? Not enough? You have to answer the phone funny and hide the earring and leave those little sideburns stranded from the rest of your hair like a tree stuck on an island?

Well. Why not? Dare to be different, they say. Besides, the way this kid is going, he could dye his hair orange and wear a petticoat to the huddle — they would still throw him the ball. And he would still catch it. Kickoffs. Punts. Pass receptions. Iowa. Michigan State. Florida State. It hardly seems to matter who or what is between him and the end zone anymore. Desmond Howard, whose nickname is Magic, just seems to materialize there, the ball in his arms, the official throwing his hands in the air.

"He's got such great quickness, that's the thing," coach Gary Moeller says of his most explosive threat. "And then of course, he can catch it. And then, on top of that, he can dodge people. And after he dodges them ..."

Uh, back to you in a minute, Mo. Because there are the X's and O's, and then there's the big picture. Desmond Howard isn't just the whirling dervish in the maize and blue uniform. He isn't just the scoring machine who averages a touchdown every third catch and who racked up four TDs in the season opener and two in every game since (around campus they joke about calling him Desmond Two-Two). At 5-feet-9, Howard isn't just the most exciting little package to hit Ann Arbor since a kid named Anthony Carter.

There's something else. When this season is over, Howard might very well be selected "The Best College Football Player in the Nation." The Heisman Trophy winner. If so, he would be the second Wolverine in history to win that award; the last guy, Tom Harmon, did it 51 years ago. Michigan does not push its players for such honors. Push? Heck, they run from Heisman hype the way senators run from Ted Koppel.

But here is the thing about Desmond Howard. He is such a talent, such a game-breaker, and such a nice kid, that — hold your breath here — you may actually find the Michigan commanders giving him a (gulp) plug.

"If he continues like he's going, then yes, I would say he deserves the Heisman," says Moeller.

Ohmigod.

You heard it here first.

"Coach Moeller said that?" Howard asks. He jerks his head in surprise and grins. "Oh, man." Howard will say things like this. Oh, man. Peace. He also wears beads around his neck, likes to meditate and has posters on his walls of Malcolm X and Martin Luther King, and a map of Africa. He signs autographs this way: "Peace my brother, Desmond Howard." In all my time covering today's college football superstars, he is the closest thing I have found to a child of the '60s. And he wasn't even born until 1970.

"I think the '60s were a really interesting time, what people did and tried to do," Howard says, making all us oldsters feel a little bit better. "They were trying to learn. Here at Michigan, I try to study my heritage as much as I can because it was never really available to me growing up. So much of the problems we have in this country have to do with education. Kids just aren't being given a chance."

He points to a small pile of posters against the wall. "A friend of mine gave me those. Each of them is about a different African king. I've been reading them. I think maybe some of that lineage is in me."

"You think you were a king in another life?" I ask.

He laughs. "I might have been one before," he says, "and who knows? I might be one again."

Now. Before you get the idea that Desmond Howard is some sort of self-absorbed hippie, let me say this: Nothing could be further from the truth. He is delightful, funny, engaging, warm, and on top of that — and I can't say this about every athlete I've met — he thinks. He looks at a situation and measures the consequences. Take his living situation. He moved far off campus — to Ypsilanti, actually — into his own apartment, by himself, because, he says, "I have a lot of work to do. If I were living in the dorms, people would be knocking on my door all the time, wanting to talk football. I would never get anything done."

He also realized that with the success he's having, there may be pressure to skip his final year of eligibility next season and go to the NFL. He has a rule about that: Desmond has to graduate. So he has taken courses over the summer and is on track to get his degree in May. This way, should the NFL make him an offer he couldn't refuse, he would still leave U-M with what he came for: an education.

"He's such a self-motivated kid, both football-wise and academically," says Moeller. "I remember when he first came here. I was the guy who recruited him. He was a running back in high school, and I said to him, 'We have a lot of running backs right now. You sure you still want to be one?' He said, 'Yeah.' Then, on the first day of practice, I saw him out there with the defensive backs. I said, 'What are you doing?' He said, 'I just want to play as soon as I can, I don't care where.' "

Fortunately, Moeller and Bo Schembechler switched him to receiver, watched him for one day, and figured that was where he belonged. Schembechler used to boast to reporters about "this crafty little devil from Cleveland, Ohio, who might just make you forget John Kolesar."

It didn't take long. Although Howard started slowly, with nine catches his freshman year, two of those were touchdowns. ("My biggest regret of that season was when we went to the Rose Bowl. I had one pass thrown to me, late in the game, and I was wide open. I could have scored. But Michael Taylor overthrew me. We could have won that game.")

He has since provided better memories. A pair of touchdowns in the Gator Bowl. The nine catches against Indiana last year (including an incredible over-the-shoulder, one-handed grab). The kickoff and punt returns that cause such excitement, Michigan Stadium seems to tremble. The 12 touchdowns this season (and we are only five games in).

And, of course, the now famous fourth-and-one diving catch that clinched revenge against dreaded Notre Dame.

"Who really called that play?" I ask.

Howard bursts into laughter. He does this, by the way, almost every time you ask a question.

"Let's just say coach Moeller called it, and Elvis (Grbac) confirmed it! Hahahaha!"

"And you delivered it."

"Yeah, basically."

Basically, my foot. There is very little basic about what Howard does, unless you consider running past the defensive backs, past the special-teams tacklers and past the big linemen a basic skill. "He's better than Rocket Ismail," says Michigan State cornerback Alan Haller. And that's a Spartan talking!

Yet for all the hoopla, Howard refuses to play the part of Big Man on Campus. True, he shares a nickname with the most famous basketball player this state has ever produced. ("My junior high school basketball coach gave me the nickname Magic, after Magic Johnson. It just kind of stuck.") Yet he does not wear that name on his chest, he does not walk to class in his football sweats, as many players do, hoping the women will spot him and point. And he does not lose sleep over the Heisman Trophy. He might give himself a special haircut should he win it, but he doesn't lose sleep.

"I didn't ask to be put in the Heisman race. For me, just to be mentioned in the same sentence means I'm on track for my goal."

Which is?

"To be the best football player I can be."

And that leads to the final question — although it won't be the last time it's asked: What if he were to be the best, if he were to win the Heisman, would he leave Michigan after this season?

"Right now, I plan on coming back and going to graduate school. I realize the college years are the best time you can have, and I want to make them last."

What if someone offered a Rocket Ismail-like contract?

He laughs again. "Then," he says, "I might have to go."

We'll see. It's not like the old days, when Harmon was playing. It's not the '60s, either. The great players may wear sideburns, but they rarely stick around college anymore. If you're lucky, you get a few fond seasons, and then they are on their way.

Still, that doesn't mean they don't learn anything. There's a moment in the movie "The Natural," when Robert Redford admits he wants people to look at him one day and say, "There goes Roy Hobbs, the greatest hitter who ever lived." I asked Desmond Howard what he would want whispered.

"Me? When I walk down campus, I want people to say, 'There goes Desmond Howard, he's a smart young man.' "

Better get a new daydream, kid. They're saying that already. ∎

The Series MVP? It's none other than Atlanta's Lemke

October 25

ATLANTA — Sooner or later in this World Series — probably Saturday night, the way the Braves are going — they will have to name an MVP, and won't that be fun? I can see the guys in the backroom, rushing to make up the trophy.

"Quick, read me the ballots."

"OK. One for Lemke—"

"Who?"

"That's what it says. Lemke."

"Lemke? You sure? How the hell you spell that?"

Of course, we could have predicted this, when Minnesota and Atlanta made the World Series and seven CBS executives immediately locked themselves in the bathroom and wept. The Twins and Braves are hardly household names. Most Americans still think the Braves have Dale Murphy, while the rest hear Minnesota and say, "Yeah, whatever happened to that Harmon Killebrew guy?"

To make matters worse, most of the supposed-to-be stars in this series (Kirby Puckett, Terry Pendleton) are taking a backseat. What we have center-stage are guys like Jerry Willard, who once quit baseball to build houses, driving in the winning run Wednesday on a sacrifice fly. What we have center-stage is a Minnesota kid named Knoblauch — I think it's a kid, it could be a sausage — and he's hitting .353. What we have center-stage is an unknown named Scott Leius (rhymes with Pay Us), who smacked a home run to win Game 2.

And what we have center-stage is Mark Lemke, a second baseman who weighs less that Kent Hrbek's lunch and whose glasses and short figure suggest an English major at Georgia Tech, rather than the hero of back-to-back World Series games. "The Lemmer," as they call him here, won Game 3 with a single in the bottom of the 12th and helped capture Game 4 with a triple in the bottom of the ninth.

Already, The Lemmer has had the CBS crew at his house to film him eating breakfast and answering the phone, just like normal people, which he used to be, before Tuesday.

"Do you watch your batting average on the scoreboard when you come to bat?" he was asked after the Braves clobbered the Twins, 14-5.

"Actually I hit so poorly during the regular season I conditioned myself to never look at that scoreboard," he said.

By the way, it should not surprise you that Atlanta has dubbed him The Lemmer (I can see that guy on "Saturday Night Live": "The

Lemmer. The Lematola. The Lemmeister. The Lem Man ...").
Personally, I doubt the nickname will stand the test of time. Willie,
Mickey, Duke ... and The Lemmer? Call it a hunch.

But, naming is a big pastime here in Atlanta, The City That Never
Sleeps, Because Another Mall Might Open. In fact, I have noticed folks
here spend a lot of time creating new and cute names for everything,
especially restaurants and shops.

Why, just this morning, I had breakfast at Yolks On You ($10.95),
picked up a newspaper at Fact 'N' Fiction ($.50), grabbed a frozen
yogurt at The Creamation Department ($2.95), got my hair cut at
Strands In The Jungle ($45), bought running shoes at Toes Up ($95), an
umbrella at Rubber Duckies ($17) and a pair of underwear at Sgt.
Skivvies ($9.50).

I can hardly wait to visit the butcher shop.

But back to Lemke. He had two triples Thursday night, three RBIs
and two runs scored (although it seemed like every Brave did that). He
is not the first guy to come out of nowhere and make a dent in the World
Series. This tradition goes way back, and includes such memorable
forgettables as Dusty Rhodes with the 1954 Giants, Al Weiss with the
1969 Mets, Brian Doyle with the 1978 Yankees.

But Lemke is the man of the moment — "I'm trying not to think
about it," he says — and if the Braves pull off this miracle, I promise
you, he won't have to buy his own beer in this town for a long time.

A nd neither will I. Our Atlanta visit is now over and my head can
finally stop throbbing from all that drum beating.

Actually, I'm sad to go. For one thing, I never got to meet Jane Fonda.

And I waited in every elevator. I even hung around that special
parking place in the stadium basement, the one marked "Ted Turner." I
figured I had an "in" with Ted — The Tedder, I call him — since we had
met back in Moscow in 1986, during his Goodwill Games. In fact, we
shared such quality time together that I know if he saw me today he
would pop right out of his car, look me in the eye and say, "Park this, will
ya?"

But I digress. We are in search of an MVP, and with the Braves on the
brink of victory, could it be ... The Lemmer? "Every player has his up
and down periods," he said. "I guess I'm in my up period."

You could say that. But who knows? This is a crazy series. And now,
it's back to Minnesota. Because of the results so far, analysts will claim
home field will win this thing. Maybe so, maybe no. We go from
tomahawk insanity in Atlanta to homer-hankie insanity in Minnesota. If
you ask me, the only difference between the two places is that you can't
blow your nose in a tomahawk.

Although I bet The Lemmer gives it a good shot. ∎

The Wilt equation:
Does it really add up?

November 5

Today we answer the most talked-about question in sports: Is it possible that Wilt Chamberlain slept with 20,000 women? Wait. Let me check my watch. Make that 20,001.

Chances are you have heard about Wilt's claim. He wrote it in his new book, "A View From Above," which I always thought referred to his height. Maybe it refers to the mirror over his bed.

Twenty thousand women. That's what he says. He told me personally, Sunday night, when we did a radio talk show together. I must admit, Wilt looked remarkably fit for a guy who has endured so much sexual activity. After 20,000 women, I expected him to be wheeled in on a slab, with a dumb grin on his face.

"So Wilt," I began, and here, being the thoughtful, intelligent type of talk-show host who gets no ratings, I paused, looking for important subjects rather than the cheap and tacky sex stuff.

"So," I said. "IS IT TRUE, OR WHAT?"

"It's 20,000," Wilt insisted. "I went back to my old datebooks and figured it out."

Which is what people across the country are doing right now. The Wilt Equation. America hasn't done this much calculating since the stock market crashed. You see men by the water coolers, counting on both hands. Let's see, if you take Wilt's age (55), figure the year he says he started (15), divide it into the total number of women (20,000), you come up with … an average, he writes, of 1.2 women a day.

Personally, it's the .2 that has me confused. Is .2 just a slow dance? Or a soulful kiss?

For me, .2 was high school. But I was always weak in math.

I had no idea people would make such a fuss over this," Chamberlain admitted Sunday. "It's a small part of the book. I didn't write it to brag. People are always asking about my statistics, how many points I scored, stuff like that. So I figured they would be interested in another statistic."

Yeah. Wait'll the fantasy leagues get a hold of this.

Actually, it's not the numbers that impress me, but the timing. If you allow for sick days, travel days and the occasional day when he just didn't feel like it (if there ever was such a day) you pretty much figure that, in order to squeeze everyone in, Wilt's conversations had to go something like this:

WOMAN: "Hi, aren't you—"
WILT: "YOUR PLACE OR MINE?"

Now. I should say here that Chamberlain does not encourage promiscuity, although coming from a man nicknamed "The Big Dipper" you take that for what it's worth. Much of his bedroom activity, he said, came during the '60s and '70s when, as he put it, "there was a sexual revolution going on."

Obviously, Wilt made general.

I also should mention that Wilt promotes Safe Sex. AS OFTEN AS YOU CAN POSSIBLY HAVE IT. No. Ha. I just threw that in because, when you sit next to a man who has lost count of how many countries he has had sex in, you feel a little inferior.

And then John Salley showed up. And I really felt like a monk.

Salley, like Wilt, is not married, hovers in the 7-foot range and has a reputation as a ladies man, although his Pistons coach, Chuck Daly, would prefer a few fewer dates and a few more dunks.

Anyhow, I figured Salley dropped by for a few tips, or maybe some of Wilt's old phone numbers. They started talking. Next thing you know, they'd be on the air saying: "Betty from Hoboken? You knew Betty from Hoboken? Last time I saw her—"

I tried to think fast: What would Dr. Ruth do?

I went back to sports. I asked Wilt about the NBA. About salaries. About the time he scored 100 in one night. Points, that is.

"Let's go to the phones," I said, satisfied I had diverted the subject. "Hello, you're on the air ..."

"Yeah, Wilt? About the 20,000 women. That's, like, unbelievable!"

Now. I know many women are reading this column, and perhaps some feel Wilt's claim is insulting. Perhaps they feel women should not be rung up like a pinball score.

To these women I say: You're right. At least I think you're right. But what do I know? I consider it a good night if a waitress takes my order.

"I love women, and I truly respect women," Wilt said. I have no doubt as to the former. And, actually, I can believe the latter. Wilt Chamberlain is not into groping, *a la* Mike Tyson. (After 20,000 love scenes, how much of a thrill can groping be?)

Wilt says he simply enjoys making love, and has done so with women of all races and nationalities. He says as far as he knew — he claims he always asked — none of his partners were married, because he does not believe in infidelity. He also says he never had sex right before a game.

I hope he told Salley that.

So is it true? Who knows? Maybe, it's like Wilt writes in his book, "There are a few of us who are fortunate enough to be in a position to fulfill our lustful desires. And I'm one of those lucky ones."

Or, as the old song goes:
Wise men say, only fools rush in
But I can't help falling in love with you
and you and you and you and you and you ... ∎

Now let's cry and cheer for AIDS' other victims

A nd now it's time to treat everyone like Earvin (Magic) Johnson. That's the real lesson of these terrible last few days. The eruption of love, support and sympathy for the stricken NBA star was a wonderful thing to see. But when you think about it, of all the patients in the world with the AIDS virus, Magic may need this the least. He is extremely wealthy, can get the finest doctors and will be honored and loved no matter how sick, heaven forbid, he gets.

What about the rest? Who loves them today?

If I were an AIDS patient watching the world since 6 p.m. Thursday, when news that Johnson was retiring because he had the virus literally burned across the nation, lighting the sky, erasing all other stories — the Detroit TV stations actually reported no other news that night — I might cry a bittersweet tear.

Where was everybody, I might wonder, when I got sick?

The truth is AIDS did not begin with Magic and it won't end with him either. If we lived in parts of Africa, I doubt we would have time to notice Thursday's news; we'd be too busy tending to the dying members of our families. If we lived in India, the story that a basketball player had been stricken might raise only a sigh, because how much can sadness is left for one when hundreds of thousands are falling all around you?

As Americans, we were squeamishly innocent about AIDS before Thursday. We turned from its glare, swept it into a corner, dismissed it as a curse for other people, weirdos, gays, drug addicts, promiscuous bar-hoppers. Even when some big Hollywood celebrity began losing weight and was photographed looking gaunt and pale, we told ourselves, "Well, it's a shame, but Hollywood people, you know how they are ... ."

This is not Hollywood. This is not India. This is right outside your door.

Can you hear it?

T wo images burn in my mind this morning. Both, not surprisingly, come from the TV screen.

The first was Friday night, when Magic Johnson bopped onstage with Arsenio Hall, who whooped and waved in his normal idiotic fashion, as the cheering audience rose to its feet.

"I'm still gonna be the same old Earvin, happy-go-lucky, living life to its fullest and having a good time," Magic said, smiling. It was a feel-good program, and you walked away believing the man is special enough to beat this thing.

Then, the other image, on ABC's "Nightline" in the wee hours Friday morning. Among Ted Koppel's five guests — four of whom were healthy and had only praise and support for Johnson — was one man from an AIDS organization who is also afflicted with the virus, a disturbing fellow named Kramer. He was not as young or as handsome as Magic. He had short white hair, glasses and a frightening expression, like the butler in a haunted house. This is what Kramer said — not even said, but yelled — at the camera:

"Magic Johnson is going to die! I am going to die! We are all going to die! There are 40 million potential victims out there. This is not an epidemic, Mr. Koppel, this is a plague!"

There was no band playing, and nobody clapped.

Somewhere between those two images, I hope, lies the clue to our next step. We cannot stop with the smiles on the "Arsenio" show, making us feel good, because this is beyond feeling good, and it is beyond sending letters to LA, telling Magic you still love him. That is a fine thing to do, sure, but let's be honest: It's easy to love Magic. He is famous, heroic; he has a smile that would melt chocolate off a Milky Way.

It may not be as easy to love the AIDS patient down the street, the gay man with the thin, bony face, the pale woman dressed in now-baggy clothes, the victims who gather outside city halls with signs asking for support. But they deserve your emotions, too.

One of the best books about the AIDS crisis was entitled "And The Band Played On," suggesting that, for all the horror, the healthy part of the world basically ignored this disease. From now on, that is unforgivable, and I am not just talking about education. Yes, education is essential — you cannot believe how many teenagers still think a condom is something somebody else wears — but we have tried for years to teach teens about birth control, and even that has been slow.

Meantime, people are dying. We need money, right now, to fight this disease, to research it, to try experimental cures, as they are doing in European countries that are far ahead of us. We need money and not just your contributions; we need money from our government, which has been all too content to have voters think of AIDS as a gay disease, since it meant less pressure to spend on a cure.

What we don't need is a cut in the budget for the Centers for Disease Control, which thanks to our administration is what will happen next year. What we don't need is George Bush conveniently admitting he "hasn't done enough" on the AIDS issue, after the Magic story breaks and Bush sees it could hurt his re-election chances if he says anything less.

What we don't need are people like Sen. Jesse Helms, who, in his disgusting fashion, actually supported legislation that forbade federal funding for AIDS education if anything in the material was "offensive."

Like what, Jesse? The word "gay"? Or "sex"? How about the word "dead"? That's the one we should find most offensive.

Magic Johnson was unlucky, and now he is being brave; we need to be the latter to avoid being the former. If you truly believe in what Magic says, and you want to prove it, you find time for other victims, the ones without any championship rings. You don't treat them like lepers. You give them your time; you give them a kind word.

And then you get on the phone and behind the typewriter and you get out in the streets and you don't stop badgering your lawmakers until they appropriate fewer dollars to their own special interests and a lot more toward saving the world from this horror that takes no names, only corpses, and is getting closer to your doorstep every minute. ∎

Juicy rematch with Bulls is really more of a lemon

November 13

CHICAGO — Well, soap opera fans, let's begin with the moment you all were waiting for: Michael Jordan and Isiah Thomas actually touching each other for the first time since last year's nasty playoff finale. It's true! I saw it! Just before game time Tuesday night, they shook hands at centercourt, and exchanged a few words. One can only imagine:

ISIAH: Hi, Mike. I hear Barcelona water gives you diarrhea.

JORDAN: Is there someone talking? I don't see anyone talking …

Actually, what they really said was: "Have a good game, man," which, put into regular talk, means, "May you drop dead in toxic waste."

And with that, the rematch began.

Unfortunately for Detroit, that handshake was as close as the Pistons would come to His Airness and the Chicago Book of the Month Club Tuesday night. By the third quarter, Jordan would be cooling his toes on the bench, resting up for tomorrow's full day of endorsements and rumor denials, his Bulls so far ahead, they were in a different ZIP code. And the Pistons? They would be playing Lance Blanks and Charles Thomas and wondering what happened to the great game everyone was predicting.

Let's examine what happened. Ready?

Detroit couldn't make a shot.

Any questions?

Defense was all right, rebounding was all right, offense was a big problem," said Chuck Daly, after watching his team miss basket after basket and get stuffed by the world champs, 110-93. "An old coach used to say, 'You gotta be able to score 100 points,' and right now, given our people, even moving the ball around, I'm not sure we could do that."

Hmm. That does not say much for Jack McCloskey, the GM, who supposedly revamped this team over the summer to score more points and better compete with athletic teams such as the Bulls. Did Jack make a mistake? More on that in a minute. Right now, soap opera fans, I know what you want. You want to hear about … The Fight!

Actually, it was more like The Shove, which it always is in the NBA. It began in the frantic third quarter, with Bill Laimbeer — Laimbeer? I am shocked! — planting himself on a Chicago fast break as Horace Grant came right at him. Bang! They collided and fell to the court, their legs tangled, and Laimbeer rose with a loose swing at the air (that, by the way, is as close as Laimbeer ever comes to a real punch). Meanwhile,

Grant — sensing that Laimbeer might do some real damage, like break his goggles — jumped up and ran to the Bulls' bench as if he'd just seen the ghost of Jimmy Hoffa.

Scottie Pippen, seeing Grant so scared, came flying in and got tangled with Isiah Thomas, who pushed him off. Joe Dumars jumped in to stop Pippen, who was going after Isiah, then Jordan jumped in to stop Dumars, but got caught up with John Salley, who was trying to figure where Hammer was sitting, so he could tell him about this new group he's found.

Meanwhile, Isiah had been yanked away by referee Luis Grillo, who was grabbing him now, pushing him back, and making the big "T" sign — and we don't mean "terrific" — and this made Isiah rush and grab him again, which caused Daly, Brendan Malone and Mike Abdenour to run out, Abdenour no doubt there to distribute ice to injured players or anyone who wanted a cool drink. Cool drink? Did someone say cool drink? Suddenly both benches cleared, while the crowd amused itself with cheers of "DETROIT SUCKS!" then "LAIMBEER SUCKS!" and back to the old favorite: "DETROIT SUCKS!"

And next thing you knew, Chicago was up by 22.

So all in all, it was a pretty average night in the Pistons-Bulls series. Except for one thing: These games are supposed to be close.

Given the fact that McCloskey revamped the team to compete with the Bulls, what did you think of how your 'new' team stacked up?" Daly was asked. He bit his lip, rolled his eyes, and said, very diplomatically: "It is my job as coach to try to find players to score."

He forced a grin. You can figure it out.

Meanwhile, in the locker room, the Pistons took the loss in stride. Dumars (1-for-11 shooting) said they were "in the game until the third quarter," when the Bulls jumped from three points up to 22 points up. And Laimbeer said, "We're just not playing well offensively right now."

When your leading scorer is Dennis Rodman (20 points), I think that's a fair assessment.

Time out! Hammer said, and I quote: "It's only one game, baby. Heh-heh. Hammer time!"

Observation on the Bulls: They played tremendous defense and seemed to have three players on every Piston who threatened to shoot.

Observation on the Pistons: If they have to rely on William Bedford all year, they're dead.

As to "The Fight"?

Said Grant: "Detroit hasn't changed a bit."

Said Laimbeer: "I didn't do anything."

So everything's back to normal. By the way, no one shook hands after this game except Detroit's Darrell Walker and Chicago's Rory Sparrow, neither of whom was with these teams last year.

Don't worry. They'll learn. ∎

Utley's best medicine:
A friend by his side

November 20

The man behind the desk marked "Patient Information" looked up at the next customer, his eyes widening slightly, as if to say, "This one must be a football player."

"I'm here to see my buddy," said Roman Fortin.

"His name?"

"Mike Utley."

The man checked the list, then gave Fortin a red pass and pointed him toward the intensive-care unit. Fortin, dressed in blue jeans and a white shirt and a blue-jeans jacket, lumbered toward the elevator in a nervous hurry, past the cafeteria and the flower shop and the newspaper boxes, one of which carried the headline: "Utley May Never Walk Again."

Fortin pressed the elevator button and stared as it lit. He had been on the sideline when it happened Sunday, the first play of the fourth quarter. Initially, he cheered with the crowd, because the Lions had scored the go-ahead touchdown. But wait. Where was Utley, his long-haired lineman buddy, his roommate on the road? How come he wasn't running back with the rest of them, shaking his fists?

Then Fortin looked out and saw why: Utley's massive body was a stiff lump in the middle of the field, the referees were kneeling over him, tapping his arms, and then the paramedics ran out with a stretcher and Fortin ran out, too. Three minutes. Five minutes. No movement. Utley's legs were dead. He said he couldn't feel them. Orders were shouted. Don't touch his neck! Leave the helmet on! "You'll be OK," Fortin told his friend, even as they tied Utley to a stretcher with enough tape to rope a steer. They wheeled him away, put him on an ambulance, and the game continued.

Now Fortin marched his big body down the quiet hospital hallway, his feet slapping against the squeaky-clean shine. "I gotta let Mike know I'm here. I just want to tell him, you know …"

What do you tell him? What do you say? That it was worth it? That everything will be OK? Neither is true. Even as Fortin pushed the door and softly entered the intensive-care room and stood over his friend, who was flat on the bed, and whispered, "Hey, Mike, how's it going?" and Mike mumbled, "Hey, Roman" — even then, both knew things were far from OK. The clock was ticking on Utley. Every minute that passed without improvement was another dollar on the square that says he never walks again. That is the ugly, brutal truth.

So is this: Football is a bloody business, where knees explode and arms pop out of sockets, and now and then, even parts of the spine snap and rupture into little pieces. Naturally, this morning, people are screaming about the violence of the sport — even though Utley's injury was the result of a freakish fall, not a hit — and of course, they are right. But what good will that do Utley now?

Here, Tuesday morning, was something that would help him more. Fortin, his fellow lineman, his friend. They met last year. They lifted weights together. They went to gun clubs together and shot handguns. And lest you think everything they did was high-testosterone, know that Fortin also brought Utley, a 25-year-old bachelor, home to his wife and kids — this wild giant with the page-boy haircut, the motorcycles,the heavy-metal music, and here he was going with the family to Pizza Hut.

Nobody really knew these guys. They weren't star players. Offensive linemen never are. "I would have liked Mike whether he played football or not," Fortin said. "You like somebody, you like him."

Fortin stayed in the room, hovering over his friend. Utley said he wished they would help him sit up. He also said he was hungry, and asked Fortin if his wife "could make me some of those chocolate chip cookies." Fortin smiled. They talked very little about football. They talked more about God, and hope, and how he would beat this thing, you'll see. And finally, visiting hours were over. "I told him that I loved him, and that I was praying for him," Fortin said in the hallway. "His spirits are real good and, um … I feel a lot better."

Fortin tapped the wall. He fidgeted. He had just seen his buddy stuck on tubes and machinery, and now he was trying not to cry. "You hear about stuff like this," he said, "but it never means anything until it happens to you or one of your friends."

And he left. A few hours later, doctors made the sad announcement: Utley had not improved. In all likelihood, he would never walk again.

Last Friday, two days before their final game together, Fortin and Utley went to a movie. They usually chose action films (naturally) but this time they just ran into any theater, didn't even know what was playing, and wound up watching "The Fisher King" — "an intellectual movie," Fortin moaned — and the whole time, Utley kept teasing. "Great choice, Roman. Really great choice."

Slapping and joking, they barely noticed the scene near the end of the film, in which Robin Williams lies hospitalized, in a coma, and Jeff Bridges sits over him and cries, realizing just how good a friend he might lose. Because it is Hollywood, Williams naturally awakes, he fully recovers, and the final scene has the two men laughing together in Central Park.

You think about Mike Utley, paralyzed for life, and you watch Roman Fortin trying not to cry in the hospital lobby, and you say to yourself, if only life worked out like the movies. If only it did. ∎

The kick is good now, and the memory is bad

November 22

TALLAHASSEE, Fla. — I placed the football on the grass and held it upright with one finger. The goalpost was 34 yards away. I asked Gerry Thomas whether he could make it now, and he said, "Oh, yeah."

He measured off the steps. He looked at his toes and exhaled. Then he rushed into the ball and thudded his foot against the leather.

It was a good kick, the ball soaring end over end, high and straight between the uprights into the empty bleachers. It landed on a concrete step and bounced into the air. You could picture the referees holding up their hands. Good! Three points!

A breeze blew. Thomas shook his head.

"I wish I had done that Saturday," he said.

Saturday was different, of course. There were 60,000 people screaming and all those Miami players coming after him with blood in their eyes. There were TV cameras in every corner, millions watching at home, Thomas' teammates on their knees, saying a prayer, his coach glaring intently. "Come on, hit it! Hit it and we win, we win, we can win the national championship! ..."

They didn't win. They lost. By one point. That final field goal, from this very left hash mark on the Doak Campbell Stadium field, missed by the length a textbook, and Gerry Thomas suffered one of those terrible sports moments when you want to grab the air of the immediate past and strangle it, punch its stomach, make it to spit up the moment so you can do it over.

But you never get it over. You have to go on.

And that's even harder than missing.

"It's still in the paper every day," sighed Thomas, a 20-year-old walk-on kicker who doesn't even have a scholarship at Florida State — but certainly has a slice of immortality. "People have been pretty nice, but they're not going to forget. I'm sure I won't forget it either, not for the rest of my life."

You wonder about college football, the pressure, the hype. It's fun for winners. But defeat can make losers feel like bugs squashed against a windshield. One minute you're flying, next minute ...

When the game between the two best teams in college football ended Saturday — Miami 17, Florida State 16, ruining the Seminoles' perfect season, wiping out their No. 1 ranking — Thomas, who had made three field goals earlier in the game, trudged to the locker room and sat with his head hung. It was not his fault — not alone, his teammates and coaches made plenty of mistakes. But suddenly, the door burst open and reporters came charging in.

"They were on top of Gerry before he had a chance," recalled Dan Mowrey, the former starting placekicker whose erratic performance had led coach Bobby Bowden to replace him with Thomas just last month. "He wasn't ready to talk. He had just missed the biggest kick of his life. So me and some of my teammates formed a wall around him. We said a few things, shoved some of the reporters. It was nasty."

Eventually, Thomas was snuck into the bathroom, where he cried for a minute. Should any kid have to endure this? Thomas is a thin young man with a Billy Bathgate innocence and a smile that seems both happy and sad. He was raised, of all places, in a town called Niceville, Fla. Niceville? No doubt he felt like going home Saturday night.

"You know, I'd make that kick nine out of 10 times," he said now, staring at the bright yellow goalposts in the empty stadium. And then, because words are never enough in sports, he began to show me. He kicked the ball when I held it. He kicked with the automatic holder. He kicked over and over, the same way every time, his head down, his leg coming through the ball and booming it into the air. Two, three, four, five times. Seven, eight, nine times. Each time, the ball rose and spun through the uprights, a game-winner, a kick of dreams, good! It was good! It should have been good! …

"What have you learned about the difference between a hero and a goat?" I asked.

"It's inches," he said. "Inches."

Not too many came around Florida State this week. The Seminoles have no game scheduled Saturday, and the national swarm of media has moved across the state, to Miami, the new No. 1.

"This campus is dead," Mowery said. "It's completely different than it was last week. It was like all year we had this man called Dream and he was with us, and then Saturday, he was killed."

No one feels his loss more than Gerry Thomas. You understand that in order to have the glory of big-time college sports, you must have a flip side, if someone wins, someone must lose with equal intensity. Such is the arithmetic of heroism. But it doesn't seem fair. Thomas is a humble kid, a sophomore computer major with only a vague idea of what he wants to be when he grows up, yet his moniker already has been decided. In the sports world, he is "the guy who missed the kick."

"It's not the end of the world; I know that," he said softly, standing on that field, tossing a football from one hand to another. "I have more things in my life than just making a kick. … But I should have made it. I can make that kick …"

Nine out of 10 times. I saw him do it.

He only wishes everyone else did, too. ∎

Ball screams cheap shot, vows to avenge his agony

December 9

Jerry Ball wanted somebody dead. He knew what had happened. He'd seen it a thousand times. Only this time it had happened to him, this nasty football trick: One guy holds you up, the other chops you low. And now it was his knee that was throbbing and his turn to sit on the motorized cart that would drive him off the field and into his street clothes, and, damn it, he wanted no part of this. Better a crane should lift him through the roof than to ride off like some wounded soldier in front of the enemy with their cheap-trick garbage. Helpless, he turned like a caged beast, maddened with this sudden inability to run or to even kick somebody, and he banged a fist down on the back of the cart and I swear you could hear it reverberate in the upper deck.

That was a call to arms, a declaration of war, and for the next three hours, that's what it was out at the Silverdome on Sunday — bloody mayhem. You would have sworn the building was under siege: so much noise, so many stretchers, so many injured and hobbling. There were cramped muscles and twisted knees and the kind of vicious hits that, were this a musical, would be underscored by cymbal crashes. Sacks. Fumbles. Players disconnected from the ball and then their senses. In the end, when the bombs stopped falling, the Lions would learn the meaning of character — just as they would likely gain entry to the promised land, the playoffs. But it cost them. They lost one of their top two defensive players, most likely for the rest of the season.

And now Jerry Ball wanted revenge. Satisfaction. Somebody dead. Something. The game was just about over, and he was doing something I have never seen done before: planting himself on a folding chair in the tunnel where the players exit. He was in a gray sports coat and black shirt, his new crutches by his side, even as photographers and reporters raced back and forth. He glared down the tunnel as the players began to trickle in.

"You waiting for (Brad) Baxter?" someone asked, referring to the fullback who had chopped Ball at the knees in the first quarter.

"I ain't waiting for Baxter," he barked. "I want Coslet."

Bruce Coslet is the coach of the Jets.

"Damn chop block," he said. "Completely illegal. They know it."

The first Jets player to pass him was cornerback James Hasty.

"You all right, big fella?" Hasty said, from under his helmet.

Ball sneered. "Yeah, I'm … nah, I ain't all right." He didn't even look at the guy.

Hasty moved on.

M ore players converged in the tunnel, their cleats clomping on the concrete floor. Jets defensive tackle Bill Pickel spotted Ball, and came over.

"Hey, you OK?"

Ball glared. Pickel moved on.

Now came Baxter, the guy whose helmet went right into Ball's knee on that second-and-five play in the first quarter — a play in which Ball was completely engaged in a standing block with center Jim Sweeney. That's supposed to be illegal, going for a guy's knees when he's engaged at the arms. Nothing was called. Ball went down. He knew his season was done.

Baxter saw Ball and trotted right to him. Big mistake.

"Yo," Baxter mumbled, "I was just trying to block someone, baby, you know how it is, everybody got to block somebody, I was just doing my job ... ."

"Hey," Ball snarled, leaning into him. "That was a f - - - - - up play. You know it."

"I was just trying to block."

"That was f - - - - - up."

"Let's go over here and talk, man."

"I can't walk!" Ball yelled.

Baxter slid away into the crowd of players.

"Where's Coslet at?" Ball said. By now the crowd was thick, players, cheerleaders, referees, cart drivers. Ball spotted some green jackets, and across the way he saw Coslet moving quickly. He couldn't get to him, so he lifted a crutch in the air and yelled — he yelled above the cleats and above the engine noise and above the field music and there was no mistaking the voice of Jerry Ball, a big man cut down.

"YO!" he screamed after Coslet. "IT WASN'T WORTH IT! 'CAUSE YOU STILL GOT YOUR A - - KICKED!"

Coslet looked over his shoulder, then turned away and was swallowed by crowd. And he was gone.

I n the end, that will be all the retribution coming to Jerry Ball this season — that, and the fact that his team, which for so many years had lacked a winning instinct, much less a killer instinct, now has managed to find both. Listen up, Detroit football fans: You can circle Sunday on your calendars, because this was the day the Lions learned just how tough they have become.

This was George Jamison making a crushing sack on third-and-one, and Dan Owens making a crushing sack on third-and-two, and Melvin Jenkins making a crushing sack that separated Jets quarterback Ken O'Brien from the ball. This was William White slamming so hard into running back Freeman McNeil you could hear his bones rattle. This was Barry Sanders being treated like a dish rag, thrown into the Jets' sideline whenever they got a chance, quite often late — no penalty flags again — yet managing to burn them for 114 yards rushing.

This was injuries and more injuries: Ray Crockett being carried off the field by four of his teammates; Bennie Blades being carted off; Tracy Hayworth lying flat on the sideline, as doctors worked on him. There was even a fan, trying to streak, who fell from the railing. He was taken off on a stretcher.

"I haven't seen so many stretchers in any game I've ever played here," Kevin Glover admitted, after the Lions held off the Jets, 34-20, in that furious, desperate and brutal 3½-hour war. "We had to suck it up and win. And we did."

He looked around the room. Eric Sanders had his knee wrapped in ice and crutches under his arm. Jamison was hobbling, Chris Spielman was hobbling. Toby Caston pulled off his uniform and just stared out.

"What they did to Jerry was wrong," Caston said. "It was a cheap shot. And we had to come together for him."

It seems this team is doing that every week, doesn't it? Coming together for a fallen Rodney Peete, for a fallen Mike Cofer, for a fallen Mike Utley, now for a fallen Jerry Ball. You wonder at what point the fallen exceeds the material needed to come together.

Apparently not yet. The Lions are 10-4, they are going to the playoffs almost certainly. And there they will need all the lessons they learned Sunday, because in the playoffs, everyone plays like this, tooth-and-nail — using their teeth and nails if they must.

So be it. Football is brutal. But it shouldn't be cheap. The Lions lost their biggest defensive threat Sunday, on a play that shouldn't be allowed. The referees went deaf and dumb. The Jets got away with murder. All Ball got to do was yell as the enemy slipped away.

"I promise you this," Ball said afterward, pressing down on his crutches and speaking loud enough for his teammates to hear. "If we ever play those guys again, I'm gonna be haunting them in their dreams."

You can bang on that. ∎

Sports' big stars come a'caroling for Christmas

December 15

Snow is falling. I hear a knock. I open my door. And look who I see doing their sports Christmas carols ...

Wayne Fontes, "Silent Night"
Silent night, roster is light,
This one's injured, that one's tight
Down went Rodney, and Jerry and Mike
Eric and Cofer, they're riding the bike
Could we get a delay-ayyy
and do the playoffs next May?

Cecil Fielder, "Santa Claus is Coming to Town"
You better not run, you better not hide
You better unlock that bank vault real wide
Cecil's agent's coming to town.
He's making a list, checking it twice,
Adding 10 zeros onto his price
Cecil's agent's coming to town.
He knows you need my home runs,
And RBIs count too,
He only wants what the market bears
Say Bobby Bonilla times two — oooh!
You better not scheme, you better not plot,
All that we want, is all that you got
Cecil's agent's coming to town.

Chuck Daly, "The Christmas Song"
Bedford missing on an open shot
Laimbeer scoring all-time lows,
Isiah's drive being blocked by a giant
Aguirre moans about his toes.
Everybody knows
We used to be the champions
Now we lose to Miami
Though it's been said, many times, many ways,
Let me ask you, God
Why me?

Keith Jackson, "Winter Wonderland"

Sleigh bells ring — Whoa Nellie!
Children sing — on his belly!
We're making a stir — a real barn burner!
Walking in a winter wonde—FUMBLLLLE!

Wilt Chamberlain, "I Saw Mommy Kissing Santa Claus"

I saw Wiltie kissing Mrs. Claus
Underneath the mistletoe last night
He said, "This might be fun
You'd be 20,001
I've had the rest, now I'll try the best
While Santa's on the run!"
I saw Wiltie kissing Mrs. Claus
Till her husband burst in on his sleigh
Then Wiltie got a shock
With saltpeter stuffed in his sock
No more kissing Mrs. Claus today.

The Red Wings' front office, "God Rest Ye Merry Gentlemen"

God rest ye Sergei Fedorov
And Dosvedanya too
We sure are glad we got you out
'Fore Russia split in two
You shoot, you score, you pass, you fly,
Fans really love your act
We hope you don't ask for "new contract"
That's a fact
We hope you don't ask for "new contract."

Rodney Peete, Randall Cunningham, Joe Montana, "I'll Be Home For Christmas"

We'll be home for Christmas
Doing therapy,
Watching soaps and horoscopes
We dream of recovery.
Christmas is depressing
While our teams still play
But we'll be back next Christmas — if they don't give our lockers away.

Bo Schembechler and Ed McNamara, "The Little Drummer Boy"

We need a stadium a new sta-di-um,
You lack the cash to build a gym-na-si-um.

That's why I came to you
stop sucking your thumb.
Don't tell us what to do
you bum-bum-bum-bum,
Who you call bum?
We want it done!
Put it downtown or else, your new sta-di-um will never come.

Desmond Howard, "Rockin' Around the Christmas Tree"

Trophies around my Christmas tree
What a happy holiday
Can't even move, with all these plaques
Got the Heisman on my knee.
Trophies around my Christmas tree
And the agents on their way
Like to stay here at Michigan—
wait, how much did you say?

John DiBiaggio and George Perles, "Blue Christmas"

We'll have a Green Christmas without you
I am not leaving, John boy, so I doubt you
It's been fun, now you're done
No more coach or AD
Hold on there buster,
You forget about paying me?
We'll have a Green Christmas without you
I stuff your stocking with horse-poop you lout, you
I am right, I have might
Hope you choke Christmas night
And you — no you — have a green — drop dead
Green Christmas. ∎

Lions are playoff-bound and homeward-bound

December 16

G REEN BAY, Wis. — For so many years, they were the orphans with runny noses pressed against the banquet window, watching other teams enjoy the feast. Now here they were, all grown up, caked with blood and dirt, chests heaving, sweat freezing into tiny icicles on their eyebrows — and they were trying to get a better look again, peering in, straining their necks, watching, this time, as the officials planted the yard markers into the frozen ground of Lambeau Field, two sticks that would finally answer the Detroit Lions' question: Playoffs, in or out?

"I was marching around in circles saying, 'Don't let them get the first down, please don't let them get it,' " Chris Spielman would say.

"Not me, I was standing right over that yard marker," Bennie Blades would attest. "You know how they move those things sometimes. ..."

It had been fourth-and-inches, late in the game, the Packers trying to steal this thing back from the Lions who had stolen it away. Fourth-and-inches in Lions territory, and the whole afternoon of desperate, error-plagued winter football had come down to this: Mike Tomczak took the snap and handed off to Vince Workman, who headed into the stack of bodies, looking for a hole, and Spielman and Blades plowed into him with every ounce of ferocity left after three hours in the Arctic Circle. A pileup. Screams both ways.

On the sidelines, coach Wayne Fontes held his breath and Kevin Glover bent over as if doing calisthenics, trying to get a better angle. Suddenly, the whole Lions team was on its knees or tiptoes: Where's the ball, where are they marking it?

"Pleeeese ..." Spielman mumbled.

Down went the sticks, into the ground, first one, then the other, the second landing a measly inch away from the football. The referee set his hands. Short. Short? SHORT! The Lions burst into the air, screaming, cheering, celebrating their rite of passage, and the playoff word they had been waiting for, what, a lifetime?

In.

"Ho-leee! This is like Star Trek!" yelled an elated Lomas Brown in the exultant Detroit locker room, after the Lions outgasped the Packers, 21-17, to make the playoffs for the first time in eight years. "You know, boldly go where no man has gone before? Explore new worlds? That's what this is like for us. A new world!"

In.

D id you ever think you would see it? Did you ever think, three years ago, when, on another frozen Wisconsin afternoon, against this same Packers team, Wayne Fontes took over this perennially sad franchise and was so overwhelmed that he cried after the victory, weeping and hugging players — did you ever think you would see this? The Lions, 11-4, tied for the third-best record in the whole NFL, assured of at least a home-field wild-card game and possibly even a first-round bye as Central Division champions?

"We finally have a chance at the dance," said Fontes, his skin beet-red as he defrosted in the locker room. "I remember my first win here. I know I shed a tear or two after that."

"Did you shed any today?" he was asked.

"If I keep talking, I might."

He smiled, and almost did.

Now granted, Sunday's victory was hardly a work of art. With a windchill of minus-20 and gusts that would suck the life from a penguin, footing was slippery and the ball was an enemy, cold and heavy, so that most of the time the quarterbacks seemed to be throwing shot puts. There were six fumbles, 19 punts, and the operative phrase of the day was "change of possession."

But the point is this: The old Lions would have found a way to lose this game, and the new Lions found a way to win it — just as they found a way to beat Chicago on Thanksgiving, and Miami on a goal-line stand, and Minnesota after trailing by 17 points. On Sunday they rallied — outdoors, mind you — with two fourth-quarter touchdowns, one a pretty, third-down timing lob from Eric Kramer to Robert Clark; the other, a Mel Gray special, a punt return from heaven, 78 yards and six missed tackles long.

And then, of course, that fourth-and-inches. The final crunch.

"Do you think making the playoffs officially ends any fears about the old Lions habits?" Spielman was asked.

"I don't think we deserve to even be compared to anything old anymore," he bellowed. "What has this team shown all year except character, desire, class and a will to win?"

Nothing. That's quite enough.

In.

A s the players undressed, the locker room grew more and more emotional, as if the idea were really sinking in. Players such as Brown and Glover, who have been with the Lions for years and have had deep talks about how valid an NFL career is if you never make the playoffs — and finally they were there, grinning, slapping each other's tired flesh. And here was Kramer, the quarterback from nowhere, a guy who seems to do a lot of things wrong except win, and once again he was surrounded by reporters, that spacy look on his face as if to say, "Two years ago I was in the Canadian League. Can you believe this?"

And here, standing quietly, was Barry Sanders, only the single biggest reason the Lions are where they are today. He had carried the ball 27 times, mobbed, as usual, on every play, but he made the critical yardage when he had to. Now he was dressed in his jacket and tie, and team owner William Clay Ford came to shake his hand.

"Congratulations," Ford said.

"Congratulations to you," said Sanders, grinning.

A pause here to take this all in. Sure, there have been some letdown moments this season — the opening-day massacre in Washington, the scalping in San Francisco, the still-unforgivable collapse against the lowly Tampa Bay Bucs. But look: The regular season is nearly over, and you can count the Lions' defeats on one hand, while you need three hands to count their victories. And don't forget, they pulled off Sunday's victory without Jerry Ball, Eric Sanders, Mike Cofer, Mike Utley or Rodney Peete, which only constitutes nearly a quarter of their starting lineup.

From amid the clamor came a sudden voice, scratchy and old. "EVERYBODY LISTEN!" It was the man they call the Brow, Joe Diroff, the unofficial Detroit sports nut, and a sort of symbol that your Motown team has made it. He was there with the Wings in 1986, and the Tigers in 1987 and the Pistons in 1988 and now, after driving all night to get here, he stood in the middle of these exhausted, bloodied football bodies, an old man with a raspy voice, and began a cheer. And remarkably, like little kids, the Lions joined in:

"Can we do it?"

"CAN WE DO IT?"

"Are we tough?

"ARE WE TOUGH?"

"We're the Lions!"

"WE'RE THE LIONS!"

"Red hot stuff!"

"RED HOT STUFF!"

And they cheered and clapped and laughed like Christmas. Can you believe it? The Lions in the playoffs, at the banquet table, for real, no more nose against the window?

"Bold new world," Lomas Brown repeated, and Captain Kirk could not have sounded more excited.

In.

At last. ∎

1992

Spielman brings passion for perfection to his work

January 8

A lone in the dark he sits, behind the projector, his thumb clicking the remote button as the players on screen move backward, then forward, then backward, then forward. He calls the action like a drill sergeant:

"Corner trap (click) ... now a sprint 15 (click) ... this is a 15 bend. See that tight end? (click) He's supposed to block No. 52. (click) He's gotta get his butt up there, now! Look, (click) he's hesitating, (click) he's hesitating (click) ... GO, RIGHT NOW! (click) ... too late!"

Coaches do this kind of film watching, gulping coffee and rubbing their eyes. And so Chris Spielman, a coach's son, does it, too. He is the only player at the Silverdome at this hour. It is Tuesday, an off day, the day other Lions are at home sleeping or playing with the kids.

And here is Spielman with his joystick.

"This is Washington's draw play (click) ... see that hole? (click) I gotta be there (click) ... ooh, (click) I'll be faster than that guy Sunday, guaranteed (click)."

You might think this unusual behavior for an athlete, even in the playoffs, but remember, we are talking about Chris Spielman, whose first tackle came at age 5, when he took down his grandmother. She had just walked in the door, and Chris wanted to play football, and he wrapped her in his arms and — whompf! — down she went.

"Jeez," I say. "Did you hurt her?"

"Nah, she's still living."

He flicks on the lights and laughs, his neck muscles rolling under his T-shirt. His hair is matted, his stubble at least three days' thick, and there is a scar on his forehead. I ask Spielman the last time he was without a scar someplace on his body, and he says, "When I was born."

There is no telling how Sunday's NFC championship game will turn out, but I can promise you the man who will bring the most spit and desire to that game will be the man behind this stack of game films. You think Chris Spielman was born to play football? When he was 3, he was racing through the house with his older brother, Rick. They were heading for the door, Chris lunged forward — and ran into the wall. Opened this bloody gash on his forehead.

"Dad, does Chris have to get stitches?" Rick asked their father.

"I think so," his father said, frowning.

Legend has it Chris said: "Goody."

But that's only a legend.

And you can't believe every legend you hear, right? Otherwise, you'd think Spielman, 26, is no more than a tightly wound instrument of destruction, a walking set of shoulder pads whose only form of expression is "GRRRRRR!"

Not true. He might be every factory worker's favorite ballplayer, all grit and gristle and overachievement, but he is also a shy, patriotic husband with a thin tenor voice, a guy who sees things simply but honestly and without pretension. He sort of reminds you of the Tom Cruise character in "Born on the Fourth of July" — before he goes to Vietnam. Life is black and white. You work hard. You strive to be the best. And you do what you have to do. Spielman hates wearing neckties, but he'll wear one if he has to. He is not much for books, but he went back to college to earn his degree.

He does not swoon at romance, but he can pull it off. The summer after he was drafted by the Lions, Spielman proposed to his high school sweetheart, Stefanie, the only girlfriend he's ever had. Here's how: He took her to a miniature golf course in Canton, Ohio, and when they reached the 18th hole, he told her he left his keys near the green, could she please go get them? When she got near the hole, she looked down and saw an engagement ring wedged inside. She began to cry.

"Then what did you say?" I ask.

"I said, 'Go ahead and putt.' "

"No, after that."

"Oh. I said, 'Stefanie, will you marry me?' She finally said yes. Afterward, the people gave us a free game because we got engaged on their putt-putt course."

See? Told you he had a romantic side.

This place has good food," he says, pulling open the door. "You ever been here?"

We are entering Klancy's on Opdyke Road, one of Spielman's favorite restaurants — largely because it's within a mile of the Silverdome. Klancy's has a Formica counter, booth tables and, according to Spielman, "great mashed potatoes." Upon spotting the football player, one of the workers immediately motions to a booth near the back. Several waitresses say, "Hi, Chris." The cook pokes his head out and says, "Chris, how ya doin'?' "

Spielman sits down, looking sheepish.

"I told them we were coming. They're kind of excited."

Spielman does not do a lot of interviews outside of the locker room. He is painfully shy about his private life, mostly because when he was in high school in Ohio, his picture was on the cover of a Wheaties box — part of the cereal's efforts to honor young athletes — and instantly, his world was turned upside down. People asked him to speak to Boy Scout troops, to make appearances, to serve as an upstanding example of American youth. That's a tall order for a sweaty teenager who mostly liked to play football, lift weights and watch TV with his buddies. He would go out with Stefanie, and guys would laugh behind his back and call him "the Cheerios boy." He chose to attend Ohio State, not far from home, and that only made his celebrity more intense. He started his freshman year, and from that moment on, everyone on campus knew who he was, every class, every lunchroom.

"The hardest thing for me to do is to let people get close to me," he says. "Mostly because of that Wheaties box thing. I only have about five people who I really let know me. With everyone else, I mostly talk football.

"Maybe because of that, there's this misconception that I'm only a football player, not a person. I always hear how intense I am, and my wife and I talk about that. She tries to get me to stop and ... what is it, smell the roses? But I can't do it. It's not me.

"After a game, whether we win or lose, if there was one play I messed up on, it haunts me for days. I'm in this constant search for perfection, I don't know why. When I come home from a game, I start walking around the house in circles. I go from the living room to the dining room to the kitchen — and I don't even realize I'm doing it. Stefanie says, 'Chris, sit down.' And I say, 'Huh?'"

To understand this intensity, you must understand his relationship with his father, Sonny, a high school coach who took his 4-year-old son to practice, pointed to a group of players and said, "Go watch them." Sonny Spielman wanted his kids tough; he demanded excellence and hard work. When Chris was 11, he took a job raking baseball fields at a summer camp — while other his age were playing on them.

"Responsibility," his father called it.

You hear stories about Chris' obsession with football: how he once smashed a window in college to break into the weight room. How he would meet the Ohio State coaches before sunrise to watch film. "My goal was to get to the building before (head coach) Earle Bruce did," he admits.

That meant 6 a.m. He did it.

Even now, he rises at that hour every day in the off-season to work out. He is so consistently excellent that no one even bothers to ask coach Wayne Fontes how Spielman played this week. He does the film thing every Tuesday and on Sunday he is the general, calling out defensive signals in the two seconds between the time the opposing team drops at the line and snaps the ball. That's not easy.

"Chris is unbelievable," his teammates will tell you, rolling their eyes in a mix of admiration and disbelief.

But he is also human. It is not hard to see beneath the whiskers and the piercing eyes, to find there a shy boy who is trying to earn the love of his father. Is that so unusual?

As he struggles to talk about himself at Klancy's, I notice he has pulled apart several toothpicks and destroyed a straw. Nerves, he says.

Nerves?

Yes. And that's the thing about Spielman. There are a lot of levels operating here. There is the guy who will be counted on to lead the Lions' defense against the Redskins this weekend, but there is also the guy who looks down when people compliment him. It is true he won the Lombardi Trophy and a Pro Bowl selection for his never-ending toughness. It is also true that he wears sweat socks under black dress socks, because the dress ones are "too thin." He swears by his country, his religion, says he would have fought in Vietnam ("definitely"), but when I ask what he would say if a son one day came to him and said "Dad, I want to be a florist" — this is what he answers:

"I'd tell him, 'Be the best florist there is.' "

And ultimately, that is the core of Chris Spielman. His obsession comes not from a desire to inflict pain, but from a desire to be the best, the way his parents taught him. Because of that, he is truly passionate about his work, football, and there are those who say this is not the healthiest obsession.

You know what I think? I think in an age of apathy, passion is not something you criticize. It could be in art, music or football — it is still passion, and it should be celebrated, at least when it blossoms in a fair and decent man, who doesn't ask for more than his share, and doesn't put himself above the mashed potato-eaters.

"I'm really not a grrrr person," he says apologetically, "it's just when I talk football, I get excited. ..."

We understand. You are what you are. So next time passion gets the better of Chris Spielman, maybe you can forgive him.

His grandmother did. ∎

Dream ends in Washington, but Lions' memories sweet

January 13

WASHINGTON — The day began to die on the second play from scrimmage, when Erik Kramer was smothered and the ball squirted loose and the Redskins picked it up as if lifting a penny off the sidewalk. You knew then, somewhere in your stomach, that the theme of this chilly championship game would be simple and sad: The dream ends here.

That it did not end quickly, that the Lions found a few moments, found some spit to blow in the face of overwhelming odds, is both a tribute to this remarkable team and quite likely its legacy. There was no joy in the start of this game and there was no joy in its lopsided finish. But like the season itself, there was something to be said for the middle.

Something good, I think.

Oh, it may be hard to see that right now. This morning, all you see is an image as unsettling as sour milk, Washington quarterback Mark Rypien standing in his backfield, alone as a city beggar, picking his receivers, playing his own personal game, throwing one bomb after another, six points, six points. The Lions never touched him. Compare that with Kramer, who had someone's helmet in his mouth on nearly every play, and you pretty much have this year's NFC championship.

"Every time I looked up it seemed like there were one or two of them," said a bedazzled Kramer, who was sacked four times and knocked down maybe a million more as the Lions evaporated one game shy of the Super Bowl, a 41-10 drubbing by the dominating Redskins.

"Will you be sore tomorrow?" he was asked.

"I'm sore right now."

No doubt they all are. And yet, there were moments. The Lions gave the Redskins maybe half a game, which is half more than most people expected. And if that sounds like we're making excuses for this team, just ask yourself if you thought the Lions would even survive this game nine days ago? The Lions probably never had enough to beat the Redskins, not in this stadium. But they got here. To the NFC championship game. That was surprise enough.

In the locker room after the game, they peeled off their uniforms for the last time. Chris Spielman left his on awhile, his silver pants covered with the mud of defeat. "They're the better team," he mumbled. "They're the better team. ..." Spielman, even more than most, had lusted for this game to be different from the season opener, which was lost to this same team in this same place, 45-0. Sunday was different.

Not different enough.

"They're the better team — right now — and that's hard for me to face. But it's true and I know it. ..."

The dream ends here.

And yet, for a few minutes, they had people wondering, didn't they? Let's face it: Against a great football team, the Lions began as badly as you possibly can begin a game — short of coming out without your clothes on. Their first ball was batted away, their second ball fumbled, their fifth dropped, their sixth intercepted. And yet somehow, come the second quarter, they found themselves trailing only 10-7. Their silver stretch offense had created open receivers, Kramer got his balance back, threw a touchdown pass, Barry Sanders worked a little magic, and the defense held off a goal-line drive, forcing a field goal, and later forced a punt.

"That's when I felt most optimistic," said Sanders, who gained 44 yards on 11 carries. "I knew we had played badly, but we were still in it."

"When did you stop being optimistic?"

He frowned. "Somewhere in the third quarter."

Indeed. As it turns out, that second quarter was the apex of the Lions' day. The Skins scored again, they took a 17-10 halftime lead, and then, in that third quarter, they came out and drove right downfield. Another field goal; 20-10. The Lions then embarked on their last meaningful march, clawing to the Washington 21, only to see an Eddie Murray field goal blocked by a guy named Jumpy Geathers. That was their last gasp. You could almost see the players slump under their shoulder pads. Rypien came out and uncorked a 45-yard bomb to Gary Clark that fell perfectly into his arms, touchdown, and the crowd went crazy. Somewhere in the parking lot, the Lions' driver started the bus.

"You want to win this game so badly that when it starts to slip away, it really hurts you," Lomas Brown said. "They were the better team today. We know that. But we got to within two games of the Super Bowl. Now we have to learn how to win those last two games."

Which is a hell of a thing to say, when you think about it. Do you remember the last time the Lions lost a game? It was Nov. 10, against Tampa Bay. Do you remember what people were saying? "Same old Lions." "Tampa Bay?" "They'll never be any good until they stop beating themselves."

Guess what? They stopped. They shed their skin. They won the next game, and the next, seven in a row, and they came into Sunday with a lot of people thinking they had a chance to upset the Redskins, maybe the best team in the game right now.

You know what they call that?

They call it progress.

And it is that progress — after the sting fades — that the Lions should sleep with this winter. That, and an incredible pastiche of memories.

"What do you think you'll remember most from this season?" someone asked Ray Crockett.

"I'll remember a bunch of guys who came together for one cause ... and I'll remember one special guy who went down for that cause, trying to be the best."

Message to Mike Utley: They went down trying. There's no shame in that. But then, Mike already knows that.

And so, the football season ends in Detroit. The two best teams, Washington and Buffalo, go on to the Super Bowl, and that is how it should be. And yet maybe the best way for Lions fans to remember this season is not by the pictures of Sunday's collapse, but by the pictures leading up to it.

Can you ever forget the sight of Sanders, dancing off tacklers, stepping backward, then bolting ahead for a 47-yard touchdown? Can you ever forget the sight of the Lions huddling at midfield, heads bowed in prayer, thumbs up, a sign to Utley, who sat in a wheelchair 2,000 miles away? Can you ever forget the sight of Jerry Ball in street clothes — about a mile's worth of fabric — screaming his team on, or Rodney Peete or Mike Cofer, faces that will be back next year, healthy, and oh, the possibilities of that!

Isn't that what this whole little adventure was about?

Possibilities? Herman Moore, becoming a receiving force? Willie Green, earning the nickname "Touchdown Machine"? The improved secondary of Crockett and Bennie Blades? Possibilities? They won't understand this in other cities, where their football teams have gone to a playoff or two, maybe a championship, but in Detroit, the biggest miracle of the year was getting people to believe in pro football again. After that, everything's going to be easy.

"You know, I'm really gonna miss these guys," said Brown, looking around the emptying room, the wet floor, the wads of used tape, the dirty towels, the now-ripped sign that read "GET MIKE HIS RING."

"I mean, I miss the guys every year, the camaraderie, the Sunday mornings, all that. But this year, you know, somehow I'm gonna miss 'em more."

And he packed and walked out, headed for the bus.

So it ends, a most remarkable little football season. There was a sign in the end zone at RFK Stadium, a sign that hung prominently in the corner, near where Willie Green caught that first touchdown pass. It read: "Silence of the Lions."

Not anymore. For the first time in a long time, the Detroit Lions made noise, crazy, surprising, beautiful noise, that scooped up our city and took it one game shy of the football rainbow. Take that with you as you head into winter, the best part of this season, the middle.

Now. How long until September? ∎

Luge gave Bonny Warner rare glimpse of the world

February 11

ALBERTVILLE, France — This is an Olympic story, the best kind, the kind that doesn't end in a medal and really doesn't have to. It's the story of a college kid who carried a torch in Lake Placid, N.Y., and, on a dare from a friend, jumped on a luge sled and sort of fell into this whole new world. Had that never happened — had she never been at the track that day, wearing a new sweater that she ripped to shreds when she scraped against the ice walls, and she didn't even care because when she finished her virgin ride she came up hollering "YEEEHAH!" and she was hooked — had that never happened, Bonny Warner might today be just another engineer in just another American company, pulling down a paycheck, watching TV, going to TGI Friday's on weekends.

Instead, she has had this incredible life, been around the world, made friends in countless nations, had one adventure after another. She ends her athletic career today and Wednesday, in the women's single luge. And then she peels off the speed suit and says good-bye. Unless she wins a medal — and she probably won't — you might never know she exists.

But you ought to.

I first met Bonny when I was a young reporter traveling with the luge team through Europe. She was blonde and loud and funny and spirited, and it seemed that everywhere we went, she had friends. It was 1983, and luge was even less known in America than it is today. The U.S. team was about a dozen stouthearted speed nuts who traveled from country to country with their sleds tied to the top of a van, their clothes packed in duffel bags and their meal money often limited to whatever a candy bar cost at a gas station. You had to love this sport to endure it; you had to love climbing onto a sled and dropping into a frozen track, which curved like a snake and whipped you to 60 m.p.h. between its horrifying ice walls.

Bonny Warner loved it. At the time, she was the best hope America had in women's luge. That first ride back in Lake Placid had piqued her interest enough that she tried a two-week luge camp — which she paid for by selling her Olympic pin collection — and that camp had been enough to make her want to train in Europe. One problem: She was a college student. Where would the money come from?

The phone rang. It was an official from Levi Strauss, who informed Bonny she had just won $5,000 in a sweepstakes contest.

Hmmm. This stuff happens only in movies, right?

"You know how I won that?" Warner said, laughing the other night. "I had been shopping with my mom at the Gap in California. She was buying something for my sister and I was bored, so I filled in this entry and dropped it in a box."

On such moments can a life turn …

Of course, Bonny could have blown the money. Bought a car. Bought a vacation. Instead she bought a sled. And a plane ticket to West Germany. And she showed up at a luge track in Konigssee and told them she wanted to learn how to do what they did. So surprised were the Germans at the sight of this American student who spoke only English and didn't even know that there were track fees to pay, that they accepted her, gave her a job, and let her learn. And learn. And learn …

By the time she rejoined her U.S. peers she was, by their standards, a player. And thus began a wonderful 12-year journey of snow-covered towns in Switzerland and Austria and East and West Germany, week after week, race after race, winter after winter. She would go to school in the warm months — at Stanford — and maintain her training by practicing on a summer sled on wheels. She worked at luge tracks, she worked as a waitress, she worked as a nanny, she worked in the college cafeteria. The money came, the money went. You didn't think about money. You thought about going faster. You thought about zipping through those narrow ice straightaways. You thought about those cramped hotels and those bumpy van rides and the new friends you made and the adventures you had …

You thought about marching in the Olympic ceremonies.

"The first time I really felt like an Olympian was in Sarajevo, 1984, when they gave us our team jacket," Warner said. "I never had money to spend on clothes, and here they were giving us this sheepskin coat. I remember thinking, 'Wow, this is the most expensive jacket I've ever owned!' And then I looked inside, and it said: 'Made especially for the U.S. Olympic team.' I was, like, wow …

"Then, when we were inside the tunnel for the opening ceremonies, I heard the noise of the crowd. And when we stepped into the stadium, I saw all those people cheering and waving flags. And I just burst into tears …"

Bonny Warner is 29 now. These are her third and last Olympics. She wept in Sarajevo. She wept in Calgary. And last Saturday, under a winter moon in Albertville, when the announcer bellowed *"Les Etats-Unis!"* she got the wet eyes again. Maybe because it was her last time. Maybe because there are still people out there — despite the Carl Lewises and the NBA marketing types — who feel that wearing USA on your back is about as big a thrill as you can get.

Bonny Warner never won an Olympic medal — her best finish was sixth in Calgary — so her career memories are not about gold, silver or bronze. If you ask me, they're better. They're about moments, funny, touching, such as the time she got lost with a Yugoslavian cab driver, who drove her around for an hour, then was so apologetic he refused to consider a tip. Or the time she worked for a German family and the father asked her, in German, to make sure she cleaned "da groh" and rather than ask what that meant, she cleaned everything in the house, only to learn that "groh" meant toilet.

The places she has gone! The things she has seen! East Germany, Russia, Romania. Places that will never be the same again. Before luge, she had never been out of North America; as of this week, she has visited more than 30 countries, has friends with whom she can stay in at least 25, and has made enough of an impression in Germany that a letter sent to her recently marked "Bonny Warner, Konigssee" was automatically delivered to her old house by a postman who remembered her from 12 years ago.

I don't know what you pay for stories such as that. I do know you can't buy them on the stock exchange.

"It's funny," Warner said the other night, sitting in the lounge of her team's hotel. "I was always a pretty good athlete. I could have gone out for basketball or swimming, the big scholarship sports. But I had this thing for the small sports. I guess I like the underdog. I like small villages like this, getting to know the people."

She laughed and looked around. There were bobsledders from around the world playing cards at the next table and lugers from around the world tapping their feet to a calypso band. As a reporter, I felt very much an outsider. Not Bonny. She belonged. A citizen of the world.

This is the part of the Olympics they never talk about, how sports can take you from a small-town kid and stretch you, enrich you, pull you around the globe and leave you on a much higher plane than you could ever have reached in your own backyard. Bonny Warner is retiring from luge Wednesday, a dozen years after that fateful first ride in her new sweater, but there is little of that college freshman left. In its place is a woman who will always see life as another adventure, the art of the possible, confident, optimistic. She has no medals. But she has perspective. She has wisdom. She has a hell of a scrapbook. For that, she can thank a sled.

"Sometimes I think where I'd be if I didn't go on the track that day," she said. "I'd probably be working for some company, just another part of the population that didn't know much about luge."

Instead, next month, she rejoins her real-life job: flying 727 jets, as a second officer for United Airlines. She says sometimes, coming through the clouds, it feels like a luge run, the whole world a white blur.

I have to smile. I remember that energetic kid riding the vans in '83, and I figure it's only fitting that Bonny Warner enter the friendly skies. That's where you end up, I suppose, when you shoot for the stars.■

Moral for Tyson: You can't always take what you want

February 12

ALBERTVILLE, France — Let's put the Olympics on hold for today and talk about the Mike Tyson rape conviction, because even over here, on a snowcapped French mountain, some things are pretty obvious:

Did he do it? I think he did. If I'm on that jury, I vote guilty, too. Not because, as a sports writer, I know of at least a dozen incidents in which Tyson has fondled women, grabbed their buttocks, walked around a nightclub with his pants off and slid up against women, groped them, talked dirty to them, tried to force-kiss them, threw tantrums when they turned him down, got charged with sexual assault twice in one disco, said to countless strangers, "I want to f - - - you," and once told a writer, "When I make love to women I like to hurt them, I like to hear them scream."

Forget all that. Even if I know nothing about Tyson going in, I still vote guilty coming out because, quite simply, Tyson and his lawyers all but tell me to do so. This was Tyson's defense: I am lewd, crude, a sex fiend, and she knew it.

That's a defense?

Nuh-uh. That's suicide. Tyson, 25, sought to drag his accuser, a college freshman, into the mud with him. Even if she knew Tyson wanted to sleep with her, so what? No is no. Rape is rape. You would figure, at $5,000 a day, Tyson's lawyers would know that.

Instead, like the weakened boxer he had become in recent years, Tyson abandoned even the slightest jab in Indianapolis. He barreled in, headfirst, and said, "This is me. Deal with it."

They did. Guilty.

When the verdict was announced Monday night, Tyson blinked, then went blank. Like many young celebrities, he is not used to hearing, "You're wrong, Mike" — not without 20 bloodsuckers retorting, "Nah, you're right." It's the Elvis syndrome: Surround yourself with hangers-on, swallow their empty praise and go down the tubes. A sad cycle. I see it over and over.

Not long ago, a Detroit athlete told me, with admiration, of how actor Eddie Murphy was so beyond cool, he didn't even talk to the women he wanted. He looked at them, nodded to a bodyguard, and the bodyguard whispered in her ear, "Eddie wants to see you later." It was just assumed she would show up. It was also assumed she would, as the expression

Gone to the Dogs   **201**

goes these days, give it up — especially if she were young and ambitious. The Murphy logic went this way: Do you want to sleep with Eddie and maybe have your life changed, or keep your values and go back to paying the rent?

No doubt, many women would choose the former. There are gold diggers out there, as Tyson's lawyers suggested. It's even possible this 18-year-old accuser who agreed to that limo ride and went to that hotel and let that door shut behind her, this woman who just put Mike Tyson away, might indeed have been impressed with the boxing star, liked his money, thought he could help her.

That only makes her dumb. Not a criminal.

And here is what we should all remember: The lesson of Room 606 in the Canterbury Hotel is not about being dumb, nor is it about being black — although I understand why some people think that. It is not William Kennedy Smith versus Mike Tyson, either. True, both men are well-known and both were charged with rape. But the cases were different, the stories were different, the victims were different and the histories of those accused were certainly different. Personally, I wasn't fond of the smug Mr. Smith, either.

But to get lost in that smoke is to miss the point entirely. The point is about men and women and respect. Here is one thing Tyson and I have in common, along with every other male on this planet: We do not know the fear of rape. We do not know the horror as a member of the opposite sex, realizing, suddenly, that you are outmuscled and outsized, you cannot make it to the door, you are about to be grabbed, pinned down, violated, humiliated, and all your strength will still not save you.

We do not know because we are men. We are bigger and stronger.

It is why we have been raping for centuries.

It is also why it has to stop.

Maybe now it will, at least a little. Critics see this verdict and say it will encourage conniving women. Frankly, I worry less about a nation full of gold diggers than a nation full of men had Tyson been acquitted. What a message that would have been! Be as lewd as you can be; it's their word against yours.

Not anymore. You feel sorry for Tyson, who could have been a wonderful story, youngest heavyweight champ in history. Instead he grabbed the crown, took the money and figured, rather than change his old street ways, he could now justify them. When women rebuked his sexual advances, he reportedly told them, "Don't you know who I am?"

Yes. A man who just got caught. Sooner or later, Tyson will go to prison for this. And when he sits in his cell, he finally might hear the voice that shocked jurors in the courtroom: his voice. For in the end, Mike Tyson became the moral of his own story. This was the moral: You can't just take what you want, no matter who you are.

That's pretty clear. Even from France. ∎

Behind Ray LeBlanc's mask lies the story of the Games

February 14

MERIBEL, France — Sometimes your moment comes right on schedule, when you are young and ambitious, ready to snap it off with your teeth. And sometimes, you wait for that moment a long and winding time. The big leagues never call. Your life stops in truck driver towns. You begin to wonder, as you pass another birthday looking out the window of a bus, whether perhaps you are meant to be no more than this, some sort of lyric in a bad country song.

You do time in Ft. Wayne, Ind., playing for the Komets; you do time in Indianapolis, playing for the Ice. You work two years as a goalie in North Carolina, Spruce Pine and Winston-Salem, something called the Atlantic Coast Hockey League. Night after night, you pull on the pads, the gloves, the mask, you take pucks in the gut, you sweat a swimming pool inside your uniform and maybe a few hundred people clap. Then you go home and flip on ESPN and see kids you used to play against skating across the NHL. You go to sleep thinking about the house payment. The years pass.

A few months ago, during the tryouts for the U.S. Olympic hockey team, Ray LeBlanc, 27 years old and a veteran of just about everywhere except the big time, asked the coach whether he could go home for a few days. He wasn't getting much work, they were bringing in other goalies to look at, a guy who had played for the Boston Bruins, a guy who had played for the Los Angeles Kings, and maybe this whole thing wasn't going to work, why should it, who was Ray LeBlanc to think he should be an Olympic goalie anyhow? So he asked Dave Peterson for a break.

"Everything all right?" Peterson said.

"Yeah," LeBlanc said. "I just need a few days to paint my house."

Paint his house? Uh, couldn't someone else do that? LeBlanc shrugged. Maybe he didn't want to say that someone else would charge about $1,500, and that was money he didn't have to spend right now. You do six years in the International Hockey League, you get financially realistic.

Peterson gave his blessing. The tryouts continued. And Ray LeBlanc, never realizing his moment was just around the corner, went home to New England to apply a fresh coat.

Thursday night, in this spirited little ski village, Ray LeBlanc stood on the Olympic hockey ice, wearing the red, white and blue mask, and he made the boys back in Ft. Wayne proud. He took all the team

Gone to the Dogs

from Finland could throw at him — and the Finns are one of the best teams in the world. He caught their shots. He smothered their shots. He fell on their shots. In three periods, they fired at him 30 times and only once did the shot get past, a point-blanker that Grant Fuhr might have missed. In his last two games, LeBlanc has made 75 of 76 pucks die unfulfilled.

The Americans haven't lost yet.

"They are a very good team," said Finnish assistant coach Sakari Pietila in the press conference after the United States upset his group, 4-1. "They did not surprise us. They played hard. And they got a very good effort from–"

He looked down the podium where LeBlanc was sitting and realized he didn't even know his name.

"–from, eh, the goaltender."

LeBlanc almost grinned. How far was this from the Flint Spirits and the Saginaw Hawks, for whom he played just three years ago? How far was this from riding the bench in Indianapolis, while the team played a younger, high-round draft pick who needed development for the NHL? LeBlanc was already Kevin Costner in "Bull Durham," a career minor-leaguer, a veteran whose time had never come. But this night, on a mountain full of snow, he had just given America its best Olympic hockey game since that Friday in Lake Placid a dozen years ago.

What is Winston-Salem thinking now?

I'm keeping everything they give us," LeBlanc admitted in the hall. "I have this box full of souvenirs. Some guys are selling them. Not me."

His voice cracked. He has a face like Bruce Springsteen's and the halting speech of a man who's really not sure how he got here. He falls back on cliches like "One game at a time" and says, "My teammates are doing it, not me." Yeah. Tell that to his family back home. LeBlanc says he calls, and all these people are screaming at the other end.

"They yell, 'Keep it up, Ray! Don't stop now!' "

No. Don't stop now. Maybe this will be a new story. Nobody needs it more than U.S. hockey, which is force-fed stale crumbs of 1980 wherever it turns. Perhaps a team like this, no-names who are virtually interchangeable, can do enough magic to make us forget Mike Eruzione and Jim Craig. Perhaps a guy like Ray LeBlanc will lead the way.

"Do you have any idea what's happening to you?" someone asked, flipping open a notepad.

LeBlanc paused. Of course he did. He remembers every minute in the IHL, the ACHL, the alphabet soup teams that have swallowed his life. He knows this is that moment he has always dreamed about, that maybe after this, nothing will be the same. But he absorbed the question, and he said the right thing and this is why you like him:

"What's happening to me," he said, "is happening to all of us."

I bet it was a good paint job, too. ∎

India's two-man team shows Games hold more than gold

February 16

MERIBEL, France — There I was, going down the mountain, when I bumped into the entire Indian Olympic team. Both of them.

"Where's the rest?" I asked the two skiers.

"Hello, yes," they said.

"No, no. The rest of your team. What happened? Miss plane? Bus go off cliff?"

"Hello, yes," they said.

There was no missed plane. No bus off the cliff. These two guys, Nanak Chand and Lal Chuni, both about 5-feet-9, with black hair and awed expressions, were indeed the entire Olympic team from India. That's India we're talking about now. New Delhi? Bombay? Sixteen to a room? That India?

This is not some tiny country like Jamaica or the Virgin Islands — both of which have more than two athletes in these Games. The last time I checked, India's population was nearly 900 million. More than three times the population of the United States. More than three times the people in Russia, or the CIS, or whatever they call it now.

Nine hundred million people.

Two athletes.

"Don't you have any skaters?" I asked.

"No skaters," they said.

"Bobsled or luge?"

"No thing like that in India."

"Well, how about other skiers? I mean there are only two of you."

"We are only two who make standard."

"You live in the mountains?"

"Live in Himalayas."

"Lots of skiing there?"

They looked at each other. "Skiing, yes. Chair lift, no."

No chair lift?

No chair lift. I had just met the only skiers in the Olympic Games who climb up the mountain, put their skis on, ski down, take their skis off, then climb back up the mountain.

That can really cut down on training runs.

"One hour to top," Nanak said. "Five minutes to bottom. Soon, you are very tired."

Like I said.

Now, just as I was wondering whether this whole thing was a setup — maybe a new TV show called "Calcutta's Funniest Home Videos" — along came an older man in an Indian team coat. He smiled as he grabbed my hand.

"Hello, hello. You are most welcome."

Turns out he was the coach, the trainer and the head of the Olympic committee. I think he also waxed the skis. His name was Singh Hukum. He spoke English. And he verified everything.

He said poverty and the political situation have kept India from developing more winter athletes — or even building chair lifts. He said the Games were not even televised in his country.

"For these boys, this is only their third mountain. They come in hope of a miracle. In our country we believe in miracles."

"What would be a miracle in their event?"

He asked them in Indian, then smiled.

"Finish the race. And not come in last."

I thought they were shooting a little high.

But who knows? After riding the chair lift, they might have so much excess energy they'll win the gold medal. You never know.

And that's the point of this column.... .

There is talk about raising the standards at the Olympics. Some of the purer athletic types have complained about the likes of Eddie (The Eagle) Edwards, the clumsy British ski jumper, or the Jamaican bobsled team, which sometimes comes down on its heads. Critics say the Olympics should be for the world's best, not the whole world.

I say no. Actually, I say let those critics walk up Nanak's mountain and try skiing down. See how pure they feel then.

The Olympics have always been about participation. For every three medalists are 50 athletes who go home with only the memory of having tried. And for most of them, that's enough.

It will be for Nanak and Lal when they ski the slalom later this week. Already they had a chance to watch the downhill competition ("Most exhilarating") and meet Italian superstar Alberto Tomba ("He is very, very better than us").

It tells you something about the state of the world when a country like India can barely afford to develop two skiers. But it also tells you how much a couple of kids might need a dream like the Olympics to give them some light. Who cares where they finish? Who cares if they slow down the race? It's once every four years. We can wait.

"Excuse us, we must train now," the coach said. And he pointed his kids to a line of people at the bottom of the mountain. Their eyes lit up, and they raced off.

I have a feeling about these guys. Here it is: I don't think they'll win the slalom.

But I bet they set a record for chair lifts. ∎

Who was that guy? Herschel, impersonating a bobsledder

February 17

LA PLAGNE, France — I rarely go to bobsled races, because I can see the same thing at a bank robbery. Two guys in masks come running out, jump in a vehicle, duck and drive away. Big deal.

But I did attend the Olympic bobsled race Sunday, because certain circumstances demanded it, such as national interest, and the fact that if I didn't go to bobsled, I had to go to figure skating, in which the ice dancers were scheduled to do the Original Mandatory Program, which this year is ... the polka! I am not making this up. Roll out ... the barrel!

Also, Herschel Walker.

He was another reason I chose bobsled. As you probably know, Mr. Walker — not a good name for this sport, when you think about it — is a famous football star who was rushed in to boost U.S. bobsledding, much the way he has boosted the Minnesota Vikings. True, the Vikings haven't won an important game since Herschel showed up three years ago, and word is they were happy he switched to an amateur sport, because at least fans would stop complaining that they weren't getting their money's worth.

But, hey. I bet those people know nothing about bobsled. Of course, neither did Herschel as of a year ago. But he has bigger thighs.

Which is why he was rushed in and given, in no particular order, a tryout, a helmet, a team jacket and the top driver. Too bad he wasn't given some instructions.

On Saturday, in Herschel's first-ever two-man race — nothing like starting at the top, as they say in bobsled — he made a boo-boo. He jumped in the sled too soon.

"I couldn't figure out why our start times weren't faster," said driver Brian Shimer, who knows that in bob — as we experts call it — the start is everything. "Then I looked at the film, and I suggested that Herschel wait a little longer, take another step or two before jumping in."

Shimer was only asking Herschel to do what Vikings coaches have been asking for years, namely stay up a little longer before going down. But, hey. If this were your first race in a supersonic sled, you might jump a little early, too. I mean, can you imagine pushing the thing so hard that suddenly it takes off without you, and you're left in the middle of the track wearing nothing but a skin-tight body suit, while all these Austrians are laughing their heads off. "Ha, ha, Gunther. Look! He is waiting for da bus!"

Herschel's rear entry wasn't Shimer's only problem. Thanks to the lack of a sled technician — U.S. team officials told him "they couldn't afford one" — Shimer learned two days before the race that his sled runners were illegal. He had to stay up nights to modify them.

Poor guy. In one race he had troubles with Walkers and Runners.

Eventually, both problems were addressed. But by that point, USA I, also known as "Herschel and the Other Guy," was out of medal contention.

"Of course I'm disappointed," Walker said after finishing seventh. "Herschel comes to win."

(By the way, Herschel likes to talk about himself in the third person. Don't ask me why. Isiah Thomas does it, too, and I never understood that, either. Like when he says, "This is what Isiah is about... ." Wait a minute. Do I have the wrong guy? Did Isiah leave the room? Did I forget my glasses and accidentally start interviewing Charles Thomas? No. Athletes just do this. And, to be honest, Mitch thinks it's pretty annoying.)

Anyhow, back to Herschel.

And another quote: "Herschel came to win a medal."

Well. All right. I can understand that. So did everybody at these Games, with the possible exception of the Honduras luge team, which probably came to avoid monsoon season.

But the thing is — and hear me out on this — I don't think we deserve a medal. Even if we had the fastest time.

To be honest, if Walker and Shimer had captured a gold Sunday, I would have immediately called for the expulsion of bobsled as an Olympic sport. Hey. If a guy can just fly over after the NFL season, take a few practice runs, never race in competition and win a gold, then the damn thing is too easy.

The Swiss team won Sunday's race, followed by the two German teams. The Swiss pair has a combined 11 years' experience.

Both German brakemen — Herschel's position — have been in bobsled since 1985. These guys go to World Cup competitions, they practice endlessly, they study sled construction, they read trade magazines. They're probably the only people to see the movie "What About Bob?" and come out saying, "No sleds. Bummer."

Now, true, these guys never took a handoff from Wade Wilson, but do you really need that? Isn't it more important to have some race experience, a sled technician or the correct runners?

What happened here, if you ask me, is the U.S. bobsled people got a little greedy. They wanted success, fast, along with publicity, two things they haven't had recently. Athletes such as Herschel — and Edwin Moses and Willie Gault — seemed to be a quick fix to their problems. And it's true, U.S. bobsled got a lot more reporters up the hill Sunday than in past Olympics. But all that meant was more journalists to chronicle a simple lesson: Practice makes perfect.

Not an NFL jersey.

"Will you compete next year?" someone asked Walker.

"You're asking me to predict the future," he said. "And Herschel doesn't predict."

"How about the 1994 Olympics?"

"Herschel doesn't predict."

"Do you think you would have done better with even one season's worth of racing?"

"That's like a prediction."

(Getting a little frustrated with this, I asked Herschel how he did in his first football game. And he said, "Pretty good." Then I asked whether he played better in subsequent games. He said, "Oh, yeah. That's the experience factor." When I asked him to apply this to bobsled, he said, "You're trying to get me to say we'd be better with more experience. But that's kinda like a prediction. And Herschel doesn't ...")

You get the idea.

Now, it's true, not everyone was discouraged by Sunday's race — even though Herschel's start times, which are basically all he's there for, were beaten in all four runs by a number of competitors, including the Swiss brakeman, who is a locksmith in real life, and a German brakeman, who is a building engineer. Maybe Herschel needs a new job.

We'll see. The four-man competition is this weekend, and with Herschel pushing, some U.S. officials are actually predicting a gold. I guess they figure a week is long enough to build a career.

You know what? I hope somebody else wins it. Not to be unpatriotic, but I'd rather applaud some team that has been working together season after season, traveling in vans, going to small races, dreaming of the Olympics.

As for coming back to watch our team? I'll pass. Like I said, if I want to watch somebody steal something, I'll go to a bank robbery. It's a lot warmer. ∎

Alberto Tomba's boasts are as big as his fantastic feats

February 19

REPORTER: "Why did you arrive by helicopter?"
TOMBA: "Because everyone else drove."

V AL D'ISERE, France — When we last left Alberto Tomba, he was riding a mob of happy, singing Italians at the bottom of an Olympic slalom in Canada. They yelled his name. They kissed his curls. Reporters asked questions, then hugged him when he answered.

"Alberto!" the chorus sang. *"Fantastico, Alberto!"*

Now here he was, four years later, at the bottom of an Olympic course in the French Alps, and the picture was the same. They leapt over fences. They screamed as he passed. Reporters fought police who fought fans who fought police, all so they could get close enough to pat his head or kiss his cheek.

"Alberto! Grazie, Alberto!"

He came. He saw. He skied. He took a bow. Such is life for Alberto Tomba, who, at 21, was the baby bombshell of the Calgary Games and at 25, is the closest thing to God on skis. At least the Italians think so. How many bus loads of worshiping fans did they send to this mountain — from Bologna, Pisa, Val Gardenia — just to wave banners and sing songs and watch him shake up history? Three Olympic races? Three gold medals?

"Alberto! Alber–"

Wait. The mob was stirring. Police, photographers, TV cameras, groupies in hot pink ski suits — what was this? Alberto was down! Alberto was down! Had he fainted?

"Alberto! Alberto? ... "

His coach held his arms out, his bodyguard shoved everyone back. But they were not concerned. Like sidemen for soul king James Brown, they knew this was part of the Big Man's show: Here, in the middle of the mountains, Alberto Tomba was on his knees, face down, kissing the snow.

Kissing the snow?

Mmmmmmmmmmwah!

"Alberto! Si, Alberto!"

H ad Tomba been an actor, he would have been Tom Cruise. Had he been a football player, he would have been Joe Namath. Yes, there is marvelous talent in those tree-like thighs, the limbs that enable him to whisk through slalom and giant slalom courses as if he were dismantling them rather than skiing them, whacking each gate as he rips past. But other skiers have talent.

What Tomba has is *brio, bravado, braggadocio* — and a lot of other words that end in "o." Only a certain kind of guy arrives for the Olympics by helicopter, then turns his ski race into the Super Bowl. Only a certain kind of guy can say, at different moments, "I AM A BEAST!" (after a victory); "I AM THE MESSIAH OF SKIING!" (another victory); "If I race you and I beat you, will you go away and leave me alone?" (to a teammate who wanted to train with him); and "Normally, I party with three girls until 5 a.m., but at the Olympic village, I will change my ways: I will party with five girls until 3 a.m."

Ego? Is that an o-word?

You bet. And that's what makes him great. That, and speed. Consider this: On Tuesday afternoon, in the cold French sunshine, Tomba stood atop the giant slalom course, about to launch his final run, and the last words he heard would have unnerved most skiers: "Girardelli did a 1:02.6."

It was Marc Girardelli of Luxembourg, the former World Cup champion, who had just finished his run. The time was excellent. Best of the day. Impossible to beat — unless you're a fellow who calls his mother on a cellular phone minutes before your Olympic race and tells her, "Watch me on TV. I am great today!"

Which Tomba once did. I kid you not.

So it was no shock when he blitzed down the hill, made up the deficit and came across the line with glory on his face, winning the gold, becoming the first Alpine skier to win the same event in two Olympics. Never mind the up-and-down years he had between '84 and '88. Never mind the weight he put on, or the seminude hot tub photos, or the passes he made at Katarina Witt, Princess Stephanie, Brooke Shields. Was this the Olympics? Was he winning again?

Any more dumb questions?

A lberto! Forza, Alberto!"
He popped off his skis, stuck them into the snow and dropped to his knees between them, as if in a chapel. He said a little prayer. The crowd went nuts. He smiled.

As James Brown would say, "Lemme kiss myself!"

"What did you eat? How will you celebrate? When will you shave your whiskers?" reporters asked afterward, questions befitting a skier/idol/millionaire.

"Chocolate … a small party … maybe this week …" he answered.

"Can you win the slalom? … Will you make a movie?"

"I can win, for sure. … Yes, maybe I make movie."

The questions came. The questions went. He laughed and rubbed his beard and winked and said he was tired. The Italian reporters nodded. He is tired! He is tired! In Italy, Tomba's words, his love life, even his boyish pranks are not only tolerated by the media, they are cherished. I asked a reporter from Il Giorno why this was, and he said: "In Italy, we have no man who says, 'I will win,' and then he wins. Tomba is the only one."

"Is he as big as the pope?"

"Ha!" the man said. "He is much bigger!"

Bigger than the pope?

And the Big Man had to go. Back to the crowds. Back to the lovefest. They waited for him. They swallowed him up. They sang and cheered and carried him off on their shoulders as they have done now in Calgary and in Alberto-ville, France. Who knows? They might do it again Saturday in the slalom and again in Lillehammer, 1994. He is the Soul Man of skiing, three Olympic races, three gold medals, a world of his own and a legend that gets bigger and bigger: He came, he saw, he flew down the mountain. Everyone else drove. ■

Dantley's inferno: A league of smoke bombs and salami

March 9

TODAY'S ITALIAN LESSON: Dove (doveh) 1. Where. As in "Where the hell is the exit?"

FORLI, Italy — Well now, here's something you don't see every day at a basketball game. A smoke bomb. Yep. The man with the balding black hair just lit the sucker and — whooosh! — it exploded like a volcano in his hand, gushing fire and pink smoke into the rafters of this thunderous arena, which is already swaying like some Holy Rollers revival, screams and hollers and horns and whistles and chants and howls and yelps and death threats. Someone will be sacrificed before they're done tonight, that's what I figure, a human sacrifice, tossed to the lions, eaten alive, maybe me, that's the kind of crowd it is. They bite their hands and leap onto seats, stomping their feet like school kids throwing a tantrum. They sing about the referee's anatomy, they bang drums and pop balloons and chant like zealots. "AYYYAAYAYA! AYYYAYAYA!" It's a union riot, an anticommunist rally — but no, it is just another basketball game here in the Land of Antipasto, Italian professional basketball, every Sunday evening, that's all they play, once a week, which, by the looks of it, gives these folks way too much time to fire up. "AYAAAYAYA! AYAAAYAYA!" Such noise! Young, old, middle-aged, teenaged, in camel-hair jackets and olive-green sweaters and denim pants and tight black skirts and cigarette smoke and bad breath and …

… What's that smell?

Salami?

Salami. Amidst all this insanity, two minutes left in the game, and the guy next to me pops out a huge salami sandwich, and he clamps his thick lips around it and chomps down, the bread crust spreading the corners of his mouth, and then, suddenly, he screams in mid-bite, because his team has scored — "AWIPIPEEE!" — and that half-eaten salami is kind of between here and there and … wait, now the guy with the kettle drum, his legs draped over the edge of the balcony, his team has scored, and it's ahead by two points, and he's pounding like Buddy Rich, BOOM-BOOM-BOOM-BOOM, right in my ears, the seats are shaking, rattling, rumbling, and I can't help it, my reaction — and this is just one way I differ from the average Italian basketball fan — my reaction is to hose these people down.

Their reaction is to light up another smoke bomb.

So now we have — whoosh! — two smoke bombs and one salami

sandwich, and the upper deck is starting to look like a birthday cake in an Italian deli, sparks and fire spritzing over our heads, and I notice all this pink smoke is spilling down from the rafters to the lower level, onto the men in alligator loafers and the women with dyed-blonde hair, onto the radio announcers who are screaming into their microphones, onto the coaches who are slapping their foreheads — *"Buffone! Che fa?!!"* — and now the pink smoke hovers over the court and the players out there in this championship game, six Italians, four Americans — believe me, you can tell the difference — shooting and running and shooting and running, like lab rats, up and down they race, as if the next basket might save us all from Armageddon ...

... And it might, because I now see the blue-suited security police in full riot gear, helmets and visors and nightsticks and uh-oh, something's up. I've heard stories about crowds attacking at the buzzer, chasing the players and trapping them in the locker room, smashing the windows, poking their heads through the glass and hollering, *"Morte! Morte!"* until the only safe exit is the back of a paddy wagon, and I can only hope the right team wins tonight, because that kind of stuff just happens here.

Here being Italy.

Which is where I am.

How did I get here again?

And someone lights another smoke bomb.

Whooooosh! ...

W hooooosh! The cars whip past the darkened front of Lido di Milano, a sports complex, and I peer into the passing windows, looking for Adrian Dantley. This is where it all begins, a week ago, this whole crazy Arrivederci Adventure. Dantley, one of the greatest scorers in NBA history, is why I have come. Dantley and players such as him, former Pistons Rick Mahorn, Darryl Dawkins, Bob McAdoo, Mark Hughes — and NBA missing persons like Alex English, Reggie Theus, Darren Daye, Dave Corzine — all of these guys are in Italy, scattered from Sicily to Venice, filling designated foreigner spots on team rosters. Some have been coming for years.

Have you ever wondered why?

This is the Afterlife for American basketball. A place you can go when the NBA spits you out or your agent says, "Better Rome than Minnesota." Italy, where the roads were built by Caesar and the pope takes his daily prayers. Italy, where strangers kiss twice on the cheek. Italy, Land of Art and Arguments. Italy, come play for us, Americano, we give you a big contract and a house and a car, come play for us.

They come. They don't know a word of Italian. They can't find the country on a map. But they come, some of them, anyhow, to be reborn, to prove themselves, almost always to get rich. Some succeed. Some are complete washouts, even good NBA players. The fact is, life overseas is not for everyone. A lot of players arrive figuring this will be one big vacation. Then they discover the bathroom.

But wait. Here comes Dantley, driving a modest gray Fiat. He brakes. I hop in. Dantley, I should say, kind of unknowingly sold me on this story with one word, when I called him from the United States.

"Adrian?" I said.

"Si?" he said.

Adrian Dantley speaking Italian? Come on. Say no to that.

"Yo," he says now as I shut the car door. He rolls his eyes and smiles. He seems genuinely glad to see me — so I know these guys must really be lonely.

"It's weird over here," he begins.

Yeah. They have a different word for everything.

An hour later, we are sitting in a lobby of a suburban hotel, which looks a little like a Ramada Inn in Iowa that I remember, green couches and gold ash trays. People pass, unaffected by Adrian's presence. This is my first clue that Italy is not the NBA. No autograph hounds. Nobody staring. A handful of men stand in the bar, crowded around a wooden-frame TV set. They are watching soccer.

"I like this hotel," Adrian says.

"Why?"

"It has ice."

Already I have heard how the team had no ice for his knees when Adrian got here, and how they practice at night, and how the washing machine in his apartment is in the bathroom, near the bidet. (The bidet?) I have heard how players travel by bus to nearly all the road games, and how Dantley's teammates watch videos of his old NBA All-Star Games, and when he scores, they yell, "Adriano! You make basket! Adriano!"

I have heard about his coach, who is only 38 years old and also, conveniently, owns the team, and how he doesn't speak English, but this morning, after a weekend defeat, he told his assistants to tell Dantley that if things don't get better fast he's going to cut him — even though Dantley is one of two players on the roster who can make a lay-up without instructions.

"Hey, that's how it is over there," says Dantley, who is averaging 28 points a game and shooting 63 percent. "I just accept it. I mean, when I came over, they made me try out for two games before they signed me. Can you believe that?"

He laughs, and it is kind of funny. Dantley had just left the NBA, where he scored more than 23,000 points. What's he going to do, forget how to shoot?

"Man, I haven't tried out for a team since junior high. I got off the plane, had lunch and played that night. I scored 30, and I wasn't even in shape ..."

He shakes his head. "This place is unbelievable."

Dantley is earning around $500,000 this season for Breeze Milano. (That's Breeze, as in Breeze deodorant, the sponsor of the team; most teams here are named after their sponsors, including my favorite, Kleenex Pistoia.) Anyhow, Breeze Milano is a team in the A2 Division. There is A1, the best and the richest, with 16 teams, and there's A2, a lower level, also with 16 teams. Each year the top two teams from A2 move up to A1, which is cause for celebration, and each year the bottom two teams from A1 fall to A2, which could mean millions of dollars lost in sponsorship money. When that happens, "you might as well jump off a bridge," Bob McAdoo will tell me.

Each team is permitted two foreign players, usually Americans, and they pay whatever they want to get them. No salary cap. Dantley's money is decent for an American player here, but not as much as, say, Rickey Mahorn, who is making nearly $2 million for an A1 team and living like an emperor in Rome. But hey. This is Italy. You take what you can get, and you hope the dryer isn't in the bathroom, too.

"Ain't got no dryer," Dantley says.

Oh.

Back to the hotel. I notice Adrian is carrying a red notebook, and I ask what's inside. He opens it and grins. There are pages full of Italian phrases, all neatly written in his penmanship. Adrian is studying the language. His way. Which is unique. Here are some of the phrases:

"Bad call, ref."

"I'm not touching the ball."

"Where is the bathroom?"

"You better get your hand out of my face."

"I'm going to hurt him, ref."

"Get me, I'm open."

Dantley sighs and closes the notebook. He looks at the men watching the soccer game.

"You gotta learn the language," he says. "It's their country."

Let me tell you about the Breeze practice. Dantley said it was kind of a joke, and I see what he means. It is Tuesday, and we are in the Centro Culturale Sportivo Aresino, which Adrian can walk to from his apartment. That is its best feature. How can I describe the place? Think of an Elks Lodge, only less fancy, with a gym. And at the moment, the gym is occupied by teenage girls, trying to do aerobics.

"Guess we got to wait," Dantley says. And we sit in the bleachers, behind a green net. There are two baskets, and one rim seems bent. I point at it. Dantley shrugs. It's a long way from the NBA. Out on the court, a fat girl in lavender sweats tries a somersault. She flops with a thud.

"Too much pasta," Dantley whispers.

Soon, the rest of his teammates wander in. I know this because Adrian says, "That guy's on the team … that guy's on the team …"

Otherwise, I would have thought they were picking up their daughters from aerobics. I won't say these guys do not look like pro basketball players. I will say one of them is wearing Bermuda shorts. And another is carrying his car radio under his arm. Also, I think the last weight they lifted was the pot of stew their mother was cooking.

"Ciao, Adriano," they say.

"Ciao," Adrian says.

He looks at me proudly. Hey! He's speaking Italian.

Fat girl tries another somersault.

We will come back to Adrian in a little bit. Back to his teammates, who, unfortunately, have trouble hanging onto the basketball when it hits them in the hands, and back to his apartment in the suburbs, where he has learned to hang his clothes out to dry, and back to his daily schedule, in which he has memorized the exact time "Barnaby Jones" comes on the English TV channel... .

But let's move along now, down the coast, past Genoa, past Pisa, down to Rome, where we hear — "BLEEP YOU, YOU STUPID ITALIAN BLEEP" — another American voice, a familiar voice that — "AND BLEEP YOUR FAT UGLY ITALIAN BUTT" — harkens back to the good old days in Detroit, the Bad Boy days.

I'll give you three guesses.

"AW, SPEAK ENGLISH, YOU BLEEP!"

Make that two ... ∎

Mahorn says he's matured, but traces of Bad Boy remain

March 10

TODAY'S ITALIAN LESSON: Credere (credereh) 1. Believe. As in, "Can you believe Rick Mahorn and the pope are in the same town?"

ROME — Whhhrrrrooooooooomm!

I am chasing the green BMW down a curving, tree-lined road that should, ideally, be taken by bicycle, permitting me to sniff the yellow and lavender flowers that — whoosh! — instead are flying past me at warp speed as my foot is jammed on the accelerator in a desperate attempt to keep up with the — screech! — BMW in front of me — look out! — which is now — ohmigod, he's gotta be — curling around a Volvo — kidding me! — and whipping back into the lane as he — no way, no way! — wants me to follow or lose him forever — hit the gas! — so here I go, like an idiot, around this narrow Italian curve and here comes a — WHOA! — truck in the same lane — CUT, CUT! — and I — rrrrRRROOOM! — swerve and miss him by inches — *"IDIOTA!"* — and, shaking now, I downshift quickly and look ahead to that green BMW to catch a rear view of Rick Mahorn, the original Bad Boy, slapping the dashboard in hysterics.

Nothing changes. Some NBA players come to Italy and try to adjust quietly, tiptoe around the language problem, write letters home, hope the paychecks come on time.

And others bust down the door and say, "I'M HERE, DAMN IT. WHERE'S MY SPORTS CAR?"

Ladies and gentlemen:

Rickey does Rome.

First of all, I hate pasta, all right? You can have it with that damn pasta. I don't like spaghetti; only thing I like in the spaghetti group is lasagna, and my wife can make that, so no more pasta, OK?"

The spaghetti group?

"Another thing. They have these team meals before the game, like five hours before the game? What the bleep for? They want us to be together or something, but they're eating all these cold vegetables, and I'm not with cold vegetables, you understand? They're like, 'Rickey, why you no like Italian food?' I'm like, 'Italian food, bleep! Just gimme my chicken subito' — that means fast, subito — and I'm outta there."

Subito?

"And here's another thing. The whole damn country closes for three hours a day for lunch. Three hours! And then when you're at the store after lunch, and it's not open yet but it's supposed to be open, they got the nerve to look at you with an attitude, like you're doing something wrong. I'm like, 'Bleep this bleep!' "

He pauses. He grins.

Obviously, Rickey is adjusting well.

We are sitting in his suburban villa in a sprawling green golf course development, miles from the noise and exhaust fumes of Rome. This was the house Michael Cooper lived in when he played with Mahorn's current team, Il Messaggero — which also once employed Danny Ferry and Brian Shaw — and the place is magnificent, balconies and terra-cotta floors and high ceilings and a sunken living room. The birds sing, the dogs romp in the yard, and the only time Mahorn meets any neighbors is when the woman next door complains that her Mercedes is being doused by his sprinklers.

Did I mention Rickey's new Mercedes?

Yes. He didn't like the BMW. Too small. The team said no problem, we'll replace it. This is how some American stars are treated here in Italy, where basketball is the second most popular sport — soccer, a religion, is first — and teams have an insatiable lust for the newest NBA guy to get off the airplane. Mahorn is even more of a prize, because, unlike many of his American counterparts, he said *ciao* to the NBA before it said *ciao* to him. Mahorn, 33, could have signed back with the Philadelphia 76ers. But then, they weren't going to give him a Mercedes instead of a BMW, were they?

Nor were they going to provide this villa, or the maid service or the furniture or the satellite dish or the stereo system or the silverware or the sheets or the utility bills, all of which are paid for as long as Mahorn stays in Italy.

Oh, yes. He gets a salary, too. Around $2 million this season.

For playing once a week.

I could learn to like pasta for that.

"Hey, it's good over here," Mahorn admits, sliding onto the couch as he eyes his CD collection. "But you know, you gotta put up with a lot."

That depends on where you are. Adrian Dantley, whom we visited with yesterday, is earning one-fourth the money Mahorn is making, and is living in an apartment outside of Milan where the sink is so low, he has to sit to wash dishes. Bob McAdoo, a legend in Italy for six years, now has been relegated to the minor town of Forli, where he collects a minor paycheck compared to Mahorn's. Meanwhile, Tony Kukoc, the Yugoslav star who has never played a minute in the NBA, is earning more than all of them, nearly $4 million playing for a team in Treviso.

Here is the biggest embarrassment in the Italian pro league — besides the way they dribble — and its biggest problem: no financial balance. No rules. No salary cap. The Haves have it all. The Have-Nots can choke and die.

So while Dantley and his teammates, who play for a small, independently owned franchise, practice at a local community center where old men play cards just outside the door, big teams like Il Messaggero Roma or Benetton Treviso (owned by Benetton, the clothing giant) can dish out fortunes, season after season. Here, have a Mercedes.

"This is our worst problem because it's an ego thing for the big teams," says Dan Peterson, an Italian TV commentator who was a successful coach for years. "Teams like Benetton sign the biggest Americans. They don't care if they lose money — of course, they're going to lose money with those kinds of salaries, their arena only seats 4,000 or so — but it's an image thing. If they win, they have the right image. That's all that counts."

Speaking of image ...

G ET YOUR FAT BLEEPING BUTT OFFA ME, YOU DUMB ITALIAN BLEEP."

"Oh, ho, Reeeky. You are Bad Boy, no?"

"BAD BOY, MY A- -, YOU MOLTO STUPIDO."

"Ha-ha, Reeeky. OK, Reeeky."

"BLEEP ALL YOU DUMB BLEEPS."

"Reeeky? Why you say?"

"BLEEP Y'ALL!"

As you can see, practice is going well. We are at the Palaoir, the large arena where Il Messaggero plays, and the guys are on center court, doing drills, racing back and forth. Mahorn, in a white T-shirt, the beefiest guy out there, is also the focus. You immediately notice a difference in his style of play versus the Italians. Although they can shoot extremely well, they are stiff, mechanical, lacking the fluid movement of an NBA guy like Mahorn. And Mahorn is hardly the most fluid man on Earth.

I attribute this to the lack of playground basketball in Italy. Believe it or not, for all the sport's popularity, most kids who play in Italy do so in controlled environments from the age of 7 or 8. They have coaches. They join club teams. There is no high school or college basketball, just this club stuff, so they get used to playing at scheduled times, under supervision, kind of like swim teams at a local Y.

No wonder they can't improvise.

As opposed to Mahorn — "TOUCH ME AGAIN AND I'LL KICK YOUR NASTY BUTT ALL ACROSS THIS FLOOR, YOU DUMB ITALIAN BLEEP!"

I should say right here that nearly every curse that comes from Mahorn's lips — which is about every other word — is released with a smile. Which only further confuses his teammates. Is he serious? Is he joking? Does he know any words that don't start with "F"?

They have no idea. So they tiptoe around him, like Lilliputians around a sleeping Gulliver, they laugh when he laughs, curse when he curses, run away when he gets mad. Mahorn keeps them guessing. Since arriving in September, he has been embroiled in several controversies: His first coach, the venerable Valerio Bianchini, winner of virtually every championship you can win in Italy, quit midway through the season because he just couldn't cope with "these foreigners and their attitudes." Mahorn was also suspended for one game after kicking an opposing player. ("He kicked me first, so I kicked the bleep out of him, the bleep.") Once, during practice, Mahorn lost his temper and hollered at a teammate: "I'll beat the bleep out of you and every other one of you bleeps, right now!" They had to send him home to cool down.

And yet, at the same time, the onetime King of the Bad Boys has indeed mellowed here in the Italian suburbs. He is married now, has a new baby daughter (born in Italy, with dual citizenship) and another child due this fall. He is home for meals, he cleans the garage, he washes clothes, he talks about coaching one day — heaven help us — and enjoying this slow life-style. If he returns to the NBA in 1993, when his Italian contract is up, it will be hard to resume the pace. "I'm definitely more mature now," he says.

Well ... then again, he did pull that stunt when I was driving. And not long ago, he and teammate Dino Radja, a former Yugoslav star, snuck up behind some Italian workers who were standing by a gas truck, and lit these firecrackers, and the workers fell to the ground in sheer panic, figuring the truck was exploding.

And Rickey and Dino ran away laughing.

So he's not that mature.

"Reeeky is a good guy; ever'body like him deep down," Radja says after practice, rubbing the blond stubble on his face.

"BLEEP YOU, DINO!" Mahorn yells.

It's a friendship thing.

In a few days, Mahorn will play against former Piston Darryl Dawkins at the Palaoir in a nationally televised game. He will push through triple coverage and fall over teammates and take their passes over his head. He will be cheered for a rebound, cheered when he dribbles up court, jeered when he misses a shot. Oh, and there will be a confrontation, between him and Dawkins, where they start to ...

Later for that. For now, things are *molto bello* in the suburbs, the soft couch in the sunken living room with the color TV and the satellite channels.

I ask whether he has any messages for his old Pistons teammates. Mahorn thinks, then flashes that gap-tooth smile.

"Yeah. Tell John Salley to get a job."

I look out the window, at the hills, at the birds and the sprinklers and the BMW, and I wonder where you go to get a job like this. ∎

Ciao, Bob: The rise and fall of an American star in Italy

March 12

TODAY'S ITALIAN LESSON: Leggenda. 1. A legend.

F ORLI, Italy — They all wanted a piece of Bob McAdoo, all those people outside the bus, screaming and waving and cheering in Italian. Through the window he saw them, and thought to himself, "I better watch my wallet." So he slipped it in the pocket of his gym bag and …

"BOB!" They were all over him. Hugging him. Slapping his shoulders. *"SI, BOB!" "CIAO, BOB!"*

He was Elvis at the Louisiana Hayride, Tom Jones at the Sahara. They hugged him and kissed him and hoisted him on their shoulders, laughing and singing as if a long-lost brother had come home from the war. When he finally escaped to a quiet corner, he saw that his bag had been ripped open and everything inside was gone for souvenirs. Everything, except …

They left him his wallet.

That was the best of times for Bob McAdoo, the year he won his first championship here in Italy, the year he took the country by storm. *Il Americano!* Such talent! Right here in the Land of Pasta! Other big-name NBA players would follow him across the sea, Joe Barry Carroll, Albert King, Michael Cooper, Danny Ferry, Rick Mahorn. But back in the mid-80s, he was the hottest American import. Hey, Bob! *Ciao,* BOB! The best of times.

And these are the worst.

When they own your rights in Italy, they really own your rights. Young Italian players are purchased as early as their teens, with the money going to whichever local sports club they play for (remember, there is no high school or college basketball here). American players who sign the big contracts find it works the same way. The first team you sign with owns your rights, and another Italian team can only acquire you if your original team agrees to sell.

Bob McAdoo was a hero in Milan for four years. In his first season, his team won everything there is to win in Italy, the league championship, the Italian Cup championship, the European Cup championship. McAdoo had a great attitude, played hard, didn't just show up asking for his check. The Italian fans loved him.

But good times burn like rocket fuel here, where owners show terrible impatience for success. Just a few seasons after those championships, Milan shook up its roster — players were getting too old, they said — and, despite his 30-point average, McAdoo was let go.

OK, he figured. Other teams are interested. But Milan wanted to make sure he didn't go to a team that could challenge it. So the owners kept passing up offers for his rights, until the team from Forli, a small town not far from the Adriatic Sea, made a bid.

Forli was no threat. It was way down in the standings. The deal was made.

And McAdoo, somewhat of a legend in Italy, was given an apartment in a strange town and told, at age 40, to go prove himself again.

I am sitting in that apartment right now, looking at the photos that hang on the wall. Outside, a dense fog hovers over the rooftops, making the whole town — with its colored concrete walls and small bridges — seem surreal. It is quiet. The oak furniture is neatly kept, American magazines are set in perfect precision on the coffee table. All around are snapshots of McAdoo's children, one inside a frame that reads: "I Love My Daddy."

They used to come with him to Italy. That was before his wife, Charlina, died shortly before last Christmas. She was 33.

"Cancer," McAdoo says, not eager to discuss the subject. "I flew back and forth four straight weeks when it got really bad. In fact, I had just returned here when they called and said she died."

How did the team react?

"Oh, they were understanding — for about a day. Then they asked if I could fly back from the funeral in time for that Sunday's game."

He shakes his head, with the sigh of a man who has seen it all. McAdoo looks nearly the same as he did during those explosive NBA days, when he dropped baskets as if shelling fish, winning an MVP award and three scoring titles. He still has the mustache and the easy grin, a little bit of Chuck Berry in his face. The lanky 6-foot-9 frame seems remarkably athletic for a man who turned 41 last September.

Yet there is a quiet edge to McAdoo now, a loneliness that is both apparent and understandable. A typewriter sits on the table, which he uses to write letters to his children. "Letters, rent a video, go to eat, that's about all I do here," he says. "This town's a lot smaller than Milan."

"You eat in restaurants by yourself?" I ask.

"Oh, yeah," he answers, as if that were a given.

At practice later that afternoon, it is apparent why Milan felt secure in sending McAdoo to Forli. His teammates are, to be generous, average. One guy wears his white shorts so high, I think he's going to choke himself. Another comes out in a cotton sports shirt, with the collar turned up, as if he's going for a cruise on a yacht. He picks up a ball and starts to shoot.

McAdoo slides into three-on-three drills, drills he probably ran harder back in high school. *"PRESSA! PRESSA!"* his coach screams. As they move up the floor, I notice some players seem reluctant to pass to McAdoo, choosing not to look his way. It suggests a common problem between the highly paid American stars and the everyday Italian players.

The salary gap is enormous: U.S. players average between $300,000 and $500,000 (some exceed $2 million a year). The natives, on average, earn less than $80,000. "There's jealousy, no doubt," McAdoo admits. I have heard the same thing from Adrian Dantley, Rick Mahorn and Darryl Dawkins. This, of course, puts the Americans in an odd situation: They are expected to chalk up tremendous statistics to justify their salaries, yet teammates often do not want to get them the ball. "Sometimes," Dantley told me privately, "I just go and get it."

After practice, McAdoo comes from the shower shaking his head. He seems a little embarrassed by the level of play. His team is in the worst situation, the bottom of the A1 standings. Every year, the lowest two teams in A1 fall to the A2 league, where the sponsorship money dries up. Everyone here is nervous.

"Hey," McAdoo says, looking down at me, "I bet you could suit up and play for this team. And I ain't never even seen you play. You wanna try?"

That night, we go to the big arena in town where, by coincidence, the finals of the Italia Cuppa are being played. Four of Italy's best teams are here, as are thousands of fans and basketball types. When we enter the arena, you can feel the electricity. The rafters shake with noise, foot stomping, whistles. It is everything McAdoo once had here, back when they ripped the bag off his shoulder. He seems energized by the excitement. He slides into the gym with his hands dug into his pockets. On the court, the players are racing up and down. Soon people begin to recognize McAdoo.

"Hey, Bob! ... *Ciao*, Bob! ... OK, Bob!"

A reporter steps up with a small tape recorder. He shoves it in McAdoo's face. "Bob McAdoo, can you tell what you think about the great Americano Vinny Del Negro?"

McAdoo allows a sarcastic grin before answering. Del Negro, the former N.C. State point guard, is a new face, and Italians love new American faces in their league. Nobody tonight gives McAdoo credit for taking the big leap in the '80s, for coming to this country and making good and sticking around for six years. Tonight, they want to know about Del Negro.

It occurs to me that McAdoo, who played for seven teams in the NBA, has been facing such adjustments his whole career. Getting too old. Sliding to another level. Still, he keeps playing. He keeps scoring. He scored nearly 19,000 points in the NBA, won two championship rings. Now he is inside an arena near the Adriatic Sea.

Later, I ask whether he ever feels forgotten.

"I don't worry about being forgotten anymore," he says. "This is my job, that's all.

"Hey, I have a son who doesn't even know who Wilt Chamberlain is, and Wilt was maybe the greatest player of all time. And I have younger son" — he laughs — "and he probably won't even remember who Bob McAdoo was."

He looks back at the court. "Everybody gets forgotten."

The hour grows late. I have a long drive to Rome. I thank McAdoo for his time. "All right," he says, turning. "You sure you don't wanna stick around here, maybe have dinner after the game or something?"

I say thanks anyhow. We shake hands. As I reach the outside doors, I look back over my shoulder at one of the greatest scorers in the history of the NBA, standing by himself, leaning against the bleachers. I step outside, and see the fog has gotten worse. ∎

Italy's a renaissance for some, last chance for others

March 13

TODAY'S ITALIAN LESSON: Finito.

ROME — Here are two moments of truth for the American basketball player who crosses the sea to find fame, glory and a paycheck in the Land of Pasta. Here are those moments of truth:

1) The first time he goes to a public bathroom and discovers the Italian answer to the toilet which, and I am being polite, can only be described as a hole in the ground with two grates to put your feet, like a Twister board, and he takes one look at this and says, "Oh, no, no, nonononono" and comes running out and yells to his teammates, "Hey, hey, there's something really wrong in there! Someone stole the toil–"

And they stare at him, blankly.

2) The games. The first time you play a game in the Italian league, especially if you are used to, say, the Forum near Los Angeles, or the Palace of Auburn Hills, you are in for a shock. And I don't just mean the zone defenses, which collapse on every American as if he were giving out money. And I don't just mean the two referees (vs. three in the NBA), neither of whom seems to have a clue as to what he's doing. And I don't just mean the crazy coaches who, during their one time-out per half — that's all they get; a good idea, if you ask me — scream at you rapid-fire even though you don't speak Italian, so it all sounds like *"uuuseee iibii dibbi TINO! TITO! JERMAINE! — OK, SI?"*

No. I am talking about the atmosphere, which ranges from the thunderous, murderous, ear-rattling, drum-beating, screaming, spitting, smoke bomb-tossing sold-out crowds when the championships are played — where riot police line up courtside, brandishing their nightsticks, and things have gotten so out of hand they actually give an award each year, the Discipline Cup, to the best-behaved fans, in hopes of getting them to abandon certain unnecessary behavior, such as strangling the opposing team — to arenas where the crowd is so sparse and thin and quiet, you would think it was a Girl Scout bake sale.

Both are pretty weird.

"The NBA player is not just a part of the train over here. He's the locomotive. He's supposed to put the team on his shoulders and go."
— **Dan Peterson, Italian broadcaster and former coach**

I see two games in my last 24 hours here. The first is in Rome, a nationally televised contest, in which Darryl Dawkins, a former Piston now of the planet Lovetron and also playing for Phillips Milan, does battle with Rick Mahorn, a former Piston now of the planet "SHUTTHEHELLUP" and also playing for Il Messaggero.

Mahorn and Dawkins are all over one another, pushing, grabbing, dunking. One time Mahorn gets past, sinking a short jump shot. Another time, Dawkins barrels through for a vicious dunk. They laugh, exchange words at the free throw line. They seem to enjoy playing someone from the old country. Unfortunately, other guys are out there, too, Italian players, some of whom don't seem to want to give the ball up, particularly to the ex-NBAers. There are, by the way, a handful of very good Italian players in this league, but most are, at best, medium college level by U.S standards. They do a lot of outside shooting, and they shoot quickly and with form. Extend the arm, follow through. Good shooters.

Dribbling, on the other hand ...

"FOUL? AIN'T NO DAMN FOUL! COME ON!" I see Mahorn screaming at a ref. I see it, but I can't hear it, because the fans are whistling and hooting so loud I think the glass backboards will shatter. The arena is large, and in the upper deck an entire section is on its feet, waving banners, the fans calling themselves *"DESPERADOS."* They chant this same deafening phrase: *"CHI NON SALTA, E' MILANESE!"*

Which means, "He who doesn't jump is from Milan!"

(OK. So it's not what Desperados would yell in America. What do you want? I'm in Italy.)

... And now I am in Milan, a small place called Palalido, where Adrian Dantley's team, Breeze Milano (also known as 1. Adrian's team, 2. Milano, 3. Breeze Deodorant!) is playing the team from Sardegna. This is the other end of the spectrum. While Dawkins and Mahorn play for A1 teams, Dantley plays in A2, where you often get crowds like this; three-quarters empty in a small, sunken gym, the noise echoing in the rafters. It is strange to see Dantley, one of the greatest scorers in NBA history, taking the ball at the top of the key and doing that old spin move past one, two, three, four defenders, weaving his way through the zone like a snake weaving through a bush, finally finding the basket and banking it in to small applause. Sometimes he looks so superior, you wonder what he's doing with these guys.

But other times, too many times, it seems, he is pulled down by the level of play around him. Passes arrive too high or too low, there is little defensive switching, he seems awkward, lost, sometimes even more so than his Italian teammates. It brings to mind a lesson nearly every ex-NBA player has told me over here: "One man will not carry a team." Bob McAdoo, stuck with a bad supporting cast in Forli, put it best: "I don't care if you bring Michael Jordan and Patrick Ewing. You stick them with bad teammates and zone defenses, they'll just get dragged down like everyone else."

And Dantley has some bad teammates. Their shots clank off the rim.

Their passes are off the mark. They play no defense. Dantley's coach is a 38-year-old man who also happens to own the team and I'm not sure what his strategy is, but with the squad falling helplessly behind, and the crowd thinning even more, he sits Dantley down, even though Adrian is the only guy able to score consistently.

"Oh, boy," says Dantley's wife, Dinitri, who is sitting next to me in the stands. She holds her baby daughter, Kalani, in her lap. Her son, Cameron, plays in the aisle. The scoreboard flashes. It is old and cheap. A man walks around selling candy bars from plastic bags. We are, I realize, in little more than a glorified high school gym, a strange place for a man who once started in the NBA Finals. I ask whether this is just an off-night crowd and Dinitri says, "No, unfortunately, it's typical."

I watch her. I watch her husband on the bench. I watch the clock run down. I know Dantley is making nice money over here, but it's hard not to feel kind of sad.

"All I knew about Italy before I came here was 'The Godfather.'"
— **Rick Mahorn**

Nobody thinks about the afterlife in sports. Not when they're coming up. There is always a higher level to go to, from high school to college, from college to the NBA, from a rookie contract to a free-agent contract. More status, more money, more fame.

But what happens when the parabola peaks? What happens when you still want to play and there are suddenly no NBA takers? What happens is Italy. Or France. Or Greece. What happens is a level of game you thought you passed a long time ago. What happens is, you start down the other side of that parabola, and sometimes it can be embarrassing even if it keeps you wealthy. "I'm not worried about what people think," Dantley told me this week. "I can still play. And I got a family to support. How many jobs you can think of pay me half-a-million dollars a year?"

Fair enough. And other players make even more. So maybe they don't get the good passes, and maybe they can't understand the plays, and maybe the lockers are chintzy and the showers are low and the apartments they give you come with a washing machine in the bathroom. Hey. You grin and bear it, or you leave.

Of course, a few survival tips might help. Here, from my week in Italy, are the things players most often suggested:

1. Learn Italian.

2. Learn to play zone defense.

3. Bring a friend, preferably one who can dribble.

4. Buy lots of videotapes. By the way, without exception, the TV was every player's favorite companion. I think this is a shame, given all the culture you could take in here. Also, I flipped through the channels, and even with satellite TV, this is pretty much all you get:

CHANNEL 1: Movie in Italian.

CHANNEL 2: Talk show in Italian.
CHANNEL 3: Fuzzy picture.
CHANNEL 4: British documentary on grasshoppers.
CHANNEL 5: "Barnaby Jones" rerun.
CHANNEL 6: Fuzzy picture.
CHANNEL 7: CNN.
You mean to tell me you can't live without that?
5. If at all possible, play for a big team in a big city.
6. Use an Italian attorney.
7. Try to avoid public bathrooms (see above).

Conosco i miei polli (I know my chickens).
— **Italian way of saying, "I know what I'm talking about."**

The first famous American to play in Italy was Bill Bradley in the mid-'60s, as a Rhodes Scholar. He wore red sneakers and helped the country in the European championships, and they adored him.

A lot has changed since then, including the multimillion-dollar contracts, the two-player-per-team foreigner limit, the huge corporate sponsorship, and the interest by NBA players not only old but young (i.e., Brian Shaw, Danny Ferry, Darren Daye).

Still, if I learned anything from this week, it is that this whole crazy deal is simply what you make it. Remember that great summer you spent backpacking across Europe? It can be like that. Remember that summer you spent in the worst job of your life? It can be like that, too.

These are the images I take from my *avventura Italiana:* Vinnie Del Negro, the former N.C. State guard, being hailed as *"paisan"* after helping his team to a victory; Bob McAdoo, who has been here six years, telling me he still drives once a week to Switzerland, just to get his letters mailed reliably; Dantley, now living in a modest three-bedroom apartment, saying, "I told my wife the other day that we have a 10,000-square-foot home in Washington, D.C., and after living here, I realize we don't need anything that big"; the meal that the Il Messagero guys had together five hours before their game, a lavish spread of pasta and meat and salad and dessert, after which they all went upstairs to their hotel rooms for a team nap; an Italian point guard named Franceso Anchisi telling me, "It is time to retire. My daughter goes to school and when they ask her what her father does for work she says, 'He plays basketball,' and they say, 'No, not for fun. What does he do for work?'"

Once-a-week games, zone defenses, 30-second clock, big contracts, enormous pressure, lasagna, the Vatican, exhaust fumes ...

And this is what it all boils down to: You can have a job, you can have an adventure. But after all the noise and the smells and the sauces, what playing in Italy means to American athletes is this: a chance. Still having a chance. And you know what? For most of them, that makes it worthwhile. Trust me on this. I know my chickens. ∎

'Do you believe us now?'
U-M advances to Final Four

March 30

L EXINGTON, Ky. — The buzzer sounded like a classroom bell, and
all five of them jumped like school kids sprung for the summer.
The fans were screaming and the band was blasting and the
scoreboard, baby, the scoreboard was on their side. Chris Webber
punched at the noise and did one of those mid-air leg kicks that
threatened to carry him up through the roof of Rupp Arena and all the
way to Minneapolis. Which is where they're going, by the way.

Fab Five. Final Four.

"DO YOU BELIEVE US NOW?" Webber screamed at the crowd,
after the young Michigan players had done what few people save
themselves expected them to do, beat Ohio State, 75-71 — in overtime,
no less! — to advance to the promised land of college basketball. "DO ...
YOU ... BELIEVE US NOW?"

How could they not? After all those passes? All those slams? All those
blocks and steals and elbow-clearing rebounds as the Buckeyes' crowd
threatened to smother them in noise? It wasn't just beating Ohio State,
which had knocked off Michigan twice this season. It wasn't just that
Michigan's five freshmen scored all but two of U-M's points. No. It was
how they did it. With poise. With confidence. With defense. With a late
comeback. It was so, well, so adult.

"DO YOU BELIEVE US NOW?"

What a moment this was! Webber flapping his arms at the crowd like
a giant pterodactyl, and Jalen Rose locked in a bear hug with Jimmy
King, and Ray Jackson dancing at midcourt as the Michigan band
pumped out "The Victors." The Final Four? Even Steve Fisher, the
coach charged with molding all this raw and dangerous talent, looked a
little stunned.

"Honestly. Are you surprised?" someone yelled at him as his kids
began to cut down the nets.

"Honestly?" he yelled back, grinning. "I am surprised. But" — he
pointed to his players — "they're not."

A nd when the happy smoke from this weekend clears, what Fisher
said is what will stand out the most. Never mind the critics. These
kids expected to do this. Nowhere during these past two weeks did
Michigan act like a young team ready to lose. If anything, the
Wolverines made their opponents — including favored Oklahoma State
and Ohio State — look like lesser teams, held their star players down.
Byron Houston of the Cowboys was made to look awful Friday. Jimmy

Jackson of the Buckeyes — who some thought was the best player in college basketball this season — was rendered merely mortal Sunday, 20 points and nine turnovers.

"They played extremely well," Jackson admitted.

"They would never let us get a good look at the basket," said Randy Ayers, his coach.

You hear that, critics? Defense? It's not just a dunk-a-thon with these guys, you know.

Although there was plenty of that. Especially from Webber (a game-high 23 points), who bounced back from a foul-laden Friday night to play in the clouds Sunday afternoon, muscling inside, slamming down one swooping jam after another, until the biggest mystery was not how many points he would score but what face he would put on after each hoop. Once he came out screaming like a man having his toenails ripped out. Another time he raced upcourt with a monster-like glare at the back of Lawrence Funderburke, who was trying to guard him. There was no stopping Webber this day. There was no stopping Rose, who dribbles and shoots with such veteran excellence that he scowls whenever he misses, as if they're all supposed to go in.

"Today was 45 minutes of hard battle," Rose said, "and it was about what team wanted it most."

He left no doubt as to which team that was.

Fab Five. Final Four.

P ICTURE! PICTURE!"
Out on the Rupp Arena floor now, they were squeezing into a group photo, players, coaches, cheerleaders. Each Wolverine had a piece of the net in his hands, or his teeth, and each was wearing a hat that read: "Final Four." Someone took a head count and noticed only Jimmy King, the leaping gnome of a guard, was missing.

"JIMMY! YO! JIMMY!"

And here came King, out of the stands, and he ran across the floor and did a headfirst slide into the group, landing in their laps and flipping over with a smile as the cameras flashed …

Nice. They looked like a team.

Snapshots? You want snapshots? Take these from this rites-of-passage weekend: Rose galloping downcourt, looking left to Webber, drawing the defender, then dishing blindly to King, who was wide-open for the slam. BANG! Or center Juwan Howard, dropping in those short jumpers and racing off the floor Friday night screaming, "WE'RE GOING TO SHOCK THE WORLD!" Or Ray Jackson, the unsung freshman, sticking to Jimmy Jackson like glue, playing the last 7:19 with four fouls and still shutting down Mr. Everything. Or junior center Eric Riley, who had to swallow his pride when these young bucks arrived, giving up his starting position, yet saving their necks against Oklahoma State, coming off the bench for 15 points and a big man's night.

"Honestly," Riley was asked, "when did you stop thinking of your teammates as young?"

"First day of practice," he said.

And he wasn't kidding. Let's face it, folks. This is not normal, five freshman starters going to the Big Dance. (It has never happened before.) But these are not normal players. They have all been through big-time pressure in high school. And from the day they arrived in Ann Arbor, they made a pact that they would rise to become all they could be, as fast as they could get there.

Now they are racing through this tournament the way a child might race through the neighbors' hedges.

"Where were you last year at this time?" someone asked Ray Jackson after the game.

"I was in high school. I remember watching the Final Four with my homeboys, and I said, 'I'm gonna get there.' And they're my boys, so they said, 'Yeah, we know you are, Ray. We know you're going.'"

They just didn't know how soon.

And now, onto Minneapolis, where they will face Cincinnati on Saturday. Suddenly, not only are they in the Big Show, but the Wolverines are favored, as the Bearcats are an even bigger surprise. What we are saying is this: Michigan. Monday Night. Championship Game. Could Happen.

Now. Some think this is good for the school but bad for the players. So much success so early could make sophomore and junior years difficult, full of letdowns and anticlimaxes. But while there might be some validity to that, what are you going to do? Tell them to lose? If these kids are talented enough to win it all their first year, well, that's their destiny. They will deal with the problems later.

"Part of us wants to win it now because we are freshmen," Rose admitted. "We know we won't ever be freshmen again."

"Tomorrow is promised to nobody," Jackson added, philosophically.

And so we have this: history in the making. Michigan beating Temple, East Tennessee State, Oklahoma State and Ohio State, following the 1989 championship path, through Atlanta and Lexington. (Fisher joked that the hotel room here that he has used both times should be hermetically sealed until Michigan returns.)

And yet, while there are parallels to the '89 team, this is different. It's like watching the Beatles in their first recording session. Like watching Edison playing around in the lab with wires. You know something big is coming. It's just a matter of time.

And the time might be getting closer.

"DO YOU BELIEVE US NOW?" Webber yelled once more, as the team disappeared into the tunnel.

We saw it. And seeing is believing. Fab Five. Final Four.

This is really some story, isn't it? ∎

When players went on strike, hockey lost its warm image

April 2

If you were driving around Tuesday night listening to the Red Wings game on radio — and as it turns out, that could be the last hockey game of the year — you might have heard a segment between periods called "Spotlight on Amateur Hockey." It's an odd little program in which announcer Budd Lynch, with his deep, resonant voice, talks to kids about hockey, in this case a 13-year-old:

"So … I see you play defenseman."

"Yeah."

"Do you enjoy that position?"

"Uh-huh."

"How's your coach?'

"He's good."

Not exactly riveting radio. But it's cute. And I bet the kid's parents like it. I sat in my driveway and listened to this squeaky little defenseman and Lynch, all coming to me between periods of a big pro sporting event, and I laughed. That's the kind of next-door feeling that has always separated hockey from other money sports. That, and players who call each other "Spudsy" and "Jonesey" and who take their teeth out and who say hello to strangers and who visit places such as Moose Jaw and Flin Flon in the off-season to do charity events.

And who don't go on strike.

Until now.

On the list of awful things I expected to see in sports — and that includes rape charges, gambling scandals, recruiting violations and Don King — I must say a strike by pro hockey players was at the bottom. They had never done it before. They never seemed the type. It would have been like watching a Boy Scout playing poker.

For me, and I think a lot of other writers, hockey was always the last bastion of sanity in pro sports, an island of normalcy in a sea of money, egos and endorsement contracts.

A clean and well-lighted place to go.

On strike?

Hockey went on strike?

I feel like I have lost a friend. Like I just watched my neighbor take up with a bunch of hoods and spit at me. It's not that I'm the world's greatest hockey expert. I am not. And it's not that NHL players don't have the right to walk out, same as any American worker. They do. It's just that I never thought they would. And I took comfort in that.

These young men skate and grunt and sweat through their pads and lose teeth and break noses and bash each other against the boards, then take a shower and slap each other and say, "Good one, eh?" Well, it seemed to me young men like this would find the whole idea of a strike repellent. A man works. A man gets paid. If he has problems with his boss, he goes in and straightens them out. But he doesn't walk out with work to be done. He doesn't say good-bye when the playoffs are one week away. He doesn't strike when his salary doesn't increase 50 percent in the last two years.

A strike? Hockey?

Right until the end, I thought they would avoid this. I thought something would click in their heads that would make them say, "Wait a minute. We're not the NFL. We're not the spoiled-rotten baseball players. We're hockey. We're different."

But they didn't. And so we have nothing. No NHL games. No playoffs to ponder. I know about the issues in this strike; to be honest, I couldn't care less. The world is full of people griping about money and about keeping their "fair share." Owners say it. Players say it. When both sides are done blustering, it all comes down to greed, ego and stubbornness. On both sides. All strikes do.

But when they happen in sport, they have this one bad side effect. Fans get angry. Fans get disillusioned. And nobody is the same when the strike is over.

A couple of years ago, I took three big-time athletes to a baseball game: Joe Dumars of the Pistons, Barry Sanders of the Lions and Steve Yzerman of the Wings. The purpose was to meet Cecil Fielder, the Tigers slugger, and see what sparks flew when four superstars stood in close proximity.

I remember introducing them, and I remember Fielder bellowing to Dumars, "Hey, Joe! I can hoop, you know!" And then he turned to Sanders and laughed, "I can play me some football, too." And here was Yzerman, off to the side, with his hands in his pockets, smiling and looking uncomfortable. Cecil didn't say much to him. I don't know if he knew who Yzerman was, to be honest. Only one of the greatest hockey players in North America. But it didn't bother Yzerman. He just smiled.

Hockey always has been a little off to the side. If you ask me, that was a strength. It might have lacked the following of baseball or football, but hockey never had the anger, either, or the cynicism, or the fans who said, "That bum! He makes all that money and that's the way he plays?"

I'm not saying that will start now. But the seal has been broken after 75 years of uninterrupted labor, hockey players have walked out, and it's over money, it's always over money, and money and sports will never fit in the same pocket of the heart.

I think about that junior hockey radio program. I think about that 13-year-old kid. I wonder what he makes of all this. I bet it's not good. ∎

With his Grandma gone, Howard finds a new family

April 3

I t was time for Juwan Howard to tell his grandmother about life as a
man, to tell her about college and basketball and the new fame he
had found in Michigan. He leaned over. He began to speak.

"I'm doing good, Grandma," he said. "College, it's, like, not as easy as
I thought it would be. But you know, I'm doing OK. I'll get good grades,
like you want. … Our basketball team is doing fine. We're progressing.
We just need a little time. The fellas are real nice and all. We're like …
this family. …"

He paused. Tears were in his eyes now. Such a big man, with that
stretched torso and those long arms and the goatee around his lips and
chin, such a big man, to have tears in his eyes. Now he leaned a little
closer. He whispered.

"I think about you all the time, Grandma. You're always in my heart.
You, you're the No. 1 person in my life and I … I miss you, Grandma."

He looked at the tombstone. He put down the flowers. And there,
above the earth where the only real family he knew was buried, the big
man cried.

People see what they want to see. And so when some folks watch
Juwan Howard this weekend as Michigan plays in the Final Four, they
will see anger. A scowl. Rebounds, elbows, hard physical play. They
might even see a replay of him strutting into the tunnel last week after a
victory, yelling, "WE'RE GONNA SHOCK THE WORLD!" and
undulating in a boastful dance, like some giant caterpillar. Maybe they
say, "Great, another one."

And as usual, they miss the point. If there is one thing Juwan Howard
is not, it is "another one" of anything. In most ways, he breaks the mold
of his circumstances. Here is a kid who never had a real mother or
father, yet grew up with more manners than John Boy in "The Waltons."
Here is a jock who has every excuse to flop around in untied sneakers
and dirty underwear, yet he irons his clothes religiously and never goes
outside until he is perfectly groomed. Here is a tall, strong, powerful kid
from the rough side of Chicago, who could have gone through life
throwing his weight around, proving his toughness, yet he never got in
a serious fight, never fell into drugs, and came out of those hard streets
with only one painful scar: He had lost his only real family.

This is the story of how he found a new one.

O ur room is right here," he says, pushing through the unlocked door
on one of the upper floors of Michigan's South Quad. The place is

small, the decoration sparse; a brown carpet remnant covers the floor. Two butcher-block desks. A poster of a rap star. TV. A few videotapes. On one bed near the window sits Jimmy King, the buoyant guard and Howard's roommate, who looks up from behind a newspaper, nods, then goes back to reading. Howard's bed is against the near wall and he is fussing over that bed right now, fluffing the pillows and straightening the ends of the blanket, as if that's the thing to do when adults enter the room, make sure the bed is made.

"It's OK," I say. "I'm not going to bounce a quarter on it or anything."

"Naw, naw," Howard, 19, says, with his deep laugh. "Gotta be neat, man. Gotta be."

There were rules on 69th Street in Chicago, in that three-bedroom apartment where he lived with his grandmother. Being neat was only one of them. Do your schoolwork. Remember your manners. Say "Yes, ma'am" and "No, ma'am." And absolutely no cursing. One time, young Juwan got mad at a cousin, and, reciting words he had heard on the street, he squeaked, "I'm gonna f - - - you up."

"What did you say?" his grandmother asked.

Next thing Howard knew, he had a bar of soap in his mouth. Not just a little. The whole bar. "To this day, I can still taste that soap," he says. "Uhhhh. It was terrible!"

He didn't curse in the house anymore.

J uwan Howard got his mother's last name. He didn't get his mother. She was only 17 when he was born, had to leave school, wasn't ready to marry the man — "She still wanted to lead her life, go out, stuff like that," Howard says with surprising understanding — and so his grandmother, Jannie Mae Howard, a Mississippi-born pistol with dark hair and a weakness for cigarettes, said she would raise the boy. She even adopted him, so it was legal. His natural father, Leroy Watson Jr., who worked for the telephone company, had wanted the child to be named after him. Leroy Watson III. The grandmother shook her head, the first of a million no's.

"If I raise him, he carries my name."

Howard. Juwan Howard.

"Hey, I'm not a Leroy type anyhow," Juwan says now. "Can you picture that? I told Jalen (Rose) I was almost a Leroy, he about cracked up laughing."

If you come from a safe, warm home in the suburbs, if you are lucky enough to know Thanksgiving meals and family vacations and walking your kid sister to school, then the idea that a mother and father could let someone else raise their son might strike you as absurd. You have not spent time in the inner city. Children find their own way there; they grow up the best they can. Aunts and grandmothers are often mother and father; cousins and friends play brothers and sisters. "Juwan grew up more attached to me than his mother," says Thelma Howard, his aunt, who lived in the apartment, too. "I would have to carry him wherever I went. You know, he never had any brothers to play with. I think he always wanted that."

"Hey, I'm not the only person in the city of Chicago who grew up the way I did," says Howard, who has what he calls a "distant relationship" with his natural parents. "It's the culture that surrounded us. I was grateful I had my grandmother."

His grandmother. Yes. She woke him every morning at 6:30 — "C'mon, Nooky," she would say, using his childhood nickname, "get out of bed, time for school." She made sure he was dressed nicely, that his teeth were brushed, his hair neat, his schoolwork done. She couldn't watch him play basketball, not in person, because she got too nervous. But hey, she knew he could shoot. She had seen him throw socks through a bent clothes hanger when he was a child.

When he needed advice, his grandmother was there. And when the gangs came around, and they always come around, Jannie Mae Howard chased them off. "They were more scared of her than they were of me," Howard says, laughing.

A boy and his grandmother.

A family.

On the morning of Nov. 14, 1990, Howard dressed for school in a rayon shirt, slacks and black dress shoes. When he hugged his Grandma good-bye, she said, "Look nice today. You're gonna be on television."

It was the day Howard was to announce he had chosen Michigan, the first of the eventual Fab Five to do so. There were reporters waiting at 8 a.m. Reporters? Well, at 6-feet-9, with a soon-to-be 27-point scoring average, Howard was already one of the top five prospects in the nation. As he sat down to sign his letter of intent, he almost couldn't believe it. He was going to the Big Ten. All the work had paid off. He was getting out of the hard life. "I was psyched," he says.

It would be the best half-day of his life.

That evening, after practice, he drove home. He saw a family friend outside the door. She looked upset.

"What's the matter?" Howard asked.

"'I'm so sorry for you,' she said.

"What are you talking about?"

"Oh. You don't know ... I shouldn't be the one to tell you."

"Tell me what?"

"About your grandmother."

He leaned into her. "What about my grandmother? ... What about MY GRANDMOTHER?"

This: Earlier in the day, just hours after Juwan had signed his future, Jannie Mae Howard had collapsed in her daughter's arms. The paramedics came. The sirens whirred. It was over quickly.

She was dead of a heart attack.

"When Juwan came home, I was sitting inside, trying to figure out how to tell him," Thelma says. "I heard this noise from outside. I looked out, and Juwan had this woman by the collar and he was yelling.

"I took him inside and told him what had happened. And he blew up. He started screaming and hollering and crying. He ran upstairs. That was the first time I'd ever seen him like that."

Juwan didn't come home that week. He stayed at his high school coach's house. Every night. Slept there. Ate. Watched TV. There was no one to tell him he couldn't. No one to tell him, "Juwan, I am your parent. Come home."

His grandmother was gone.

So was his childhood.

G ood luck on Saturday," the waiter says, pouring some ice water. Howard smiles and says thank you. He is unusually polite, and unusually mature. When he doesn't understand something, he says, "Could you repeat the question?" When he agrees with something, he says, "Yes, yes. Certainly." You wonder how he got this reputation as a tough guy. Maybe it's the goatee.

"I think it is, yes," he says. "I grew it in high school because I wanted to be like Magic Johnson and Charles Smith. But people say it makes me look mean. Maybe I'll shave it off."

He rubs his chin. " 'Course, I told the guys that I would shave my head if we made it to the Final Four, but now I don't want to. I'm gonna take a beating for that."

"A beating?" I ask.

He laughs. "Yeah. That's the way we are. If we say something, we have to stick with it, or else we beat on each other."

We. We. There is talk about these Fab Five freshmen, how tight they seem for kids who really only came together seven months ago. Some of it, for sure, is the success they are enjoying. Like the early Beatles, the Michigan players are finding fame is something you share exclusively, selfishly, only you and the others know what you are feeling.

Yet in Howard's case, it is more than that. From the first day he arrived at Michigan, he found something he had been looking for. He says he does everything with his teammates now. Goes to malls. Movies. "It's like, it doesn't feel right if I'm not with at least one of them. I'm so happy that I took a gamble and came here, and they all came, too."

What do you do when you have no real home left? You find another one. So more than any other member of the Fab Five, Juwan Howard now revels in the team. He tells everyone about the things they will do. He says he is behind each of them "100 percent." Even if they decide to leave school early.

"Unless we haven't won a national championship," he adds quickly.

"First we have to do that."

We.

W hen Howard was in high school, he took the ACT exam three times before he passed. He was determined not to be shackled when he got to college. He wound up a member of the National Honor Society and homecoming king. "He has always been like that," says his old coach, Richard Cook. "Serious and focused. Even during practice, he never took a shot that wasn't useful. He started with lay-ups, backed up to the foul line, then to the three-point line."

And now he has gone all the way to the Final Four. It seems almost pre-destined. According to his aunt, the last thing Howard said to his grandmother before they closed the casket at her funeral was, "I'm going to Michigan. And I'm going to win everything for you."

"I know she's watching," he says now. "And she has the best seat in the house. Maybe even better than the press."

He laughs. Sometimes basketball is about shooting and dribbling. And sometimes it's about finding your place. There are those who watch the Fab Five and say they're too young for all that is happening to them. Maybe some of them are. But when Juwan Howard takes the court Saturday, and the ball goes up, and he can see them all from the corner of his eyes, Jalen, Jimmy, Chris and Ray, together, forever, in a hardwood circle — with Grandma watching above — it is all he ever needed and he is right where he wants to be: in the cradle of loved ones, home at last. ■

Fab Five's loss in title game isn't the end of their story

April 7

MINNEAPOLIS — As the seconds ticked away on their fabulous lives as freshmen, the expressions were suddenly different. The eyes were dazed. The mouths hung open. Chris Webber watched Duke's Antonio Lang slam down an uncontested dunk; Webber turned up court with a weary look. Jalen Rose watched Grant Hill hang on the rim after another slam; Rose clenched his jaw in disgust. This was not right. This was all wrong. The Wolverines suddenly were a team full of genies corked and stuck inside the bottle. Only when the buzzer sounded were they free to do their magic, but by that point, it was too late. The Duke players were the ones leaping and hugging and living out the dream. The Wolverines sat on the bench with their heads in their hands and covered their teary eyes with towels.

End of chapter.

The story continues.

This was no funeral, this 71-51 title-game loss to the defending champions of college basketball, the Duke Blue Devils, who showed the world in the second half how to get the most from an exhausted yet intelligent bunch of players. Oh, it might have looked bad, especially those last few minutes, when Duke left the Wolverines in the dust. But a death knell? Not for Michigan. Hey. Come on. They're kids. They're 19 years old. They made it to within one victory of a national championship. You going to bury them over that?

"When I was sitting on the bench in that final minute, I thought people were gonna misconstrue this," Webber said, fighting back tears in the locker room. "They'll say we lost because we were kids, we couldn't handle the pressure. That's not it at all.

"We lost because Duke was a better team tonight."

Exactly. Hey. A lot of teams in America sigh after they play Duke. Here was a Blue Devils team that was playing beneath itself, turning the ball over, not hustling. Even its star players were missing shots and drawing fouls. And yet, there is a reason the Blue Devils have been to the championship game three years in a row and won the last two. They come back. They play smart. They turned up the defense on Michigan, and, suddenly, getting a shot was as hard as finding a good candidate in the presidential campaign. Michigan stumbled. Michigan fell. And Duke climbed the ladder to cut down the nets.

But before you place Duke in another league, remember that three years ago, when Christian Laettner and Bobby Hurley were just getting started, Duke lost to UNLV in the final by 30 points.

Under that standard, Michigan is ahead of the game.

"We'll be back," Juwan Howard promised from his seat in the Wolverines' locker room. "We got three more of these to go."

End of chapter.

The story continues.

B ad finish aside, this will always be a great tale for the Wolverines. Were it a movie, you would have been mesmerized from the opening credits. Jimmy King, a leaping gnome from Texas, the most sought-after player in his high school. Rose, a slinky fireball of confidence, the most sought-after player in his high school. Howard, a dominating big man with an uncanny soft shot, the most sought-after player in his high school. Ray Jackson, a bundle of offense and defensive pressure, the most sought-after player in his high school. Webber, the prototype big forward, muscled beyond his years, agile beyond his frame, the most sought-after player in the country.

All five? At the same school? Let's face it. This was a team that made news on move-in day. From the time that Fisher unhooked the bridles and let all five of them start — Feb. 9, 1992, mark that on your sports calendars — they became more than kids tossing around a basketball; they became an event. A thing. A moving, jelling, growing, laughing, learning, twirling, rebounding, shooting, boasting, toasting, dunking, ker-plunking single unit of basketball talent. Oh, they lost games, but the defeats always seemed more accident than inability.

The early-season loss to Duke was followed by five straight victories. A blown game to Ohio State was avenged by a big victory over Indiana. All the time, they were learning to play together, building their machine, fitting the screws and attaching the pipes, until, by tournament time, they were on line and running. Five freshman starters. Beating Temple. Beating East Tennessee State. Beating Oklahoma State — once ranked No. 2 in the nation — and beating Ohio State, everyone's favorite from the Big Ten. Then coming here. Beating Cincinnati. Going to Monday Night in Minneapolis, against the defending national champions.

"We're the No. 2 team in the country, I guess," Webber said in the locker room. "That's higher than we've been ranked all year, right?"

R ight. It was no fun to watch the closing scenes of this championship, the sad Wolverines staring at the Blue Devils' celebration, or Webber telling cameramen to "get out of my face" in the tunnel, or Rose putting his arms around Webber as they rode to their final press conference of the tournament, holding their heads together, crying, or Howard telling reporters that he felt "so drowsy out there," because of the cold he has been fighting.

In fact, from a pure basketball point of view, this game was not much to watch, either. It was more a slugfest than a dunk-a-thon, more marked by fouls than baskets, more dotted with turnovers than assists. The Blue

Devils won because they turned 49 percent shooting by Michigan in the first half into 29 percent shooting in the second. They won because they outrebounded U-M. And they won because of Grant Hill, son of former football star Calvin Hill, who started in place of the injured Brian Davis and with 18 points is the biggest reason Duke wears the crown this morning. Laettner and Hurley were sub-par by any standards.

But as a team, Duke was good enough. And so these were the pictures Michigan was left to ponder: Rose, limited by foul trouble, scoring just 11 points and winding up on his back in the lane, as the final seconds ticked down, no foul, no help, no mercy; Ray Jackson, who didn't play well — or even many minutes — in the last two games of his freshman year, flicking a towel in disgust; Jimmy King shooting 3-for-7; Howard grabbing only three rebounds.

"We just unraveled in that second half," coach Steve Fisher said. "I don't know if it was nerves, or youth, or a little of both. I think mostly it was Duke. ...

"You know, you see the look of disappointment on the kids' faces as that horn sounds, and you see how happy the Duke kids are, and you realize what a roller-coaster business we are in."

And so it ended. On the down side.

Now. There will be those who say it is better this way. Too much success too soon can drown a team. Maybe they are right. You won't get Michigan to admit it. "The memory I'll take from this season?" Webber said, gritting his teeth. "This loss. I will never forget it."

OK. But to let the season end in sadness, to put on a maize-and-blue sackcloth this morning, that would simply be foolish. Remember, this was the championship game. What was Michigan doing here at all?

No. Better to remember these Wolverines in happier poses: Webber, throughout this tournament, slamming dunks that were matched in ferocity only by the expressions on his face. Or Rose, slicing through the lane like a rabbit slices through hedges, tossing up a soft shot that contradicts his speed, yet curls in anyhow. Or Howard, posting up, turning and banking, the classic big man move. Or King, flicking the jump switch and soaring to the backboard for a dunk.

Or James Voskuil and Eric Riley, coming to the rescue with big games. Or Fisher, sipping water on the sidelines, staying calm with all this youthful mayhem.

Better to remember them on Sunday, when they sat before the nation's media, laughing, joking, walking around a hotel lobby with people trailing behind them as if it were the most natural thing on Earth. It wasn't stardom that threw them Monday night. It wasn't pressure. It wasn't youth. It was simply a team that, on this night, was better. No failure. When you dream, you can never fail. You just dream again.

End of chapter. The story continues. Get yourself a candle and a comfortable chair; this will be a good read before it's over. ∎

Pistons' dominant era ends on a May day in New York

May 4

NEW YORK — As they showered and dressed for the last time together, zipping the bags on their fading legacy, they seemed lost as to where to go next. Once upon a time, they had lived for these showdown moments, they were potent, unbeatable, they went all the way to the final buzzers and took all the final buzzers to June.

Now, here, on a Sunday afternoon in early May, in a Madison Square Garden that couldn't even sell out, they were finally and completely mortal — and they died like so many teams had died against them, heaving desperation three-pointers as a hostile crowd sang farewell.

"NA-NA-NA-NA ..."

Joe Dumars missed a jumper.

"NA-NA-NA-NA ..."

John Salley missed a jumper

"HEY, HEY ..."

Isiah Thomas missed a jumper.

Good-bye.

"It was eerie, it was ... weird," Dumars said of the final minute of the 1992 season, after the Pistons — not so long ago the NBA champions — exited the playoffs in the first round, losing to the Knicks, 94-87. "To think there are three more rounds of playoffs and we're not in any one of them. ... I don't even know what to do now."

Here's what you do: You go home. Camelot has been closed. The illusions are over. The Detroit hockey team will play longer into this spring than the Detroit basketball team, and Lord knows the last time that happened. On this final Sunday, even the ball seemed to wave farewell. It ricocheted over Mark Aguirre's head on a missed free throw. It jumped out of Salley's palms as he tried to slam it. It left Thomas's fingers and went smack into the swat of Patrick Ewing, who rejected it with a roar.

The Pistons could no longer score. They could no longer intimidate. When the final horn sounded, and the young Knicks were hugging in celebration, Bill Laimbeer, once the symbol of Detroit's smug dominance, pushed through the crowd and grabbed several of his vanquishers. He made no threats. Instead, he said the only thing that seemed appropriate:

"Congratulations. Now go bleep up the Bulls."

Say good-bye.

This is the end of this team, the real end. Even last season, when the Pistons were dethroned by Chicago, they did not go gentle into the good night. "We'll let the Bulls have the trophy for one year," Thomas had said then, smirking. "Next year, we'll come back for it."

There were no smirks this time. And they won't be coming back for anything. The Pistons weren't dethroned Sunday, they were defrocked.

And now they will be dismantled.

Chuck Daly is gone. History. He could make the announcement this week or he could wait for months, but know this: He has coached his final game in Detroit. And when the coach changes, everyone else is fair game. It is quite possible you will not even recognize this team in two years. Between the players Jack McCloskey would like to trade and the players Thomas would like to trade, there are few — if any — safe lockers.

"If Chuck goes, I'll remember him for all the success we had under him as a team," Thomas said diplomatically in the locker room, already laying out the farewell speech. "All of my success as a professional has come under him."

Some would suggest it was over him.

But that is an issue for another time.

Sunday was a time for endings, bitter as they often are. It was a time to realize that although the Pistons were once the newest model, state of the art, the NBA teachers, they are now watching their students surpass them. Chicago beat them last year with the Detroit paw print, defense. The Knicks, no great team, beat them Sunday with defense and toughness.

"They play," Laimbeer said, "like we used to."

And the Pistons do not. Oh, they can still make you sweat to score, but not as much as they do themselves. Watching this team try to put the ball in the basket is like watching Sisyphus try to push that boulder up the mountain. It is painful. A migraine headache. No better symbol of the empty tank of Pistons offense came during the second quarter Sunday, a quarter in which Detroit managed just 12 points. Midway through the period, they cleared out for Aguirre, who tried muscling inside, dribbling, dribbling, finally leaving the floor and forcing an ugly baseline shot that missed everything — only to be caught by Laimbeer, who followed with another shot that missed everything.

Two air balls in a row?

Jake O'Donnell, the veteran referee, came downcourt after that one and yelled at a reporter: "What's the deal, first one to 70 wins?"

Say good-bye.

Now the reporters and TV cameras were pushing their way into the cramped and steamy room. The questions flew. What about Daly? What about McCloskey? What about the future?

"Ask Chuck," came the answers.

"Ask Jack."

"Who knows?"

In one corner, Aguirre talked about "not being sad, because I'm realistic." In another corner, Laimbeer said, "It's not how high you jump anymore, it's how much space you take up. And New York is such a big, physical basketball team …"

Off to one side, Dennis Rodman, only a towel around his waist, kept walking in small circles, like an expectant father. He would shrug off strangers with a "no comment," then see a familiar face and begin to gush.

"The saddest part isn't that we lost," he said, his eyes ready to moisten, "the saddest part is, we're not a team."

How different this was from just two years ago, when they all hung together in a happy champagne shower, singing and whooping and feeling like they would live forever. They had won two championships in a row. They were as good as they could get and as bad as they wanted to be. They were Joe and Zeke and Buddha and VJ and Lam and Dennis and Mark and Sal-Sal. They were a unit defined by winning. They were the embodiment of success.

But defeat erases your blueprints, so you tinker, you disrupt. James Edwards was dealt. Vinnie Johnson was released. Scott Hastings, Tree Rollins, gone. New bodies were brought in, but they could only be bodies, they could not have shared the experience, and a steaming resentment began in the locker room. Things were said. The hunger dried up. The players got older. The opponents got smarter …

You get nostalgic when greatness fades; you wish you could have frozen everything before it took a downturn. You wish the Pistons could have stayed in those parade cars rolling down Woodward Avenue. You wish they could have kept their cocky smiles, laughing at the world, saying, "Hey, who's got the ring, you or us?"

You wish.

But Detroit's basketball wishes have been used up for now.

Say good-bye.

And, finally, they did just that, walking one by one out into the Garden tunnels. The arena was nearly empty. Through the opening, you could see the basketball court being taken up in favor of ice for the evening's hockey game. Brendan Suhr, Aguirre and Laimbeer walked slowly down the concrete ramps. Daly was already gone. He had commented on the game, wished the Knicks well, then disappeared without taking questions, because he knew what those questions would be. He did say, "Everything is a consequence of your actions." He was talking about the Pistons' play. He could have been talking about his future.

Back in the locker room, only Dumars and Thomas remained. They had been the cornerstones of the championship teams, Dumars the

NBA Finals MVP the first year, Thomas the second. But now the burdens were too great. Thomas, who tried one last desperate time to win it by himself Sunday, scoring the Pistons' last 19 points, nonetheless, shot a miserable 34 percent for this series. And he was left in the dust several times Sunday by Knicks rookie Greg Anthony, who hadn't even hit puberty when Isiah entered the NBA. And Dumars, still an excellent player, simply cannot do everything.

"We played hard," Thomas kept saying, "but …"

Once Upon a Time, they put their footprints in the sand and they were kings of the beach, stronger and tougher than anybody out there. They shook up their city. They shook up basketball. Once Upon a Time, when the baskets came easier, nobody could best them in the final quarter of the final game. They said, "This is our moment." And it was.

"May," Dumars said now, picking up his bag, "I don't even know what goes on in May.

"I guess I'm gonna find out."

And that is the end of Once Upon a Time. ∎

Wings' season of promise stops at red light in Chicago

May 9

CHICAGO — The game ended the way they all seemed to end, the way this whole damned, crazy postseason has ended. Bang — and you're dead. Less than 100 seconds left on the regulation clock, the crowd on its feet, screaming like beasts. Paul Ysebaert bumped into Sergei Fedorov deep in his own end. The puck squirted loose, here came Chicago's Greg Gilbert, scraping it out, shoveling it to a driving Brent Sutter, who pushed it past Tim Cheveldae for the only goal that mattered — which was also the only goal of the night. Game over.

Darkness.

"I watched that whole play like I was in slow motion," said a teary-eyed Shawn Burr after the Red Wings were swept from the playoffs with a heartbreaking, 1-0 loss to Chicago. "I was screaming for someone to pick up Gilbert, just screaming, 'Get him! Someone get him!' "

No one got him. And a few terrible moments later, the Wings skated off the ice, heads down, showered in beer cups and noise. As coach Bryan Murray made his exit, a broom flew from the stands and landed at his feet.

Red light.

Darkness.

"It's going to be so weird getting up tomorrow with no hockey," Cheveldae said. Home for the summer? The Red Wings? Already? That's like watching the Rolling Stones leave the stage after two numbers. Like mowing half the lawn. Like shaving the left side of your face. Talk about incomplete! I'm still waiting for the Wings to play a good game against Chicago, a team they beat five times during the regular season.

It's not going to happen.

"They were the better team; they won four games; they played better in all four," Cheveldae said. He looked at his feet. How sad a picture he was, dressed in the bright yellow sport jacket that had brought him luck in the Minnesota series. He had vowed to use it only in desperate situations, such as Friday night, with the Wings down to their last gasp of the year.

Now here he sat, his hair wet, like a little kid waiting for his folks to pick him up after swimming practice.

"You're gonna give up on that jacket now?" he was asked.

He forced a chuckle. "I'll sell it to you."

Red light.

Darkness.

M an, what a lousy week for Detroit! First the Pistons. Now the Red
Wings. Was it something we said? Did we forget to shower?
Detroit sports fans are now forced to watch the 1992 Tigers — which
ranks right up there with watching "Who's the Boss?" reruns. The worst
part is we are all still trying to figure out how the Wings lost this series.

And so are they.

What happened to that offensive machine that used to wear these
uniforms? In three of the four games against Chicago, the Wings scored
a total of two goals. Two? With the talent they have?

Here they were again Friday night, this group with more potential
offense than the Houston Oilers, and they simply could not find the net.
Sometimes they couldn't even find the puck. Whenever you looked up at
the shots-on-goal numbers, it was Chicago 7, Detroit 1, or Chicago 10,
Detroit 4.

There were moments when the Wings seemed to be playing as if
trapped in a foxhole. They fought back, but they never seemed
confident. Sluggish at times, off balance at times, they appeared to be
waiting for the other shoe to drop. Even a string of power-play
opportunities did nothing to put zip in their skating. It was as if with
every failed opportunity they came back saying, "Geez, it's getting
worse. It's getting worse!"

It did. They managed to equal the shots on goal. Even take an
advantage. But they kept hitting Ed Belfour's pads, or his stick, or a
Chicago defender's sprawling body. It was that kind of series. A series in
which the Wings' best players put in a lot of time on the power play, and,
getting nothing there, perhaps were a bit worn out for the regular play.
A series in which Chicago's lesser lights shone brightly — guys such as
Gilbert and Dirk Graham and Jocelyn Lemieux.

It was a series in which the Hawks seemed always to be falling on top
of a Detroit puck, or holding a Red Wing back with a stick, or
shadowing him with the body. At times it was like trying to separate two
magnets.

"If you could have one moment back from this whole thing, what
would it be?" Steve Yzerman was asked.

"The first face-off of Game 1," he said. "I just want to start the series
again."

Red light.

Darkness.

A nd now, the morning after. There will be theories galore as to why
this playoff hit the iceberg and sank so quickly. One — perhaps the
most sensible — is that the seven-game Minnesota series took so much
out of the Wings, they needed to take a breath — only the breath came
during Games 1 and 2 against Chicago, two games they lost. By the time

the Wings collected themselves, they were in a foreign building, and they dropped a one-goal game in the final five minutes.

That quick. The series was over.

That's one theory. Others include 1) the always popular "blame the goaltender" approach; 2) the overused "Bryan Murray and his mediocre playoff history" approach; 3) the frequent "Where are the star players like Yzerman and Fedorov, and why aren't they scoring more?" theory; and 4) Lee Harvey Oswald.

OK. So I stuck that last one in. What's the difference? The fact is, what happened here cannot be summed up in any single paragraph, or blamed on any single player. It was a combination of bad plays, bad breaks, funny bounces, individual lapses and — did we all forget? — the opponent's playing some pretty good hockey. Give Chicago credit. That physical, dumping, bumping style of hockey might not beat everybody, but it sure neutralized the Red Wings. The Hawks got terrific goaltending and timely scoring. Their whole performance seemed to be summed up by that game-winner by Sutter.

"What was it like watching that red light go on so late in the game?" Jimmy Carson was asked afterward.

"It was like freeze-frame," he said. "I don't think anyone out there who hasn't played with this team, who hasn't competed and traveled and lived with these guys since Sept. 7, watched us progress, shared our dreams, all the high hopes, and then to be out there and see that goal score and just like that, it's … done."

Just like that. The shame of this — beyond the obvious — is that the Wings' wonderful accomplishment in the regular season (98 points) will be obliterated by the bad taste of these playoffs. But maybe that's how it should be. Maybe hockey teams should stop spending time patting themselves on the back for the regular season, since it means absolutely nothing. The Wings learned some valuable lessons about upping their game in the early rounds of the playoffs — and those lessons, in the end, might be worth far more than the 98 points ever could be.

So the Wings go home now, to their wives and kids and fishing trips and golf games. Their challenge will lie in not destroying all the confidence they built from November to March. The management's challenge will be to improve the roster without destroying it.

And the fans' challenge?

To sit through the next five months of baseball and try not to leap out the window.

Good luck. ∎

From Athens to Barcelona, the Olympics' naked truth

July 23

They ran naked, for one thing.

Really. In ancient Greece, or so the legend goes, Olympians sometimes ran their races in the raw. Nude. A-buffo. Today, Russian athletes don't have a flag or even an anthem. But they have shoe contracts.

Progress, right?

To moan that the Olympics "ain't what they used to be" is to say Shirley Temple doesn't wear pigtails anymore. Tell us something we don't know. From a small, simple ritual that featured one race and a prize of an olive wreath, the Games have evolved — if you can call this evolution — into TripleCast, a $125 act of stupidity in which the American couch potato can watch everything from water polo to the modern pentathlon minute-by-minute, day-by-day, on his cable TV. Even Zeus couldn't handle that. I don't care if they all ran naked.

These days, the Olympics are big. I mean BIG. Looking back on where they came from and where they are now gives you the feeling of a farmer who put a male and female rabbit in a cage, then returned one year later. Whoa! Where did all this come from?

Ah, but the Olympics rarely look back — not on the bad stuff, anyhow. Although they almost died several times this century — the 1904 Games in St. Louis were such a fiasco that the Greeks put on another Summer Games two years later just to convince people the Olympics should continue — the closing ceremonies still end with the words, "See you in ..." (wherever the next Games are scheduled). Already, they are building stadiums in Atlanta for 1996. Already, hotel rooms are booked. Already, Jane Fonda has picked out a dress.

And we haven't even found out who the world's greatest athlete is this year.

Think about what the Games have become! Reebok. Butch Reynolds. Yugoslavia. Steroids. Badminton. Charles Barkley. These concepts would have baffled the ancient Greeks. And they invented math.

Yet as we head toward the year 2000, there is no stopping the whopping. The Olympics continue to bloat into this massive flying zeppelin, swelling fatter and fatter with demonstration sports, corporate sponsorships, professional teams, drug tests and camera wires.

Who would have ever guessed that from Point A, as in Athens, we'd now be at Point B, as in Barcelona? A few Olympic traditions, and their modern-day counterparts:

Ancient Greece: The Olympics consist of one event, a footrace, that takes less than a minute.

1992: Sixteen days, 28 sports, about 10,000 athletes and 9,000,000,000 commercials.

Ancient Greece: Boxers try to get an edge by sticking nails in their hard leather gloves and shred their opponents' faces.

1992: Boxers must fill a urine beaker before they can exit the building.

Ancient Greece: The Games feature an event called Pancration, a bloody man-to-man battle in which anything — scratching, kicking, eye-gouging — is allowed.

1992: Badminton is an Olympic sport.

Ancient Greece: Emperor Nero insists on competing in the Games, accompanied by 5,000 bodyguards.

1992: Michael Jordan arrives in Barcelona.

Ancient Greece: Nero competes in the chariot races, falls out of his vehicle but is helped up by fearful competitors, who let him win the race without a struggle.

1992: Larry Bird.

Ancient Greece: All wars are suspended during Olympic Games.

1992: Yugoslavia.

Ancient Greece: The mother of Peisidorous, a boxing champion, disguises herself as a man to be in her son's corner.

1992: Sandra Farmer-Patrick runs the 400-meter hurdles in a two-piece, sequined, bikini track suit.

1896: A Greek water carrier named Spyridon Louis wins the marathon but refuses a barber's gift of free haircuts for life because he wants to preserve his amateur status.

1992: The U.S. basketball team is staying in a $900-a-night hotel.

1908: Dorando Pietri, an Italian marathon runner, hobbles into the stadium, dazed, weak, and is helped across the finish line by sympathetic Olympic officials.

1992: Butch Reynolds sues the Olympics to let him compete.

1904: The St. Louis Games, due to poor organization, take 4½ months to finish.

1992: NBC begins its promotion campaign.

1904: The St. Louis Games feature a competition between "uncivilized tribes."

1992: British soccer fans arrive in Barcelona.

1912: Jim Thorpe is stripped of his two gold medals and erased from Olympic history books because he was paid $2 a game for playing semi-pro baseball the summer before.

1992: Reebok spends $20 million on a Dan vs. Dave ad campaign — before either one qualifies for the team.

1920: The swimming competition is held in a moat.

1992: Olympic swimmers will wear warm-ups designed by Henry

Grethel.

1920: Charley Paddock, a barrel-chested Californian, wins the 100 meters after drinking a prerace glass of sherry and a raw egg.

1992: Ben Johnson is back again.

1924: A French spectator pokes an American student for "loud rooting."

1992: "USA! USA! USA! ..."

1932: The first full-scale Olympic village is used, and athletes love it so much that some cry when they have to leave.

1992: Carl Lewis books his hotel suite.

1952: The USSR competes for the first time.

1992: The Unified Team competes for the first time.

1976: East Germany wins more gold medals than the United States.

1992: East Germany?

1976: African boycott.

1980: U.S. boycott.

1984: Soviet boycott.

1988: South African and Cuban boycott.

1992: No boycott.

And that's just a taste of it. There is no stopping the Olympic explosion. Big goes to bigger. The Games are like that giant marshmallow man in the film "Ghostbusters" — massive, frightening and yet appealingly childlike at the same time.

After all, the idea of the Games — the best athletes in the world, brought together in one single, harmonious competition — is exactly what the ancient Greeks were hoping for. Of course, they never figured on Nike, Chuck Daly, Latvia, Estonia, Summer Sanders, Bob Costas or the synchronized swimming team.

But, hey, they ran naked. What did they know?

Let the Games begin. ■

Matador left without a fight as Spain embraces Olympics

July 27

BARCELONA, Spain — In the old, bloody days, when his was the only sport worth talking about in this country, the young man's courage would make him a hero. Kings would applaud. Senoritas would throw roses into the ring.

Now he stands alone in an old brick arena. It is Sunday morning, the first full day of the Summer Olympics, which might as well be a million miles from here. There are no Olympic symbols in the Placa de Toros. There are only faded posters and a sound that echoes from the wooden stalls below — *ca-clump, ca-clump* — the sound of bulls that will die tonight. He folds his arms. He watches them move.

"Most men, they do not like to see the bulls before they fight," he says. "But I am an exception. I come even when I do not have a fight."

He nods his head. "Just to look."

Here stands the lonely matador, in cotton slacks, black loafers, short brown hair and a jeweled crucifix around his neck. He is only 27, his name is Manolo Porcel, and he lives with his parents and his six brothers in a cramped apartment by the airport. He is part of a dying breed that once symbolized this nation, macho men ready to stab the beast. You wouldn't even think of an Olympics here in the 19th Century without a bullfight. Now they can't push it far enough away.

"Politicians," he says, sighing.

Across the city, little girls are diving off a platform, and some NBA millionaires are pretending to give a game to a team of Angolans. Here, in the land of his birth, Manolo gazes at the bulls and wishes he were in action tonight, waving the sword, tipping his hat. Where are his Olympics, he wonders?

It is no longer politically correct for Spaniards to love bullfights, especially not in Barcelona, where they have cut the season to a few lonely months and turned one of the two main bullrings into a concert arena. The country that inspired Ernest Hemingway to write "Death in the Afternoon" wants no more bulls dead, the hell with tradition. Catalonia, where the Games are held, wants to throw a blanket over the thing altogether.

"The people who make these Olympics want the world to see how we are modern as all of Europe," Manolo says. "This, they think, is primitive."

Some old men walk up. They wear caps and smoke cigars and have bellies that hang over their belts. Bullfight fans. One is asked what he thinks of Manolo, and he wags a finger.

"Good," he croaks. "Very good matador."

There was the night Manolo fought with exceptional style and was awarded the bull's ear by *el presidente*. There was the night he had to leap into the ring and kill the bull that just moments before had gored his fellow matador in the stomach. There was the special night he wore *el traje de luces*, the suit of lights. There was even the night in Barcelona, not long ago, when he heard the cheers of *"Ole!"* on a warm Sunday evening.

But bullfights grow scarce, and Manolo — who, like most young matadors is following the path of an older relative, his uncle, a retired matador — is lucky if he gets 15 *corridas* a year. Unlike Carl Lewis, he has no agent. Unlike Summer Sanders, he books his own dates. He phones organizers, or they phone him. He goes where there is work.

"I hope, one day, to support myself only as a matador," he says. "But for now, I also do *taxidermista.*"

Taxidermy. He specializes in bulls heads.

The sun grows hotter. The sand in the ring is packed and hard. Manolo, who trains like any other athlete — "running, cycling, weight lifting" — might practice his technique on a day like this, but the training school on Montjuic has been closed for the Olympics. It is in the shadow of the main stadium, and the organizers said sorry, no access.

Manolo walks through the gates and out toward the Gran Via. No one recognizes him. A few blocks down, an entire office building is covered with the image of Michael Jordan. This is what it has come to in Spain: A bullfighter gets no attention. A kid from North Carolina gets his own building.

"When I go out with senoritas, I do not even say I am a matador," he says. "I wait until I know them better. Sometimes they laugh.

"But this is my love. And there is no fooling here. When you drive to work as a matador, you may never drive home. How many sports ask you to risk your life, every time?"

It is hot and bright and dusty, the kind of day Hemingway once wrote about. Across the city, they are swimming the breaststroke and punching a volleyball over a net.

The matador squints. In the old, bloody days, he might have been a hero. But today, he is just another Barcelonan without a ticket. He says he will go home now, to his apartment by the airport, and make himself something to eat. ∎

You call this badminton? They don't even have beer

July 30

BARCELONA, Spain — Now, wait a minute. I think we've taken this "all sports are equal" thing a little too far here. Badminton? Badminton is an Olympic event? You win a medal for slapping a birdie over a net? What's next? Olympic hot dog grilling?

"Badminton's cool," someone says. "Go see it."

Listen, pal. I know badminton. I know the roots of badminton. The roots of badminton are in your basement, in a box that sits untouched until the Fourth of July barbecue, when you take it out and pray the moths haven't eaten the rackets.

Here is what happens next:

First, you spend an hour untangling the net.

Then you have a beer.

Then you hold the birdie under the faucet to wash off the mildew.

Then you have another beer.

Then you call in your kids, and you give them the rackets, the birdie and the net — which you still haven't untangled, so it looks like something a New England fisherman would pull in over the side of the boat — and you say a few inspirational words, such as, "Here. Try not to kill yourselves."

Then you have another beer.

So I know badminton, OK? But because I am a curious man, I take a trip to the Olympic badminton "venue." And I'm thinking, "Venue? Don't they mean 'backyard'?"

And I walk inside.

And I'm thinking "inside?"

And this is what I see: four large, hard courts with perfectly straight nets, and these ridiculously healthy-looking players, racing around, slapping birdies a la Boris Becker. Some are even wearing kneepads.

Where I come from, wearing kneepads to play badminton is like playing checkers in a helmet.

And I don't smell any burgers.

Where the hell is the grill?

You have come to interview the Malaysians?"

Well, sure, I say. I mean, I'll interview whoever has the barbecue sauce.

The official points to three well-built men, with jet-black hair and stringy mustaches. They are in full badminton action, looking very much like tennis players, running and grunting as they whack the birdie at tremendous speeds. They do drop shots. Overhead smashes. Someone should stop them, I figure, before they knock over the beer cooler.

"They are brothers," the official says. "The Sidek family. Very good players. Medal favorites."

Hmm. They must celebrate the Fourth of July every month in Malaysia.

Their practice ends. I approach the brothers. They are Razif, 30, Jalani, 29, and Rashid, 23. I figure they will be totally thrilled that a journalist has come to talk to them, and maybe offer me a burger. I introduce myself to Razif. This is the first thing he says:

"Didn't you interview me yesterday?"

I have been pretty patient with the Olympics. I said nothing when they added synchronized swimming, even though you can see the same thing in an Esther Williams movie. And I kept quiet about rhythmic gymnastics, which should be called "Olympic ribbon waving."

I put up with taekwondo and field hockey and yachting — amateurs? yachting? — and I even looked the other way when some genius tried to make bowling an Olympic sport. ("If he gets this 7-10 split, Chris, he'll have the gold medal... .") But I will not — will not! — tolerate an attitude from a badminton player.

"No," I snap. "I was not here yesterday."

Razif shrugs. "I do many interviews."

He must be joking.

He is not joking. In Malaysia, badminton is big, and so are the Sideks. They get stopped for autographs. Women bat their eyes flirtatiously. These guys — who have been offered $100,000 each by their government if they win a medal — are the Malaysian Dream Team.

Go figure.

"At first, I like the attention," Rashid says, "but now, it can be troublesome."

Yeah. Everyone wants you to sign a birdie.

By the way, the Malaysians do not use the word birdie, or the British equivalent shuttlecock, which has to be the worst name in sports since pigskin.

This is what the Malaysians call a birdie: "*Bulutangkis.*" As in "Boy, I really smashed that *bulutangkis!*" Or, "OK, everyone, watch the *bulutangkis!*"

(By the way, these birdies — or *bulutangkis* — are not cheap. Nor are the top-flight badminton rackets, which can cost $100 — or $98.01 more than an entire badminton set costs in America. And ours comes with a box.)

"You know," I tell Razif, "in my country, badminton is quite different—"

"Yes, I know," he says. "You play on grass. Ha ha. Is very funny."

He pulls off his kneepad and zips his $100 racket inside a leather case. I decide not to bring up the cooler thing.

Instead, I ask the Sideks how they got started in the sport. They say their father pushed them. They say they "wanted to be football (soccer) players," but Papa made them play badminton instead. I can see this happening in Texas, can't you?

But what the heck? These are the Olympics. All sports welcome. Even ones that come in a box.

"It was always our father's dream to be badminton champion," Rashid says. "Now, he gets his dream with us."

Maybe. What he doesn't get is a burger.

And as far as I'm concerned, it ain't really badminton until he does. ∎

Olympic gymnastics training robs girls of precious youth

July 31

BARCELONA, Spain — So where does Kim Zmeskal go for a refund? Where does she go to get back the childhood she sacrificed for gymnastics, or the school she left to spend eight hours a day in the gym? Where does she go to get fresh bones, never broken or sprained, or fresh muscles, never pulled or torn? Where does she go for fresh confidence, never shattered into a million pieces like it was Thursday night, in front of the whole world?

Tell me where. Then tell her. I love the sport of women's gymnastics; it is breathtaking, like dance, the purest command of the human body. But I defy anyone to attend an Olympic gymnastics competition — at least anyone who loves children — and not walk out terribly upset.

Seeing Zmeskal, a tiny, 4-foot-7 creature who was a pre-Olympic favorite, step awkwardly out of bounds during her first event Thursday, hearing the crowd groan, seeing her face collapse into tears on the sidelines because she knew, instantly, that there was no way she could come back from that, her Olympics were dying in front of her, and she still had three events to go — seeing that, you wanted to leap the railing, grab her under your arm and run out the door, yelling: "What's the matter with you people? Can't you see she's just a child?"

And despite the glory that was showered on other gymnasts, despite the wonderful gold-medal performance by the Unified Team's Tatyana Gutsu, the riveting final vault that launched 15-year-old Shannon Miller all the way to the silver medal, the overall impression you have leaving the building is simply this:

It is just not worth it.

There was a girl in this competition, perhaps you saw her, a North Korean named Kim Gwang-Suk. She had the body of a 9-year-old, no curves, no chest, no sign of puberty. Her face was grade-schoolish, with a little ponytail, and she was missing one of her front teeth. Some say it hasn't grown in yet.

She is listed as 17 years old.

This is just one of the lies in this sport. Faking ages to enter competitions (the minimum age for the Olympics is 14) is quite common in certain countries. A bigger concern is why the sport has shifted its emphasis from grace and form — remember the older Russian gymnasts of the '70s? — to lift, flight and power. And the fact is, a tiny, prepubescent body can bounce off a vault or flip though midair much better than one laden with the extra flesh of a blossomed teenager.

"The sport is for the little girls now," says Bela Karolyi, the Svengali who coaches Zmeskal.

But at what price? At least half a dozen times Thursday night, I saw girls fall off the bars and land flat on their faces, or overshoot their dismounts and bounce onto their heads. And these are the best gymnasts in the world.

Did you know that many young female gymnasts never develop enough body fat to start a menstrual cycle? That they can go years in this unnatural stage, as if someone roped their hormones and held them captive?

And they are considered the lucky ones?

For this, parents send their children away from home. Have them live with foster families. Have them spend sunup to sundown with a guy like Karolyi, who once said of the championship building process: "These girls are like little scorpions. You put them all in a bottle, and one scorpion will come out alive. That scorpion will be the champion."

I don't know about you, but I don't want to raise a scorpion. I don't want my daughter's wrists broken, her back aching, her knees operated on before her 16th birthday. I don't want her in therapy for years, learning how to cope in the real world she left so long ago.

Which brings us back to Zmeskal. Just how normal do you think her life will be now? A world champion, a heavy favorite, the cover girl of Time magazine — and she slips in the first 10 seconds of her best event Sunday, barely qualifies for the all-around competition, then makes a beginner's mistake Thursday and steps out of bounds during her floor routine. Shaken, upset, she follows with another little slip on the beam, and boom! That's it. Bye-bye, glory. She finishes 10th, behind a Spanish girl who couldn't manage a single 9.9 from the judges.

"I didn't have the meet of my life," Zmeskal said, fighting tears in the floor area after the competition. Her hair was pulled back in its tight blond ponytail. She came up to the waist of most of the reporters. "It wasn't the best night of my life."

She looked like she wanted to fly to another planet.

Look, this is not picking on gymnastics. All sports require sacrifice. All sports have physical dangers. But few demand that young girls peak at age 14 or 15, that they be ready to take on the world by then and not slip even the slightest bit on a four-inch beam or a pair of wooden bars. Few sports are so unforgiving of maturity.

There will be no next Olympics for Kim Zmeskal. At 20, she'll likely be too old. If she doesn't salvage a medal in one of the individual apparatus events – which are all that remain now – she'll go down as one of the biggest busts of Barcelona, a terribly heavy burden to bear.

And where are the people responsible for this?

Well, there is Karolyi, the ex-Romanian turned American star-maker, who sneaked out of the gym to avoid reporters after Thursday's competition. I caught Karolyi just before he got on the bus. This is what he said of his prize student's collapse:

"Her nerves gave up. It was something I expected. She became a victim of her own success."

And his feelings toward her now?

"I really feel sorry for this little girl. She could have been shaped into an Olympic champion. But the inside politics, all this dirtiness about the selection procedure, all this hocus-pocus, led to the destruction of her greatest ability: her confidence."

Right. When in doubt, blame politics.

It might be good that Karolyi is quitting gymnastics after these Olympics. Fewer Americans will be tempted to race down to his Houston academy and hand their kids over on a leash — just because he once sculpted Nadia Comaneci and Mary Lou Retton. Last I saw, wasn't Comaneci a bit of a dizzy defector, living in Canada? And Retton, now in her 20s, doesn't seem to have advanced much beyond a Kewpie doll, at least from my conversations with her. Is that how you want your daughters to grow up?

As the arena emptied Thursday, Dave Zmeskal, father of the fallen champion, stood by the railing, looking out on the floor. He was asked whether he still thought it was worthwhile, the leaving school, the injured wrists, the screaming by Karolyi, the non-returnable hours of his daughter's adolescence?

"Oh, yes," he said. "I have no regrets."

He ought to. Kim Zmeskal is too young to know any better. So is Shannon Miller. So is that tiny girl from North Korea who is being used in something that — when you consider the bandages, the bruises and the verbal lashings — is just shy of child abuse. We watch these Olympics, year after year, and this situation gets worse and worse, younger and younger. And ultimately, it must be the parents who put a stop to it.

"They're just kids," Dave Zmeskal said, looking at the floor where his daughter lost her dreams. "They're just kids. They make mistakes."

Right.

What's your excuse? ∎

Dimas is last but not least among U.S. Olympic heroes

August 3

B ARCELONA, Spain — Now the flashbulbs were snapping like crazy. He had to laugh at that. Last summer, someone shot a flash as he ran toward the vault, right in his eyes, and, blinded, he missed the vault completely and landed on his head. He was knocked unconscious. The medics had to help him out.

You could have seen that on every blooper show from here to Albuquerque. It was the most famous thing Trent Dimas had ever done.

Until Sunday night.

You wait for greatness. You wait for heroes. And you wait for the perfect Olympic moment. So here was Dimas, a 21-year-old gymnast with a full flashing smile and dark, wavy hair that had Spanish girls cooing when he walked past, and here he was, just sitting around, no one paying attention. He was like an extra in a Batman movie. The setting was big, but who was he? Just another American gymnast.

And American gymnasts — especially the men — had done a pretty big belly flop at these Games.

So he waited. He stood up. He sat down. He had qualified for only one event in the apparatus finals, and wouldn't you know it? It was the last one. The high bar. Dimas had come to the arena at 5 p.m. and now it was almost midnight, and he still hadn't gone.

"Guy could have gone out for a hamburger and had time to digest it," someone joked.

Trent Dimas was the last American on the last event on the last night of gymnastics. All across Barcelona, there seemed to be more important things to see. Jackie Joyner-Kersee was winning her heptathlon gold medal at Estadi Olimpic. The U.S. boxers were grumbling over a rob job out in Badalona. The Dream Team was busy slicing up the Spaniards in front of the hometown crowd. Gymnastics? Who needed it? If a handful of U.S. reporters were there, it was a lot.

Now it was after midnight. The escalators had stopped their climb up Montjuic. People were hailing cabs outside. The arena was half-empty.

Dimas ran through his routine in his mind, the back flips, the release moves. Finally, the last American gymnast in the last event on the last night heard his name called over the loudspeakers.

"TRENT DIMAS, USA."

And somewhere, the sky began to open.

I can't believe it!" he kept saying over and over when it was done, when he had pulled off the impossible and won a gold medal, the first

American gymnastics gold in a non-boycotted Games since 1932. "I can't believe it! I can't believe it!"

He hugged his coach, Ed Burch, who has been with him since he was a kid. He grabbed his head in disbelief. He looked to the stands. He hugged his coach again. "Numb!" he said. "I am totally numb!"

What had he done, this New Mexico kid who skipped college to concentrate on the Olympics? Just the most mesmerizing high-bar routine of the Games, complete with three release moves, including one in which he lets go, does a back flip and somehow finds the bar between his legs. Don't ask me how. He owned that bar. His body was wooden when he needed it straight, and a rubber pretzel when he needed it bent. He swung with such force, it seemed he would lift off into space. He scissor-kicked. He slid through his own arms.

And when he finally let go for good, he tumbled backward twice in mid-air and landed smack in the middle of history. The place erupted, like an opera house when the diva hits her last magnificent note.

Golden.

"It all came together when I needed it," Dimas gushed. "After I stuck my dismount, I was afraid to move. I wanted the judges to see how I stuck it."

They saw. They were impressed. They gave him a 9.875, the winning mark. An American? Yes. Although the night belonged to another star from another country — the Unified Team's Vitaly Scherbo set a record for gold medals, winning the rings, pommel horse, vault and parallel bars — this one thing, this last event on the last night of gymnastics, could not be taken away.

Call it a parting snapshot.

These Games, so far, have been a disappointment to some U.S. fans. They say we're lacking Olympic heroes. They sigh because there are no feel-good faces to take into the night, no Mary Lou Rettons or Greg Louganises as there were in Olympics past.

Here is a feel-good face, America. Take a look at the kid who barely made this team, the kid who was blooper material last summer, who wasn't supposed to have a chance against the former Soviets and the Chinese.

Take a look at that smile, that wavy hair — the whole package looks like a cross between gymnast Mitch Gaylord and actor Vincent Spano — and then look a little deeper. Look at the eyes moistening on the victory stand. Look at the lungful of air he exhales. Look at those lips singing along. "And the rocket's red glare ..."

That's the Olympics you're seeing there, folks. The last American in the last event on the last night of his competition. They were flashing the bulbs now, taking his picture and capturing the moment. But this time, under all that hot light, he didn't fall, he didn't blooper and land on his head. He was standing there, like destiny, and he didn't even blink. ∎

Lean on me, father tells son as he struggles to finish line

August 5

BARCELONA, Spain — The son went down as if he had been shot, grabbing his leg, falling to the track. The father, watching from the stands, felt something sink in his stomach. He lowered his head. The memories flashed back: the park, near the old house, the boy, 6 years old, racing alongside him, grabbing his body.

"Where's the finish line, Dad?" he would say, laughing. "Carry me to the finish line. ..."

The finish line. The noise of the crowd snapped him back to reality. Cheering? What were they cheering? He looked up to see his son, face twisted in pain, rising to his feet on the red oval track, waving off the medics who carried a stretcher. Derek Redmond, a British sprinter whose Olympic dream was over, whose right hamstring had just snapped like a Popsicle stick, was trying to complete his 400-meter race. He had half that distance to go. Because he couldn't walk, he began to hop. He hopped like a wounded fugitive. One step. A grimace. Two steps. A yell.

The son was crying. And the father had to come.

He doesn't really remember all the steps down from section 131, row 22, seat 25. He doesn't really remember leaping over the railing or landing on the field, or pushing off security guards too stunned to stop him. The Olympics? He was not at the Olympics anymore. Jim Redmond was a parent outside a burning house, hearing a cry through the window. And all he knew was "my son, I had to get to him."

And suddenly, he was alongside him.

"Dad," Derek said, grabbing him, throwing an arm around his shoulder and burying his head to hide the tears. "Dad ... get me back to Lane 5. I want to finish."

And leaning on each other, just like the old days, father and son made their way down the track, while stunned officials looked on, frozen, and the crowd, and the whole world watching, got this lump in its throat.

You can set the stage for heroism. You can plan your Olympics for maximum exposure, light the skies with fireworks, invite kings and queens and NBA stars. But you can never create the magic of real life. It just happens.

"If I tried to do that again, I don't think I could," Jim Redmond admitted after this burst of real life was over Monday night, after he had taken his 26-year-old son where his son wanted to go, across the line, into the finish area, where the medical staff once again came running with a stretcher.

"No stretcher!" the father barked.

He knew what his son wanted. He had been with him all these years, through the good times, when he made the Olympic team, when he set the British record in the 400, and through the bad times, the four operations on his Achilles tendon, the countless other injuries that left him on crutches, unable to run as late as six weeks before these Games.

"Derek's pride was at stake out there," he said. "If he had been taken out on a stretcher he would never have run again. We had agreed, no matter what, that he was going to finish the race. He was going to say he got through the semifinal of the Olympic 400 meters.

"All he needed was a little support. I'm his father. I'm supposed to provide it."

And so he did. And when he was sure his son was OK, when the hamstring had been iced and wrapped and the tears had dried, Jim Redmond made his way back to his seat, stopping to apologize to every official along the way, because, "I didn't want the British to get a bad name for disrupting the Olympics. ..."

You couldn't make up a story like this. Back in North Hamptonshire, in the small village they call home, Redmond's wife, daughter and son-in-law were watching this whole drama on TV. The daughter, nine months pregnant, saw her brother crying in agony, then saw her father, filling up the screen with his heavy-set form, the crowd rising to applaud him — Dad? On the track? — and, apparently, this was all too much. She felt this sudden spasm. Next thing you know, the doctor was at the door ready to deliver a baby.

As it turned out, that was a false alarm. But the idea was wonderfully real. Right here, in the middle of an Olympics weighted down with commercialism, sagging with drug rumors, fighting its own largess, we have a plain old family in a plain old town that seems so tied into one another, when one feels pain, the other twinges. And goes to help.

Even if it means leaping onto the Olympic track.

"In an emergency," Jim Redmond said, "you don't need accreditation."

He is almost 50 years old. Two decades ago, he started a business he still owns. A machinery shop called "J. Redmond & Sons."

"I had hoped Derek would take over, but he has other ideas. That's OK. He's a good kid. He keeps my name clean. You can't ask for more than that."

Or more than this, maybe the best story of the 1992 Games. Like most Olympians, Derek Redmond came here dreaming of gold, the fantasy, the end of the rainbow. Instead, he got his own backyard. Here they were again, arm in arm, headed for a finish line; J. Redmond & Son, together as usual.

Come to think of it, what could be more golden? ∎

Screams! Threats! Thuds!
Wrestling is whole lotta sole

August 8

BARCELONA, Spain — I knew these Olympics were open to the pros. I didn't know that meant pro wrestling. But after what I just saw, anything is possible. After what I just saw, I half-expect Hulk Hogan to battle the Iron Sheik for the gold medal.

What I just saw, in Olympic wrestling, featured two Russians bouncing on their rear ends, one Russian slamming his shoes on the mat, a screaming Bulgarian, a group of Iranians spitting and throwing caps, and an American in Spandex flexing his muscles while circling the floor, growling, "I AM THE CHAMPION! I AM THE CHAMPION!"

It's the Olympics or the WWF, one or the other.

Did I mention the Russian Mafia threatening the judge?

Wait. This gets complex. Why don't I give you a play-by-play, as it happened. Ready? …

OK. It's high drama time. The gold-medal wrestling match at 180.5 pounds. On one side is American Kevin Jackson, who grew up in Lansing, Mich., lives in Iowa and looks like a middle linebacker with no hair. On the other side is the Russian, Elmadi Zhabrailov, who looks like John Stockton on steroids.

They wrestle. It's a close match. It's 0-0 with time running out. Suddenly the Russian gets Jackson in a grab move, has him on his hip, and Jackson is trying to retaliate but is also bouncing toward the out-of-bounds line. He gets there.

The referee whistles, separates them and awards no points.

Here's where the fun starts.

Out storms the hulking Russian wrestling coach, Ivan Yarygin — let's call him Ivan the Terrible. Alongside him is a smaller assistant; we'll call him Mr. Excitable. And they're both out on the mat, waving their arms, screaming at the judges that their guy should be given a point, that Jackson was running away. Mr. Excitable drops to his butt and begins bouncing, like a baby, to imitate Jackson, which is pretty dangerous, because Jackson is standing right behind him. Meanwhile, Ivan the Terrible is gesturing wildly at the referee, as if to say, "Give us a point, or I will eat you for breakfast!"

All this, remember, while the match is still in progress.

Wait. We're just getting started.

Somehow they get these two back to their seats, and the match goes to sudden-death overtime. The crowd is roaring. And wouldn't you know it? Jackson completes a takedown move and the referee signals one point. It's over! American wins! Uh-oh.

"I KILL YOU! I EAT YOU! I CHEW YOU!" Ivan the Terrible seems to be screaming as he charges the referee. The defeated wrestler, Elmadi, is screaming, too, and suddenly he plops down in front of the judges and he's not moving. He's going to sit there, as long as it takes, until they change their minds. What's he going to miss back home? Another revolution?

Meanwhile, Mr. Excitable, the assistant, who, by the way, is wearing green paisley shorts and a hat full of Olympic pins — I know the ex-Soviets are hurting for team uniforms, but there's gotta be something better than this — he suddenly takes off his shoes and begins slamming them on the mat. Over and over. Thud! Thud! Thud! Thud! And he's screaming in Russian!

By now, the crowd is half-cheering, half-booing. A group of Iranians begins to shower the mat with caps and bottles. Some spit. Others whistle. And in the middle of all this, Kevin Jackson, who had just won a gold medal, I think, is trying to celebrate the way any normal, red-blooded American who hasn't eaten real food in weeks would do: He is circling the ring like a grizzly bear, arms high, yelling, "WHOO! I'M THE OLYMPIC CHAMPION! WHOO!"

A protest is filed.

We pause for this commercial break.

OK. We're back. Now we're outside the jury room, where the judges are reviewing the tape. With us is Ivan the Terrible, the grumbling Russian coach, and Mr. Excitable, who looks a lot like the losing wrestler, Elmadi, and now we know why: He is his older brother. Whoa! No wonder he's upset.

Out comes the jury. One member, wearing a blue sports coat, gives the thumbs-down sign. The protest is denied. Uh-oh.

"YOU SAW IT! I SAW IT!" screams Ivan the Terrible. "I want to know what is in this referee's brains?"

If he's still in the building, probably very little.

But you needn't worry about that. The referee, a Bulgarian named Todor Groudev — Todor the Bulgarian, beautiful, no? — already has a bad history with the former Soviets over a previous match. The way I figure it, old Todor is out of here already, on the next flight to Plovdiv.

So the jury has to take the grief. The poor guy in the sports coat is trying to explain, in a nice calm voice, why the jury cannot overturn the decision. "Look, the Russians feel they are right. The Americans feel they are right. We can only look at the tape."

This makes sense to me. But then, up steps this small, seedy-looking guy, who says he is Russian and demands to know what nationality the jury member is.

"I am Italian," the juror says.

And this is what the Russian says: "We know you Sicilians and your

Mafia ways. But we have our ways, too."

Then he bangs his fist into his palm and gives the juror a glare.

I figure that's Russian for "You sleep with the fishes."

Let's jump to the medal ceremony. Such drama! The place is buzzing! Will the Russian show up? Will he accept his silver? The music begins, and out comes Jackson and the bronze medalist, an Iranian — but no Russian. The crowd hoots and jeers. He's not coming! He's refusing the medal! …

But wait. Out of the far right corner of the building … yes … here comes Elmadi, being dragged by two of his teammates. He is weeping, shaking his head, as if to say, "No, really, I can't accept that silver medal." But he keeps walking toward the medal stand. He buries his head, turns back, then continues on, then turns back, then continues on. I swear, I saw this same routine at the end of a James Brown concert once. Except James had a cape.

Meanwhile, poor Kevin Jackson. All he did was wrestle, and now they're booing him like George Bush. When his name is called as "gold medalist," the roof almost collapses.

Then Elmadi's name is called. He steps up, and the well-dressed official tries to put the silver medal around his neck. Elmadi pushes it away. The official, who has no doubt been practicing this move on his wife for months now, is insisting. "I must put it around your neck."

"Hell with that," Elmadi is saying.

"Your neck! Let me put it around your neck!"

"No neck! No neck!"

"But I must–"

"No neck!"

Finally, Elmadi just grabs the thing, and the official rolls his eyes. Meanwhile, Elmadi's brother has — you guessed it — taken off his shoes again, and he is pounding the floor, trying to get people to drown out "The Star-Spangled Banner," or trying to shrink his size 10s down to size 9s, one or the other. So the crowd begins to stomp its feet, while American fans sing "the rocket's red glare." The Iranians are whistling and booing. Elmadi is bent over, weeping or laughing. Ivan is still screaming. The brother is playing "A Whole Lotta Sole." The place is like Armageddon, any minute now, the walls cave in …

And that's it. I guess you have to tune in next week to see the finish. I will tell you that an hour after all this happened, the loser was sitting outside doping control, smoking a cigarette.

Meanwhile, Kevin Jackson was trying to explain his Olympic experience: "It was total chaos. It was ridiculous. It made them look bad. It made their team look bad.

"It really was unprofessional."

In wrestling? Are you kidding? That's as close to professional as it gets. ∎

Ilitch comes dressed in blue, but he's white knight to fans

August 27

It was like one of those arranged marriages in the old country. The bride wore yellow balloons and offered fresh fruits and cakes. The groom arrived in a fine blue suit and brought his family. He complimented the lady on her grace, despite her years. He listened to her sing "Take Me Out to the Ball Game" through her aging loudspeakers. For a moment, he appeared to blush, as if overwhelmed by the ceremony. He was really hers? She was really his?

"Talk about a field of dreams," Mike Ilitch said, sighing.

I have witnessed many Opening Days at Tiger Stadium. I have never seen one with as fresh a feeling as Wednesday, a balmy afternoon in mid-August. There were white tablecloths on long buffet tables — all set up in rightfield. There were waiters circling home plate with desserts. There were frills and gimmicks — but more than that. There were smiles and sighs of relief. It was some sort of rebirth down at Michigan and Trumbull, like the morning after Noah's flood. Everything was bright and dewy and ready for rebuilding.

Which is exactly what this baseball team needs, of course. Rebuilding. Rejuicing. Rejuvenating. Mike Ilitch — who began his new era by letting go of several top front-office people — might have worn blue for his first official day as Detroit Tigers owner, but he was the white knight to fans. And the questions from the media reflected that:

"Will you keep Tiger Stadium?"

"Will you sign Cecil Fielder?"

"Will you bring back Ernie Harwell?"

If Ilitch did everything that was asked of him Wednesday, he would need another lifetime — and maybe a couple of tablets to write his Ten Commandments. Yet he smiled, he answered the questions. He even made jokes, suggesting that he really wanted Fielder to play for his hockey team.

And in simply doing the one thing he does best — handing over the money and making the purchase — Ilitch accomplished a feat that had grown nearly impossible in the old Tigers regime:

He gave this franchise hope.

And isn't hope the basis of all good marriages?

I dream of the day when the buses come rolling down here from all across the state," Ilitch said, sounding like a Kennedy running for office. "I dream of the day when moms and dads take their kids to a game again. ..."

"When you first started with the Red Wings you gave away a free car each night to boost attendance," a reporter said. "Would you do that again with the Tigers?"

"Hey, if I have to," Ilitch answered, "I'll give away free limos."

Free limos. He made promises like that. He talked of winning and spending money. He talked of signing old stars and going after new ones. He said everything right, everything the old regime, under kooky Tom Monaghan, would never say.

Example: They said no more Tiger Stadium? Ilitch said he would consider keeping Tiger Stadium.

They said no more Ernie Harwell? Ilitch said he might bring Harwell back.

They said, "We'll move if we don't get our way?" Ilitch said, "I will never take this team out of Detroit, never."

The white knight.

Now, normally, a fellow like this comes along, and the media slice him apart, as if he were a kid wearing a new suit to reform school. And yet you won't find any cynicism in this column. And you might not find it elsewhere this morning. Here is why: Mike Ilitch is a rare bird.

He actually means what he says.

And because of that, this was a fine day in Tigers history. Maybe now we can blow away that stale, crusty air that always hung over this team and bring it into the 1990s. Maybe now we can look forward to going to the ballpark — if Ilitch delivers on his promise to "make it an exciting place, for kids especially."

It is true, only hours after Ilitch's introduction party, several front-office people, including Joe McDonald, who oversaw player development; Jeff Odenwald, the top marketing guy; Mike Wilson, the controller; and Ralph Snyder, the stadium operations man, were let go (or not offered new employment, to be technical). But hey. You wanted change? You got change. I see nothing surprising here. Ilitch's own people have long been specialists at marketing, accounting and arena operations, which explains the good-bye to Odenwald, Wilson and Snyder. And McDonald was no doubt cleared out to make room for whomever takes over the day-to-day baseball operations.

Anyhow, these changes are small pebbles compared to the biggest change: the philosophy of the owner. Tom Monaghan once said he bought the Tigers to make up for the fact that he was cut from his eighth-grade baseball team. The poor kid turned rich, ready to get back at all his enemies.

Ilitch harbors no such vindictive thoughts. He is not trying to prove his macho by buying a team he could never dream of making. On the contrary, the Tigers are a team that Ilitch once came close to making, as a minor league player in their farm system. So he is not so much buying a new dream as picking up an old one, a dream he interrupted for the rigors of real life and one he now returns to, at age 63, with the same boyish enthusiasm he once showed running the bases. His former coach at the minor league level remembers him as "a guy with as much hustle as Pete Rose, a guy who loved the game."

Wednesday, Ilitch talked about love, too.

"You can do a lot on love," he said, explaining how he will balance this new burden with Little Caesars, the Red Wings, the Detroit Drive and all the other things he owns. "Every hour that I put in here will be out of love. It won't feel like work. This whole thing is a labor of love."

N ow. We can only hope that Ilitch doesn't get his parade rained on by the realities of 1992 baseball. Many a new owner has sniffed the stadium grass and stood on the pitcher's mound and proclaimed, "Wow, this is the greatest!" — and a few years later, he is holding his head and moaning, "Why did I ever get into this business?"

It could happen — even to Ilitch. The greed of the players, the egos of the owners, the expense of a stadium, the fickle nature of fans, all could conspire to wipe the smile off an owner's face. Admit this is true. But there was no removing that smile Wednesday afternoon. Not from that chiseled, curly-haired face that now owns 100 percent of the major sports teams that play in this city.

"I'm not a savior of anything," Ilitch warned. "All the things I've done, if you broke them down, you'd see a lot of it was the people behind me. ...

"But I'm excited. I want to bring baseball back to where it once was with this franchise. I'll probably spend every spare minute I have here. This is the game I love."

While he spoke, a waiter moved through the crowd holding a silver tray with slices of dessert. "Piece of cake?" the waiter asked. "Piece of cake?"

Not really. It only felt that way. ∎

etc.

Columns from the Free Press
Sunday Comment Section

Wouldn't it be wonderful if all the news was fit to print?

August 26, 1990

After awhile, even journalists get tired of bad news. It seems as if every time you pick up a paper, the stories are shocking, depressing or disgusting. And that's just the sports pages.

Wouldn't it be nice if, just once, you could control the news flow? Then we might see stories such as these:

WASHINGTON — A federal judge today ruled oil company presidents do have every right to charge higher prices for gas. However, the judge also ruled that, for the rest of their lives, those presidents must pay $700 a gallon for drinking water, $900 for a loaf of bread and $2,000 for clean sheets.

HOLLYWOOD — After a six-month absence, singer/actress Cher appeared at a press conference at least 60 pounds overweight. "I don't know what happened," she said, munching from a Dunkin' Donuts bag. "One day someone put this stuff called 'food' in front of me and, geez, it's good. ...."

PARIS — For the first summer ever, not a single tourist visited this famous city, leaving the citizens to deal only with each other, after which one exclaimed, "*Sacre bleu!* We truly are rude and obnoxious!"

LOS ANGELES — Dr. Ruth Westheimer admitted today that she has been making it all up, and she hasn't had a date in years.

CHAPEL HILL, N.C. — The results were eye-opening this weekend when a group of 100 TV evangelists were forced to actually read the Bible. "Did you see this?" one asked. " 'Thou shalt not steal'? Whoa. When did that get in here?"

WASHINGTON — President Bush officially abolished algebra, calculus and trigonometry from all high school curricula, saying, "I've been running the country for two years and I've never seen a logarithm."

Instead, high school teens will study How to Speak Without Whining.

ATLANTIC CITY, N.J. — Financiers who last week agreed to bail out Donald Trump from his enormous debt have apparently changed their minds.

"We held a long meeting," said the group's spokesperson, "and we came to this conclusion: The guy's a dweeb. Let him sink."

NEW YORK — Major League Baseball announced that from now on, all players must spend two years working in the real world, just to see what it's like.

HOUSTON — NASA scientists today announced they are recalling the famous Hubble telescope from space because, "We don't know what the hell we're looking at anyhow. ..."

WASHINGTON — A federal insurance investigator has determined that every American with insurance is owed at least $10,000 in refunds. "I can't believe this business," said the investigator. "You give them all this money for years, and then, when you have an accident, they raise your rates. Boy, wait till I tell the president. ..."

NEW YORK — The American Society of Book Publishers voted unanimously never to publish another book by Shirley MacLaine because, as one member put it, "She's a ditz."

WASHINGTON — The Defense Department admitted today that $875 is indeed too much to pay for a screwdriver.

NEW YORK — After the stock market jumped 400 points then fell 200, weary Wall Street analysts finally admitted, "We have no idea what makes it work. The thing has a mind of its own. We quit."

BIRMINGHAM, Ala. — Doing what many felt was long overdue, country clubs across America today opened their doors to all minorities. The minorities, however, said, "Nah, golf is boring.'

WASHINGTON — Despite the alarming rise in gun-related murders, the NRA continues to insist that every American should have the right to a gun. So today, the companies that make bullets voluntarily went out of business.

DETROIT — Famous rock singer Madonna returned home this weekend and abruptly announced her retirement — after her father said, "Shame on you!" and sent her to her room.

CHICAGO — Scientists were greeted with cheers and hugs when they announced that, after a decade of research, they had determined, beyond a shadow of a doubt, that extra-cheese pizza is the healthiest and least fattening food on Earth.

NEW YORK — ABC, NBC and CBS announced that from now on, news anchors will be chosen by their knowledge of current affairs, not their hairstyles.

SOUTH PACIFIC — The ship carrying George Steinbrenner, Don King, Bob Arum and Brent Musburger mysteriously disappeared today. No traces were found. ∎

Big Apple glows blood red with Brian Watkins' death

September 9, 1990

NEW YORK — I went to see Brian Watkins' deathbed. His mattress was concrete. His sheets were silver gum wrappers. All that remained was a splotch of blood on the bottom step near the token booth, where he collapsed Sunday night chasing the strangers who put a knife in his chest because they wanted money to go dancing.

"*Mire*," said a fat man in Spanish, pointing out the whole thing to a friend. He pointed to the D train platform, where the knife was first pulled, and he pointed to where the Watkins family, visitors from Utah, saw their peaceful life turn to horror. They had spent the day at the U.S. Open, mother, father, two brothers, brother's wife. They loved tennis and it was 10:20 p.m., and now they were going for something to eat.

And then, suddenly, here were these horrible kids flying down the steps and grabbing at them and slashing the father's leg and grabbing his wallet, and the mother screamed and they punched her face. Brian, the son, instinctively said, "They can't do that" and lunged for them, and it was welcome to New York City. A "butterfly" knife — four-inch blade, maybe it cost $20 on 42nd Street — went into his chest.

And still he chased them. He and his brother, they chased after these wild kids who had punched their mother, up one flight of steps, across a platform, another flight of steps, they ran, the blood spitting out of Brian, until the wild kids were gone and Brian couldn't stand up anymore. He fell at the foot of a big wall poster of "Cats," now showing at the Winter Garden Theater.

"*Mire*," the man said again, pointing now at the bloodstain on the filthy concrete. He and his friend shook their heads and the friend said, "Ooo-eey."

I shivered. I know this subway station. Back when I lived in this city, it was my stop, 53rd Street and 7th Avenue. I rode the subway here every day, ignoring the danger, hoping, like thousands of others, that these trains would carry me to some exhilarating life, a flashy career, the stuff that leads people to New York in the first place.

The stuff that led Brian Watkins here. He dreamed of being a pro tennis player; it lured him every summer. His family would get tickets to the Open, and Brian would watch and recall how he had been a state high school champion in Utah. And although he was 22, he still thought, "If I keep training, with a little luck ..."

But New York is no place for luck, it is a city from hell, a city where they shoot you for breathing, for turning a corner, a city where a gang of

19-year-olds want to go dancing so they leave the house with no money, figuring to pick some up from the nearest available victims. They even have a name for this. They call it "getting paid."

Brian Watkins paid. And his family will never stop paying. Every vacation, every tennis tournament, things they once loved will now be full of tears, and the mother will always wonder, "What if I didn't scream?" And the father will always wonder, "If only I had jumped in …"

Eight strangers caused these nightmares. Five of them were arrested after the stabbing at Roseland Dance Hall. They were dancing at street level as Brian Watkins died in the subway. They were dancing on his grave.

What have we come to? What kind of place is this where the victims don't know the killers and the killers don't care. You could be a priest, you could be a grandmother, you got a couple dollars, down you go. Sports writers in New York boast of their tennis tournament's gutsy atmosphere, the noise, the heat, the tough crowd, the legacy, but this is part of the legacy now, too: Family from Utah loses son in subway. Attend U.S. Open at your own risk.

The tennis goes on. The crowds ride the subway. But they look over their shoulders now and see Brian Watkins' ghost, the ghost of random violence, crime without provocation. It can hit anyone, any time, sports lovers, innocent people, and so it is chilling, the breath of fear. It is what New York City is all about these days.

Down in the 53rd Street station, a transit worker ripped the "Cats" poster off the wall. I asked whether he had been here Sunday night. "I don't work weekends," he said, and moved the bucket closer to Brian Watkins' deathbed. You wonder how much time the killer will get for this one.

As they shipped the body back to Utah, a police spokesman said Watkins "did what every red-blooded American hopes he has the courage to do." But all that is left of the red-blooded American is red blood, dried and fading on the subway steps. A kid who came to see tennis. Since when did you need courage to do that? ∎

Mollycoddling of athletes creates locker-room louts

September 30, 1990

L et's say your sister goes to the office one day and a group of guys surround her and start giving her trouble. One pulls down his pants. He says, "Is this what you want?" They're laughing. They think this is funny.

Your sister is humiliated. She comes home, visibly upset. And you're ready to kill these guys, right? You want them fired. Now. They can't get away with this.

Victor Kiam, the owner of the New England Patriots, would like to get away with it. So would his employees, the four or five football players who harassed a reporter named Lisa Olson in their locker room recently and set sports behavior back 20 years. Not that it was very advanced to begin with.

What they did was stick their private parts near her face and make suggestive comments. And now, having exposed their flesh, they're ready to expose their audacity. They and Kiam — who reportedly called Olson "a classic bitch" after the incident — are diving into a very old safety net in sports: "She didn't belong there in the first place."

And across the country, people who would load the rifle if this happened to their sisters are somehow, unbelievably, acting as if these football players are right.

L et's get a few things straight: First of all, Olson belonged in that locker room as much as the next guy, and I mean guy, because right now those are the rules. Women are allowed to cover pro teams. Same as men. You don't like it? Fine. Pick a better way to protest than getting naked and doing an Andrew Dice Clay impression.

But this is beside the point. This incident is not about sports writers, or access, or why male reporters don't go into women's locker rooms. (Name one sport in which that is necessary.)

No. This is about the terrorizing of a human being. What the Patriots did to Lisa Olson you don't do to a woman, you don't do to a man, you don't do to a dog.

I have seen this kind of behavior before in locker rooms. Gang mentality. Come on. Let's get so-and-so. Remember, many of these players have been protected since high school, bailed out by coaches, agents and public relations people, then patted on the back and told, "That's OK, big fella. Just win on Sunday."

Thus spoiled, they figure there are two sets of rules, one for them, one for everybody else. And the line is the locker room wall. No less an authority than Bo Schembechler, who is usually smarter, recently blamed an ugly incident between Tigers pitcher Jack Morris and a female reporter on the fact that sports writers — both men and women — don't understand "the sanctity of the locker room."

Maybe not, Bo. But as long as that locker room is in America, there are laws to obey. And I don't mean curfew.

Y ou want to know the sickest part of this whole thing? The New England players accused Olson of leering at them the day before. She explained that she was waiting for an interview; they claimed she was hanging around, giving them the eye.

I doubt it. Let me explain something about locker rooms: They are open places, with no place for a reporter to sit. So you have to stand, rather foolishly, in the middle. And wait. You would rather be anywhere else, you try to avert your eyes, but lest you risk your subject running out the back door, you have to stand there. It's uncomfortable, but that's how you gather information for stories — the stories that help make these guys famous and rich.

Male reporters can do this and don't get accused of leering. But, apparently, many players still feel that women, deep down, are basically cheerleaders, wanting only to jump in the sack with a football star. Consider the horrifying amount of sexual assault charges in recent years against pro and college athletes. Everything from fondling to rape.

That is no coincidence, folks. That is the sad result of a culture that teaches star athletes to take what they want.

But they can't take a person's dignity. This is unforgivable. Can you imagine if a group of white players surrounded a black reporter and began taunting him with racial slurs? It would be on "Nightline" for a week.

Olson's case is no different. It was the terrorizing of a human being, and every Patriot involved should be suspended by the NFL. Kiam, the worst kind of owner, a rich bigot, should be suspended as well.

And after all this, if you still think these athletes were somehow justified, imagine if it was your sister they had harassed.

Because one day, it might be. ∎

'20/20' gaffe isn't o-tay with Little Rascals' Spanky

October 14, 1990

Whenever I get a spare moment, I try to think deep and meaningful thoughts, such as what is life, who invented the split pea, and, of course, whatever happened to Buckwheat?

I thought I had the answer to the last one recently, when the ABC-TV show "20/20" aired a segment claiming to have found Buckwheat, a former star of the Little Rascals comedies. According to the show, Buckwheat was working as a grocery bagger in Tempe, Ariz.

Naturally, "20/20" went to interview him. Buckwheat, whose real name was Billy Thomas, said he had changed his name to Bill English and had stopped signing autographs because it "interfered with my work." I guess bagging is tougher than it looks.

Now, at first, this story struck me as something you'd see in the National Enquirer. "BUCKWHEAT FOUND AT STOP-N-SHOP, SAYS TOMATOES ARE O-TAY!"

But hey, I'm the suspicious type. And since "20/20" is hosted by Hugh Downs — who used to host "Concentration," a very serious show where two people try to guess the secret of a 30-foot puzzle — and Barbara Walters — who was last seen batting her eyelashes at Warren Beatty and saying, "You're sensitive, aw-went you?" — well, you figure they must be telling the truth.

I mean, they research these things, right?

As it turns out, the man "20/20" interviewed — the man to whom it devoted a whole segment on national television — was not the real Buckwheat. He was an impostor. A fake. The real Buckwheat would have stood up and said so, except for one thing: He's dead. He died 10 years ago, of a heart attack.

Now. Call me a workaholic. But this seems like the kind of thing you might discover in your research, no? There are books written on the Our Gang crew, and the authors could have told you the bad news about Buckwheat — and Alfalfa and Froggy, if you wanted.

Also, there is a company called Buckwheat Enterprises, in LA, operated by Buckwheat's real son, William Thomas Jr. I'm sure he would have provided information about his father, and maybe a few posters, too.

But, alas, "20/20," which got the grocery bagger story in a letter from a viewer — and we all know how those letters can be trusted, especially the ones written in crayon — well, old "20/20" laid an egg. Hugh Downs had to apologize on Friday's show. The producer has reportedly resigned, so I guess his next project, "Life On Mars," will be scrapped, too.

To be honest, a TV show making a boo-boo such as this doesn't really surprise me. Many TV programs — particularly talk shows — are in such a hurry to get high ratings they are often shoddy on research.

What surprised me was that anyone would pretend to be Buckwheat in the first place. Especially if all it got him was a job in a grocery store. So I called George (Spanky) McFarland, another ex-Little Rascal, who now lives in Ft. Worth, Texas. McFarland, 62, is pretty easy to find, except, obviously, to the people at "20/20."

"That guy didn't even look like Buckwheat," he said. "These imitators are all over. They pretend to be Buckwheat, or Darla, or me. One fellow in LA said he was me and tried to become a movie producer. He was renting equipment and everything. I opened my mailbox one day and I was getting his bills.

"Another time there was this woman in Florida who said she was me. And people believed her. I mean, they could look at her and see she was a girl."

Spanky is pretty ticked off over this whole Buckwheat mess. He's also kind of mad at "Saturday Night Live," which, in the early '80s, had Eddie Murphy doing a regular spoof on Buckwheat, prancing around the stage saying "O-tay!"

"Buckwheat never said 'O-tay,' " Spanky said.

"He what?"

"He never said 'O-tay.' That was Porky."

"How could so many people be wrong?"

"They stuck a phony Buckwheat on network TV, didn't they?"

Good point.

Anyhow, Spanky said he was glad "20/20" apologized. He also said Porky and Butch are still alive, in case you see any more reports.

All of which reminds me of that "Saturday Night Live" skit in which they mocked (ironically) ABC's "Nightline" in a report claiming "Buckwheat has been shot!" In the skit, the "murderer" is Alfalfa. He was mad because Buckwheat put a frog down his pants in grade school. But in the end, Buckwheat comes back to life. Why? Because Alfalfa put blanks in the gun!

Hmm. Maybe there's something to this. And I think we should investigate. It may sound a little farfetched, but then again:

It's not as farfetched as "20/20." ■

An abode cannot abide being jilted for another

October 28, 1990

The house is not talking to me. She is upset. I cannot blame her.
"Forgive me," I say.
She says nothing.
"I was confused," I say.
She says nothing.

She is gone, the house. She is no longer mine. A few weeks ago, in a well-lit office with lots of papers, I sold her. I sold her to a person I had never met before.

It seems cruel now, a thing I would not have done four years ago. We were in love then. She was everything I had dreamed of. She wore her entrance way like proud plumage, the glass on her windows was clean and reflected sunlight. Her rooms were white and inviting, like vanilla ice cream. I walked inside her and pointed like a proud lover.

"Isn't she beautiful?" I said to friends. "This is where we will sit together, by the fireplace. And this is where we will eat together, in the kitchen. This is where we will sleep together, in the bedroom. Isn't she beautiful?"

All my friends agreed. She was beautiful. We were a couple. The house and I. Together forever, right?

"I'm sorry," I say now, as I pack up a carton of books. "I really am."
The house says nothing.

Once, I brought her flowers. I put them in her kitchen. I gave her a fresh coat of paint and put furniture by her walls. It wasn't fancy furniture. But she didn't mind. She accepted my picture frames, she accepted my bookshelves. She accepted my boots in her front hall closet.

"Remember when we first got the dog?" I say. "And he got so excited that he — well, you remember. On your carpet?"

She accepted. She never complained. She was there to protect us. In the winter, she would catch the snow and hold it against her shingles while we sat inside, drinking hot chocolate. In the summer, she would stop the sun and take the heat on her bricks while we slept inside, cool and quiet.

Once in a while, she coughed up water in her basement. And now and then her plaster skin would crack and peel. But she stood tall. We were proud of her.

Over the years, we would have parties and buff her up, and her wood floors would shine and her carpet would be soft. Guests would gather inside her and say how lovely she looked.

"Yes," I would sigh. "She is lovely. She could use another bedroom. And her backyard is a little small, don't you think?" They would shrug and say I was probably right.

"I didn't mean it," I say now, packing clothes in a garment box. "Really, I didn't."

My house says nothing.

What happened to us? How did our relationship collapse? Was it that classic problem of the '80s — did we both need our space? I seemed to take up more of hers; she seemed to have less to give me.

Soon, I grew distant. I drove through other neighborhoods. Then, not long ago, I saw ... her. She was tall and inviting and had a huge backyard. Lots of trees. Fancy neighbors. She sang of space, of growth, of high ceilings and track lighting.

She wore a "FOR SALE" sign.

I stopped. I went inside.

When I returned to my old house, she seemed ... different. Her charm had withered. Her bookshelves were stuffed. Her floors needed waxing.

She was everything she always had been, of course, proud and loyal and true. But my eyes were dazzled. I told friends about my new love. I drew pictures on napkins. "This is where we will sit together, by the big fireplace, and this is where we will eat together, in the big kitchen, and this is where we will sleep together, in the big bedroom."

I told my old house that maybe she should see other people, too. I allowed them to come in and look her over. One day, a young man took a liking to her. He offered me money.

And a few weeks ago, in a well-lit office full of papers, I sold her to him.

Almost immediately, I felt a sense of doom, as if I'd done a terrible thing. Sure enough, a few days later, the new house fell through. Bad deal. Our relationship was over.

And so now I sit, amongst the boxes, looking for a new place to live. And suddenly, my old house seems like all I could ever want. Did I really sell her? To a stranger? I think back to the first time I lit a fire in her fireplace, and how we sat together and shared in the warmth. It was nice. It was cozy. Why, I wonder, are we never satisfied?

"Forgive me," I say.

She says nothing.

"I was confused," I say.

She says nothing.

"But you are my home," I say.

"I was your house," she corrects.

And then she says no more. ■

Otis Day, my man, you are a five-minute screen legend

November 25, 1990

I am sitting with a legend. I want to pinch myself. I want to run to the phone, call my friends, and say "MY GOD, DO YOU KNOW WHO I AM TALKING TO?"

He is not the president. He is not a sports hero. He has never won a Nobel Prize, and probably never will, unless they give it out at a toga party.

Basically, he is an entertainer who made a handful of small films — and one very big one. He was on the screen for maybe five minutes. Five wild and crazy minutes. Five legendary minutes.

I am sitting with Otis Day.

OTIS, MY MAN!

"You know," he says, in a scratchy voice, "if I had a nickel for every time someone said that, I'd have $15 million by now. At least."

In case you don't know, Otis Day is the man who sang "Shout!" in the film "Animal House" — while John Belushi and his fraternity pals wiggled in togas. It was silly. It was wild. It was also the quintessential party scene in the history of the movies — better than the Elvis films of the '50s, better than the beach party films of the '60s. The "Shout!" scene has been replayed everywhere from MTV to halftime of Pistons games.

Maybe it was that hairdo. Maybe it was that soulful singing. Maybe it was the movie itself, which became a cult classic among 20- to 40-year-olds. But somehow, Otis Day, with five minutes on the screen, became folklore, larger than life. He was the singer we wanted to be at the party we always wanted to attend.

And here he is, in front of me, about to perform at a local radio convention. Good God! I feel like crushing a beer can on my forehead.

Now, before we go any further, I must explain a few things to my fellow "Animal House" fans. Yes, Otis still has that enormous energy. He screams. He shouts. He cackles with laughter.

Then again, why not? Otis is only 39 years old. And he's not really Otis — at least he wasn't born Otis. He was born DeWayne Jessie, an actor who barely knew the song "Shout!" when the folks from "Animal House" hired him for the part.

"People meet me and think I'm 97 YEARS OLD!" he bellows, jumping up, then sitting down again. "They think I'm some long lost blues singer from Mississippi! Sometimes, I play along. I tell them, yeah, that's me. 'The Still of the Night.' 'Earth Angel.' I WROTE ALL THOSE SONGS!

HAHAHAHA!"

Actually, Otis — uh, Jessie — was hired for "Animal House" strictly because of his looks. He was only supposed to lip-sync that party scene. But he convinced them to let him sing for real. Wearing a wig and a sequined jacket, he belted out the number, threw his hands in the air, made all those crazy faces … .

And picked up his paycheck. The whole scene, he says, took three hours to film. "I figured, you know, that was fun. But it was just a part."

And then the film opened. And people went nuts. OK. Men went nuts. A lot of women think "Animal House" is stupid and boorish. But hey, they said that about another classic, "Caddyshack." So what do they know?

Anyhow, the offers came flooding in. For Otis, not for Jessie. People wanted to book him. At this club. At this party. At this frat house. As a singer.

And so Otis — uh, Jessie — formed a band, and began to tour. The money increased. The offers grew larger. He played Prince's club in Minneapolis. He played at Caesars Palace. He played on the floor of the Stock Exchange. Fans screamed. They wore their togas. "OTIS, MY MAN!" they yelled.

Amazing. DeWayne Jessie had done what Dr. Frankenstein had always dreamed of.

He had given his creature life.

And today, after nine years and $350,000 in fees and lawyers, he owns the name. He is Otis Day. Which has its ups and downs.

"One time I got on this airplane, and just as I got to my seat, the pilot came over the loudspeaker and said, 'OTIS, MY MAN!' I wanted to DIE!

"Another time, I was pulled over by the cops in LA. 'What's your name?' the cop said. I said, 'Otis Day.' He said, 'OH, MY GOD. I JUST RENTED YOUR TAPE LAST NIGHT!' "

Amazing. Five minutes in a movie. A lifetime career. I watch him do his act. He sounds familiar. When the first notes of "Shout!" are played, the crowd goes bananas.

Amazing.

"You know," he says afterward, "I'm glad people like Otis. But to tell the truth, the 'Shout!' scene really wasn't my favorite scene in the movie. I liked the part where John Belushi shoots a gun and the horse has a heart attack. I cracked up! I mean, that horse just killed me!"

I wonder what he's doing now? ∎

Let children be children – hold out for a pencil box

December 16, 1990

I am walking through the toy store. I am shopping for the holidays. I am looking for one item — and one item only — something that, to me, always symbolized the magic of this season.

I am looking for a pencil box.

"We have a discount on Nintendo," says the toy salesman, yanking me toward the computer section. "Ten percent off Swords and Serpents, Magic Johnson's Fast Break, Tradewest Super Off Road and, of course, Mindscape Gauntlet II."

"I am looking for a pencil box," I say.

"Heh-heh," he says. "That's a good one. Look, if you don't like Nintendo, how about a miniature LCD game, maybe Top Gun by Konami, or Batman by Tiger Electronics? Kids love those. And we're running a special. Batteries not included, of course."

"Pencil box?" I say.

"Keyboards!" he says. "How about these electronic keyboards with 16 pre-sets for rhythm and instrumental tracks? Cool, huh? Or this miniature Hot Lykx guitar? Check this baby out. Make the kid feel like Van Halen."

"Pencil box?" I whisper.

"Van Haaaaalen," he sings.

I do not want the kid to feel like Van Halen. I do not want the kid to blow fighter jets out of an electronic sky. I want the kid to have the same simple burst of wonder that I had when I first got the pencil box years ago, and I pulled back the white-ribbed door and watched it magically disappear into the red plastic.

It did not require batteries, this pencil box. It did not come with an LCD readout. It was simply a place to store your pencils, or erasers, or whatever. That was the joy. You could hide anything in there. You shut the white-ribbed door and it was safe, yours forever. Such a feeling! At an age when your mother still cut your lamb chops, and your father still pinned the mittens to your jacket, the pencil box meant responsibility. Privacy. Your own secret storage.

"Vehicles!" says the salesman, dragging me to a display area that resembles a miniature car lot. "We've got the whole line of Power Wheels. We've got race cars. We've even got this battery-powered Barbie Corvette."

"Barbie Corvette?" I say.

"Great, huh? Your little girl can cruise the neighborhood. Goes 3½ miles an hour. Power-lock brakes. Only $149.99. Even a make-believe car phone on the dash."

"Look, I —"

"How about this?" he says, pushing over a small jeep that looks like it could cross the Kalahari. "For $269.99, we've got this battery-powered Jeep Safari. Opening doors. Realistic dash. A pretend engine with a real dipstick. Great, huh?"

A dipstick?

I do not want dipsticks. I do not want car phones. I do not want something that will make the kid feel like an adult. There is too much time in life to feel like an adult. And not enough to feel like a kid.

With the pencil box I felt like a kid. It was the first present I ever received. I would take it to school and sneak peeks at it under my desk top. I would slide the white-ribbed door back and forth and imagine it was the trap door to the universe, or a tiny magic carpet.

Oh, the things I could hide in there! A paper clip. A penny. A magic rock. And when the teacher caught me daydreaming, I would tell her I was just checking to see if my pencils were sharpened. And she bought it!

"Ninja Turtles!" yells the salesman. "The kid has to be into Ninja Turtles! Or these Bart Simpson dolls by Mattel!"

"No," I say.

"Board games! I've got Electronic Battleship. Or Heartthrob. Or Let's Go Shopping."

"Nuh-uh," I say.

"Look, I've got this Spectra-Sound Drum Set, complete with sticks. Or this Matchbox Motor City Carwash. Say, I've got a great price on this radio control Mini-Typhoon Hovercraft, good on land or water."

"I just want a pencil box," I say.

"A pencil box," he repeats.

He shrugs and takes me to the office equipment section. I see computers. I see printers. I see full-color monitors and electronic slide rules.

I do not see any pencil boxes. I wonder where they have gone. I wonder what ever happened to the simple presents that grew in a child's imagination, grew and grew, until they were something spectacular — instead of the spectacular presents that can only dull as the batteries wear down.

"You sure you don't want the Mini-Typhoon Hovercraft?" asks the salesman. I tell him thanks, I will keep looking. I am dreaming of little yellow pencils in a red plastic box, and wishing I still had my mittens. ∎

Ugly sign of racism lies just beneath the surface

December 30, 1990

Snow covers most of the house now, the front door, the mailbox, the circular driveway. From the outside, it is just another suburban home, a place where children might build a snowman on the front lawn. But there are no children here, no snowman. The doors and windows are shut tight. People whisper and point when they pass. Here is why: Beneath the snow, the word "NIGGER" is written in the grass. Someone took weed killer one night and burned it in giant letters.

This is not Mississippi. This is not Alabama. This is Michigan — worse, this is my neighborhood, Farmington Hills. The home belongs to a black family who, as far as anybody knows, never bothered anyone. They went away on a trip this summer, and when they came home, there was the message on the lawn.

I used to drive past this place almost every day, the way children go past a haunted house. I stared at the letters, which could be read from across the street. How could someone write that, under the sky, out in the open? What's that saying — "It can't happen here"?

It can happen anywhere. We are about to begin a new year, but in many ways, this snow-covered house is still a reflection of America, white on top with a hatred burning underneath. I work in sports, where the races meet every day — black man tackles white man, white man pours champagne on black man — and, of all places, you would figure, racism could not survive here.

Yet this year alone we had the Shoal Creek controversy. We had Arizona and the Super Bowl. We had a high school basketball game here in Michigan, in which white kids taunted a player by yelling, "Nice shot, black boy!"

Disturbing? Sure. But what is more disturbing is this: Lately, when these issues arise, there seems to be impatience, even annoyance. "Does everything have to be racism?" people moan. "They're always complaining. It's just a little thing."

No, it's not.

Sadly, there is no such thing as a little prejudice. It's like being a little pregnant. Remember that once, in the South, it was considered a little prejudice that blacks had to sit in the back of the bus. Yet this summer, an elderly man named Louis Willie, who once rode those buses, became the first black member of Shoal Creek Country Club in Alabama — only because the club, as host of the PGA Championship, was embarrassed into accepting him. Even up to a few weeks before

Willie's admission, the founder of the club insisted: "We will not be pressured into accepting blacks. ..."

A little prejudice.

Rodney Peete is one of the most intelligent and personable athletes I know. He is also black. A few years ago, while attending Southern Cal, he played a baseball game in Alabama. Peete hit a single. He danced off the bag, threatening to steal second. Suddenly, a woman rose from the stands and yelled, "Get that black boy off the bases! Put the chains on him! Put the chains on him!"

A little prejudice.

This summer, a young white Tigers player said to me: "The Latin ballplayer does not understand fundamentals. He is only interested in being flashy. We all know that." He did not smile. He was serious.

A little prejudice.

It is nothing new. Think about the number of black athletes versus the number of black managers, coaches or owners. Think about the racial remarks you hear all the time at sporting events. "He's fast — for a white guy." "He's hot-tempered, like all Latinos." In truth, these are hateful things to say.

The problem is, as whites, in the majority, we don't always realize it. And now, it seems, we grow weary of racism complaints. "OK," we sigh, "we get the point." But we don't always get the point. Try to imagine it from the other side. White fans routinely mob black athletes for autographs. They say, "We love you!" Yet, as Peete observes, "How many would let us date their daughters?"

Think about it.

Now. I am not saying no progress has been made. Nor am I saying that no athlete has ever used racism as an excuse. But I do feel that when you're in the majority, you have to guard against insensitivity. Prejudice is not some boulder you can drag most of the way up the hill, then abandon. It will roll back down.

On the day before Christmas, I returned to the house in Farmington Hills. I knocked on the door; no one answered. So I stood there, on the lawn, and thought about Shoal Creek, and the Super Bowl, and how many of us shook our heads and said, "Such a fuss over nothing."

Then I looked down, at the snow, and thought about what was beneath it, the message spelled out in weed killer. And I wondered, as I do today, whether you can ever make enough of a fuss over anything. ∎

Her left foot is gone –
but cheerleader cheers on

February 24, 1991

T he doctor said she had two choices: Irradiate the foot, hoping the cancer would die, or cut the foot off and keep the disease from spreading. Beth Hardman looked at her parents. She was 16 years old, a high school student with the smile of an angel, the kind of smile that gets you elected, as she soon would be, homecoming princess. And now she had to decide whether to keep a foot. Her Left Foot. They don't make movies about kids like this. Maybe they should.

"I think we ought to take it off," Beth told the doctor. "Let's set up the appointment."

"Are you sure?" he asked. "Don't you want to think about it?"

"No," she said, "if I change my mind, I'll call you."

She went to school the next day. She told her cheerleading coach. And then she told the team. They sat in a circle, listening to her words. When she said "amputated," her friends began to cry. "They would call me up at night and say, like, 'No, it can't be.' And I'd say, 'Yeah, it is.' "

By the following week, it was.

For a while, after the operation, she wore a cast; she walked on crutches. When classmates would stare at Her Left Foot, she would laugh and say, "Hey, I'm up here." Then, when the cast was removed, she went to soak in the tub and saw the stump for the first time in the bathroom mirror. "I thought I was gonna faint," she says. "It was like some horror movie." The next few weeks were tough. Sometimes she would come home from school and drop on the bed and cry.

And then, one day, the crying stopped. Maybe it was this football game in the fall of 1989. As homecoming princess, she had to walk out on the field, in front of all her schoolmates, and she was simply determined not to look weak and crippled. She threw away one crutch and hobbled out with the other, in her cheerleading outfit. The crowd applauded. And then she figured, what the heck, and she stood stiff alongside her cheerleading teammates and began to yell, a big smile on her face:

Hey, No. 1 fans,
yeah, you in the stands!
We wanna hear you
clap your hands!

Maybe you think cheerleading is silly. Maybe you think homecoming and letter jackets are queer items of adolescence. But you're wrong;

sometimes, they are a badge of courage. Next weekend, Beth Hardman, now a senior at Sterling Heights, will compete with her teammates for the last time in the state cheerleading championships in Saginaw. She will jump. She will spin. She will lunge and do handsprings. All on Her Left Foot.

It's about time someone clapped for her.

S he's really an incredible story," says Terri Cassels, the Sterling Heights cheerleading coach. "She wanted to rejoin the team as soon as possible after the operation. I said OK, but I would make her attend every practice, just like the other girls. I wasn't going to give her special treatment.

"She came all the time, sometimes right after therapy when she was still in pain. She would sit and watch, and at times she got pretty down. I remember when she first showed me what was left of her foot, I had to force myself to say, 'Oh, that's not bad at all!' Then I went home and cried my eyes out."

But things got better. Today, Beth's Left Foot is a rubberized prosthesis that fits below her ankle. It looks like a foot, flesh colored, has toes and nails. "I even put polish on them," Beth says.

More than that. She walks. She drives. She plays baseball and basketball. Last year in Florida, she strolled the beach without embarrassment. When you ask about the change in her life, she flashes a smile that could light up a closet. "It's no big deal," she says.

No big deal. What gives a high school kid such character? What makes a girl, a child, really, at an age when a pimple on your face is considered unfair punishment from God, mature enough to lose a foot but never a stride?

"When I look back, I don't even know why I chose to do it," she says, sitting in the gym after practice, her T-shirt wet with sweat, her hair pulled in a ponytail. "It's kind of a blur. Kind of like shock. My parents wanted me to make the decision, because I had to live with it. Chemotherapy wouldn't work on my kind of cancer. And I guess I felt safer if they took it off, so the cancer couldn't spread.

"As for my new foot, it's cool, I can walk around in shorts and stuff. But when I get home, I take the foot off and just walk around natural, with a sock on. It's easier. And I don't mind. Everyone in my house is used to it. So are all my friends."

You ask what makes her so special.

She says, "I'm not special."

Last Thursday, the Sterling Heights cheerleaders, the defending Class A champions, gathered to practice for their upcoming competitions. It was a tough afternoon, long and sweaty, like an Army drill. They jumped and hopped and dropped and spun and lifted one another on their shoulders. They did jumps that resembled something from a Russian ballet, a scissors kick in mid-air. And all the time they kept giant smiles on their faces, cheering through the pain.

That's the way to do it,
let's hear more.
When we yell "Stallions,"
you yell "Score!"

Beth Hardman did every move. Even the Russian jump. She has practiced and worked her muscles until they allow her to excel nearly the way she did before this incident. There are only 12 girls in a competitive cheerleading squad. If one messes up, the team loses points.

Believe me: You would not know, from watching the Sterling Heights squad, that only 23 of the 24 feet were natural.

"Beth coming back," says Cassels, "it wasn't just a victory for her. It was like a victory for all of us."

We hear so many comeback stories in sports, but they often involve professional athletes, guys with big money in the bank, guys who have TV cameras film their rehab. Rarely do we hear about the simple courage an active teenager can show. It's our loss.

"What have you learned from all this?" Beth Hardman is asked.

"Think positive," she says, looking down at her foot. "You can take any situation and make it better by bringing yourself up."

Spoken, you might say, like a true cheerleader. Isn't it strange how life sometimes picks on the young — and even stranger how well they handle it? This weekend, in Saginaw, one brave teenager and Her Left Foot will show the judges how well she can cheer for other people — when really it should be the other way around. ∎

Tough veneer couldn't veil Uncle Eddie's good heart

May 5, 1991

There is one less tough guy in the world this morning: We buried Eddie yesterday.

Even as I write this, I can still see him, punching me in the arm when I was a kid and saying, "Put em up, buddy boy" — then striking a pose like one of those 1920s boxers. I can still feel his steel-hard muscles when he lifted me into the air, and the sandpaper edge of his whiskers when I kissed his cheek.

He was a short man, a squat, powerful body with a thick neck and a voice that growled as it told stories. We loved to hear those stories around the dinner table — hard, gutty tales about the war, the Depression, or the time, as a New York City cab driver, that he looked in the rearview mirror just as his passenger was pulling a knife and coming toward his throat. Eddie grabbed the knife with his hand and squeezed the blade to protect his Adam's apple. The attacker jumped out and ran away, leaving Eddie bleeding, the knife stuck deep in his palm.

"What did you do?" we kids would ask.

"What the hell do you think? I parked the cab and got myself to a damn doctor!"

We squealed. Tough guys.

Did you ever have a relative you couldn't wait for your friends to meet? Someone who was older than you, but somehow connected? That's the way I was about Eddie. He was my great-uncle, my grandmother's brother, 82 years old, and I was crazy about him — partly because they don't make guys like that anymore. Men of my generation, we think, we talk, we negotiate, we worry. Eddie had a simpler approach to life: There was family — and there was everyone else. And if anyone from the second group tried to mess with the first, they would have to deal with him. Put 'em up, buddy boy.

Over the years, we would always visit, and as I grew, he would measure me with his fists, smiling at my size, then saying, "I can still lick you, buddy boy." And even later, in his 70s, when he was sick and his breathing labored, he would walk past me and poke a rabbit punch into my chest. "Just remember, buddy boy," he would say.

His toughness was his shield. It got him through World War II, and through his working years, through the warehouses, the docks, the hard-labor jobs that swallowed much of his life. It was his way. To yell. To bark. To curse. And yet, he would always slip you some money or give you a hug when no one was looking. When you came to him with personal news — of college or a new job or a new girlfriend — the tough veneer would crack and his eyes would light up. "Hey, that's swell," he would say, like something out of a Mickey Rooney movie.

In the mid-1970s, he had heart surgery. He later told me that during the operation he felt his soul rise from his body and look down on the doctors, frantically trying to revive him. "Then I saw this light," he said, "and this tunnel, and my dead mother and father and brothers and sisters were all there at the end, calling to me."

"God, what did you do?" I asked.

"I yelled, 'Go away, you sons of guns! I ain't ready for you yet! Leave me alone!'"

And the next thing he knew, he was back in his body.

I believe that story. I always have. My Uncle Eddie could even tell heaven to wait.

He lived another 17 years, if you can call what happens to some old people living. His heart, his lungs, his kidneys all went bad. The last time I saw him, last month, in his apartment, he was attached to an oxygen machine, which hooked to his nose and trailed him like a leash. He was wearing a bathrobe when he answered the door, and he had not had time to put in his false teeth. "I'm sorry ... I ... look like crap ..." he mumbled. "Geez ... it's swell ... to see you."

We talked, as much as he could. I teased him about still being able to lick me, and he forced a smile and said, "Nah ... I ... these days, I don't think so." I had a video camera with me and I wanted to record some of his stories, but my aunt said no, not when he looked so bad. Maybe next time.

There was no next time. Last week he was rushed to the hospital, his heart and lungs failing. He was put on a respirator. Robbed of his speech, he could only scribble notes. A floor doctor came in, someone Eddie didn't know — and if he didn't know you, naturally, he didn't like you — and after the guy left, Eddie, barely conscious, handed a note to his son: "THIS DOCTOR STINKS."

Those were his last words.

He's gone now. And I will miss him forever. I can picture him in heaven, punching some angel in the chest and saying, "Hey, buddy boy, who's in charge here?"

Of all the people I have met in my life, no one has ever touched me the way my tough-guy uncle did. I wonder whether anyone ever will. ∎

Bill Murray keeps us guessing – and laughing

May 26, 1991

G reat. As if Michael Jordan weren't enough, now we've got to deal with Bill Murray? That's right. Bill Murray. The actor. The comedian. Mr. Ghostbuster himself ...

A Bulls fan?

He told me so. The other day. Said he might just show up at a Detroit-Chicago playoff game, ready to taunt the Pistons. "Maybe I'll wear one of those Bill Laimbeer masks," he said. "You know, I heard Laimbeer never really suffered a cheek injury. He's just having his face lifted. It's true. He's getting redone so he can do TV work when he's finished with basketball."

Let me tell you how I came to talk with Murray, the wisecracking former "Saturday Night Live" cast member who is now the only movie star that a hippie and a yuppie can agree on. He was in New York. I was in Detroit. And we were speaking through a satellite TV screen. He could see me. I could see him. I am not making this up. Someone once wrote that as long as Bill Murray is on the screen, rolling his eyes and looking for the meaning of life, the '60s are not dead. But this was definitely the '90s. I sat in a studio and suddenly, like Captain Kirk, Murray appeared on the screen, slumped behind a desk, wearing pink shorts and a white sweatshirt. He looked like a beach bum who had wandered into a lawyer's office to collect his inheritance.

"Hi," he said. "I'm Bill. What's your name?"

"Mitch. From Detroit. How about those Pistons?"

Murray grinned. "My Chicago boy, Mark Aguirre, helping you guys out."

"Isiah Thomas is from Chicago, too."

"Yeah," Murray said, "but we don't claim him. He's too weird."

Now. I want to state right here that I have never before had a conversation with a major appliance. But Murray could make me do it. I would talk to him through a TV screen. I would talk to him through a wall. I have been watching his work for years, and I think he is a unique figure in American entertainment — a bridge for people who want to enjoy pop culture but don't want to feel like morons. You can catch Murray, even in a blockbuster movie, and still feel cool. He's like an FM radio station that never got too big.

Not many actors, for example, can star in a typically silly Army comedy, yet have a line such as this: "Chicks dig me because I rarely wear underwear, and when I do, it's often something unusual. ..." Not many actors can star in a typically silly supernatural comedy, yet approach a female ghost this way: "Excuse me? Miss? Where are you from ... originally?"

Not many actors can portray Hunter S. Thompson.

Murray has. I like watching him on screen. He kind of slides along, shoulders slumped, belly out, his arms and legs too stiff, as if someone had been tightening the screws that attach them. And then there is that look. A vacant stare, big eyes, tight lips, the perfect set-up for ... what? Sarcasm? Tenderness? Insanity? That's the thing about Murray. You never know what's coming. Funny? Poignant? Or both? In his newest film — "What About Bob?" — he plays a obsessive psychiatric patient who follows his analyst on vacation. In one scene, the analyst, played by Richard Dreyfuss, asks why Murray's marriage fell apart.

"There are two kinds of people in the world," Murray sighs. "Those who like Neil Diamond, and those who don't. ..."

Murray grew up in Chicago — which explains his Bulls loyalty, as well as his obsession with Cubs baseball. He goes to Wrigley Field. He has a son named Homer Banks Murray (named after Cubs great Ernie Banks). He even did a guest stint once as Cubs broadcaster during a game. ("This umpire is terrible!" Murray moaned. "Somebody find out what hotel this guy's staying at. ...")

Personally, I always thought Murray would make a good sports writer. He's got the unshaven look, the messed-up hair, the deadpan sense of humor. He's got the clothes.

I told him that. About the clothes. And I thought I upset him. He stared at me, his eyes narrowed. He grumbled, "What the hell is that supposed to mean?"

And then he laughed. And he stood up to show me his pink shorts. "You're right. I do have the clothes. Take a look at these, huh? Tell me these wouldn't get you into the Super Bowl pregame party."

Murray is a great kidder, maybe the best in the world. He could kid his way past a Russian border guard. He could kid his way onto the space shuttle. He could be talking to the Queen of England, then suddenly grab her by the head and say, "Queenie. Honey. Loosen up. Here are those noogies you ordered last Christmas. ..."

I asked Murray whether he ever has a problem being taken seriously.

"Don't you?" he asked.

"Well, I ... uh ..."

"No," he continued, "actually, I have a tremendous problem with that. People think I'm kidding all the time. All day long. I just got finished working with a director who never knew if I was kidding. I made this guy cry a few times. And I was kidding. I said, 'Don't cry. Don't you remember? I did this joke two days ago ... '

"People who know me know when I'm kidding, like my family. I come from a big family, and they all know when ... wait, I take that back. There are two oddballs in our family. They don't know when you're kidding. This one brother — I love this story — I was talking to him on the telephone, we were talking about nothing, really, and all of a sudden, he says, 'I got that, by the way.' "

Murray laughed. "Whooooa! I don't know what the hell he was talking about! I didn't say anything funny or gettable at all. But he got it."

Of course, Murray should be used to people getting more than he intended. He is the only actor on the planet who routinely has his lines quoted and requoted by American males, ages 25 to 40. Good Lord! Nearly every sports fan in America seems to do an imitation of Murray as the rumpled greenskeeper in "Caddyshack" who plays an imaginary round of golf in the flower bed:

"Cinderella story ... former greenskeeper, about to win the Masters, the crowd is going wild ... OOOH! He got all of that one, he has to be happy with that. ..."

"If I hear that one more time," I said to Murray, "I'm gonna vomit."

"Thank you," he said.

"No, I mean, you must hear it, too. What lines do people recite when they come up to you?"

"Well, that's a big one. And then there's, 'I want to party with you, cowboy,' which is something I said in 'Stripes' after a guy told a story about making love to a cow. And there's, 'That's a fact, Jack!' People are always yelling that at me from truck windows. ..."

Murray, those people should know, is not only a collection of lines. He takes the craft of acting more seriously than you'd figure. Surely you recall Murray's years on "Saturday Night Live" and all his diverse characters, including the nerd with the pants hitched up above his waist ("Helloooo, Mrs. Loopner") and the celebrity reporter ("Liz, honey, we love you. Don't ever change ... ") and the oily lounge singer ("Star Waaaars! Nothing but Staaaar Wars! Everybody, sing along! ...").

But if you ask Murray for the best character he ever did on that show, he'll choose a part that lasted all of four seconds. "I played this dumb actor in a sketch in which John Belushi was the star. He was this famous stunt man, and I was the actor he was replacing. I do a scene where I'm about to fall off a fire escape, and they yell CUT! And Belushi comes in to fall something like, I don't know, 18 inches. And he gets hurt. They have all these props, with his name on it and everything, and it's just this tiny little fall ...

"Anyhow, they ask me, the dumb actor, if I can find my way back to my trailer. And I go (long pause), 'Yeah ... I think I can.' That was the best thing I've ever done on TV. It was just this one moment, but I was trying a new kind of acting at that point, going from this straight manic stuff I'd always done to something different, where I was messing with the timing a little, using my body in a different way. It was scary, like changing your golf swing. Like going from briefs to boxers. But I did it. I went (long pause), 'Yeah ... I think I can.' "

He smiled. "Best thing I've ever done."

Hmmm.

So Murray is not just a kook. Someone once described him as "a cross between Harpo Marx and Clark Gable." That's not bad. You do believe it when he plays the clown. But you also believe it when pretty girls fall in love with him. In "Stripes," he seduces a female army officer by tickling her with a spatula. "Your problem," he tells her, poking her like a pancake, "is that no one has ever given you the Aunt Jemima treatment. …"

And, yes, you do believe it when Murray plays a nut. In this new movie, he walks around with a goldfish around his neck, saying things like, "I need, I need, I neeeeed!" And yet by the end of the film, you love him. And you hate the analyst. Murray himself is not all that big on psychiatry:

"Most of the people I know who have gone through therapy, they genuinely need help, but they go to someone who reinforces the way they're already living. That is totally baffling to me. It's like, 'That's you! You're supposed to annoy people! You're just being you! That's you!' It's like people say, 'My shrink says it's OK that I'm a bulimic.' I mean, I don't get it.'

The truth is, Murray has too much sense to be crazy. That is his gift.

Now, if we could only straighten him out on this Pistons thing.

"Bull Pride, Bull Power," he said deadpan and made a fist. Then he looked over, and saw the people in New York telling him to end the interview.

"They say I gotta go," he said.

I told him thanks.

"Good luck," he said. "And as far as the Pistons, uh, maybe we'll see you in the World Series."

And he disappeared.

What the hell was that supposed to mean? ∎

No news is good news
on a road less traveled

July 28, 1991

I took a vacation. I went to France. When I go away, I like to go far away, someplace where they don't speak English. I do this not because I enjoy ordering what I think is a hamburger, only to have the waiter bring me ox brains.

I do it because going someplace where they don't speak English is the only way to escape my addiction.

My addiction is the news.

When I am here, I cannot avoid it. The news greets me on my doorstep. It hollers from my car radio. It is my life. My work. My addiction. The news. Who's dead? Who has been elected? Who has been traded? Maybe it's different if you don't work in this business. All I know is, after a while, the news just finds me no matter where I am.

And at some point each year — usually when the weather gets hot — I suddenly don't want to know anymore. I overdose. I turn off. The stories are no longer absorbed. Instead, they pile on top of me like dead leaves. I am smothered. News sick. I cannot hear about another death. I cannot hear about another drug bust. I cannot listen to another athlete complain that a million dollars is lunch money.

There is only one cure for this: Go away. Where they don't speak English. I took a vacation. I went to France.

It worked. For a while.

I got a bicycle there. I went riding. Every day, through the southern countryside of Provence, I pedaled my seven-speeder with a small group of friends, our wheels spinning tirelessly, gears clicking in rhythm. The roads were empty. The sun was hot. Like quiet wind, we whistled past olive groves and peach trees. Past vineyards thick with grapes. Now and then we would glide past a farmer tending his crop, and he would look up, wipe the sweat from his brow and shake his head at these fools on wheels, out in the heat when they didn't have to be. We said nothing. We rolled on.

I liked that part, saying nothing. I was not there to talk. I was there to disappear, to blend in, to smell the aroma of fruit trees, to feel the sweat dripping down my arms, a victim of the same French sunshine that baked the red tile roofs and left dogs panting under shade trees. This was what I wanted: to join the picture for once instead of analyzing it or reporting it. I gripped the handlebars of my bicycle and tried to forget about the U.S. trade deficit and the latest teenager to be shot for his sneakers.

By the third day, it was working. I felt cleansed, lighter. I no longer felt the need to pull off the road and click on CNN. Instead, I ate breakfasts of fresh bread with jam and listened to the insects that sang in the trees. I walked through the water beneath an ancient bridge. I bought yellow plums from a vendor who had just picked them.

One day, while riding, a large bee flew into my face, startling me so much that I crashed into another cyclist and we both tumbled into the grass. Unhurt, we looked up and began to laugh uncontrollably, like kids who had just fallen into mud. The day was hot and dusty, and you could hear our laughter a half-mile down the road.

This lasted two weeks, and when my plane touched down in Detroit, I was still feeling good. I had a nice tan and strong legs from all the cycling. I vowed to continue my healthy eating and went to the supermarket for fresh tomatoes and cucumbers.

And at the supermarket I finally bought a newspaper. And this was the first story I read: A man in Milwaukee had been arrested for murdering at least 17 people. He not only killed them — drugged them, strangled them and cut their bodies to pieces — but he also had sex with some of their corpses.

He took pictures of them with arms missing, heads cut off. There were even reports that he ate their dead flesh; he claimed to have cut one victim's heart out and put it in his freezer "to eat later."

He told the police all this in a calm voice, and as I read it I felt the breath leave me, as if I'd been kicked in the stomach. Lord, how on earth is a man like this created? What happened in his childhood to turn him into such a monster? And all those victims! Their families, no doubt wondering where their sons had gone, now learning they are not only dead but in pieces, perhaps even … eaten. Is there any understanding this?

I felt a sudden shiver and then a familiar oozing, sinking feeling. The news. The news. My job. My addiction. I was home. I folded the paper and put it into the bag. A humid breeze blew. For a moment, I thought about France, the breads and jams, falling off my bicycle and laughing beneath the olive trees. And then I thought about this lunatic in Milwaukee, slicing the heads off his victims, licking his lips. And I realized, like most people who take a vacation from the news, that I already need another one. ∎

MTV's music videos preempt the wonder of imagination

September 8, 1991

Nobody listens to pop music anymore; they watch it. They flick on MTV, plop onto a couch and let the images take over. What was once a drumbeat is now a cue for the video editor, jump cut, jump cut, dancing bodies, lips, hair, ocean waves, naked girls, gangs waving their fists, guitar players sticking their tongues out.

This is killing pop music, if it's not dead already. Perhaps you were unlucky enough to be near a television Thursday night, when the "MTV Video Music Awards" aired. With Arsenio Hall as host — that should tell you something right there — they actually gave awards for things such as best choreography, art direction, cinematography and "breakthrough video."

Can I ask a simple question: What does any of this have to do with music?

When I was 12 years old, I went to a dance. It was my first. I mingled nervously as Janis Joplin and Marvin Gaye played on the stereo. I ate potato chips while Otis Redding sang about the dock of the bay. There was this girl my age. She had brown hair. Wore hip-hugger jeans. Although she made me shiver just being around her, somehow, toward the end of the night, I found the courage to ask her to dance. The music was slow. She said OK. We awkwardly hooked bodies, her arms around my neck, mine around her waist, and we swayed back and forth in the corner, the first time I was ever that close to a girl. The music was "So Far Away" by Carole King. If I died today, I would remember that song tomorrow.

So far away,
doesn't anybody stay in one place anymore?
It would be so fine to see your face at my door.

Every time I hear that music, I am a teenager again, my eyes closed in her hair, my heart pounding softly.

I need no video to paint that picture. That's the wonder of music. You hear it, and all by itself it can strum your emotions, make you sad, happy, nostalgic, wistful.

Video, on the other hand, robs your imagination. It packages the pictures with the song until the two become inseparable. During the MTV broadcast, they made a big deal of naming a special award for Michael Jackson. Sure, Jackson is a talented singer and dancer, but his videos are so arresting — and so frequently played — you can't forget them. As a result, whenever you hear his song "Bad," you picture a bunch of gang members dancing in a subway; "Thriller" makes you picture Jackson growing hair on his hands and turning into a werewolf.

I believe this sells a lot of CDs and videos. I don't believe it helps music. Not at all. Kids are no longer interested in instrumentals, for one thing. They have no appreciation for melody. They hear a song today and they say, "Have you seen the video for that yet? It's great."

Listening is out. Watching is in.

O f course, this keeps folks such as Madonna in business. Madonna might be the single biggest beneficiary of MTV, as well as its biggest star. Her music is usually too mechanical to stand on its own. Half the time it's nothing more than an electronic drum beat with a few vocals thrown on top. Try whistling "Justify My Love." It's not much of a melody.

But as background music to her latest shock video — it's terrific. And that is all it is. The music becomes the picture. The picture becomes the marketing. The marketing sells the records.

And that is exactly what the record company wants.

Record companies like image. It can be controlled, shaped and sold. It's easier to create an image than to trust your artistic ear — the way Sam Phillips once did when Elvis walked into his studio, or Berry Gordy did when he heard Smokey Robinson sing.

I was a musician once. Dreamed of writing hit songs. This was in the early '80s, just when MTV was starting up. One day, I heard that a European group called a-ha had been signed to a record contract based solely on its photo. No one had even listened to the group. Its members looked right — cute, long hair, high cheekbones. "We'll make them work," the record company figured.

Shortly thereafter, I left the business.

After MTV on Thursday, I have no regrets.

But this is my fear: We are raising a generation that won't be able to appreciate music unless it comes with special effects. They are missing all the magic. There's a story about Gustav Mahler, the 19th Century composer, who drew his musical inspiration from the scenery in his native Austria. Once, when a friend came to visit his country home, Mahler said, "Don't bother looking at the view. I have already composed it."

Today, they would say, "Don't bother listening to the music; we already filmed it."

And Gustav would be wearing Spandex. ∎

Sex is the ringmaster
in Thomas-Hill circus

October 20, 1991

A week ago I was racing through an airport and noticed a crowd of people around a coffee shop television. This was a Saturday afternoon, and I figured it must be a football game.

I was wrong. All those people were watching the Clarence Thomas-Anita Hill hearings, hanging on every word. I found this at first encouraging. And then kind of sad. For once, in a nation full of trivial pursuit, we, the people, were discussing politics.

But the reason was sex.

That might prove the real shame of the whole Thomas controversy, that it took large breasts, pubic hair and someone named Long Dong Silver to get us even momentarily interested in our judicial process. Face it. Without the sex, this was just another political debate, and most Americans would rather watch soap operas. Only when the hearings became soap opera, did those same Americans find their interest, shall we say, aroused?

So enrapt were we with who was lying, however — he or she? Did she want it? Was he after it? — that we overlooked the most important questions: What kind of judge was Thomas? Where did he stand on issues? Why was he nominated in the first place, and did he deserve to be a Supreme Court justice for life — helping shape America for the next 30 to 40 years — based on his record? The answer has nothing to do with pubic hair.

But that became the focus. Time magazine called the hearing "an ugly circus." Yet if Hill was theatre, she was just another act.

Go back to July, when President Bush nominated Thomas. He said he was "picking the best man for the job based on merits."

Come on. That was surely theatre. Black and white groups alike will tell you a 43-year-old judge with a short history on the bench and an even shorter list of written opinions is hardly the best man "based on merits." There are many more qualified people, of all races and sexes. Bush chose Thomas for two reasons: 1) He liked his conservative views and 2) Thomas is black. There is nothing inherently wrong with No. 2, by the way. Thomas would take the place of Thurgood Marshall, a black man, who is retiring. It seems only fair in a democratic country that blacks have a voice on the nation's highest court. The same holds for Hispanics, Asians and other minority groups.

But wouldn't it have been better — and more honest — for Bush to say this, much the way Lyndon Johnson told the nation when he appointed Marshall in 1967: "It is the right thing to do, and the right time to do it"?

Instead, Bush began with a song and dance, and it just continued.

Thomas went before the Senate and turned into a clam. He avoided all tough questions. Is this proper behavior for a Supreme Court nominee?

Thomas was acting, having been coached by White House handlers in the art of political theatre. Why was he so shocked when his opponents played the same game?

When Anita Hill came forward, Thomas suddenly rediscovered his voice. He got angry. He accused the Senate of a "high-tech lynching for uppity blacks." This argument loses steam when you realize Hill is black. But words such as "lynching" are tinderboxes. And Thomas knew it.

Meanwhile, Republican senators were enjoying the fact that, for once, they could accuse Democrats of being racist, and maybe steal some of the black voters who traditionally went the other way. So on prime-time TV we saw a disgraceful display of showmanship, speeches that had far more to do with getting re-elected than with wisely selecting a judge. That was the issue, wasn't it? Wisely selecting a judge?

Too late. The focus, like a circus spotlight, had jumped to one of the sideshows, the one about sex. And there it stayed.

Eventually, Thomas was approved by a narrow margin, 52-48. This begged for a heated debate: 1) Shouldn't becoming a Supreme Court justice require at least a two-thirds majority? 2) Should the Supreme Court have a minimum age? 3) Should we limit the terms of justices? 4) How can we de-politicize the nomination process?

Unfortunately, nobody has sex in these issues, so they went unspoken.

And now Thomas is on the court. We can only hope he shows wisdom, but most Americans will never know, because they rarely read Supreme Court opinions. Next time I see a crowd around an airport TV, it will probably be a touchdown or a porn star on Oprah Winfrey's show. And maybe the saddest lesson from Thomas-Hill will be just this: Titillation makes us tick.

I wish the Supreme Court could do something about that. ∎

We must treat Indians like people, not mascots

October 27, 1991

ATLANTA — If someone named a sports team the Washington Negroes, you can be sure the black community wouldn't stand for it.

And if someone named a sports team the Atlanta Jews — had a dancing rabbi as their mascot — the Jewish community would never allow it.

This week, a group of American Indians stood up and complained that enough was enough, all these sports teams named Braves, Redskins, Chiefs — with their whooping, war-painted, tomahawk-waving mascots — this was insulting to their heritage. Please stop.

They were told to sit down, shut up.

In some ways, it was the most shameful scene in sports in a long time: Atlanta-Fulton County Stadium, the World Series, a small band of Indians holding signs that read, "We Are People, Not Mascots" and "Please Respect Our Culture" — and they had to be protected by armed guards from angry Braves fans, who were dressed like Indians, painted like Indians, yet were screaming at real Indians, "Get lost!" and "You're only here for publicity!"

Once again, a great show of compassion from a ticketholder with a beer. Get lost? Correct me if I'm wrong, but isn't every one of us a stranger to this land if you go back far enough — every one except the Native Americans, the Indians?

Get lost? What happened to our compassion? Before Game 4 of the World Series, an Indian leader named Wabun-Inina (Man of Dawn) pleaded for baseball fans to lay down their toy tomahawks in a pile. "Do the right thing," he said.

When I looked, not a single tomahawk had been surrendered.

Oh, everyone had an explanation. Like the father who said, "Give it up? I just paid five bucks for this." Or the beer-bellied fellow who yelled, "CUSTER WAS RIGHT!" and giggled as he walked away.

Everyone had an explanation, a justification for ignoring the issue. Here were some of the popular ones:

1) Where were these Indians last year? You might ask the same thing of the "loyal" Braves fans, who used to hold their noses and pretend the team didn't exist. The tomahawk chop, the war paint, that annoying chant Braves fans sing — these weren't center stage last year. They are now. So the protest is here. What's surprising about that?

2) Why do they want the team name changed now — after all this

time? The fact is, Indians have protested names such as Braves, Chiefs and Redskins — can you imagine a team called Blackskins? — for years. Their protests have been largely ignored.

3) Why are they mad at something that honors them? Since when is it for us to determine what honors someone else? The fact is, real Indians do not paint their faces to be a mascot; face-painting is a sacred ritual. Same goes for chanting and drum-beating, which, in Indian culture, are mostly a form of prayer, not a war cry.

"Really?" we say. "We didn't know that." Of course not. Most of what we know about Indians comes from cartoons and westerns: whooping, horse-riding, scalp-chasing Injuns. We expect them to fit those stereotypes. That's like expecting Mexicans to behave like the Frito Bandito.

Do you know what Tonto means?

It means fool in Spanish.

They should be honored with that, right?

I find this a simple issue. If you are a compassionate person, then you must agree with the Indian protesters and give up the tomahawk, the feathers, the face-painting. You can't be sensitive to one minority group and not to others.

Or can you? Maybe the saddest sight in Georgia this week was that of laughing black fans who marched past Indian protesters swinging tomahawks and singing, "AHHH-AH-AH-AH-AH-AH" to try and drown out their speeches. Black people did this? In Georgia? A place where, not long ago, there were water fountains that read "white" and "colored"?

Shame on them. And shame on all of us who for some reason figure the sympathy runs out when it comes to sports. "We're just having fun," we say. But it's not fun if it hurts. And this is hurting a lot of people, who, sadly, have had the stuffing kicked out of them ever since we set foot on their land.

In the 1830s, white settlers took most of the Cherokee, Choctaw, Chickasaw, Creek and Seminole nations and literally moved them out of the way, marched them to Oklahoma, where they began a slow and steady death. Indians call this "The Trail of Tears."

Today, when we ought to know better, we show the same kind of cruelty.

"GO HOME!" a fan screamed this week.

"We are home," answered an Indian.

He's right. But how would you ever know? ∎

Teenager's senseless death symptom of an age of anger

December 29, 1991

H e was running from them now, a teenager running from other teenagers, and he felt the terror you feel in dreams when someone is gaining on you and you can't get away. His friends were running ahead of him, and they made it to the car and dived inside and locked the doors. But he kept running, the way he used to run down a lacrosse field, heart pumping, legs churning. He ran to the front of the school, but the others caught him, tripped him, pushed him to the ground. They were around him now, and they began to kick. One to the stomach. One to the head. Another to the head. Maybe he tried to say something, like "No" or "Please," but you wouldn't have known it because he was sucking air by this point, gasping, and they were all too young to understand that life had begun to ooze out of him. Another head kick. Another.

It was Friday night, teenagers doing another teenager, but this was not inner-city violence. This was not about money or drugs or a new coat. This was about nothing, a fight after a dance, suburban macho. Some of the kids barely knew whom they were kicking! And they kicked him again. Eight times. Nine times. Now he was on his hands and knees, halfway into blackness, and the kid who had at least partly started all this, the skinny teenager from the initial fight that was supposed to be one-on-one, came staggering up from behind, his eye bleeding, and he stood over his fallen rival and allegedly said, "This is for breaking my gold chain." And he kicked him in the face.

Alex Stachura never got up again. He was rushed to the hospital. His parents were called. As they drove to the hospital, they thought "auto accident" because that's what you think when you live in the suburbs and you get a call from the hospital, right? Auto accident? You never figure your 16-year-old boy got his head kicked in.

"There'll be an operation," his mother told herself in the waiting room. "He'll be sick, but I'll nurse him. I can do it, I am his moth—"

The doctor came out.

Alex was dead.

This is a story about how violent we have become, even our most pleasant neighborhoods, and how this all has to stop, this teenage fury, because it's so senseless. They act tough, they talk tough, but they have no idea what their bodies can do — and soon we have one more mother's son buried in the earth, and four others facing a second-degree murder charge.

"They're just kids," you want to say.

Yes. They are.

"This is Alex," says Walter Stachura, sliding a high school yearbook across the table. He is sitting in the kitchen of his home, the same place he was sitting that night when the phone rang. Across from him sits his wife, Alicia, who is biting her lip and dabbing her red eyes, because this is the first time she has talked about her son's death with a reporter. In between is their 14-year-old daughter, Colleen, and their eldest child, Jason, a college freshman whose blond hair and pout give him strong resemblance to his dead brother. Both boys played lacrosse at Warren De La Salle High, and the yearbook photo shows Alex running down a field, stick in hand. He earned a junior varsity letter in the sport and once bragged about a game in which he scored two goals and checked his opponent really hard. So he was not afraid of contact, but fighting was not his thing. He had a quick wit. He could cut you up verbally. He didn't need to throw punches. But someone else did.

"These boys who fought Alex, some of them had called and threatened him before," his mother says. "Once they got Jason on the phone by mistake and threatened him."

"It was your typical teenage stuff," Jason says. "They said, 'We're gonna come beat your head in.'"

On the final night of his life, Alex Stachura knew he would fight. He knew where. He knew the opponent. A kid named Nicholas Del Greco, who used to attend De La Salle but had transferred that semester to Sterling Heights High, had been stirring a feud with Alex since last spring. It began over a girl, but the girl was now history, yet the anger lingered. Why? Who knows? Why do teenagers stay mad over anything?

On more than one occasion, Alex tried to stay clear of Nick. Once, according to the Stachuras, Nick and his buddies even pursued Alex in a high-speed car chase. Alex got away. By autumn, things had come to a head: Without the parents knowing it, Alex and Nick agreed to fight Sept. 20 after the dance.

Alex reportedly told a friend, "I'm going to get my ass kicked tonight." He went anyhow. Because of that, he is not blameless. But in this story, nobody is.

They met behind an elementary school. Alex came in a car with three friends. Nick arrived in a four-car entourage, maybe a dozen kids. A judge would call them "a gang," but truth is, many barely knew Del Greco or Stachura. They came to watch, which is even more sick.

What happens next depends on your witness. Most agree the two boys traded punches, then began a grab-and-roll on the asphalt. After a few minutes, Alex had clearly won the scuffle, and they disengaged. There was yelling. Alex began to walk away, he might have screamed at the crowd, and Nick hollered something like "Get him!" and then Alex began to run. And suddenly, the group, these children, took on the bloodthirsty coloration of the moment, and they began to chase him, kick him …

Cause of death was head injuries, swelling of the brain. Witnesses suggest Alex was kicked 11 to 15 times by the four Sterling Heights students who were arrested and charged: Del Greco, 16; Matthew Trout, 16; Arthur Zrodlo, 15; and Marek Sobotka, 17. The prosecutor asked for second-degree murder charges — he said you kick someone in the head, you know what you're doing — and another thing: He wanted them tried as adults, not juveniles. The judge agreed.

So now the four teenagers, if convicted, could be sentenced to life in prison.

In the meantime, three of them are back in high school.

"They're just kids," you say. …

I nside the Stachura home, upstairs in Alex's room, the bed is neatly made, as if he might be home soon. His lacrosse stick stands in the corner, and a picture of him in his lacrosse uniform sits atop the bureau. There is a Bible on the desk, with his doodles on the edge of the pages. One of them reads: "You can die before you get old, but me, I'm gonna live forever."

Sixteen years is not forever. And Alex is never coming home. Downstairs, the house is quiet, save for the hum of the refrigerator and the sound of a mother crying into a tissue.

After Alex was pronounced dead at Macomb Hospital Center, the very hospital where he was born, Alicia and Walter were permitted a few minutes with the body. A nurse said, "Be quick." Walter pushed aside the curtain and saw his son on a gurney, a tube still stuck in his mouth, the red blotches on his chest where they had tried to revive him.

Alicia leaned over to kiss Alex, and his skin was cold. "I kept remembering how he liked to stay in bed in the morning," she whispers now, her eyes beginning to crumble in tears. "You kind of had to wiggle him out … and … I used to wake him up by kissing him and … I would kiss him and he was always so warm, so warm, and now he was so cold and oh, this is … so final! So horribly final!"

She is trembling, squeezing her eyes shut. Her husband begins to weep with her. "They keep saying it gets easier," Alicia says, "but it … it doesn't get easier. Every day Alex gets further and further away …"

W here is the lesson in all this? By all accounts, Alex Stachura was a good kid — not a saint, but a responsible young man who helped out at his church and worked summer jobs and liked music and had friends. And the others were supposedly good kids, too. Played on the sports teams, played in the band. No previous crimes.

So how could this happen, that their lives and families are now soaked by this bloodshed? For what? Teenage pride? Outside of Del Greco, the others barely knew Alex. How could someone do this to a stranger? Kick him in the head? Allow others to do so? What kind of children are we raising? Do they think it's not real? Is it all those violent movies we let them watch — Chuck Norris, Steven Seagal? Is it sports, from football to pro wrestling?

Or is it simply the age we live in — an age of anger and blaming others and feeling good when we flatten someone? A recent poll was conducted among Macomb County students. They said their top problem is no longer drugs or alcohol. It is "student conflict." Kids making war on other kids.

What does that tell you?

Not long before he died, Alex Stachura wrote a composition about God. These are his words:

"I believe God is different things at different times in your life. Right now, I think God is a stand-up comedian trying out his act on the human race."

How sad a world we give to our young. The new year is upon us, and if you make no other resolution, make this one: to spend more time with your children, deal with their anger, teach them peace, before we have another Alex Stachura story, one dead, four arrested.

"They're just kids," you say.

Not anymore. ∎

Fame is fleeting when Terminator calls the tune

April 12, 1992

N EW YORK — Andy Warhol said everyone gets his 15 minutes, and I guess I just had mine.

Actually, it was only five minutes. With Arnold Schwarzenegger. And one minute with Dyan Cannon. And seven seconds with Donald Trump, who really needs a new haircut. I mean, his hair just kind of creeps up his forehead, like a raccoon climbing a tree. I wanted to say, "Donald. Here's five bucks. Go down to the barber shop, ask for Al ..."

But I digress.

How did I come to be here, at the mecca of pop culture, Planet Hollywood, standing among the celebrities, hoping no one mistook me for a busboy?

Here is how: I have a past.

Not like Bill Clinton has a past. But years ago, before I worked for newspapers, I was a fledgling musician. I lived in New York. I played piano, wrote songs. I like to refer to those as My Happy Years — as in, if someone didn't throw me out of his office, I was happy. I had as much success as a songwriter as Alfred E. Neuman had on the most recent presidential ballot. Eventually, I found more rewarding employment: as a security guard.

When that didn't work, I tried journalism.

Anyhow, a few months ago, an old college roommate named Stan Brooks — a guy we used to tease back at school for watching too many movies and naturally today is a successful Hollywood producer making zillions of dollars and laughing at us as if we were tadpoles in his toilet — called me up and asked whether I wanted to write a song for a TV movie he was making. Which Arnold Schwarzenegger was directing. Which Dyan Cannon was starring in. Which was going to receive massive buildup in the press and be released as a feature film overseas.

And I said, "Who is this?"

W ell, I wrote the song. A big band tune. I got the best singer I know, Janine Sabino, who lives in Detroit, to sing it. And we recorded in the studios of that soon-to-be-world-famous band, DC Drive, who are also from Detroit and, more important, were the only musicians I knew who wouldn't explode into laughter when I sat down at the piano.

Besides, their studio is near this really good pizza place.

So we sent it off.

The song. Not the pizza place.

And a few weeks later, Stan Brooks called back and said, "Arnold loved it!"

Now. At the time, the only Arnold I knew was Jim Arnold, the balding Lions punter who collects Elvis postcards in his locker. That was about to change. The new Arnold in my life, Schwarzenegger, was the biggest name in Hollywood. The Terminator Man. Pump You Up. *I'll be baaaaack.*

And he was going to use our song as the closing song in his movie.

"Arnold and I would love for you to come to the premiere in New York," Stan said.

"Premiere?" I said.

"Yeah. They show the movie. And then there's this big party. All the stars will be there."

"Who is this?" I said.

(By the way. The movie, titled, "Christmas In Connecticut," airs Monday night at 8 on TNT. The producers told me to say that, or I couldn't eat any more of their chocolate-covered strawberries.)

Which brings us to the premiere. Such a big night! And what to wear? Being a sports writer, my wardrobe was fairly limited. I had 1) the blue blazer with the white shirt, or 2) the blue blazer with the pink shirt.

Janine wore a nice black dress.

And we went to New York. And we went to the theater. And our cab pulled up, the door opened — and Holy Hollywood! There were fans behind barricades, and mobs of reporters and TV cameras, and they all seemed to stare right at us and say, in a big, excited show business voice: "Who the hell are you? Where's Schwarzenegger?"

Thankfully, Arnold arrived, in a limo. And Dyan Cannon, and a bunch of other celebrities. I know this because I heard people screaming while Janine and I were stuck at the front desk, trying to find our names on the guest list.

"They're not here," the woman said.

"Are you sure?' I said.

"Who are you with?"

"Well," I said, "I, uh, wrote this song at the end of the movie."

She laughed. I knew I would never record in her studio.

Eventually they let us in — Who would actually make up such a reason for being there? — and we took a seat. And the movie started. And after the final scene, sure enough, here came our song — called "Cookin' For Two" — blasting over the loudspeakers. I must admit, it was a kick. I got goose bumps. Which is why, when I saw someone get up to leave before the song was over, I yelled, "Hey! Sit down!"

It was Dyan Cannon.

So I guess I won't be recording in her studio, either.

But enough about the movie. You want to hear about THE PARTY at Planet Hollywood, the fabulously popular nightclub co-owned by

Schwarzenegger, Sylvester Stallone and Bruce Willis, a place where, on an ordinary night, I would not be admitted until 4 a.m., when they needed help with the trash.

Instead, Janine and I were ushered inside and — Bam! Another wall of TV cameras, clawing fans, would-be starlets, paparazzi, all staring at us and saying: "Out of the way! Arnold's coming!"

And we were shoved past the bar and the tables and past the glass-enclosed memorabilia, which includes an arrow from the movie "Robin Hood" and John Travolta's white suit from "Saturday Night Fever."

And suddenly, a publicity person grabbed us and said: "Arnold will meet you now. Hurry up." And we were dragged through another roomful of humanity that reminded me of an embassy during the fall of Saigon, and with one final push, we were suddenly biceps-to-biceps with the big man himself.

Arnold.

Who was talking to other people.

"Arnold," someone said, gently tapping him on the shoulder, "I'd like you to meet …"

But Arnold turned to someone else.

"Arnold," he tried again, "I'd like you to meet …"

And he turned to someone else.

"Arnold, I'd like you to meet …"

And suddenly, he was looking at us. He grinned, and said, "Da song wasss faan-das-dic."

And I said, "Thank you."

"You haf a faan-das-dic voice."

And Janine said, "Thank you."

The publicity person said, "Arnold, we'd like you to meet …"

And someone bumped into me.

And I turned, and it was Donald Trump.

And I wanted to say to him, "Hey, D-man. Can't you see I'm rapping with Arnold here? Get a job, you bum." But I didn't, because I was too busy staring at his hair, which I wanted to whack with a machete. And by the time I turned, Arnold was gone.

And so was Trump. With Marla Maples. Who has a nicer haircut than he does, and a bigger ring.

And soon, I was back at the food table, watching the entire cast of "Saturday Night Live" come by to chat with Arnold. So this was the Big Time. I thought back to my old days as a piano player, and I figured life has a funny way of working out. Who knows? Maybe Arnold will call again. Maybe he'll need another song. Maybe they'll find our names on the guest list.

And maybe not. Just in case, as I left the scene, I did what any normal person would do if his 15 minutes were coming to an end: I grabbed as many chocolate-covered strawberries as I could. *Hasta la vista, baby.* ∎